NOVELL'S

IntranetWare™ Administrator's Handbook

NOVELL'S

IntranetWare™ Administrator's Handbook

KELLEY J. P. LINDBERG

NOVELL PRESS®

Novell Press, San Jose

Novell's IntranetWare™ Administrator's Handbook

Published by
Novell Press
2180 Fortune Drive
San Jose, CA 95131

Library of Congress Catalog Card No.: 96-78238
ISBN: 0-7645-4517-5
Printed in the United States of America
10 9 8 7 6
1P/SZ/QX/ZZ/IN
Distributed in the United States by IDG Books Worldwide, Inc.

Distributed by CDG Books Canada Inc. for Canada; by Transworld Publishers Limited in the United Kingdom; by IDG Norge Books for Norway; by IDG Sweden Books for Sweden; by IDG Books Australia Publishing Corporation Pty. Ltd. for Australia and New Zealand; by TransQuest Publishers Pte Ltd. for Singapore, Malaysia, Thailand, Indonesia, and Hong Kong; by Gotop Information Inc. for Taiwan; by ICG Muse, Inc. for Japan; by Norma Comunicaciones S.A. for Colombia; by Intersoft for South Africa; by Eyrolles for France; by International Thomson Publishing for Germany, Austria and Switzerland; by Distribuidora Cuspide for Argentina; by LR International for Brazil; by Galileo Libros for Chile; by Ediciones ZETA S.C.R. Ltda. for Peru; by WS Computer Publishing Corporation, Inc., for the Philippines; by Contemporanea de Ediciones for Venezuela; by Express Computer Distributors for the Caribbean and West Indies; by Micronesia Media Distributor, Inc. for Micronesia; by Grupo Editorial Norma S.A. for Guatemala; by Chips Computadoras S.A. de C.V. for Mexico; by Editorial Norma de Panama S.A. for Panama; by American Bookshops for Finland. Authorized Sales Agent: Anthony Rudkin Associates for the Middle East and North Africa.

For general information on IDG Books Worldwide's books in the U.S., please call our Consumer Customer Service department at 800-762-2974. For reseller information, including discounts and premium sales, please call our Reseller Customer Service department at 800-434-3422.

For information on where to purchase IDG Books Worldwide's books outside the U.S., please contact our International Sales department at 317-596-5530 or fax 317-596-5692.

For consumer information on foreign language translations, please contact our Customer Service department at 1-800-434-3422, fax 317-596-5692, or e-mail rights@idgbooks.com.

For information on licensing foreign or domestic rights, please phone +1-650-655-3109.

For sales inquiries and special prices for bulk quantities, please contact our Sales department at 650-655-3200 or write to the address above.

For information on using IDG Books Worldwide's books in the classroom or for ordering examination copies, please contact our Educational Sales department at 800-434-2086 or fax 317-596-5499.

For press review copies, author interviews, or other publicity information, please contact our Public Relations department at 650-655-3000 or fax 650-655-3299.

For authorization to photocopy items for corporate, personal, or educational use, please contact Copyright Clearance Center, 222 Rosewood Drive, Danvers, MA 01923, or fax 978-750-4470.

IDG BOOKS WORLDWIDE

John Kilcullen, *President & CEO, IDG Books Worldwide, Inc.*
Brenda McLaughlin, *Senior Vice President & Group Publisher, IDG Books Worldwide, Inc.*
The IDG Books Worldwide logo is a trademark under exclusive license to IDG Books Worldwide, Inc., from International Data Group, Inc.

NOVELL PRESS

Rosalie Kearsley, *Publisher, Novell Press, Inc.*
Novell Press and the Novell Press logo are trademarks of Novell, Inc.

Welcome to Novell Press

Novell Press, the world's leading provider of networking books, is the premier source for the most timely and useful information in the networking industry. Novell Press books cover fundamental networking issues as they emerge — from today's Novell and third-party products to the concepts and strategies that will guide the industry's future. The result is a broad spectrum of titles for the benefit of those involved in networking at any level: end-user, department administrator, developer, systems manager, or network architect.

Novell Press books are written by experts with the full participation of Novell's technical, managerial, and marketing staff. The books are exhaustively reviewed by Novell's own technicians and are published only on the basis of final released software, never on prereleased versions. Novell Press at IDG Books Worldwide is an exciting partnership between two companies at the forefront of the knowledge and communications revolution. The Press is implementing an ambitious publishing program to develop new networking titles centered on the current IntranetWare version of NetWare and on Novell's GroupWise and other popular groupware products.

Novell Press books are translated into 12 languages and are available at bookstores around the world.

Rosalie Kearsley, Publisher, Novell, Inc.
David Kolodney, Associate Publisher, IDG Books Worldwide, Inc.

Novell Press

Publisher
Rosalie Kearsley

Associate Publishers
Colleen Bluhm
David Kolodney

Associate Acquisitions Editor
Anne Hamilton

Communications Project Specialist
Marcy Shanti

Executive Managing Editor
Terry Somerson

Editorial Assistant
Sharon Eames

Development Editor
Cynthia Putnam

Copy Editor
Carolyn Welch

Technical Editors
Howard Olson
Alan Jex
Russ Miller
Stephanie Leavitt
Mark Hinckley
Greg Angell
Brad Young
Nick Brailas
Don Doyle
Tim Huntley
Diane Heckman
Mark Shapiro
Robert Wong
Brian Connolly

Production Director
Andrew Walker

Production Associate
Christopher Pimentel

Supervisor of Page Layout
Craig A. Harrison

Media/Archive Coordination
Leslie Popplewell
Melissa Stauffer

Project Coordinator
Ben Schroeter

Production Staff
Stephen Noetzel
Andy Schueller
Deirdre Smith

Proofreader
Christine Sabooni

Indexer
Matthew Spence

Book Design
Kurt Krames

About the Author

Kelley J. P. Lindberg, a Certified Novell Engineer (CNE), joined Novell in 1986. As senior project manager, she has managed projects such as NetWare 3.12, NetWare 4.1, NetWare 4.11 and IntranetWare, and other Novell products. She has also written several other books about NetWare products, including the award-winning *Novell's Guide to Managing Small NetWare Networks*. She lives in Salt Lake City, Utah.

Preface

As the administrator of a NetWare 4.11 or IntranetWare network, you are responsible for ensuring that the network is installed correctly and runs smoothly. To do this, you may arm yourself with a variety of information sources: manuals, online documentation, magazines, books, and maybe even the phone numbers of a few knowledgeable friends. Because there is so much flexibility and functionality built into NetWare 4.11 and IntranetWare, there is a tremendous amount of information available to help you manage your network.

Sometimes, however, all you really want is a quick way to find just the information you need. You don't need a full-scale discussion of every aspect of managing the network. You don't want to wade through stacks of magazines or hypertext your way through three dozen manuals to find the information you know you saw once before. What you really want is a brief refresher, if necessary, and instant access to the command, utility, syntax, or parameter setting you want. This book was written with you in mind.

Filled with lists, tables, and installation checklists, this handbook is a vital tool in your administrator's bag of tricks. The Instant Access pages at the beginning of each chapter help you immediately identify the utilities or commands you use to complete a specific task. If you, like most other busy network administrators, don't have a lot of time to spend looking for information, you'll want to keep this book handy.

What's the Difference Between NetWare 4.11 and IntranetWare?

NetWare 4.11 is the best-selling core networking software that provides the essential services of a network: connectivity, security, file and print services, Novell Directory Services, the NetWare Web Server, and so on.

IntranetWare consists of NetWare 4.11, along with components that allow workstations to easily access intranet and internet services such as Web servers and FTP servers. These components are:

- Novell IPX/IP Gateway
- NetWare Multiprotocol Router
- WAN extensions for Wide Area Network connectivity
- FTP Services and FTP management utilities

This book covers both NetWare 4.11 core services and the additional IntranetWare components. Throughout this book, all references to IntranetWare also hold true for NetWare 4.11.

What You Need to Know

This book is designed to provide quick-reference access to essential data and facts about setting up, reconfiguring, managing, and troubleshooting your NetWare 4.11 (or IntranetWare) network. While the explanations provided throughout the book equip you with the basic concepts behind each NetWare feature, you should be somewhat familiar with how an IntranetWare network operates.

You should also have access to the online documentation that came with your IntranetWare operating system, in case you need more detailed instructions or explanations of concepts that are unfamiliar to you.

Finally, you should be familiar with the operating systems that run on the workstations you'll be maintaining, such as DOS, Windows 3.1, Window 95, OS/2, or Mac OS.

Using Windows-Based vs. DOS-Based NetWare Utilities

In many cases, IntranetWare provides you with more than one way to complete the same task, usually by supplying you with two utilities: one that runs in DOS, sometimes referred to as a character-based utility, and one that runs in Windows 3.1 (or Windows 95), often called a GUI (graphical user interface) utility.

The primary utility that network administrators use to manage an IntranetWare network is the NetWare Administrator utility, which runs in Windows 3.1 and Windows 95. There is a DOS-based utility, called NETADMIN, which allows you to perform many of the same tasks as the NetWare Administrator utility. However, NetWare Administrator has more features than NETADMIN, and because of its graphical interface, NetWare Administrator can be easier to use in some situations. In addition, due to conventional memory limitations, NETADMIN may have difficulty working with NDS Directories that contain several thousand objects in a single context. Therefore, most people prefer to use the NetWare Administrator instead. For this reason, NETADMIN is not discussed in this book.

What This Book Contains

All of the major components of IntranetWare are explained in the chapters and appendices of this book.

- Chapter 1 describes the network topologies and network cabling architectures that you can use when setting up an IntranetWare network.
- Chapter 2 explains how to install an IntranetWare server, and how to upgrade a server from a previous version of NetWare.
- Chapter 3 discusses the various ways you can manage, maintain, and monitor the performance of an IntranetWare server and its storage devices.
- Chapter 4 describes how to install and upgrade network workstations running DOS, Windows 3.1, Windows 95, OS/2, or Windows NT.
- Chapter 5 provides an overview of Novell Directory Services (NDS), including explanations of how to set up and manage NDS objects, bindery services, NDS partitions and replicas, and NetSync. It also explains how to merge NDS trees and how to troubleshoot your NDS setup.
- Chapter 6 includes instructions for creating and managing users and groups on the network. It describes how to create a user template to simplify the creation of users. It also explains how to set up login scripts and menus to automatically set up your users' access to network directories and applications.
- Chapter 7 covers the various security tools provided in IntranetWare, which you can use to make sure your network is as secure as you need it to be.
- Chapter 8 discusses file management, including tips on how to plan the directory structure, conserve the server's disk space, manage volumes, back up and restore files, and protect databases using NetWare's Transactional Tracking System (TTS). It also covers the utilities you can use to work with files and directories and explains features such as data migration and file compression.
- Chapter 9 covers both the Quick Setup and the Custom methods for setting up NetWare print services.
- Chapter 10 explains how to connect Mac OS workstations to your IntranetWare network, as well as how users can share PC and Mac OS files.

- Chapter 11 provides an overview of the protocols supported by IntranetWare (IPX, TCP/IP, and AppleTalk) and explains the utilities you can use to configure them.
- Chapter 12 explains how to set up and use the online documentation that came with your IntranetWare network operating system.
- Chapter 13 provides tips on disaster planning and recovery.
- Chapter 14 explains how to install and manage the NetWare Web Server.
- Chapter 15 describes how to install and use the Novell Internet Access Server (including the Novell IPX/IP Gateway) and FTP Services for IntranetWare.
- Chapter 16 is an alphabetical reference to the utilities and NLMs (NetWare Loadable Modules) you can use in IntranetWare.
- Appendix A lists all the available parameters that can be used in each workstation's NET.CFG file.
- Appendix B lists all the available SET parameters that can be used to modify your server's performance.
- Appendix C describes a variety of additional resources you can turn to for more help or information (such as user groups, Novell's Internet site, Novell publications, and so on).
- Appendix D supplies you with a variety of worksheets you may want to use to document information about your network, such as its hardware inventory, configuration settings, and backup schedules.

This book also includes an index to help you quickly get to the information you need.

Acknowledgments

With a final digital flourish, I click the Send button on my e-mail, and this book's creation process comes to a close. As with every book I've written, this one has been an adventure that has taught me more than I thought I had the time to learn, and not just about NetWare 4.11. I've met new people, tapped into new sources, and explored the boundaries of those pesky physical limitations of time. (Twenty-four hours in a day is a woefully short period of time.)

This is always my favorite part of writing a book — when I get to thank the people who helped me get through the last few months.

First, genuine thanks go to Novell, for allowing me to spend the last decade of my life helping make NetWare the most superior networking system in the world. I also thank Novell for allowing me to spend my so-called spare time writing about NetWare products.

Next, I want to thank the people at IDG Books, who are always top-notch. Cindy Putnam, my editor, has all the qualities writers dream of in an editor — great editing skills, of course, but also those important intangibles like patience, efficiency, and a calm voice that reassures the writer that everything's under control. She has bent over backwards to help make this book the best it can be. Thanks, Cindy! Thanks also go to the IDG Books folks who've managed to become not just incredibly helpful business associates, but also good friends: Anne Hamilton for maintaining an infectious positive attitude (and for working out the business issues), David Kolodney for always being full of brilliant ideas and poems and funny stories (and for being a steadfast believer in me), and Carolyn Welch for coordinating the editing and production and tying up the loose ends.

Rose Kearsley, another good friend and the publisher (until just recently) of Novell Press, deserves my continuing thanks for her encouragement and enthusiasm (as well as congratulations on her new position). Colleen Bluhm and Marcy Shanti also helped me with their encouragement and quick attention to details.

A huge vote of appreciation goes to Doug Hascall and Cindy Eckerman at the Compaq-Novell Enterprise Computing Partnership, who supplied me with a couple of great machines (a Proliant and a Prosignia VS) to help with my research. Thanks again to everyone at Compaq.

My technical reviewers for this book were terrific. First, I want to thank Henry Sprafkin for helping with the IntranetWare chapter and Jim Bowman for helping with the Web Server chapter. I really appreciate their knowledge and willingness to help. Thanks, guys! Next, I want to thank Howard Olson. As always, he came through with patience, answers, suggestions, and a ready sense of humor whenever I showed up at his door. Despite the fact that he was already working long hours on his own project, he still found time to review several key chapters for me. Alan Jex, Russ Miller, Stephanie Leavitt, Mark Hinckley, Greg Angell, Brad Young, Nick Brailas, Don Doyle, Tim Huntley, Diane Heckman, Mark Shapiro, Robert Wong, and Brian Connolly also helped keep me honest by graciously reviewing chapters in their respective areas of expertise. This book is much stronger for all of their efforts, and I can't thank them enough.

Of course, I am very grateful to my friends and family, who think I've chosen an odd way to spend my evenings and weekends, but who put up with me anyway. Above all, I want to thank my husband, Andy, for being the best thing that ever happened to me.

(IDG Books Worldwide would like to give special thanks to Patrick J. McGovern, founder of International Data Group, who made this book possible.)

Contents at a Glance

Contents

CHAPTER 1

Network Topologies and Architectures

Planning the Network Architecture

- Ethernet, currently the most common network architecture, provides good performance at a reasonable cost, and it is relatively easy to install.
- Token Ring generally works well in situations that involve heavy data traffic because Token Ring is reliable. It is also fairly easy to install, but it is more expensive than Ethernet networks.
- AppleTalk networks can run on several different network architectures: LocalTalk, EtherTalk, and TokenTalk. AppleTalk, a networking protocol suite built into every Macintosh, provides peer-to-peer networking capabilities between all Macintoshes and Apple hardware.
- High-speed network architectures, the newest generation of architectures, are capable of supporting speeds up to 100 Mbps. Most of these architectures use fiber-optic cabling.

The format in which a network is laid out is called its topology. For example, a network can be laid out in a bus format (see Figure 1.1), a ring format (see Figure 1.2), or a star format (see Figure 1.3). Variations or combinations of these topologies are also commonly used.

The cabling scheme that connects the nodes together into these topologies can be called the *network cabling architecture*, or just network architecture. The most common network architectures currently are Ethernet, Token Ring, and AppleTalk. (ARCnet is an older, slower architecture, which is no longer supported in IntranetWare.) High-speed architectures, such as Fiber Distributed Data Interface (FDDI), Thomas Conrad Network System (TCNS), and Fast Ethernet, are becoming more and more prevalent.

Because each of these network architectures handles data in a different way, each requires a unique type of network hardware.

FIGURE 1.1 *Bus Topology*

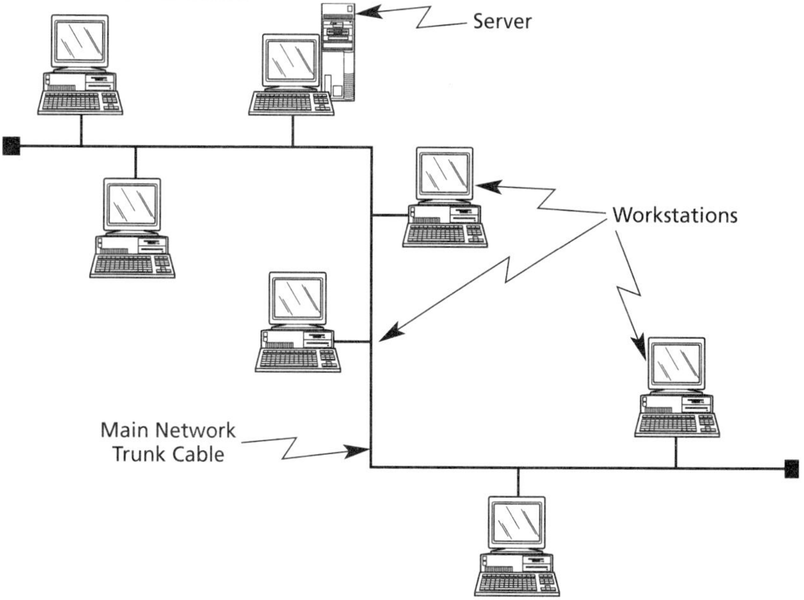

FIGURE 1.2 *Ring Topology*

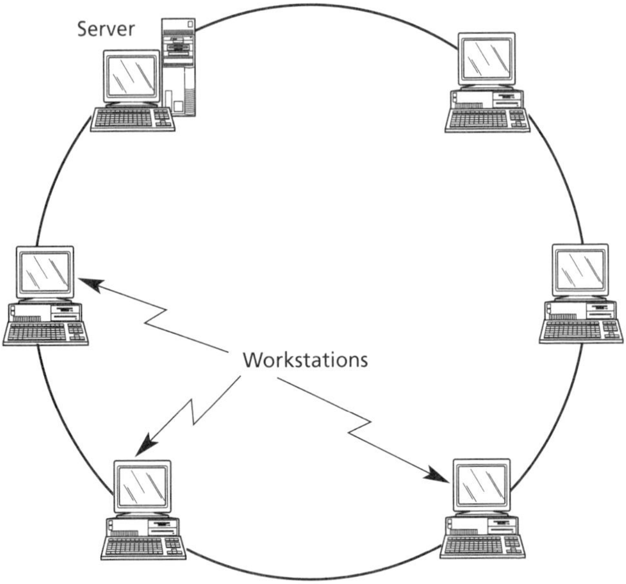

FIGURE 1.3 *Star Topology*

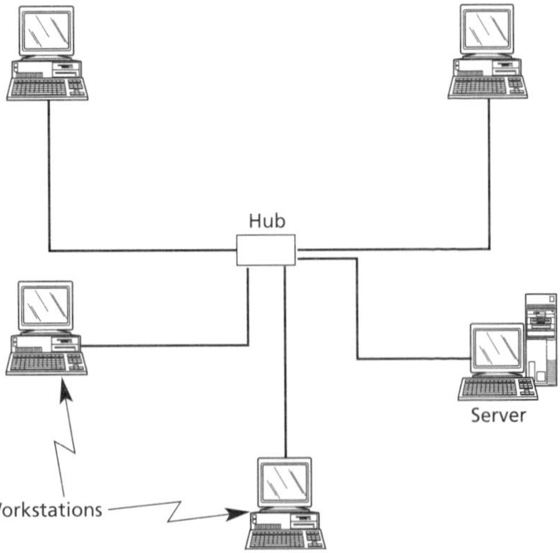

Network Hardware — An Overview

Networking hardware consists of the following components:

- *Network boards.* These special circuit boards, installed in each workstation or server, connect the computer to the network cables. (Some computers come with the network boards integrated into the rest of the computer system hardware. These boards are sometimes called built-in adapters.)
- *Cables.* Network cables connect each workstation and server to the network. These cables can be coaxial (also called coax), unshielded twisted-pair, shielded twisted-pair, or fiber-optic. The type of cable you use depends on the requirements of the topology you install.
- *Connectors and terminators.* Each type of cable requires different types of connectors to join cables together or connect them to other pieces of hardware (such as network boards). Some types of cable also require special connectors known as terminators to be attached to the open ends of any cables. Terminators keep electrical signals from reflecting back across the network, causing bad packets on the network.
- *Hubs.* Some network architectures require that the cables attached to workstations all feed into a separate piece of hardware before being connected to the main network cable. *Passive hubs* simply gather the signals and relay them. *Active hubs* actually boost the signals before sending them on their way. (The terms active hub and concentrator are often used interchangeably.)

Ethernet Network Architecture

Ethernet is currently the most commonly used network architecture. Ethernet is relatively easy to install at a moderate cost. Because it has been so widely used for many years, its technology has been well tested. Ethernet networks can use either bus or star topologies.

There are several variants of Ethernet, each of which packages *data packets* (units of information packaged into a sort of electronic envelope and sent across the network) in different ways. These different types of Ethernet packet formats are called *frame types.* In some cases, a given network will support only one Ethernet frame type. However, NetWare allows a single network board to support more than one frame type by configuring the LAN driver for the server's network board to recognize two or more types.

ETHERNET FRAME TYPES

The four Ethernet frame types are shown in Table 1.1.

TABLE 1.1 *Ethernet Frame Types*

FRAME TYPE	DESCRIPTION
Ethernet II	This is the original "official" Ethernet frame type. It is used on networks that use AppleTalk Phase 1 addressing or TCP/IP, and on networks that communicate with DEC minicomputers.
Ethernet 802.3	This is the default frame type supported by NetWare 3.11 and earlier versions of NetWare. This frame type can support either a bus or star topology. It is also called the *raw frame type* because it uses only the defined 802.3 header and doesn't include the standard header extensions defined by the 802.2 and SNAP variants of Ethernet. Ethernet 802.3 is not a standard IEEE 802.2 frame type, and it was used primarily by Novell in earlier versions of NetWare. Don't use this frame type on networks that use protocols other than IPX.
Ethernet 802.2	This frame type can support either a bus or star topology. Because it is an IEEE standard, NetWare 3.12, NetWare 4.1, and IntranetWare use this frame type by default. If you are upgrading a NetWare 3.11 (or earlier) network to IntranetWare, or adding an IntranetWare server to an existing 3.11 network, you have two choices. You can either make the LAN drivers in the 4.11 server recognize both frame types, or you will have to change all LAN drivers in the older servers and workstations so they will recognize 802.2 instead of 802.3. The latter solution is preferred because it allows for easier growth in the future and it doesn't generate as much packet traffic on the network as supporting two frame types. Ethernet 802.2 packet frames have both the 802.3 header and the 802.2 header extension.
Ethernet SNAP	This is a variant of the 802.2 packet format. It is used on networks that have workstations using protocols such as AppleTalk Phase 2 addressing. Ethernet SNAP packet frames have both the 802.3 header and the SNAP header extension. SNAP stands for Sub-Network Access Protocol.

ETHERNET CABLE OPTIONS

In an Ethernet topology, the cables that connect the machines together are laid out in a specific fashion. The cables you use will fall into three general types of functions. These are described in Table 1.2.

TABLE 1.2 *Cable Functions in an Ethernet Network*

CABLE'S FUNCTION	DESCRIPTION
Trunk cable	The trunk cable is the backbone of the network. All other nodes (workstations, servers, and so on) are connected to this trunk.
Drop cable	The drop cable can be used to connect a node to the trunk cable in a thick Ethernet network.
Patch cable	The patch cable can be used to connect two hubs.

How these types of cables are laid out depends on the cabling hardware (physical wiring) you select. Ethernet networks can be wired using any of the following types of physical cables:

- Thin coaxial cable (also called Thin Ethernet cable)
- Thick coaxial cable (also called Thick Ethernet cable)
- Twisted-pair cable

These types of cables are explained in the following sections.

Thin Ethernet Cable

Thin Ethernet cable is RG-58 (50-ohm) coaxial cable. It is 3/16 inch in size. It is also called ThinNet, CheaperNet, and 10Base2. Thin Ethernet cabling is more popular than Thick Ethernet cable because it is less bulky, more flexible, and relatively easy to handle.

Thin Ethernet, like most coaxial cable, is covered with PVC so it can be run through air conditioning and heating ducts. However, PVC-covered cable cannot be used in the space between a false ceiling and the next floor (called the *plenum space*) because PVC is quite toxic if it burns. Another type of cable, called *plenum cable*, must be used in those areas. If you use thin Ethernet, you will need the following types of hardware components:

- Ethernet network boards are necessary for each workstation and server.
- BNC barrel connectors are used to connect lengths of the trunk cable together into one trunk segment.

- BNC T-connectors are used to connect each node to the network cable.
- BNC terminators are used to terminate one end of each trunk segment.
- BNC grounded terminators are used to terminate and ground the other end of each trunk segment.
- Repeaters, if needed, regenerate the signal and pass it on to another trunk segment, thereby extending the normal limits of the network.

Thin Ethernet cable, like all cable, has limits and restrictions (described in Table 1.3) that will affect how you can set up the network.

TABLE 1.3 *Limits and Restrictions of Thin Ethernet Cable*

NETWORK ITEM	LIMITS AND RESTRICTIONS
Trunk segments	Maximum segment length (segments can consist of several shorter cables linked with BNC barrel connectors) is 607 feet (185 meters).
	Maximum number of segments per network (linked by repeaters) is five, for a total of 3,035 feet (925 meters). Only three of the segments can be populated with nodes, however.
	All trunk segments must be terminated at one end and terminated and grounded at the other end.
Nodes	Maximum number of nodes per trunk segment (including repeaters, which count as nodes) is 30.
	Maximum number of nodes (including repeaters) on the entire network is 90.
	Minimum cable distance between nodes is 1.6 feet (0.5 meters).

Thick Ethernet Cable

Thick Ethernet cable is RG-8 (50-ohm) coaxial cable. It is 3/8 inch in size. It is also called ThickNet, Standard Ethernet, or 10Base5. Because Thick Ethernet cable is bulkier, stiffer, and more difficult to handle than Thin Ethernet cable, it is usually used as the trunk cable, with twisted-pair drop cables used to connect the nodes to the Thick Ethernet trunk.

Thick Ethernet, like most coaxial cable, is covered with PVC so it can be run through air conditioning and heating ducts. However, as previously mentioned, PVC-covered cable cannot be used in the space between a false ceiling and the next floor because PVC is toxic if it burns. Another type of cable, called plenum cable, must be used in those areas.

If you use Thick Ethernet, you will need the following types of hardware components:

- Ethernet network boards are necessary for each workstation and server.
- N-series barrel connectors are used to connect lengths of the trunk cable together into one trunk segment.
- Transceivers (one for every node) connect the nodes' drop cables to the trunk segment.
- N-series T-connectors or vampire taps attach the transceivers to the trunk cable.
- Drop cables (also called transceiver cables) connect the network board in the node to the transceiver. The drop cable must have DIX connectors on each end.
- N-series terminators are used to terminate one end of each trunk segment.
- N-series grounded terminators are used to terminate and ground the other end of each trunk segment.
- Repeaters, if needed, regenerate the signal and pass it on to another trunk segment, thereby extending the normal limits of the network.

Thick Ethernet cable, like all cable, has limits and restrictions (described in Table 1.4) that will affect how you can set up the network.

TABLE 1.4 *Limits and Restrictions of Thick Ethernet Cable*

NETWORK ITEM	LIMITS AND RESTRICTIONS
Trunk segments	Maximum segment length (segments can consist of several shorter cables linked with N-series barrel connectors) is 1,640 feet (500 meters).
	Maximum number of segments per network (linked by repeaters) is five, for a total of 8,200 feet (2,500 meters). Only three of the segments can be populated with nodes, however.
	All trunk segments must be terminated at one end and terminated and grounded at the other end.

(continued)

TABLE 1.4 *Limits and Restrictions of Thick Ethernet Cable (continued)*

NETWORK ITEM	LIMITS AND RESTRICTIONS
Nodes	Maximum number of nodes per trunk segment (including repeaters, which count as nodes) is 100.
	Maximum number of nodes (including repeaters) on the entire network is 300.
	Every node must have its own drop cable connected to its own transceiver to connect to the trunk.
	Minimum cable distance between transceivers is 8 feet (2.5 meters).
	Maximum drop cable length between node and transceiver is 165 feet (50 meters).

Twisted-Pair Cable

There are two types of twisted-pair cabling: unshielded and shielded. Unshielded twisted-pair cable is commonly used as telephone wire. Shielded twisted-pair cable uses heavier-gauge wire and is protected with insulation and foil shielding.

Unshielded twisted-pair cable, although commonly found in abundance in buildings, is a poorer choice for network cabling because it can be very susceptible to electromagnetic interference from sources such as fluorescent lights, elevators, and telephone ring signals. This type of cable is also called UTP Ethernet or 10BaseT.

Shielded twisted-pair cable is a better choice for networks because of its extra insulation and foil shielding.

If you use twisted-pair cabling, you will need the following types of hardware components:

- Ethernet network boards are necessary for each workstation and server.
- Wiring hubs can be used to connect nodes to the network. *Stand-alone hubs* are devices with their own power supply. *Peer hubs* are boards that can be installed in one of the computers on the network and physically connected to that computer's network board.
- Twisted-pair cables connect the nodes to wiring hubs.
- An external concentrator, if needed, connects nodes that use coaxial or fiber-optic cable to the network.

- Punch-down blocks, if desired, make cable termination easier to change.
- RJ-45 connectors are used to connect the cables to wallplates, network boards, and wiring hubs.

Twisted-pair cable, like all cable, has limits and restrictions (described in Table 1.5) that will affect how you can set up the network.

TABLE 1.5 *Limits and Restrictions of Twisted-Pair Cable*

NETWORK ITEM	LIMITS AND RESTRICTIONS
Hubs	The maximum distance between a node and a wiring hub is 330 feet (100 meters).
	A twisted-pair network can have up to four linked wiring hubs.
Nodes	All nodes must be connected to a wiring hub, either directly (through a cable) or through a wallplate or concentrator.

Token Ring Network Architecture

A Token Ring network is cabled like a star, but it acts like a ring. Data flows from workstation to workstation around the ring. Because the network is cabled like a star, however, the data ends up going through the central point between each workstation on the trip around the ring.

Token Ring networks can run on twisted-pair (either shielded or unshielded) or fiber-optic cables. They generally work well in situations that involve heavy data traffic because Token Ring is reliable. It is also fairly easy to install, but it is more expensive than Ethernet networks.

Unshielded twisted-pair cabling is a poorer choice for network cabling because it can be very susceptible to electromagnetic interference from sources such as fluorescent lights, elevators, and telephone ring signals.

Shielded twisted-pair is a better choice for networks because of its extra insulation and foil shielding.

There are two different versions of Token Ring — one that supports a 4 Mbps transmission speed and one that supports 16 Mbps. A single network can run only one or the other, but networks of differing speeds can be connected through a bridge or router.

If you use Token Ring, you will need the following types of hardware components:

- Token Ring network boards are necessary for each workstation and server.
- *Multistation Access Units* (MAUs) are wiring concentrators. Nodes connect to these MAUs, which in turn are connected to other MAUs to form the ring. The wiring inside a MAU forms a ring of the attached nodes.
- Cabling is necessary to connect the MAUs in the main ring.
- Patch cables are used to connect the nodes to the MAUs.
- Repeaters, if needed, regenerate the signal and pass it on, thereby extending the normal limits of the network.

IBM defined different types of cabling for use in Token Ring networks. These cabling types are as follows:

- Type 1 cable is shielded twisted-pair cable. It has two pairs of 22-gauge solid wire and can supply data-quality transmission. It can be used for the main ring (similar to a trunk cable in an Ethernet network) or to connect nodes to MAUs.
- Type 2 cable is a hybrid cable, containing four pairs of unshielded 22-gauge solid wire for voice transmission and two pairs of shielded 22-gauge solid wire for data transmission.
- Type 3 cable is unshielded twisted-pair cable, which is only required to support voice-quality transmission. It can have two, three, or four pairs of 22-gauge or 24-gauge solid wire, with each pair having at least two twists per foot. This cable is not recommended for Token Ring networks.
- Type 4 cable is undefined.
- Type 5 cable is fiber-optic cable, with two glass fiber cores. Type 5 cables are used to cable the main ring in a Token Ring network and can also be used to extend the distance between MAUs or to connect network segments between buildings.
- Type 6 cable is shielded twisted-pair cable, with two pairs of 26-gauge stranded wire. Type 6 cable is commonly used as an adapter cable to connect a node to a MAU.
- Type 7 cable is undefined.
- Type 8 cable is shielded twisted-pair cable, with two pairs of flat,

26-gauge solid wire. It is designed to run underneath carpeting.

- Type 9 cable is shielded twisted-pair cable, with two pairs of 26-gauge solid or stranded wire. It is covered with a plenum jacket and is used to go between floors.

Token Ring cable, like all cable, has limits and restrictions (described in Table 1.6) that will affect how you can set up the network.

TABLE 1.6 *Limits and Restrictions of Token Ring Cable*

NETWORK ITEM	LIMITS AND RESTRICTIONS
MAUs	Maximum number of MAUs on a network that uses Type 1 or 2 cabling is 33.
	Maximum number of MAUs on a network that uses Type 6 or 9 cabling is 12.
Cabling	Maximum distance between a node and a MAU is as follows:
	For Type 1 and 2 cable: 330 feet (100 meters)
	For Type 6 and 9 cable: 220 feet (66 meters)
	For unshielded twisted-pair: 150 feet (45 meters)
	Maximum distance between MAUs is as follows:
	For Type 1 and 2 cable: 660 feet (200 meters)
	For Type 6 cable: 140 feet (45 meters)
	For unshielded twisted-pair: 400 feet (120 meters)
	For fiber-optic cable: 0.6 miles (1 km)
	Maximum number of cable segments (separated by repeaters) in a series is three.
	All cable segments must be terminated at one end and terminated and grounded at the other.
Nodes	Maximum number of nodes is as follows:
	For networks using Type 1 and 2 cable: 260
	For networks using Type 6 and 9 cable: 96
	For networks using unshielded twisted-pair: 72
	Minimum cable distance between a node and a MAU is 8 feet (2.5 meters).

AppleTalk Network Architectures

AppleTalk is the networking protocol suite developed by Apple Computers. It provides peer-to-peer networking capabilities between all Macintoshes and Apple hardware. AppleTalk capability is automatically built into every Macintosh.

AppleTalk can run with several types of architectures:

- LocalTalk was Apple's built-in architecture in most older Macintoshes. A Macintosh doesn't need a separate network board to communicate over LocalTalk cables, but it does need a separate network board to use other topologies.
- EtherTalk is Apple's implementation of Ethernet. EtherTalk Phase 1 was based on the Ethernet II version of Ethernet. EtherTalk Phase 2 is based on the Ethernet 802.3 version. EtherTalk Phase 2 has replaced LocalTalk as the built-in networking architecture in most newer Macintoshes.
- TokenTalk is Apple's Token Ring implementation.
- FDDITalk is Apple's implementation of the 100 Mbps FDDI architecture.

For more information about using AppleTalk with IntranetWare, see Chapter 11.

High-Speed Network Architectures

Several new types of high-speed network architectures are currently being developed. These architectures are capable of supporting speeds up to 100 Mbps. Most of them use fiber-optic cabling. Because fiber-optic technology is relatively new and still evolving, most knowledgeable people in the industry recommend hiring a qualified, experienced vendor to take care of the network hardware installation. It's also important to get your vendor to guarantee that the components it installs will work together.

The following are some of the new high-speed architectures that are gaining in popularity:

- Fiber Distributed Data Interface (FDDI) is a new network architecture for using fiber-optic cables at very high speeds. It supports speeds of up to 100 Mbps, and it uses a dual-ring topology in which data can travel in opposite directions.

- Thomas Conrad Network System (TCNS) can use coaxial, shielded twisted-pair, or fiber-optic cabling. It, too, can support speeds of up to 100 Mbps.
- Fast Ethernet is being designed to transmit 100 Mbps over unshielded twisted-pair cable.

CHAPTER 2

Installing and Upgrading Servers

Instant Access

Installing

- To install a new server using default options (the quick and easy way), run INSTALL from the *NetWare 4.11 Operating System* CD-ROM and select the Simple Installation of NetWare 4.11 option.
- To install a new server using advanced features, run INSTALL from the *NetWare 4.11 Operating System* CD-ROM and select the Custom Installation of NetWare 4.11 option.

Upgrading from NetWare 4.0x or 4.1

- To upgrade a NetWare 4.0x or 4.1 server, use INSTALL.NLM and choose the Upgrade to NetWare 3.1x or 4.x option.

Upgrading from NetWare 3.1x

- To upgrade an existing NetWare 3.1x server, use INSTALL.NLM and choose the Upgrade to NetWare 3.1x or 4.x option. (This is the simplest upgrade option.)
- To transfer all the NetWare 3.1x server's data to a new machine on which IntranetWare has already been installed, use the across-the-wire migration feature of the DS Migrate workstation utility.

How you install your IntranetWare server depends on whether you are installing a new server or upgrading one from an earlier version of NetWare. This chapter discusses three different scenarios:

- Installing a new server
- Using INSTALL.NLM to upgrade an existing NetWare 4.0x, 4.1, or 3.1x server to IntranetWare
- Using the DS Migrate utility and the File Migration utility to migrate the bindery and data from a NetWare 3.1x server to a IntranetWare server

Before you install or upgrade your server, you need to make sure you're prepared with all the necessary information, as described in the next section.

Preparing to Install or Upgrade a Server

Regardless of whether you are upgrading or installing a new server, there are several decisions you have to make about your server. You may want to refer to the "Server Installation and Configuration" and "Volumes" worksheets in Appendix D to help you plan your server's installation. If you answer all the questions on these worksheets before you tackle the actual installation procedure, the process may go more smoothly.

Before starting the installation or upgrade, you should have the following information about the server:

- *The server's name.* The name can be between 2 and 47 characters long, using letters, numbers, hyphens, or underscores.
- *The server's memory.* A IntranetWare server should have a minimum of 20MB of RAM. Depending on the size of the network (the number of servers, number of users on the server, total disk space on the server, and so on), you may want even more memory. Novell recommends that you multiply the amount of your server's disk space by 0.008, and then add that amount to the base 20MB of RAM. (For example, a 500MB disk times 0.008 equals 4MB of RAM.) Then add up to 4MB more for additional cache buffer RAM to increase performance. Therefore, for a server with a 500MB hard disk, you may want a minimum of 28MB of RAM.
- *The server's internal IPX network number.* A number will be generated randomly for you, or you can specify your own. Each server on the network must have a unique internal IPX network number. (IPX, for

Internetwork Packet Exchange, is NetWare's native network protocol.)

- *The server's Directory tree.* You must know the name of the Directory tree into which the server will be installed. For more information about Novell Directory Services, see Chapter 5.
- *The server's type of time synchronization.* You may have Single Reference, Reference, Primary, or Secondary time servers. By default, the installation program will make the first server in the tree into a Single Reference time server, and all others will be Secondary time servers. For more information about time synchronization services, see Chapter 3.
- *The server's time zone.* You'll need to know the acronym for the server's time zone and whether that time zone supports Daylight Saving Time. (This information will probably be filled in automatically during the installation, but you'll want to verify it.)
- *The server's location (name context) in the Directory tree.* Before you install the server, be sure you are familiar with Novell Directory Services and how you want your network to be laid out in the Directory tree. In the Custom Installation, you'll need to specify to which Organization object or Organizational Unit object this server belongs. In the Simple Installation, you are simply asked for the name of your organization (for instance, your company name). This Organization object name will become the tree name, as well. For more information about Novell Directory Services, see Chapter 5.

You should also know the following information before starting the installation or upgrade:

- *The protocol you will use on the network.* See Chapter 11 for more information about protocols. IPX/SPX is the default; TCP/IP and AppleTalk are optional.
- *The types of network boards you will install in the server.* You'll need to know the type of board, the name of its corresponding LAN driver, its settings, and the frame type you will use (such as Ethernet 802.2, Ethernet 802.3, Ethernet SNAP, Ethernet II, Token Ring, or Token Ring SNAP). IntranetWare's default Ethernet frame type is Ethernet 802.2. For TCP/IP only, you will also need the board's IP address and subnet mask.
- *The amount of hard disk space you will allocate for a DOS disk partition.* The DOS partition is the portion of the hard disk that is reserved for

DOS system files and other DOS files that you want to store on the server. The rest of the disk becomes a NetWare partition, which stores the NetWare files and network data. Plan for at least a 20MB DOS partition, but a rule of thumb is to add 1MB to the DOS partition for every MB of server RAM installed. The first hard disk will have a DOS partition and a NetWare partition (or just a DOS partition, if you have other disks that can hold the NetWare partitions). All other disks can have only one NetWare partition each. (Each NetWare disk partition can have up to eight volumes on it, however.) You should create the DOS disk partition before running the installation program. (The installation process will create the partition for you if you want, but it's generally easier to do it yourself so that you can avoid having to reinstall the CD-ROM drive's drivers and other configuration information.)

- *Whether or not you want to mirror or duplex the hard disks.* Disk mirroring and duplexing let two disks store identical copies of network files so that if one disk fails, the other will keep working. Disk mirroring mirrors two or more disks. Disk duplexing mirrors the disks plus uses duplicate disk controller boards and cables. (For more information about disk mirroring and duplexing, see Chapter 3.)
- *Whether you want to install SFT III.* SFT III lets you set up two identical servers so that if one fails, the other continues to operate. For information on how to install SFT III, see Chapter 3.
- *Whether you want to install NetWare SMP (Symmetric Multiprocessor) or NetWare/IP.* NetWare SMP allows you to use a server with more than one processor, and NetWare/IP lets you install a network that will use the IP protocol family. For more information about installing these optional variations of NetWare, see the documentation that comes in the IntranetWare package.
- *The name of the disk controller board.* You should know the disk controller board's settings and the name of its corresponding disk driver.
- *The size of NetWare volume SYS.* A volume named SYS is mandatory for NetWare system and utility files. You should allocate at least 100MB of hard disk space for SYS, or if you plan to install the NetWare online documentation, at least 140MB for SYS.
- *The size and names of any additional NetWare volumes.* It's often a good idea to reserve SYS for NetWare files only and create a separate volume for regular applications and data files. In addition, if you will be supporting Macintosh files, you may want to create a volume just for those files.

If you choose to let NetWare create your volumes automatically, NetWare will assign the entire NetWare disk partition on the first hard disk to SYS. Each additional disk will have its own volume named VOL1, VOL2, and so on. You must choose the Custom Installation if you want the option of changing the sizes and names of the volumes before NetWare creates them. If you want to create more volumes than just SYS, you should use the Custom Installation.

- *Whether you want to use file compression on any volumes.* File compression typically can save more than 60 percent of your hard disk space by compressing unused files. By default, all NetWare volumes are enabled for file compression. However, just because a volume is enabled for compression doesn't mean the files will be compressed — you must turn on file compression for specific directories. For more information about file compression, see Chapter 8.
- *Each volume's block size and whether you want the volume to use block suballocation.* A *block* is a unit of disk space that is allocated to store a file. *Block suballocation* divides a block into 512-byte suballocation blocks so that several smaller files can share a single block. By default, block suballocation is turned on automatically. (For more information about block suballocation, see Chapter 8.) The default block size depends on the volume's size, as shown in the following list.

Volume Size	Block Size
0 to 31MB	4K
32 to 149MB	8K
150 to 499MB	16K
500MB to 1999MB	32K
2000MB or more	64K

- *Whether you want data migration turned on.* Data migration lets little-used files be migrated off the server's hard disk onto an external storage device, such as a tape, hard disk, or optical disk. These files are automatically "demigrated" back onto the server's hard disk when a user accesses them. For more information about data migration, see Chapter 8.
- *Whether you want any volumes to support Mac OS, OS/2, Windows 95, Windows NT, or UNIX files.* Because these non-DOS file systems support longer file names and different file formats, you must load a special type of program, called a *name space module,* on the server. Then you must assign that name space to the volume that you want to store

those files. The name space for Mac OS files is called MAC.NAM; the name space for UNIX files is called NFS.NAM; and the name space for Windows 95, Windows NT, and OS/2 is called LONG.NAM.

Installing a New Server

If you are setting up a new IntranetWare server, you have two choices. You can either use the Simple Installation, which will set up a basic NetWare server with default choices and a simple Novell Directory Services implementation, or you can choose the Custom Installation, which will let you configure more aspects of your network.

SIMPLE INTRANETWARE INSTALLATION

The Simple Installation method works very well in most smaller networks (fewer than 100 users). If you have a larger network, you probably want to use the Custom Installation to specify more details about your server and volumes.

The Simple Installation's Default Settings

When you use the Simple Installation procedure to install IntranetWare, the server and Novell Directory Services are set up with the following default characteristics. If you want different characteristics than these, use the Custom Installation described later in this chapter.

- The server has a name that you specify.
- The server has a randomly generated internal IPX network number.
- If this was the first server in the Directory tree, it becomes a Single Reference time server. If it was installed into an existing tree, it becomes a Secondary time server. See Chapter 3 for more information on time servers.
- The Directory tree has only one Organization object, named with your organization's name. The server, its volumes, and a user named ADMIN will be created under this Organization object. (The Organization object's name is also the name of the Directory tree.) For more information about Novell Directory Services, see Chapter 5.
- The server is set up to use the protocol IPX/SPX.
- The LAN drivers you select (or that are automatically detected) will be bound to the network boards in the server. Ethernet boards are set to use the default frame type Ethernet 802.2. If this server is being

installed into an existing network, the existing frame type will be detected automatically.

- The DOS disk partition you set up on the server's first hard disk before running the installation program still exists. (A minimum of 20MB is recommended.) The rest of the hard disk's space is created as a NetWare partition.
- Disk partitions are not set up to support disk mirroring or duplexing.
- NetWare SFT III, NetWare SMP, and NetWare/IP are not installed.
- The NetWare disk partition on the server's hard disk is set up to be a single volume, named SYS. All NetWare files are copied into this volume, and all other applications and data files are stored in this volume as well. If the server has more than one hard disk, each additional disk will contain a single NetWare partition, and the volume on that partition will be named VOL1, VOL2, and so on.
- The server supports DOS files by default. To support long file names used by Mac OS files, Windows 95 files, or other file system formats, you will have to load the name space for those files after installation.
- File compression is enabled for all volumes, but it is not turned on for any directories yet. For more information about file compression, see Chapter 8.
- Block sizes are set to the default size, which is based on the volume's size. (See the preceding list.) Block suballocation is automatically enabled in both the simple and the custom installations. For more information about block suballocation, see Chapter 8.
- Data migration is turned off. For more information about data migration, see Chapter 8.

The Simple Installation Procedure

To perform the Simple Installation of IntranetWare, complete the steps in the following checklist.

1. Set up the server hardware.

   a. Install and configure the network boards in the server. Refer to the network board manufacturer's documentation for configuration instructions.

   b. Using the DOS FDISK and FORMAT commands, create a DOS disk partition of at least 20MB. Leave the rest of the disk space free. (If the computer you're using doesn't have DOS installed, you can boot from the license diskette that came with IntranetWare. The necessary DOS commands to reformat the server's hard disk are contained on that diskette.)

c. Install the CD-ROM drive as a DOS device on the server, following the manufacturer's instructions.

d. Using the DOS DATE and TIME commands, verify that the computer's time and date are set correctly and change them if necessary.

2. Install the NetWare operating system.

a. Insert the IntranetWare Operating System CD-ROM into the computer's CD-ROM drive.

b. From the DOS command prompt, change to the CD-ROM drive's letter (usually D) and enter the following command:

```
INSTALL
```

c. Choose the language you want to use.

d. Choose Readme Files if you want to read the information in the readme files that was written too late to be printed in the manuals.

e. Choose NetWare Server Installation, choose IntranetWare, and then choose Simple Installation of IntranetWare.

f. Enter a name for this server.

g. In some cases, you may be asked to specify the country code, code page, and keyboard mapping for your server. (To select these, press Enter and choose the correct selections from the lists that appear.) If you're using United States English DOS, you usually won't see this screen.

3. The IntranetWare installation program can automatically detect many disk types and automatically select and load the necessary drivers. If the installation detects and loads your disk drivers, skip to Step 4. If the installation doesn't detect your disk driver, select the disk drivers for your server's hard disk controller board and CD-ROM drive controller board from the list that appears, and then specify their settings. If the driver you need doesn't appear in the list, press Insert and insert the diskette that contains the driver, and then press F3 to specify the correct path to the driver.

4. The IntranetWare installation program can automatically detect many network boards and automatically select and load the necessary LAN

drivers. If the installation detects your LAN drivers, skip to Step 5. If the installation doesn't detect your LAN drivers, select the LAN drivers for your server's network boards from the list that appears, and then specify their settings. If the driver you need doesn't appear in the list, press Insert and insert the diskette that contains the driver, and then press F3 to specify the correct path to the driver.

5. In some cases, you may need to select whether to access the CD-ROM as a DOS device or as a NetWare volume. To avoid a possible driver conflict, you should allow INSTALL to mount the CD-ROM as a NetWare volume. If the keyboard locks up, repeat the installation and choose Continue Accessing the CD-ROM via DOS option instead.
6. If you are asked whether to delete any existing nonbootable partitions, select Yes. At this point, files are copied to the server's boot disk.
7. If you are installing this server into an existing NetWare Directory tree, select the correct tree into which this server will be installed. (To create a new tree, press Insert.) If this is the first server in the tree, select "Yes, this is the first NetWare 4 server."
8. Select the time zone in which this server will exist.
9. If this is the first server in the Directory tree, enter the name of your organization (such as your company name). Keep the name short. This will become the name of your Directory tree and your only Organization object.
10. Enter a password for the ADMIN user. If this is the first server in the tree, enter any password you want. If this server is being installed into an existing NDS tree, type in the ADMIN password that has already been assigned.
11. If you are installing this server into an existing tree, enter the name context (location in the NDS tree) for this server.
12. When prompted, insert the license diskette. When the server has accepted the license, it will begin the "main file copy," copying the IntranetWare files to the server's SYS volume.
13. After the remaining files are copied to the server, the Other Installation Options screen appears. From this screen, choose the Make Diskettes option if you want to make a set of installation diskettes that you can use to install client software on your network workstations. If you plan to upgrade existing workstations that are already running a previous version of NetWare client software, you can choose the Create Client

Installation Directories on Server option. This will place the installation files into SYS:PUBLIC so that you can upgrade the existing workstations directly from the network, eliminating the need for making diskettes. (You can also install clients directly from the CD-ROM, so making diskettes may not be necessary for your situation.) See Chapter 4 for more information about installing workstations.

14. Choose other installation options or additional products you want to install, or choose Continue Installation if you don't need to install any additional products.
15. When the final installation message appears on the screen, press Enter to exit the program. You will be returned to the server's console prompt. The server is now functioning.
16. Reboot the server (type **DOWN** and then **RESTART SERVER**) to make all the necessary changes take effect.

CUSTOM INTRANETWARE INSTALLATION

The Custom Installation method lets you specify exactly how your server is set up, how partitions are created and mirrored, what frame types to use, what volumes to create, and so on. The following is a checklist of the steps you perform for the Custom Installation of IntranetWare.

1. Set up the server hardware.
   a. Install and configure network boards in the server. Refer to the network board manufacturer's documentation for configuration instructions.
   b. Using the DOS FDISK and FORMAT commands, create a DOS disk partition of at least 20MB. Leave the rest of the disk space free. (If the computer you're using doesn't have DOS installed, you can boot from the license diskette that came with IntranetWare. The necessary DOS commands to reformat the server's hard disk are contained on that diskette.)
   c. Install the CD-ROM drive as a DOS device on the server, following the manufacturer's instructions.
   d. Using the DOS DATE and TIME commands, verify that the computer's time and date are set correctly, and change them if necessary.
2. Install the NetWare operating system.
   a. Insert the *IntranetWare Operating System* CD-ROM into the computer's CD-ROM drive.

b. From the DOS command prompt, change to the CD-ROM drive's letter (usually D) and enter the following command:

```
INSTALL
```

c. Choose the language you want to use.

d. Choose Readme Files if you want to read the information in the readme files that was written too late to be printed in the manuals.

e. Choose NetWare Server Installation, choose IntranetWare, and then choose Custom Installation of IntranetWare.

f. Enter a name for this server.

g. Either accept the default IPX internal network number, or enter your own.

h. Accept the default destination path for the NetWare server startup (boot) files so that they are copied to the DOS partition on the server.

i. Choose the country code, code page, and keyboard mapping for your server. (To select these, press Enter and choose the correct selections from the lists that appear.)

j. If you want to add any SET parameters to the server's startup files now, select Yes and enter them. (Press F1 to read help about commands you can and cannot add to these files.) Otherwise, select No.

k. Specify whether you want the AUTOEXEC.BAT file to automatically load the server (SERVER.EXE). If you do not add this command to AUTOEXEC.BAT, you will have to load the server by typing SERVER at the DOS prompt any time the server is rebooted.

3. The IntranetWare installation program can automatically detect many disk types and automatically select and load the necessary drivers. If the installation detects and loads your disk drivers, skip to Step 4. If the installation doesn't detect your disk driver, select the disk drivers for your server's hard disk controller board and CD-ROM drive controller board from the list that appears, and then specify their settings. If the driver you need doesn't appear in the list, press Insert and insert a diskette that contains the driver, and then press F3 to specify the correct path to the driver.

4. The IntranetWare installation program can automatically detect many network boards and will automatically select and load the necessary LAN drivers. If the installation detects your LAN drivers, skip to Step 5.

If the installation doesn't detect your LAN drivers, select the LAN drivers for your server's network boards from the list that appears, and then specify their settings. If the driver you need doesn't appear in the list, press Insert and insert the diskette that contains the driver, and then press F3 to specify the correct path to the driver.

5. You can choose to add or modify existing drivers at the next screen that appears, or you can choose to continue the installation if the listed drivers are correct.
6. If you want to load protocols besides IPX, choose View/Modify Protocol Settings and select the board you want. Then specify the protocols, frame types, and other items you want the board to use. Specify an IP address and IP mask numbers if you are using TCP/IP. Press F10 to save your settings. Then choose Continue with Installation.
7. In some cases, you may have to select whether to access the CD-ROM as a DOS device or as a NetWare volume. To avoid a possible driver conflict, you should allow INSTALL to mount the CD-ROM as a NetWare volume. If the keyboard locks up, repeat the installation and choose Continue Accessing the CD-ROM via DOS option instead.
8. Select whether you want to create disk partitions automatically or manually.
   a. The automatic option assigns all free space on the first hard disk to volume SYS and creates separate volumes named VOL1, VOL2, and so on on any additional disks. If you choose the automatic method, skip to Step 11.
   b. Use the manual option if you want to set up disk mirroring, assign more than one volume per hard disk, or assign one volume to span multiple hard disks.
9. (This step covers manual disk partitioning only.) Select the Create, Delete, and Modify Disk Partitions option and choose the disk you want to partition. Then choose Create a NetWare Disk Partition. If you want to change the default size of the partition and its Hot Fix redirection area, do so.
10. (This step covers manual disk partitioning only.) If you want to set up disk mirroring, choose Mirror and Unmirror Disk Partition Sets. Select the disk partition (also called disk device) you want to mirror and press Enter. Then press Insert to choose an available disk partition to

mirror to the first partition. When asked if you want to change the partition's size, choose Yes to make sure the installation program makes the partitions the same size. Press F10 when you are finished mirroring partitions.

11. The Manage NetWare Volumes screen shows the volumes that the installation will create for you.

    a. To change the volume's name, change its block size, disable file compression or block suballocation, or enable data migration, select the volume, press Enter, and make the desired changes. Note that file compression and block suballocation cannot be turned off once the volume is created.

    b. To change the volume's size, press Insert or F3, select the volume, and change the volume's size.

    c. To add an additional volume, first decrease another volume's size, and then select the "free space" that will be shown, press Enter, and specify the new volume's information.

    d. To accept the proposed volumes and to mount them, press F10.

12. Verify the source path and press Enter so the installation program will begin copying files to the server.

13. If you are installing this server into an existing NetWare Directory tree, select the correct tree. (To create a new tree, press Insert.) If this is the first server in the tree, select "Yes, this is the first NetWare 4 server," and then give the new tree a name when you are prompted for it.

14. Select the time zone in which this server will exist and accept or change the time synchronization information that appears. ("DST offset from standard time" means the number of hours you are ahead or behind Greenwich Mean Time.) Press F10 to save the time information and continue. See Chapter 3 for more information about time synchronization.

15. Create a name context for the server. By entering the name of the organization (such as your company) and the names of descending levels of Organizational Units (such as a division and a department), you actually create the branch of the NDS tree that will contain this server if the branch doesn't already exist. If a branch already exists, press Enter on each field and select the Organizational Unit objects you want. You can enter up to three Organizational Unit names by

typing the names in the available fields. If you want to create more, use the Server Context field and type in the server's full name, with periods delimiting each Organizational Unit.

16. Enter a password for the ADMIN user. If this is the first server in the tree, enter any password you want. If this server is being installed into an existing tree, type in the ADMIN password that has already been assigned or enter the name and password of another User object already in the NDS tree. This User object must have enough NDS trustee rights to add the server to the context specified. See Chapter 7 for more information about NDS trustee rights.
17. When prompted, insert the license diskette.
18. If prompted, specify whether you need to install NetWare SMP (Symmetrical Multiprocessing).
19. Review the STARTUP.NCF file that appears on the screen. Information you entered during the installation process so far is already placed into this file. Press F10 to save the file and continue.
20. Review the new AUTOEXEC.NCF file that appears on the screen. Information you entered during the installation process so far is already placed into this file. If necessary, add any additional commands to the AUTOEXEC.NCF file. For example, you can add a command to mount all the server's volumes automatically whenever the server boots (MOUNT ALL), and you can add commands to load NLMs (NetWare Loadable Modules) automatically. Press F10 to save the file and continue.
21. After the remaining files are copied to the server, the Other Installation Options screen appears. From this screen, choose the Make Diskettes option if you want to make a set of installation diskettes that you can use to install client software on your network workstations.

    If you plan to upgrade existing workstations that are already running a previous version of NetWare client software, you can choose the Create Client Installation Directories on Server option. This will place the installation files into SYS:PUBLIC so that you can upgrade the existing workstations directly from the network, eliminating the need for making diskettes. (You can also install clients directly from the CD-ROM, so making diskettes may not be necessary for your situation.) See Chapter 4 for more information about installing workstations.

22. Choose other installation options or additional products you want to install, or choose Continue Installation if you don't need to install any additional products.
23. When the final installation message appears on the screen, press Enter to exit the program. You will be returned to the server's console prompt. The server is now functioning.
24. Reboot the server (type **DOWN** then **RESTART SERVER**) to make all the necessary changes take effect.
25. If you want the server to be able to store Mac OS files or other non-DOS files that use longer names than DOS allows, you must load the appropriate name space on the server, and then add the name space to one or more volumes.
    a. To allow the server to store Mac OS files, enter the following command at the server console, replacing *name* with MAC for Mac OS files, NFS for UNIX files, or LONG for Windows 95, Windows NT, or OS/2 files:

       ```
       LOAD name
       ```

    b. Then specify a particular volume that will store these files by entering the ADD NAME SPACE command in the following format (replace *name* with MAC, NFS, or LONG, and replace *volumename* with the name of the volume, such as SYS or VOL1):

       ```
       ADD NAME SPACE name TO VOLUME volumename
       ```

26. Make a backup of the new IntranetWare server.

Upgrading from Previous Versions of NetWare

There are two methods for upgrading servers from previous versions of NetWare to IntranetWare. The method you use depends on the version of NetWare you're currently running and the type of data transfer method you prefer.

UPGRADING FROM PREVIOUS VERSION OF NETWARE 4.x

To upgrade an existing NetWare 4.01, 4.02, or 4.1 server to IntranetWare, use INSTALL.NLM and choose the Upgrade NetWare 3.1x or 4.x option. This is the most simple way to upgrade a server. With this option, INSTALL.NLM will copy new NetWare files and the new IntranetWare operating system onto the existing server. It will also upgrade Novell Directory Services. (This option can also be used to upgrade NetWare 3.1x servers to IntranetWare.)

In most cases, it's best to upgrade all NetWare 4.0x and 4.1 servers to IntranetWare as soon as possible, to avoid maintaining a mixed network. IntranetWare fixed several problems with the older versions of Novell Directory Services, and it is easier to maintain NDS if all servers are operating at the same level.

For a checklist of steps to follow to upgrade a NetWare 4.01, 4.02, or 4.1 server, see the section "Upgrade Using INSTALL.NLM."

UPGRADING FROM NETWARE 3.1x

There are two options for upgrading a NetWare 3.1x server to IntranetWare:

- Upgrade an existing NetWare 3.1x server to IntranetWare. You use INSTALL.NLM to upgrade an existing NetWare 3.1x server, just as you do if you are upgrading from NetWare 4.0x or 4.1. See the section "Upgrade Using INSTALL.NLM" for a checklist of upgrade steps.
- Transfer all the NetWare 3.1x server's data to a new machine on which IntranetWare has already been installed. This is called an across-the-wire migration (because the data is transferred to another machine across the network cabling) and it requires the DS Migrate and the File Migration workstation utilities. This migration method of upgrading a server allows you to see and modify a model of how your Directory tree will look before you actually finish the migration. See the section "Upgrade Using DS Migrate" for a checklist of upgrade steps.

When upgrading a NetWare 3.11 or 3.12 server, the server's existing bindery data is upgraded into a Novell Directory Services (NDS) database. All of the server's bindery objects become NDS objects, and they are all placed in the same location (name context) in the Directory tree as the server. In fact, the server itself will appear as a Server object in the Directory tree. (If you use the DS Migrate option to upgrade the server, you can change where the NDS objects reside if you wish.)

Binderies are specific to particular servers. This means that if you want user John to access three different NetWare 3.1x servers, you have to create John as a separate user on all three servers. With NDS, a single NDS database is common to all servers in the network. Therefore, you only need to create John once, and then just give him trustee rights to files on those three servers.

Keep this in mind if you are upgrading several NetWare 3.1x servers into a IntranetWare Directory tree. If you have multiple instances of user John on different NetWare 3.1x servers and you install the servers into the same location (name context), the installation program will ask you if you want to delete, rename, or merge the user with the one that already exists. If one of the NetWare 3.1x users named John is actually a different person than the other two Johns, you should rename one of them before starting the upgrade to ensure that they don't merge.

UPGRADE USING INSTALL.NLM

INSTALL.NLM can be used to upgrade NetWare 3.11, 3.12, 4.01, 4.02, and 4.1 servers to IntranetWare. With this utility, new files are copied from the CD-ROM to the existing server to upgrade it.

NOTE

To upgrade a NetWare 4.x server to IntranetWare, the NetWare 4.x server must be currently running a version of DS.NLM that is 4.89 or higher. To see the DS.NLM version, run the MODULES console utility. If you are not running version 4.89 or above, you must update the existing DS.NLM before you can upgrade the server to IntranetWare. Do this by following the instructions in the readme file on the CD-ROM. If you are running NetWare 4.0x, see the READUPGD.TXT and DSREPAIR.DOC files in the PRODUCTS\NW402\ENGLISH directory. If you are running NetWare 4.1, see the READUPDS.TXT file in the RODUCTS\NW410\ENGLISH directory.

If you are upgrading from NetWare 3.1x and you want to upgrade your printing services from NetWare 3.1x to IntranetWare, you will also have to use PUPGRADE.NLM.

To upgrade a NetWare 3.1x, 4.0x, or 4.1 server to IntranetWare, complete the steps in the following checklist.

1. Because deleted files in NetWare 3.1x and 4.x remain on the server in a salvageable state, you may want to see whether there are any deleted files you want to salvage before you upgrade the server. The upgrade process will purge any deleted files still on the server.

2. Make two backups of all network files.
3. Copy the server's LAN drivers and AUTOEXEC.NCF files from the SYS: volume onto a diskette so that you can have backups of these files if necessary.
4. If necessary, edit the existing AUTOEXEC.NCF file to specify the Ethernet frame type you want. IntranetWare uses Ethernet 802.2 by default. (NetWare 3.11 used Ethernet 802.3 by default.)
5. Bring down the existing server by entering the console command

   ```
   DOWN
   ```

   and then the command

   ```
   EXIT
   ```

6. From the server's boot directory, copy the server's boot files (.BAT files, .NAM files, disk drivers, INSTALL.NLM, SERVER.EXE, STARTUP.NCF, VREPAIR.NLM, and V_namespace.NLM files) to the same diskette you used in Step 3.
7. If you are upgrading from NetWare 3.1x, rename the SERVER.31x directory to NWSERVER. (Use DOS's RENDIR command to change a directory's name.)
8. Insert the *NetWare 4.11 Operating System* CD-ROM into the computer's CD-ROM drive, change to the CD-ROM drive's letter (usually D), and enter the following command:

   ```
   INSTALL
   ```

9. Choose the language you want to use.
10. Choose Readme Files if you want to read the information that was written too late to be printed in the manuals.
11. Choose NetWare Server Installation, choose IntranetWare, and then choose Upgrade NetWare 3.1x or 4.x.
12. Specify the destination directory, which is the directory that will contain the server boot files C:\NWSERVER. The new server boot files are now copied to the directory.
13. If necessary, change the country code, code page, and keyboard mapping for this server. (To select these, press Enter and choose the correct selections from the lists that appear.)
14. The IntranetWare installation program will automatically load any disk drivers it finds in the original STARTUP.NCF file of the server

you're upgrading. If it cannot find a disk driver in that file, the installation program can detect many disk types and automatically select and load the necessary drivers. If the installation detects and loads your disk drivers, skip to Step 15. If the installation doesn't detect your disk driver, select the disk drivers for your server's hard disk controller board and CD-ROM drive controller board from the list that appears, and then specify their settings. If the driver you need doesn't appear in the list, press Insert and insert the diskette that contains the driver.

15. In some cases, you may have to select whether to access the CD-ROM as a DOS device or as a NetWare volume. To avoid a possible driver conflict, you should allow INSTALL to mount the CD-ROM as a NetWare volume. If the keyboard locks up, repeat the installation and choose Continue Accessing the CD-ROM via DOS option instead.
16. When prompted, insert the License diskette.
17. If prompted, specify whether you need to install NetWare SMP (Symmetrical Multiprocessing).
18. When the message appears describing a temporary AUTOEXEC.NCF file, review it to see if you must edit it. In this temporary file, commands that may cause problems during the upgrade are disabled with a REM command. Edit the file only if there are commands that must execute, and then continue with the installation.
19. The IntranetWare installation program can automatically load any LAN drivers it finds in the original AUTOEXEC.NCF file of the server you're upgrading. If it cannot find a LAN driver in that file, the installation program can detect many network boards and automatically select and load the necessary LAN drivers. If the installation detects your LAN drivers, skip to Step 20. If the installation doesn't detect your LAN drivers, select the LAN drivers for your server's network boards from the list that appears, and then specify their settings. If the driver you need doesn't appear in the list, press Insert and insert the diskette that contains the driver.
20. (NetWare 4.x upgrades only) If you are upgrading a NetWare 4.x server, enter the password for user ADMIN when prompted. A message will appear telling you that the NDS schema will be updated. Press Enter to continue, then skip to Step 26.
21. (NetWare 3.1x upgrades only) If you are upgrading a NetWare 3.1x server into an existing NetWare Directory tree, select the correct tree.

(To create a new tree, press Insert.) If this is the first server in the tree, select "Yes, this is the first NetWare 4 server," and then specify a name for the new tree.

22. Select the time zone in which this server will exist and accept or change the time synchronization information that appears. See Chapter 3 for more information about time synchronization.

23. Create a name context for the server. By entering the name of the organization (such as your company) and the names of descending levels of Organizational Units (such as a division and a department), you actually create the branch of the NDS tree that will contain this server if the branch doesn't already exist. If a branch already exists, press Enter on each field and select the Organizational Unit objects you want. You can enter up to three Organizational Unit names by typing names in the available fields. If you want to create more, use the Server Context field, and type in the server's full name, with periods delimiting each Organizational Unit.

24. Enter a password for the ADMIN user. If this is the first server in the tree, enter any password you want. If this server is being installed into an existing tree, type in the ADMIN password that has already been assigned or enter the name and password of another User object already in the NDS tree. This User object must have enough NDS trustee rights to add the server to the context specified. See Chapter 7 for more information about NDS trustee rights.

25. INSTALL.NLM will check the AUTOEXEC.NCF file for frame types and will inform you of any problems. Review the new AUTOEXEC.NCF file that appears on the screen. Information you entered during the upgrade process so far is already placed into this file. If necessary, add any additional commands to the AUTOEXEC.NCF file. Press F10 to save the file and continue.

26. After the remaining files are copied to the server, the Other Installation Options screen appears. From this screen, choose the Make Diskettes option if you want to make a set of installation diskettes that you can use to install client software on your network workstations. If you plan to upgrade existing workstations that are already running a previous version of NetWare client software, you can choose the Create Client Installation Directories on Server option. This will place the installation files into SYS:PUBLIC so that you can upgrade the existing workstations directly from the network, eliminating the need for making

diskettes. (You can also install clients directly from the CD-ROM, so making diskettes may not be necessary for your situation.) See Chapter 4 for more information about installing workstations.

27. Choose other installation options or additional products you want to install, or choose Continue Installation if you don't need to install any additional products.
28. When the final installation message appears on the screen, press Enter to exit the program. You will be returned to the server's console prompt. The server is now functioning.
29. (NetWare 3.1x upgrades only) If you are upgrading a NetWare 3.x server, load INSTALL.NLM again to turn on block suballocation and file compression if you want to use them. From the main INSTALL menu, select Volume Options, choose a volume, and then change the File Compression and Block Suballocation fields to On.
30. Reboot the server (type **DOWN** and then **RESTART SERVER**) to make all the necessary changes take effect.

UPGRADING PRINTING OBJECTS WITH PUPGRADE.NLM

If you want to upgrade NetWare 3.1x printing objects to NDS objects on a IntranetWare tree, you must use PUPGRADE.NLM. Upgrade printing objects after you've upgraded the server itself. To upgrade your NetWare 3.1x printing objects, complete the steps in the following checklist.

1. (Optional) To upgrade printing objects, copy the file PUPGRADE.NLM from the IntranetWare server's SYS:SYSTEM directory into the NetWare 3.1x server's SYS:SYSTEM directory.
2. Load PUPGRADE.NLM on the NetWare 3.1x server.
3. Enter the Admin user name (or equivalent user) and password.
4. If you want to upgrade your PRINTCON database of print job configurations, select Upgrade PRINTCON Database. (After the upgrade, read the log file PRINTCON.UPG in SYS:SYSTEM to see if any errors occurred.)
5. If you want to upgrade the PRINTDEF database of printer definitions, select Upgrade PRINTDEF Database, and then specify the correct context in the NDS tree. (After the upgrade, read the log file PRINTDEF.UPG in SYS:SYSTEM to see if any errors occurred.)

6. If you want to upgrade your print server and printers from bindery objects to NDS objects in the NDS tree, select Upgrade Print Server and Printers. From the list of NetWare 3.1x print servers that appears, select the print server you want to upgrade. (After the upgrade, read the log file in SYS:SYSTEM to see if any errors occurred. The log file is named with the print server's name, followed by the extension .UPG.)
7. Exit PUPGRADE.
8. Using the NetWare Administrator utility from a workstation logged in to the IntranetWare server, add user ADMIN as an authorized user and operator of the upgraded print queues and print server. (Since user ADMIN doesn't exist in NetWare 3.1x, it isn't automatically added to these newly upgraded print objects.)
9. Make a backup of the new IntranetWare server.

NOTE

If you had been running the NetWare Auditing feature on this server, auditing was disabled during the upgrade. You will need to set up auditing again on this server if you want to continue to use auditing.

UPGRADE USING DS MIGRATE AND FILE MIGRATION

DS Migrate, in conjunction with the File Migration utility, can be used to upgrade NetWare 3.1x servers to IntranetWare. Use this upgrade method if you want to replace your old server computer with a new computer and if you want to see and possibly modify the way your Directory tree will look before you migrate the bindery information into NDS.

To upgrade (migrate) a server this way, you actually install a new IntranetWare server elsewhere on the network (using the procedure described in the section "Installing a New Server"). Then you log in to both the NetWare 3.1x network and the IntranetWare network from a workstation that's running the NetWare Administrator utility. You launch the DS Migrate utility from the NetWare Administrator's Tools menu. DS Migrate transfers the NetWare 3.1x server's bindery information into the DS Migrate database. In this database, the bindery objects appear in a graphical structure that looks like an NDS tree.

NOTE

Because you are moving information from one server to another, this form of upgrade is often called "migration."

With this graphical tool, you can safely model the proposed NDS information so that it will be converted into the NDS tree the way you want it. You can add or delete objects, move them around, assign trustee rights, and so on without actually affecting the tree. When you have modeled the objects into the form you want, you will log into the IntranetWare server, and then use DS Migrate to merge the bindery objects into the NDS tree.

The bindery information that gets migrated includes all user accounts and their properties, printing objects, the system login script (which gets added to the NDS container's login script), print job configurations, and trustee assignments. The only items that are not migrated are the printer definition database and users' passwords. You will have to assign new passwords during the modeling procedure.

After you migrate the bindery information, you use the File Migration utility to copy all of the regular network data files from the old server to the new server. The File Migration utility will migrate all files except those in the NetWare 3.1x server's SYS:SYSTEM and SYS:PUBLIC because there is no need for those directories' files on the new IntranetWare server.

When you've evaluated the new server's final state, you can erase all the information from the old server and convert it into a workstation.

Running DS Migrate

To migrate a NetWare 3.1x server to IntranetWare, complete the steps in the following checklist.

1. Because deleted files in NetWare 3.1x remain on the server in a salvageable state, you may want to see whether there are any deleted files you want to salvage before you upgrade the server. The upgrade process will purge any deleted files still on the server.
2. Run BINDFIX on the old server to delete any MAIL directories for users who no longer exist.
3. Make two backups of all network files.
4. If you haven't already, install the IntranetWare server on a new machine. See the section "Installing a New Server" earlier in this chapter.
5. Log in to the NetWare 3.1x server as Supervisor, and log in to the IntranetWare server as Admin.
6. Launch NetWare Administrator by double-clicking its icon, and then choose DS Migrate from the Tools menu. (Click Continue on the introductory screen.)

NOTE DS Migrate expects the F drive to be mapped to a network drive. If it is mapped to a local drive, you'll need to remap it to a network drive.

7. From the File menu, choose New View, and then choose Bindery View (or simply click the Bindery Discover button on the toolbar).
8. Enter a name for this view, specify the author, and click OK.
9. Select the NetWare 3.1x server you want to migrate and specify the type of information you want DS Migrate to "discover." DS Migrate will then create a report containing all the information it was able to find. Any errors it finds are listed at the bottom of the report. (The report, called BINDDISC.LOG, is stored on the NetWare 3.1x server.)
10. When you've reviewed the report, close it.
11. All the bindery objects now appear in a graphical format, with all the objects located in an Organizational Unit object named with the server's name.
12. Now you can move objects around as necessary until you achieve a model of your NDS tree that describes where you want these bindery objects to reside. You can drag and drop objects into different areas, change the names of volumes and servers that the objects use, or use the Find and Replace option from the View menu to change trustee assignments and so on. If the NetWare 3.1x server and the IntranetWare server have different names, you may have to change the properties of Print Queue objects, login scripts, and print job configurations to specify the new volume names and print queue names.
13. Click the Tree button to highlight all objects, and then choose Verify Object Dependencies from the View menu. (Click OK.)
14. From the View menu, select Resolve References for Selected Objects, and then click OK.
15. From the File menu, select Open View, choose the view you want to use (the same one you named in Step 8), and then click OK.
16. Activate the view.
17. From the Tools menu, select Options and click the Configure button.
18. Uncheck the box next to Create Trustee Directories If They Do Not Exist (because you will be migrating those directories later) and make any other changes as necessary in the Configure dialog box. This

includes setting the options for passwords and for merging the objects into the NDS database.

19. From the View menu, select Configure All Objects. DS Migrate will check the configuration to make sure there are no errors before it actually merges the objects into the tree. If it finds errors, it will display the errors, and you can click Cancel to go back and fix the problems. If there were no errors, click OK to start the configuration of the objects (merging them into the IntranetWare NDS database).

When the migration of bindery objects into NDS objects has finished, you can use the File Migration utility to migrate the files from the old server to the new one, as explained in the following section.

Running File Migration

After you've migrated the bindery objects from a NetWare 3.1x server to a IntranetWare server, you can migrate the data files. To migrate files from a NetWare 3.1x server to IntranetWare, complete the steps in the following checklist.

1. On the NetWare 3.1x server, you will have to update some NLMs in the SYS:SYSTEM directory with the following new ones from the *NetWare 4.11 Operating System* CD-ROM (these files are located in the PRODUCTS\NW3X directory on the CD-ROM):
    - SPXS.NLM
    - TLI.NLM
    - CLIB.NLM
    - AFTER311.NLM
    - A3112.NLM
    - SMDR.NLM
    - STREAMS.NLM
    - MAC.NAM (for NetWare 3.11 servers that support Mac OS files only; NetWare 3.12 servers don't need this updated file)
    - TSA311.NLM (for NetWare 3.11 servers) or TSA312.NLM (for NetWare 3.12 servers)
2. On the NetWare 3.1x server, load the new TSA31x.NLM.

3. If the server you're migrating is a NetWare 3.11 server that supports Mac OS files, dismount the volume and unload the MAC.NAM file. Then reload the new MAC.NAM file you copied in Step 1 and run VREPAIR.NLM.
4. Launch the NetWare Administrator utility (if you haven't already) and select File Migration from the Tools menu.
5. Click the Next button.
6. For the Source Server, click the down arrow and select the NetWare 3.1x server.
7. For the Source Volume, select a volume to migrate, and then click Next to continue.
8. Enter the Supervisor's password for the NetWare 3.1x server and click Next to continue.
9. For the Destination Server, select the IntranetWare server to which you are migrating the files.
10. For the Destination Volume, specify the IntranetWare volume to which you want to migrate the files.
11. For the Destination Directory, specify the directory to which you want to migrate the files and then click Next to continue.
12. Enter the IntranetWare Admin user's password and then click Next to continue.
13. Click the Migrate button to begin the migration.
14. When that volume is finished migrating, you can choose another volume to migrate or you can exit the utility.

The bindery and file migrations are now complete.

CHAPTER 3

Managing the Server

Optimizing Performance

- To monitor performance, use MONITOR.NLM.
- To optimize performance, use MONITOR.NLM, SET parameters, and SERVMAN.NLM.
- To manage server memory, use MONITOR.NLM and the MEMORY, MEMORY MAP, and REGISTER MEMORY console utilities.
- To see a history of errors that have occurred with the server, the volume, or TTS, use a text editor or EDIT.NLM to read the error log files: SYS$LOG.ERR, VOL$LOG.ERR, TTS$LOG.ERR, and ABEND.LOG.
- To capture server messages to a screen so you can read them for diagnostic purposes, use CONLOG.NLM.

Protecting the Server

- To use an uninterruptible power supply (UPS) to protect the server from power outages, use UPS.NLM (or UPS_AIO.NLM for serial port connections), the UPS STATUS console utility, and the UPS TIME console utility.
- To protect the server and network from virus infections, use a virus detector, assign executable files the Execute Only file or Read-Only attributes, and warn users against loading files from external sources.

Maintaining the Server

- To display a server name, use the NAME console utility.
- To display the server's hardware information, use the CONFIG and SPEED console utilities.
- To display the server's version information, use the VERSION console utility.
- To display a list of the server's volumes and the name spaces they support, use the VOLUMES console utility.
- To bring down the server, use the DOWN console utility, followed by the EXIT console utility.
- To reboot the server, use the DOWN console utility, followed by the RESTART SERVER console utility.

- To obtain patches, use NetWire (Novell's online service on both CompuServe and the Internet).
- To control the server from a workstation, use the Remote Console feature. Load REMOTE.NLM and either RSPX.NLM or RS232.NLM on the server, and then run the RCONSOLE.EXE workstation utility.
- To control server startup activities, use the server startup files AUTOEXEC.NCF and STARTUP.NCF. (Edit these files by using EDIT.NLM and SERVMAN.NLM.)
- To manage workstation connections, use MONITOR.NLM and the ENABLE LOGIN and DISABLE LOGIN console utilities.
- To manage protocols, use INSTALL.NLM and INETCFG.NLM. (See also Chapter 11.)
- To charge for server usage, use the accounting services in the NetWare Administrator utility and ATOTAL.
- To monitor or modify a server's time, use the SYSTIME workstation utility and the TIME, SET TIME, and SET TIME ZONE console utilities.
- To load, unload, or display currently loaded NLMs, use the LOAD, UNLOAD, and MODULES console utilities.

Managing Storage Devices

- To add a new hard disk or replace an existing one, use INSTALL.NLM.
- To protect network data by mirroring hard disks, use INSTALL.NLM and the MIRROR STATUS, REMIRROR PARTITION, and ABORT REMIRROR console utilities.
- To protect network data by mirroring complete servers, use the NetWare SFT III feature. Install SFT III by using INSTALL.NLM; manage SFT III with SERVMAN.NLM, INSTALL.NLM, and the HALT console utility.
- To protect network data from bad blocks on the hard disk, use the Hot Fix feature. (Set up Hot Fix in INSTALL.NLM. Monitor the number of bad blocks found with MONITOR.NLM.)
- To manage CD-ROMs, use CDROM.NLM and the CD console utility.
- To manage High-Capacity Storage Systems (HCSS), use INSTALL.NLM, HCSS.NLM, and the NetWare Administrator utility.

Managing Routing Between Servers

- To list networks, use the DISPLAY NETWORKS console utility.
- To list servers, use the DISPLAY SERVERS console utility.
- To execute protocol configuration commands made using INETCFG.NLM, use the INITIALIZE SYSTEM and REINITIALIZE SYSTEM console utilities.
- To configure protocols, use INETCFG.NLM.
- To configure IPX, AppleTalk, and TCP/IP protocols, use INETCFG.NLM.
- To configure RIP/SAP packet filtering, use FILTCFG.NLM.
- To display routing information, use the TRACK ON and TRACK OFF console utilities.

Managing an IntranetWare server involves many different types of tasks, from monitoring performance to adding new hard disks to charging customers for their usage. This chapter explains how you can accomplish these tasks.

Console Utilities and NLMs

There are two types of tools you can use when you work with the IntranetWare server: console utilities and NetWare Loadable Modules.

Console utilities are commands you type at the server's console (keyboard and monitor) to change some aspect of the server or view information about it. These console utilities are built into the operating system, just as internal DOS commands are built into DOS. To read online help for console utilities, enter

```
HELP
```

at the server console.

NetWare Loadable Modules (NLMs) are software modules that you load into the server's operating system to add or change functionality. Many NLMs are automatically installed with the IntranetWare operating system. Others are optional; you can load them if your particular situation requires them. There are four different types of NetWare Loadable Modules that you can use to add different types of functionality to your server: NLMs, name space modules, LAN drivers, and disk drivers. These NLMs are described in Table 3.1. Many third-party software manufacturers create different types of NLMs to work on IntranetWare.

TABLE 3.1 *Different Types of NLMs*

TYPE OF NLM	FILENAME EXTENSION	DESCRIPTION
NLM	.NLM	Changes or adds to the server's functionality. Such an NLM might allow you to back up network files, add support for another protocol, or add support for devices such as a CD-ROM drive or a UPS (uninterruptible power supply).

(continued)

TABLE 3.1 *Different Types of NLMs (continued)*

TYPE OF NLM	FILENAME EXTENSION	DESCRIPTION
Name space module	.NAM	Allows the operating system to store Macintosh, OS/2, Windows NT, Windows 95, or NFS files, along with their long file names and other characteristics. Name space modules support file naming conventions other than the default DOS file names.
LAN driver	.LAN	Enables the operating system to communicate with a network board installed in the file server.
Disk driver	.DSK	Enables the operating system to communicate with a disk controller board installed in the file server.

You can load and unload NLMs while the server is running. Many NLMs have their own status screen that displays on the server. To move between NLM screens on the server's console, use Alt-Esc to cycle through the available NLM screens and use Ctrl-Esc to bring up a list of available screens, from which you can select one.

To work with NLMs, you can use commands from the server console. These commands are shown in Table 3.2. (The server console may be either the physical console or the Remote Console, as explained in the next section.)

TABLE 3.2 *NLM Commands*

COMMAND	DESCRIPTION
LOAD *nlmname*	Loads the NLM. You do not need to type the NLM's filename extension. In most cases, if an NLM requires other NLMs to also be loaded, it will automatically load them.
UNLOAD *nlmname*	Unloads the NLM.
MODULES	Lists all the currently loaded NLMs.

Using Remote Console to Control the Server from a Workstation

To control the server from a workstation, you can temporarily transform your workstation into a "remote console." With the Remote Console feature running, you can enter console utilities and load NLMs, and the commands you execute will work just as if you were using the server's real keyboard and monitor. Using Remote Console enables you to access the server from any workstation on the network, which gives you greater freedom when administering your network.

You can use Remote Console over a direct connection to the network or via asynchronous lines through a modem.

To run Remote Console over a direct network connection, you must first load REMOTE.NLM on the server. When you load REMOTE.NLM, you are asked for a password. Enter any password you choose. (You will have to supply this same password when you use Remote Console from the workstation.) After loading REMOTE.NLM, load RSPX.NLM on your server. Then, from a workstation, map a search drive to SYS:SYSTEM to give the workstation access to the Remote Console files. Finally, to execute the Remote Console on the workstation, enter

```
RCONSOLE
```

at the workstation's DOS prompt and enter the Remote Console password you assigned when you loaded REMOTE.NLM.

To run Remote Console via a modem connection, load REMOTE.NLM on the server. When you load REMOTE.NLM, you are asked for a password. Enter any password you choose. (You will have to supply this same password when you execute Remote Console from the workstation.) After loading REMOTE.NLM, load RS232.NLM, AIO.NLM, and a communications port driver, such as AIOCOMX.NLM, onto your server. Then copy the following files from SYS:SYSTEM to a directory on the workstation to give the workstation access to Remote Console files:

- RCONSOLE.EXE
- RCONSOLE.HEP
- RCONSOLE.MSG
- IBM_RUN.OVL
- _RUN.OVL

- IBM_AIO.OVL
- _AIO.OVL
- TEXTUTIL.HEP
- TEXTUTIL.IDX
- TEXTUTIL.MSG

Finally, to execute Remote Console on the workstation, enter the command

```
RCONSOLE
```

at the workstation's DOS prompt and enter the Remote Console password you assigned when you loaded REMOTE.NLM.

When using Remote Console, you cannot load NLMs directly from your workstation's local drive. You can, however, load NLMs from the SYS:SYSTEM network directory. Therefore, when you are running Remote Console, press Alt-F1 and select the Transfer Files to Server option. With this option, you can copy files from your local drive to SYS:SYSTEM. Once they are in SYS:SYSTEM, you can load the NLMs with Remote Console as usual.

The keystrokes shown in Table 3.3 let you navigate through the Remote Console screen after you've executed RCONSOLE.

TABLE 3.3 *Remote Console Keystrokes*

KEYSTROKE	DESCRIPTION
F1	Displays help
Alt-F1	Displays the Available Options menu
Alt-F2	Quits the Remote Console session
Alt-F3	Moves you forward through the current server screens
Alt-F4	Moves you backward through the current server screens
Alt-F5	Shows this workstation's address

Monitoring and Optimizing Server Performance

When you monitor the server's performance, you look for key indicators that the server is functioning at an optimal level. Some of the things you should monitor include the utilization percentage of the server's processor, the number of cache buffers and packet receive buffers being regularly used, and the server's memory allocation.

Every network has different needs and usage patterns. By default, server parameters are set so that the server will perform well on most networks, but it's a good idea to monitor the server's performance periodically anyway. By doing so, you can track how your server performs under different conditions, discover potential problems, and make improvements.

Server parameters, also called SET parameters, control things such as how buffers are allocated and used, how memory is used, and so on. You can change these parameters by loading SERVMAN.NLM, or by typing the full SET command at the server's console prompt. Using SERVMAN.NLM is much easier because you can select the SET parameters you want from menus, and SERVMAN will automatically save the command in the correct server startup file. For more information about SET parameters, see Appendix B.

The server optimizes itself over a period of time by leveling adjustments for low-usage times with peak-usage bursts. Over a day or two, the server allocates an optimal number of buffers for each parameter, such as packet receive buffers. If you bring down the server and reboot it, the server will automatically be reset to the default allocation for all parameters.

To speed up the optimization period, record the allocations after one or two days of server usage, and then set the given parameters to the recorded values. To set these parameters, use SERVMAN.NLM to select the parameters and change them. Then, when you exit SERVMAN, it will ask you if you want to save the new settings in the STARTUP.NCF and AUTOEXEC.NCF files. Say Yes, so that these settings will be executed by those files the next time the server is booted.

The following sections describe some of the ways to monitor and optimize your server's performance.

MONITORING PROCESSOR UTILIZATION

If one or more server processes monopolize the server's CPU, the server's performance can be degraded, or other processes may have trouble running appropriately.

To see the total percentage utilization of the processor, load MONITOR.NLM and note the percentage in the Utilization field. (This field is in the General Information screen that appears when MONITOR is first loaded.) If the utilization is high, one or more processes may be monopolizing CPU time.

Use MONITOR's Scheduling Information screen to list all server processes and to see which ones have consistently high Load values. If you want to change some of the values on the Scheduling Information screen, use the + and - keys to increase or decrease the values displayed in the Sch Delay column. Experiment with the Sch Delay times until the CPU load value is acceptable.

MONITORING CACHE BUFFERS

If directory searches are slow, you may need to change some SET parameters to increase the allocation and use of directory cache buffers. Use SERVMAN.NLM to change the following SET parameters that relate to directory cache buffers: Directory Cache Allocation Wait Time, Maximum Directory Cache Buffers, and Minimum Directory Cache Buffers parameters.

If disk writes are slow, use MONITOR's General Information screen to see if more than 70 percent of the cache buffers are "dirty" cache buffers. Dirty cache buffers are the file blocks in the server's memory that contain information that has not yet been written to disk, but needs to be. Then use SERVMAN.NLM to increase the Maximum Concurrent Disk Cache Writes, Maximum Concurrent Directory Cache Writes, Dirty Directory Cache Delay Time, or Dirty Disk Cache Delay Time parameters.

See Appendix B for more information about these SET parameters.

MONITORING PACKET RECEIVE BUFFERS

If the server seems to be slowing down or losing workstation connections, use MONITOR's General Information screen to see how many packet receive buffers are allocated and how many are being used. If the allocated number is higher than ten but the server doesn't respond immediately when rebooted, or if you are using EISA or microchannel bus master boards in your server and "No ECB available" error messages appear after the server boots, you may need to increase the minimum number of packet receive buffers. To do this, use SERVMAN.NLM to increase the SET parameter Minimum Packet Receive Buffers so that each board in the server can have at least five buffers.

You can also increase the Maximum Packet Receive Buffers parameter in increments of ten until you have one buffer per workstation. (Again, if you are using EISA or microchannel bus master boards in your server, increase this parameter until each board can have at least five buffers.)

After a couple of days of average network usage, use MONITOR to see how many packet receive buffers are being allocated and compare that with the maximum number. If the two numbers are the same, increase the maximum value by 50 buffers. Continue to monitor the buffers periodically and increase the maximum value until the allocated number no longer matches the maximum.

When you've determined the optimal maximum number of packet receive buffers for your system, use SERVMAN to set both the maximum and minimum values in AUTOEXEC.NCF, so that the server can quickly optimize these values if it is rebooted.

See Appendix B for more information about these SET parameters.

MONITORING MEMORY USAGE

One of the most common causes of server performance problems is a lack of adequate memory in the server. If the network seems to be operating slowly, or if you don't have enough memory to load NLMs, you may need to add more RAM to the server.

Use MONITOR's Cache Utilization screen to track the percentage of Long Term Cache Hits. If Long Term Cache Hits shows less than 90 percent consistently, add more RAM to the server.

You can use the MEMORY and MEMORY MAP console utilities to see how much memory the server is using.

To provide more memory to NLMs without adding RAM, use SERVMAN.NLM to change the Minimum File Cache Buffers and Maximum Directory Cache Buffers parameters, which limit the memory for file and directory caching. Then reboot the server. However, only use this as a temporary solution until you can add more RAM to the server.

If you're using an ISA bus or PCI bus in the server, remember to use the REGISTER MEMORY console utility to register any memory above 16MB for an ISA bus or 64MB for a PCI bus.

MONITORING THE ERROR LOG FILES

There are five different error log files that you can monitor to see if any error messages have been generated by your network. You should make a practice of reviewing these files on a regular basis to ensure that nothing out of the ordinary is happening to your network.

- SYS$LOG.ERR logs error messages for the server. It is stored in the server's SYS:SYSTEM directory. All of the messages or errors that appear on the server's console are stored in this file.
- VOL$LOG.ERR logs error messages for a volume. Each volume has its own log file, which is stored at the root of the volume. Any errors or messages that pertain to the volume are stored in this file.

- ABEND.LOG tracks any abends that may have happened on the server. (An abend, which is short for "abnormal end," is a serious error that stops the server from operating.) IntranetWare has a new feature that allows the server to shut itself down and restart automatically after most abends, so you may not be aware that the server has abended unless you view this file. This file is created on the server's boot partition but gets copied to SYS:SYSTEM when the server restarts.
- TTS$LOG.ERR logs all data that is backed out by the NetWare Transaction Tracking System (TTS). This file is stored in the SYS: volume. To allow this file to be created, use SERVMAN.NLM to turn the TTS Abort Dump Flag parameter to On.
- CONSOLE.LOG is a file that can capture all console messages during system initialization. To capture messages in this file, load CONLOG.NLM in the AUTOEXEC.NCF file. CONSOLE.LOG is stored in the SYS:ETC directory. To stop capturing messages in this file, enter the following command at the server console:

  ```
  UNLOAD CONLOG
  ```

To view any of these error log files, you can either use a text editor from a workstation, or you can use EDIT.NLM from the server. To use EDIT.NLM, enter the command

```
LOAD EDIT
```

and then specify the path and name of the desired log file.

To limit the size of the CONSOLE.LOG file, you can specify its maximum size in the command that loads CONLOG.NLM. In addition, you can specify that the previous CONSOLE.LOG file be saved under a different name. For example, to specify that the previous file be saved and named LOG.SAV, and to limit the new CONSOLE.LOG file to no more than 100K in size, you would use the following command:

```
LOAD CONLOG SAVE=LOG.SAV MAXIMUM=100
```

To limit the size of SYS$LOG.ERR, VOL$LOG.ERR, and TTS$LOG.ERR, use SERVMAN.NLM to change the appropriate SET parameters. Server Log File Overflow Size=*number* lets you specify the maximum size (in K) that the SYS$LOG.ERR file can become. Likewise, Volume Log File Overflow Size=*number* sets the maximum size for VOL$LOG.ERR, and Volume TTS Log File Overflow Size=*number* sets the maximum size for TTS$LOG.ERR.

To specify what happens to a log file when it reaches the maximum size, use SERVMAN.NLM to change the Server Log File State=*number* parameter, the Volume Log File State=*number* parameter, or the Volume TTS Log File State=*number* parameter. With these parameters, replace *number* with 0 (leaves the log file in its current state), 1 (deletes the log file), or 2 (renames the log file and starts a new one). The default is 1.

Protecting the Server

Protecting the server is a very important safeguard that cannot be overlooked. Damage to the server can affect the entire network. The following types of activities can help you protect your server. In addition, see Chapter 7 for information about preventing other types of problems, such as unauthorized access of files.

PROTECTING THE SERVER FROM PHYSICAL DAMAGE

If the server is in an exposed public area where anyone can have access to it, accidents may happen. For example, someone might unplug the power cord or turn off the server thinking it had been left on accidentally.

Be sure to store the server in a locked room. In fact, you may also want to remove its keyboard and monitor and access it only with the Remote Console feature when necessary.

Secure the server to a desk or counter if you are in an earthquake-prone area. Even a small shake can knock a computer to the floor.

PROTECTING THE SERVER FROM ELECTRICAL POWER PROBLEMS

Because electrical power is not always consistent, you need to ensure that your server will not be damaged and files won't be corrupted if a brownout, surge, spike, or outage occur.

Use a UPS for the server. This provides the server with a backup battery in case of a power outage, which allows enough time for the UPS to shut down the server cleanly, leaving no open files exposed to corruption.

If possible, attach each workstation to a UPS, too. If a UPS isn't feasible, at least use surge suppressors on the workstations and peripherals (such as printers) to prevent electrical surges from damaging the equipment.

Typically, UPS manufacturers provide software to manage their UPS products. Use the manufacturer's software to manage your UPS whenever possible. However, if you don't have software from the UPS manufacturer, you can use IntranetWare's UPS.NLM or UPS_AIO.NLM to support the UPS on the server.

If your UPS is attached to a serial port on the server, use UPS_AIO.NLM. Otherwise, use UPS.NLM.

Using UPS.NLM

To install a UPS on a server using Novell's UPS.NLM, complete the following steps.

1. Attach the UPS to the server using the manufacturer's instructions.
2. Load the UPS hardware driver on the server.
3. If you are using a disk coprocessor board (DCB) to connect the UPS to the server, load the DCB.DSK driver on the server.
4. Load UPS.NLM on the server, specifying the correct parameters in the following format:

   LOAD UPS TYPE=*type* PORT=*number* DISCHARGE=*time* RECHARGE=*time* WAIT=*time*

   (You can also just type LOAD UPS and select the parameters from menus that are displayed.)

   In this format, *type* is the number of a possible board type. The port *number* available is dependent on the type of board you use. (See Table 3.4 for the type number and port number you need.)

   The discharge *time* is the number of minutes that the server can operate on battery power (check the battery manufacturer's documentation). The default value is 20 minutes, but values can range from 1 to 3976821 minutes.

   The recharge *time* is the number of minutes the battery needs to fully recharge. The default value is 60 minutes, but values can range from 1 to 3976821 minutes.

   The wait *time* is the number of seconds the UPS should wait after a power outage before it takes over. The default value is 15 seconds, but values can range from 1 to 300 seconds.

If you want the UPS to be configured the same way every time the server is rebooted, put the LOAD UPS command in the server's AUTOEXEC.NCF file.

TABLE 3.4 *UPS Board Types*

BOARD TYPE	PORT NUMBERS
DCB (default)	346, 34E, 326, 32E, 286, 28E (no longer supported)
Stand-alone	240, 231
Keycard	230, 238
Mouse	No port is required.
Other	Refer to the manufacturer's documentation.

To see the UPS's status after UPS.NLM has been loaded, use the UPS STATUS console utility by entering

```
UPS STATUS
```

at the server's console.

To change the UPS's recharge or discharge times, use the UPS TIME console command. The general format of this command is as follows:

```
UPS TIME DISCHARGE=time RECHARGE=time
```

The discharge *time* is the number of minutes that the server can operate on battery power (check the battery manufacturer's documentation). The default value is 20 minutes, but values can range from 1 to 3976821 minutes.

The recharge *time* is the number of minutes the battery needs to fully recharge. The default value is 60 minutes, but values can range from 1 to 3976821 minutes.

Using UPS_AIO.NLM

To install a UPS on a server using Novell's UPS_AIO.NLM, complete the following steps. Use this module if your UPS is connected through a serial port.

1. Attach the UPS to the server using the manufacturer's instructions.
2. Load the UPS hardware driver on the server.
3. Load an AIO device driver on the server. AIOCOMX.NLM is the default driver that comes with IntranetWare.
4. Load UPS_AIO.NLM on the server, specifying the correct options in the following format (the options are explained in Table 3.5):

   ```
   LOAD UPS_AIO options
   ```

If you want the UPS to be configured the same way every time the server is rebooted, put this same command in the server's AUTOEXEC.NCF file.

TABLE 3.5 *UPS_AIO Options*

OPTION	DESCRIPTION
Downtime = *value*	The time, in seconds, that the server will run on battery power before shutting down. Default: 300. Values: Minimum 30 seconds (no maximum).
MSGDelay = *value*	The time, in seconds, before the system sends a message to users about the approaching shutdown. Default: 5. Values: Minimum 0 (no maximum).
MSGInterval = *value*	The time, in seconds, between broadcasts. Default: 30. Values: Minimum 20 (no maximum).
DriverType = *value*	The AIO device driver type. See manufacturer's documentation for the type. Default: 1 (AIO-COMX). Values: 1, 2, or 3.
Board = *value*	The AIO board number. See manufacturer's documentation for the number. Default: 0.
Port = *value*	AIO port number. See manufacturer's documentation for the number. Default: 0.
Signal_High	Sets normal RS232 signaling state to "high." Use the high setting only if your system uses high values instead of low values to determine if the power is low. See manufacturer's documentation for more information. Default: none.

PROTECTING THE SERVER FROM VIRUSES

Unfortunately, software viruses are a fact of life. Use a third-party product to check for viruses and to disinfect your network if one is found. Several companies are manufacturing virus detectors for NetWare networks.

Because new viruses are being created all the time, keep your virus detection software up to date (get all available updates of the software, follow manufacturer's procedures for updating, and so on).

If necessary, establish policies against users loading their own software on the network or downloading software from outside online sources or e-mail messages, or provide diskless workstations to the users.

To prevent viruses from infecting executable files, you can assign those files the Execute Only file attribute, or you can remove users' Modify right from the directory that contains the executable files and assign the Read-Only attribute to the executables. If a user still has the Modify right to a file, the virus can change the Read-Only attribute to Read-Write, infect the file, then change the attribute back. Therefore, it's important to remove the Modify right from the user if you are going to use the Read-Only attribute for virus protection.

PROTECTING THE SERVER FROM HARDWARE FAILURES

To protect your server from hard disk problems, the NetWare feature called Hot Fix monitors any bad blocks that develop on the hard disk. (Hot Fix is explained in the "Using Hot Fix" section later in this chapter.) For more protection, you can use disk mirroring and disk duplexing to store identical copies of all network files on two disks so that if one disk goes bad, the data is still available from the other. This protection feature is explained in the "Using Disk Mirroring and Duplexing" section later in this chapter.

For extremely mission-critical data, duplicating the entire server may be necessary. The *System Fault Tolerance Level III* (SFT III) feature lets you set up two identical servers that mirror each other's data. Should one server fail for any reason, the other takes over seamlessly. This provides more protection than disk duplexing because all of the server's hardware is duplicated, including network boards, hard disks, cables, and so on. SFT III is explained in the "Managing SFT III (Duplicate Servers)" section later in this chapter.

Performing Server Maintenance

From time to time, you may find you need to perform some type of maintenance on your server. For example, you may need to add a new hard disk, load the latest patches (bug fixes or enhancements) on the server, or clear a workstation connection. The following sections explain how to do some of these common maintenance tasks.

DISPLAYING INFORMATION ABOUT THE SERVER

You can see information about the server by executing various console utilities at the server's console. Table 3.6 lists the types of information about the server that you can see and the console utilities you use to display that information.

TABLE 3.6 *Console Utilities Used to Display Server Information*

TYPE OF INFORMATION	CONSOLE UTILITY TO USE
The server's name	NAME
The server's directory tree	CONFIG
The server's bindery context	CONFIG
The server's hardware information	CONFIG
All currently loaded NLMs	MODULES
The server's processor speed	SPEED
The server's version number and license information	VERSION
A list of all volumes mounted on the server	VOLUMES

BRINGING DOWN AND REBOOTING THE SERVER

If you need to bring down the server or reboot it, you can use the methods listed in Table 3.7.

TABLE 3.7 *Utilities Used to Bring Down or Reboot the Server*

TASK	HOW TO DO IT
Bring down the server but leave it connected to the server so that it continues to receive packets.	Enter the command DOWN
Bring down the server and exit to DOS. (This disconnects the server from the network.)	Enter the command DOWN then enter EXIT
Reboot the server.	Enter the command DOWN then enter RESTART SERVER

TABLE 3.7 *Utilities Used to Bring Down or Reboot the Server (continued)*

TASK	HOW TO DO IT
Reboot the server from a Remote Console.	First, make sure the AUTOEXEC.BAT file automatically executes SERVER.EXE. Then enter the command REMOVE DOS then enter DOWN then enter EXIT

INSTALLING PATCHES

As with almost all software products, no matter how thoroughly the product is tested, there is always some flaw or unexpected behavior that crops up after the product has shipped. Usually, these types of flaws show up when the product is used in a customer configuration that varies from the testing configurations used within the manufacturer's labs.

To fix these problems, Novell releases software patches, which are modules that can be installed on your IntranetWare server. Not all patches are needed in most customers' configurations, but it's often a good idea to get the patches and install them anyway, just to ensure that you protect your server from possible problems or downtime.

Novell releases these patches in a variety of ways. Users with CompuServe accounts can obtain the patches through the NetWire forum (GO NETWIRE). The patches are also available via the Internet:

- World Wide Web: http://www.novell.com
- Gopher: gopher.novell.com
- File Transfer Protocol (FTP): anonymous FTP to ftp.novell.com

If you are accessing these areas from Europe, use .de instead of .com.

The patches are also released on the Novell Support Encyclopedia (NSEPro), which is updated monthly and sent out to subscribers.

For more information about all of these sources, see Appendix C.

MONITORING WORKSTATION CONNECTIONS

Some types of server maintenance require you to break a workstation's connection to the server or to prevent users from logging in while you're completing the maintenance task. Use the utilities listed in Table 3.8 to perform these tasks.

TABLE 3.8 *Utilities Used to Monitor Workstation Connections*

TASK	UTILITY TO USE
See what workstations are connected and what files they have open.	MONITOR.NLM's Connection Information screen
Clear the workstation connection if the workstation has crashed and left files open on the server.	MONITOR.NLM's Connection Information screen (select the connection and press the Delete key)
Prevent users from logging in.	DISABLE LOGIN console utility
Allow users to log in again after you've disabled login.	ENABLE LOGIN console utility

BINDING PROTOCOLS AND LAN DRIVERS TOGETHER

Whenever you load a LAN driver to support a network board, you must also bind a protocol to the LAN driver.

During installation, the LAN driver and the IPX protocol are bound together automatically by the INSTALL program. After the initial installation, you can load additional LAN drivers and bind protocols to them by using either INSTALL.NLM or INETCFG.NLM.

INSTALL.NLM lets you load drivers for additional network boards, load drivers reentrantly (more than once for the same board) to support multiple frame types, and bind IPX to a LAN driver. INSTALL.NLM detects network addresses on the boards automatically to help reduce possible network address conflicts. INSTALL.NLM stores the commands to load the LAN drivers and bind IPX in the AUTOEXEC.NCF file.

Use INETCFG.NLM if you want to bind AppleTalk, TCP/IP, or another non-IPX protocol to the LAN driver. You can also use it to bind IPX to a LAN driver. When you first load INETCFG.NLM, you are asked if you want to transfer all the commands that load LAN drivers and bind protocols to them into the file that INETCFG.NLM uses (NETINFO.CFG) instead of AUTOEXEC.NCF. Once you use INETCFG.NLM and transfer the commands to NETINFO.CFG, you must always use INETCFG.NLM to configure drivers and protocols.

Working with Hard Disks

One of the most annoying problems that can happen to a server is a hard disk failure. There are several NetWare features, explained in the following sections, that can help you monitor and work with your server's hard disks. (For information about volumes, see Chapter 8.)

USING HOT FIX

NetWare provides a feature called Hot Fix, which monitors the blocks that are being written to on a disk. When NetWare writes data to the server's hard disk, NetWare writes the data, then verifies that the data was written correctly by reading it again (called read-after-write verification). When a bad block is encountered, the data that was being written to that block is redirected to a separate area on the disk, called the disk redirection area, and the bad block is listed in a bad block table.

Some manufacturers' hard disks maintain their own version of data redirection and do not need to use NetWare's Hot Fix feature. If your disk does use Hot Fix, the size of the redirection area is set up by default when you first create a volume on the disk.

You should monitor the NetWare Hot Fix statistics periodically to see if a disk is showing a high number of bad blocks and is filling up the allocated redirection area. To see the number of redirection blocks being used, use MONITOR.NLM's Disk Information screen. Track the number of bad blocks being found over time so that you can see if the disk suddenly starts to generate bad blocks at an undesirable frequency. (You may want to use a worksheet such as the Hot Fix Bad Block Tracking worksheet in Appendix D.) If more than half of the redirection space has been used for redirected data, or if the number of redirected blocks has increased significantly since the last time you checked it, the disk may be going bad. Use the manufacturer's documentation to try to diagnose the disk problem.

USING DISK MIRRORING AND DUPLEXING

Another way to protect your network data from possible disk corruption is to implement disk mirroring, which ensures that data is safe and accessible even if one disk goes down. When you mirror disks, two (or more) disks are updated simultaneously with network data so that both disks contain identical copies of all network files. If one disk fails, the other takes over so that the network operates normally. Users don't typically see any difference in services.

If the mirrored disks are using the same disk controller board, it's simply called *disk mirroring*.

If the mirrored disks are using separate disk controller boards, it's called *disk duplexing*. Disk duplexing provides more security than disk mirroring because it duplicates not just the disk but also the controller channel. Disk duplexing also increases the data reads and writes because the server will send reads and writes to both controllers. Whichever controller is least busy services the requests.

With mirrored or duplexed disks, if a disk problem causes the server to stop, you should turn off the server, remove the bad disk, and restart the server. Then replace the bad disk as soon as possible. When you install the new disk, the server will remirror the new drive with the existing one, which also means the server will copy all the data onto the new disk automatically.

Having disk mirroring or duplexing does not eliminate the need for keeping regular backups of your network. Be sure you always have a current backup of your network data before you change disks or change the server's hardware configuration.

Managing Mirrored or Duplexed Disks

You can use the utilities shown in Table 3.9 to work with mirrored disks.

TABLE 3.9 *Utilities Used to Manage Mirrored Disks*

TASK	UTILITY TO USE
Set up, monitor, and change disk mirroring or disk duplexing.	INSTALL.NLM
Show the status of mirrored disk partitions.	MIRROR STATUS console utility
Stop the server from remirroring a disk partition.	ABORT REMIRROR console utility
Restart the remirroring process if something halted the server's remirroring	REMIRROR PARTITION console utility

Recovering Files from an Out-of-Sync Disk

Usually, when a mirrored disk partition becomes unmirrored, its status in INSTALL (under Disk Options) is listed as Not Mirrored.

If the disk is listed as Out of Sync, NetWare does not recognize any volume information on the disk. To salvage the data from this partition, you must rename the partition so that it can be mounted as a separate volume. To do this, complete the steps in the following checklist.

1. At the server's console, load INSTALL.NLM.
2. Choose Disk Options, and then choose Mirror/Unmirror Disk Partitions.
3. Select the out-of-sync partition and press F3.
4. If another volume of the same name exists on another disk, you'll receive a warning message that the partition you selected contains the name of a volume that is already defined. Press Esc to continue.
5. When asked if you want to rename the volume segment, answer Yes.
6. Enter a new, unique name for this volume segment.
7. Answer Yes when asked if you want to salvage the volume segment.
8. Mount the segment as an independent volume.

ADDING A HARD DISK TO A SERVER

To install a new hard disk in a server, complete the following steps.

1. Bring down the server and turn off its power (or the power to the disk's subsystem).
2. If necessary, install a new disk controller board.
3. Install the hard disk and cable it to the server as necessary.
4. If necessary, configure the computer to recognize the new disk.
5. Reboot the server.
6. Load INSTALL.NLM to load the disk driver and create a new NetWare partition for the disk.
7. Use INSTALL.NLM to either mirror the disk to another existing disk, create a new volume on it, or add its partition to an existing volume.

REPLACING A HARD DISK IN A SERVER

To replace an existing hard disk in a server, complete the following steps.

1. Back up the files on the existing hard disk.
2. If the disk is mirrored, use INSTALL.NLM to dismount all of the disk's volumes and to unmirror the disk.
3. Bring down the server and turn off its power (or the power to the disk's subsystem).
4. Remove the original disk.
5. Install the new disk and cable it to the server as necessary.
6. If necessary, configure the computer to recognize the new disk.
7. Reboot the server.
8. Load INSTALL.NLM to load the disk driver.
9. Use INSTALL.NLM to delete any existing partitions on the new disk and to create a new NetWare partition on it.
10. Use INSTALL.NLM to either remirror the disk to the original disk's partner or re-create the volumes that were on the old disk (then restore the files from a backup).

Working with CD-ROM Drives and Other Storage Devices

With IntranetWare, a CD-ROM mounted in a drive that is attached to the server can appear as a NetWare volume. Users on the network can access the CD-ROM just like any other volume, except that it is read-only.

Because a CD-ROM is read-only, do not enable file compression or block suballocation on the CD-ROM volume, or you will corrupt the CD-ROM's volume index data. (If you do, use the CD console utility to rebuild the CD-ROM's volume index file.)

To mount a CD-ROM as a NetWare volume, use CDROM.NLM. This NLM supports the High Sierra and ISO 9660 formats, along with HFS (Apple) extensions. (This means you can access Mac files on the CD from a Mac workstation.)

To work with the CD-ROM after it is mounted as a volume, use the CD console command. For help using the CD command, enter

```
CD HELP
```

To install a CD-ROM and mount it as a NetWare volume, complete the following steps.

1. Install a NetWare-compatible host bus adapter (HBA) that supports CD-ROM drives.
2. Boot the server and make sure volume SYS is mounted.
3. Load the HBA's disk driver and any other associated driver on the server.
4. If your driver automatically loads the ASPITRAN.DSK driver, you must also load either ASPICD.DSK or CDNASPI.DSK on the server.
5. Load NWPA.NLM (the NetWare Peripheral Architecture driver) on the server.
6. Load CDROM.NLM on the server.
7. Use the CD DEVICE LIST console utility to see the ID number of the CD-ROM, or use the CD VOLUME LIST console utility to see the CD-ROM's volume name.
8. Using either the CD-ROM's volume name or ID number, mount the CD-ROM volume using the following command format:

   `CD MOUNT` *`volume or number`*

9. If you want the CD-ROM to be mounted as a volume every time the server is rebooted, put the commands that load the drivers (steps 3, 4, and 5) in the STARTUP.NCF file and put the commands that load and mount the CD-ROM (steps 6 and 8) in the AUTOEXEC.NCF file.

Using HCSS to Increase the Server's Storage Capacity

One way to expand your server's storage capacity is to use NetWare's High-Capacity Storage System (HCSS) to integrate an optical disc jukebox into the NetWare file system. (An *optical disk jukebox* is a storage device that holds several optical disks. The jukebox uses an autochanger to mount and dismount the disks as needed.) With HCSS, less frequently used files are migrated off the server's hard disks onto the optical disks. When accessed, the files on the optical disk are "demigrated" back onto the hard disks.

Users are seldom aware that the files they are accessing are on the optical disk system.

HCSS also lets you archive files by removing the optical disks with the files on them and storing the disks in another location.

To set up HCSS on your server, install a jukebox, and then create an HCSS volume, complete with its own file system structure, on the server's hard disk. The HCSS file system consists of the HCSS volume, which can contain one or more domain directories. Each domain directory contains pairs of directories that correspond to the media labels on each side of an optical disk.

You will set up a workstation to use the HCSS "snap-in" module for the NetWare Administrator utility. You must use this utility to manage HCSS directories and activities. Do not use other utilities to change HCSS directories, or you may corrupt the HCSS file system.

To see and modify the status of HCSS once it's set up, you can use either NetWare Administrator or the HCSS console utility.

To set up HCSS support on your network, complete the following steps.

1. Install the jukebox and its SCSI adapter board according to the manufacturer's documentation.
2. Load the jukebox's driver on the server, specifying any necessary options as described in the manufacturer's documentation.
3. Load HPCHGR.NLM (Novell's driver) on the server.
4. To register the jukebox with the NetWare operating system, enter the following command at the console:

   ```
   SCAN FOR NEW DEVICES
   ```

5. Use INSTALL.NLM to create a volume on the server's hard disk specifically for HCSS. This volume should be at least 10 percent of the total capacity of the jukebox.
6. With INSTALL.NLM, set whether you want file compression turned off or on. Then turn on data migration. Finally, set the volume block size.
7. Mount the volume.
8. Load HCSS.NLM on the server.
9. If the jukebox begins ejecting media, remove the media and enter

   ```
   MEDIA REMOVED
   ```

   at the console, and then enter

   ```
   HCSS EJECT MEDIA OVERRIDE=ON
   ```

   to prevent it from ejecting more media.

10. At a workstation, log in as ADMIN and edit the NWADMIN.INI file to add the following lines under the heading [Snapin Object DLLs]:

```
Vis HCSSDecider=hdecsnap.dll
Vis HCSSObject=hobjsnap.dll
Vis HCSSMedia=hmedsnap.dll
```

11. Begin creating the HCSS directory structure by opening the NetWare Administrator utility and selecting the HCSS volume.
12. From the Tools menu, select HCSS Create and type in the name you want to give the first domain directory in the HCSS Directory field. If you want to create additional domain directories, select Create Another Directory. Then click on the Create button to create the directory.
13. Next you will assign labeled media to the domain, so make sure the cartridges are labeled with the names of the two media-label directories you plan to create.
14. From the Tools menu, choose HCSS Media, and then choose Import Media.
15. Insert the media into the jukebox and choose OK.
16. (This step is optional.) If the media is unformatted, choose Format, enter the media label names, and choose OK. (If the media already contains files you want to keep, do not format it.)
17. From the HCSS Assign Media screen, select an HCSS directory from the HCSS Directory field, and then choose OK.
18. To add more media, repeat Steps 14 through 17.

Modifying Server Startup Activities

When you start up or reboot the NetWare server, its boot files execute in the following order:

1. The DOS system files load and then run AUTOEXEC.BAT, which sets up a basic environment and can be set to execute SERVER.EXE automatically.
2. SERVER.EXE runs the IntranetWare operating system on the computer, which turns the computer into the NetWare server.

3. STARTUP.NCF automates the initialization of the NetWare operating system. It loads disk drivers, loads name space modules to support different file formats (Macintosh, OS/2, or NFS), and executes some SET parameters that modify default initialization values.
4. AUTOEXEC.NCF loads the server's LAN drivers, specifies the server name and internal network number, mounts volumes, loads any NLMs you want loaded automatically (such as MONITOR), and executes additional SET parameters.
5. Additional .NCF files, if they've been created, can be called from the AUTOEXEC.NCF file or executed from the server's console.

The STARTUP.NCF and AUTOEXEC.NCF files are created automatically during the installation process. They contain commands that reflect the selections you make during installation. (Other types of .NCF files can be created, too, depending on the products that you install on the server.)

You can edit these .NCF files after installation to add new commands or modify existing ones. Table 3.10 describes the utilities you can use to edit the STARTUP.NCF and AUTOEXEC.NCF files.

TABLE 3.10 *Utilities Used to Edit Server Startup Files*

UTILITY	DESCRIPTION
EDIT.NLM	A text editor on the server that lets you manually edit the files. To use EDIT.NLM, enter LOAD EDIT then enter the name of the desired file.
INSTALL.NLM\	Lets you modify the same options you set during installation. Automatically updates the appropriate file with the new information you've specified.
SERVMAN.NLM	Lets you add, delete, or modify SET parameters by selecting them from menus. Automatically updates the appropriate file with the new information you've specified.

Managing Connections Between Servers

With NetWare, multiple segments of a network or multiple networks can all be connected and can communicate with each other. (Multiple networks connected together form an internetwork.) These network segments can all use the same topology and protocol (such as IPX, the NetWare default protocol), or they can use differing protocols, such as AppleTalk and TCP/IP.

NetWare uses *routing* software to enable these different segments of the network to communicate. Routing software in the NetWare server receives packets of data from a segment of the network, determines how to handle that packet, and then sends it along the most efficient path to its destination.

Each server's routing software keeps track of the internetwork's configuration in a routing table. In both NetWare 4.1 and earlier versions, each server updates the rest of the internetwork's configuration information by periodically broadcasting Router Information Protocol (RIP) and Service Advertising Protocol (SAP) information. RIP and SAP broadcasts are used to determine which servers are up and running and which routes will be the most efficient for transferring packets. Time servers also advertise their services using SAP broadcasts.

In IntranetWare, NetWare Link Services Protocol (NLSP) is used by default, rather than straight RIP and SAP routing. With NLSP, routing and service information is sent out only when a route or service on the network changes, instead of being broadcast periodically.

NLSP also supports RIP and SAP emulation, so that routers that rely on RIP and SAP will continue to function properly.

You can use the utilities listed in Table 3.11 to help you monitor the status of your internetwork and routers.

TABLE 3.11 *Utilities Used to Manage Routers and Protocols*

UTILITY	DESCRIPTION
DISPLAY NETWORKS console utility	Lists all networks that the server's router sees.
DISPLAY SERVERS console utility	Lists all servers advertised with SAP.
INITIALIZE SYSTEM console utility	Executes commands in NETINFO.CFG at server startup to enable the multiprotocol router configuration.

(continued)

TABLE 3.11 *Utilities Used to Manage Routers and Protocols (continued)*

UTILITY	DESCRIPTION
REINITIALIZE SYSTEM console utility	Reenables the multiprotocol router configuration after you've made changes to NETINFO.CFG.
INETCFG.NLM	Configures AppleTalk and TCP/IP packet routing across network segments. Configures IPX/SPX parameters. Loads LAN drivers and binds protocols to them. Enables NLSP.
FILTCFG.NLM	Configures RIP/SAP packet filtering.
RESET ROUTER console utility	Resets the router table on the server if it has become corrupted.
TRACK ON console utility	Displays the routing information that your server is broadcasting and receiving.
TRACK OFF console utility	Turns off the display of routing information.

Managing SFT III (Duplicate Servers)

NetWare 4.11 SFT III (System Fault Tolerance Level III) is a form of IntranetWare that lets you install the operating system on two identical servers that work in concert with each other. If one server fails, the other takes over seamlessly and continues to run the network. Although the SFT III capability is built into NetWare 4.11, you cannot enable SFT III functionality unless you have purchased an SFT III license.

SFT III duplicates all of the server hardware, including monitor, keyboard, disks, network boards, and cables. It joins the two servers with a special high-speed network link to ensure that all data is instantly duplicated between the two servers. The network boards that form this high-speed link are called *mirrored server link* (MSL) boards. For a list of MSL boards that have been certified for use with IntranetWare, use one of the following numbers:

- Fax Back information (to get information automatically faxed to you): 801-861-2776 or 800-414-5227

- Hotline: 801-861-5544

With SFT III, the operating system is split into two pieces: the *mirrored server engine* (MSEngine) and the *I/O engine* (IOEngine). The MSEngine is the portion of the operating system that mirrors all the network data and operations. The IOEngine is the portion of the operating system that handles the hardware input and output for this particular server computer. The IOEngine is not mirrored.

To install NetWare 4.11 SFT III on your servers, complete the following steps.

1. Make sure the two servers you intend to mirror are identical, or nearly so, in terms of model, memory, disk space, hardware, and so on.
2. Attach a CD-ROM drive to the first server and install regular IntranetWare on it, as explained in Chapter 1.
3. On the second server, create a DOS partition that is the same size as the DOS partition on the first server.
4. Format three high-density diskettes and label them Disk 1, Disk 2, and Disk 3.
5. Install the MSL boards in both servers and cable the boards directly to each other according to the manufacturer's instructions. Record the MSL boards' addresses and interrupt numbers. (You can record the boards' information in a worksheet such as those in Appendix D.) For more protection, you can install a second pair of MSL boards in the servers, too.
6. Insert the *NetWare 4.11 Operating System* CD-ROM in the CD-ROM drive on the first server and boot DOS on the first server.
7. From the CD-ROM's root directory, run the installation program by entering the following command at the first server's console:

   ```
   INSTALL
   ```

8. Select NetWare Server Installation, choose NetWare 4.11 SFT III Installation, and then choose Convert NetWare 4.11 to SFT III.
9. Enter the MSEngine name (you can use the name you first gave the server, or you can change it now).
10. Assign IPX internal network numbers for all three engines (the MSEngine and each of the two IOEngines). You can either accept randomly assigned numbers by selecting Continue with Installation, or you can assign your own numbers by choosing Modify Network Numbers.

11. Specify the first server's DOS boot directory and the location of the AUTOEXEC.BAT file. (Because SERVER.EXE will be changed to MSERVER.EXE, the installation program checks to see if SERVER.EXE is executed from AUTOEXEC.BAT and, if so, it changes the command to execute MSERVER.EXE instead.)
12. Insert Disk 1 into the first server's disk drive and press Enter so that it will copy SFT III files onto it. Insert the other two diskettes as prompted.
13. Specify the driver for the MSL board installed in the first server. (If you've installed a second MSL board in the server, specify that one, too.)
14. Now that the first server is up and running, boot DOS on the second server.
15. Insert Disk 1 in the second server's disk drive, change to that drive letter, and run the installation program from that diskette by entering

    ```
    INSTALL
    ```

    INSTALL copies of the SFT III files onto the second server. (Insert the other two diskettes when prompted.)
16. Specify the driver for the second server's MSL board. (If you installed two MSL boards, specify the driver for the second one, too.)
17. Select the LAN and disk drivers for the second server, and then select Continue Installation.
18. Press Enter two more times to continue the installation.
19. Create a NetWare partition on the second server's hard disk. If the two servers' hard disks are the same size, you can choose Automatically, and the program will create the NetWare partition and mirror it to the partition on the first server. If the disks are different sizes, choose Manually and create the NetWare disk partition to the size you want and mirror it to the first server's disk. Then continue with the installation.
20. When prompted, insert the license diskette.
21. Exit the installation program. SFT III is now installed and the disks are being mirrored. The status of the mirroring is displayed on the screen.

The startup files for the SFT III servers are different from the regular NetWare startup files. Instead of a single STARTUP.NCF file and a single AUTOEXEC.NCF file, SFT III requires two of each: one for each server's MSEngine and one for each server's IOEngine. These files are explained in Table 3.12.

TABLE 3.12 *SFT III Server Startup Files*

FILE	DESCRIPTION
IOSTART.NCF	Specifies the IOEngine's name and IPX internal network number, loads the disk drivers and MSL board drivers, executes IOEngine SET parameters, and loads NLMs that run in the IOEngine and don't need the MSEngine running.
MSSTART.NCF	Executes commands and SET parameters that affect the MSEngine.
MSAUTO.NCF	Executes commands after the servers are mirrored and volume SYS is mounted. This file includes commands that can execute in or affect network services that run in the mirrored portion of the operating system. For example, it loads most NLMs, loads Novell Directory Services, initializes time synchronization, and so on.
IOAUTO.NCF	Loads LAN drivers and binds protocols to them. Loads NLMs that must run in the IOEngine but require the MSEngine to be running (such as backup and print services).

Once SFT III is up and running, any problem on one server will cause the second server to seamlessly take over network operations. The first server installed is the primary server, and the second server is the secondary one. If the primary server fails, the secondary server will become the primary server. When you bring the failed server back online, it will mirror itself to the "new" primary server and become the secondary server.

To manage your SFT III servers, you can use the utilities shown in Table 3.13.

TABLE 3.13 *Utilities Used for Managing SFT III Servers*

UTILITY	DESCRIPTION
MSERVER.EXE	Starts the server (replaces SERVER.EXE).
SERVMAN.NLM	Allows you to configure SFT III options by changing SET parameters.
HALT console utility	Stops the IOEngine in one server, forcing the other server to take over.
RESTART console utility	Reloads a stopped IOEngine while the IOEngine in the other server continues to run, or forces a server to switch from being primary to secondary.
INSTALL.NLM	Allows you to recover orphaned disk partitions.

Charging Customers for Server Usage

With NetWare, you can charge users for using a server's resources. You can base charges on the following criteria:

- The number of minutes that they are connected to your server
- The number of service requests they make to the server
- The total number of blocks they read
- The total number of blocks they write to
- The total number of blocks of disk storage they use per day

Bear in mind that the accounting feature tracks these items for each individual server. It does not support Novell Directory Services, so if you want to charge for a user's activities across the network, you'll have to set up accounting on each server the user might access.

To manage accounting on a server, you use two utilities: the NetWare Administrator utility, which runs in Windows, and the ATOTAL utility, which is a command-line utility.

To set up accounting, use the NetWare Administrator utility from a workstation. (See Chapter 6 for instructions on setting up the NetWare administrator utility on a workstation.) First select the Server object. From the Object menu, choose Details. Then open the Accounting page and set up accounting information, such as the charge rate. The accounting charge rate is the amount you will charge for each unit used. To obtain the charge rate, you divide the total amount of money you want to accrue by the total number of units you expect to be used. For example, if you want to charge a total of $1000 per month for your disk storage, and you expect users to use a total of 50,000 disk blocks per month, the formula would be:

100,000 (cents) / 50,000 (blocks) = 2 cents per block

If you set the multiplier to 0, the charge amount will be "No Charge."

To display daily and weekly totals for each of the items that are tracked by accounting services, use the ATOTAL utility by entering the command

```
ATOTAL
```

at the workstation's DOS prompt. To redirect the display to a text file that you can read with a text editor, use the following command format:

ATOTAL > *filename*

Synchronizing the Servers' Time

Because IntranetWare maintains a networkwide Directory of network objects and information, all servers on the network must maintain a common, relative time so that all updates to that database happen in the correct order, regardless of the server that originated the update.

To ensure that the servers are keeping the same time, a NetWare feature called Time Services is implemented on each IntranetWare server. With Time Services, certain servers are designated to be the main timekeepers. The other servers all synchronize their times with these timekeepers.

When you install IntranetWare on a server, you designate how you want this server to participate in Time Services with the other servers on the network.

Table 3.14 describes the four different time server designations you can give a server.

TABLE 3.14 *Time Server Types*

TIME SERVER	DESCRIPTION
Single Reference	The sole server that maintains the network time, a Single Reference server is often used on small networks. All other servers are Secondary time servers. Single Reference servers provide the time to Secondary servers.
Primary	A Primary server synchronizes its time by polling one or more Primary or Reference servers. Together, the Primary servers determine an average time, and then each one adjusts its time to approach that average. If a Reference server exists, the Primary servers adjust their time to approach the Reference server's time because the Reference server won't adjust.
Reference	Similar to a Single Reference server, a Reference server is used on larger networks where additional Primary servers are desired. Reference servers participate with other Primary servers to determine the correct time, but they do not adjust their own time. Instead, Primary servers migrate their time to match the Reference server's time. If more than one Reference server exists, they must all be synchronized with the same external time source, such as an atomic clock, or each Reference server's time will drift independently and the network will never be synchronized.
Secondary	A Secondary server obtains the time from one of the other time servers. Secondary servers do not participate in determining the time; they merely obtain it for their own use and to provide the time to their workstations.

Set up time services on the server during installation. Time services are controlled by TIMESYNC.NLM, which is loaded automatically when the server is started up. If you want to modify the time synchronization after installation, you can edit the TIMESYNC.CFG file to modify its SET parameters.

You can use SERVMAN.NLM to change the SET parameters, but SERVMAN.NLM will not add the parameters to the TIMESYNC.CFG file. You must still edit the TIMESYNC.CFG file if you want the time synchronization parameters to be in effect the next time you reboot the server.

You can use EDIT.NLM to edit TIMESYNC.CFG.

Time synchronization uses, by default, SAP broadcasts to keep all time servers synchronized. This should be adequate in most cases. However, if you find that the SAP traffic is too heavy or that you frequently have servers joining and leaving the network (for testing or other purposes), you might want to turn the SAP synchronization off and tell the server exactly which time servers you want it to use.

To do this, edit the TIMESYNC.CFG file and add the following commands to it:

```
TYPE= server type

SERVICE ADVERTISING=OFF

CONFIGURED SOURCES=ON
```

For *server type*, specify whether this server is a Reference, Single Reference, Primary, or Secondary server. For example, enter

```
TYPE=PRIMARY
```

Then add the list of the time servers you want this server to contact, in order of priority. Add the following commands:

```
TIME SOURCE= server1

TIME SOURCE= server2

TIME SOURCE= server3
```

For *server1*, *server2*, *server3*, and so on, indicate the name of the time servers you want this server to contact.

Additional utilities you can use to work with a server's time are described in Table 3.15.

TABLE 3.15 *Utilities Used to Manage Time Services*

UTILITY	DESCRIPTION
TIME console utility	Displays the server's date, time, daylight saving time status, and time synchronization information.
SET TIME console utility	Lets you change the server's date and time.
SET TIME ZONE console utility	Lets you change the server's time zone information.
SYSTIME workstation utility	Lets you synchronize a workstation's time with the server's time.

CHAPTER 4

Installing Workstations

Instant Access

Installing

- To connect DOS or Windows 3.1x workstations to the network, install the new NetWare Client32 workstation software for DOS/Windows. (Alternatively, you can install the NetWare DOS Requester, which was the client software used in earlier versions of NetWare.)
- To connect Windows 95 workstations to the network, install the new NetWare Client32 workstation software for Windows 95.
- To install OS/2 workstations, use the NetWare Client for OS/2.
- To install Windows NT workstations, use the NetWare Client for Windows NT, available on NetWire (www.novell.com).
- To install Macintosh workstations, use NetWare Client for Mac OS. (See Chapter 10 for instructions.)
- To upgrade workstations to NetWare Client32, use the Automatic Client Upgrade (ACU) feature or the NetWare Application Launcher.

Logging In

- To log in after installing NetWare Client32, use the NetWare GUI Login program.

On an IntranetWare network, you can have any combination of the following types of workstations:

- DOS and Windows 3.1x (software included in IntranetWare)
- Windows 95 (software included in IntranetWare)
- OS/2 (software included in IntranetWare)
- Windows NT (software available on the NetWire CompuServe forum and Novell's Internet site, www.novell.com)
- Macintosh (software included in IntranetWare)

The following sections explain how to set up Client32 for Windows 3.1x, DOS, and Windows 95, as well as how to set up OS/2 and Windows NT workstations. See Chapter 10 for instructions on setting up Macintosh workstations.

To allow a workstation to communicate with an IntranetWare network, you must install NetWare client software on the workstation. (On a NetWare network, workstations are often called clients because they request services from the network.)

There are two different types of NetWare client software for DOS-based or Windows 3.1x-based computers: NetWare Client32 and the NetWare DOS Requester. You must install one of these on every DOS-based or Windows 3.1x-based workstation that will connect to the NetWare 4.11 network. If you are using Windows 95, you must install Client32 for Windows 95.

NetWare Client32 is the newest type of client software. It offers greater performance and more features than the older NetWare DOS Requester. It's recommended that you use the new Client32 software, but the older NetWare DOS Requester software is included in IntranetWare for compatibility. (If you have thousands of workstations using DOS or Windows 3.1x, you may not want to upgrade all of your workstations right away, so the NetWare DOS Requester allows you to install new workstations with the same type of configuration you're used to during the interim.)

Installing NetWare Client32 Software

NetWare Client32 offers several advantages over the NetWare DOS Requester:

- It allows the workstation software to run in protected memory mode, which means other applications running on the workstation won't conflict with the memory being used by Client32.

- It requires less memory than DOS Requester — less than 5KB of conventional memory and 1MB of extended memory.
- It has a larger cache for better performance.
- It allows a user to log in to more than one NDS tree at a time.

Client32 also has an automatic reconnect/retry feature, which can reconnect the workstation to the network service after the network service reappears. This feature will also reopen files and file locks that the workstation was using before the network service was lost.

The NetWare Client32 installation program automatically copies all necessary NetWare files to the workstation and edits any DOS, Windows 3.1x, or Windows 95 files that require modifications.

You can choose one of three methods for installing Client32 on your workstation:

- You can install Client32 directly from the *NetWare 4.11 Operating System* CD-ROM.
- You can install Client32 from installation diskettes you create from the CD-ROM. To create installation diskettes, load INSTALL.NLM on the server, choose Product Options, and then choose Make Diskettes. You'll need eight blank diskettes.
- If you are upgrading an existing NetWare workstation to Client32, you can install Client32 from the CD-ROM, from diskettes, or from a network directory on the server. To use the network directory method, you must put the client installation files into a directory on the server. Load INSTALL.NLM on the server, choose Product Options, and then choose Create Client Installation Directories on Server.

NOTE

You can also download Client32 from Novell's site on the Internet. Periodically, Novell releases updated clients with new features. It's a good idea to check this location (www.novell.com) for these updates.

INSTALLING CLIENT32 FROM WINDOWS 3.1x

The Client32 installation program for both DOS (INSTALL.EXE) and Windows 3.1x (SETUP.EXE) accomplishes the same tasks during installation. If your workstation runs Windows 3.1x from the network instead of from a local drive, use the DOS installation version. Otherwise, you can choose whichever version you prefer.

To install Client32 from Windows 3.1x, complete the steps in the following checklist.

1. Install a network board in the workstation according to the manufacturer's documentation. Be sure to record the board's configuration settings, such as its interrupt and port address. (You may want to use a worksheet such as the "Workstation Installation and Configuration" worksheet in Appendix D.)
2. Cable the network board to the network, using the correct cabling hardware, including terminators, hubs, or any other hardware required by your topology. See Chapter 1 and your hardware manufacturer's documentation for more information about limitations and guidelines for installing network hardware.
3. From the Windows File Manager, select Run from the File menu.
4. Click Browse to locate the SETUP.EXE file in the client installation directory. If you're installing from a network directory, the path to SETUP.EXE is generally PUBLIC\CLIENT\DOSWIN32\IBM_6.

   If you're installing from the CD-ROM, the directory is PRODUCTS\DOSWIN32\IBM_6.
5. Select the language you want to use.
6. At the introduction screen, you can view the readme file or click Continue.
7. Select Yes to accept the license agreement.
8. Click the Next button to accept the default target directory (the location on the workstation where you want to install the client files) and the workstation's Windows directory.
9. If you already have a LAN driver installed on the workstation, the Client32 installation program may detect the driver, or you may have to install one. You can specify whether you want to use a 16-bit or 32-bit driver. (Use a 32-bit driver if one is available for your network board.) If the driver you need isn't on the CD-ROM, you will need to have it on a diskette. (Drivers are available from the network board's manufacturer.)
10. Select the driver you want and then click Next.
11. Specify that you allow the installation program to modify the workstation's AUTOEXEC.BAT file and click Next.
12. When the installation is complete, restart the computer to make the new client take effect.

When the computer reboots, the NetWare GUI Login icon will appear in the NetWare Tools program group on your Windows desktop. (GUI stands for Graphical User Interface.) To log in to the network, double-click the icon, and then enter your login name and password when prompted. (See Figure 4.1.)

FIGURE 4.1 *The NetWare GUI Login Screen*

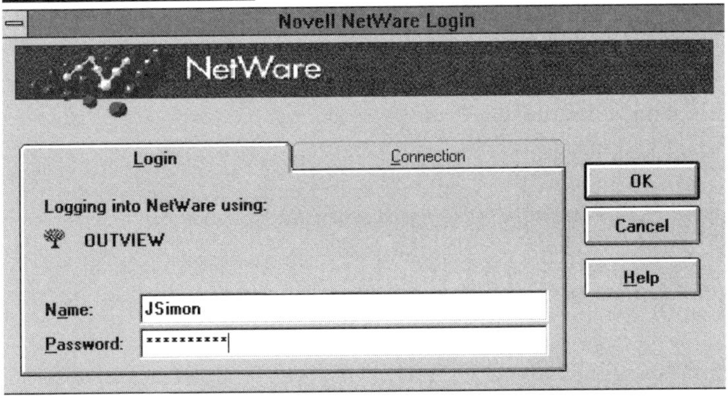

You can set up the NetWare GUI Login program so that it executes automatically whenever you start up the NetWare Client32 in Windows 3.1x. This way, whenever you first load Windows, the NetWare GUI Login screen will prompt you for your user name and password. If you use this login program, you do not need to put the LOGIN command in your AUTOEXEC.BAT file.

To make the NetWare GUI Login program execute automatically, double-click on the NetWare User Tools icon on your desktop. Then click the Hot Key button (the button that shows a picture of a key with flames). Click on the Startup tab to open the Startup page and then mark the Launch on Startup button under the Windows Login heading. (See Figure 4.2.) Under the Login tab, you can set whether the NetWare GUI Login window by default logs you into a tree or into a server. When you're finished, close the NetWare User Tools.

FIGURE 4.2 *Configuring the NetWare GUI Login Program*

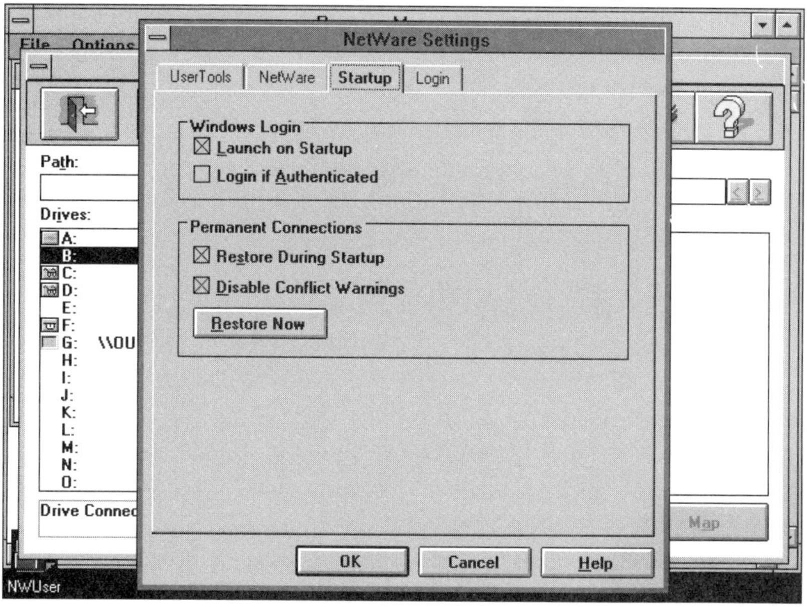

Now, when you start Windows, which automatically launches the Client32, the NetWare GUI Login screen appears. Enter your name and password and then click OK. To change the server or tree to which you want to log in, click the Connection tab to open that page, and enter your desired tree or server.

INSTALLING CLIENT32 FROM DOS

To install Client32 from DOS, complete the steps in the following checklist.

1. Install a network board in the workstation according to the manufacturer's documentation. Be sure to record the board's configuration settings, such as its interrupt and port address. (You may want to use a worksheet such as the "Workstation Installation and Configuration" worksheet in Appendix D.)
2. Cable the network board to the network, using the correct cabling hardware, including terminators, hubs, or any other hardware required by your topology. See Chapter 1 and your hardware manufacturer's documentation for more information about limitations and guidelines for installing network hardware.

3. Go to the installation directory for Client32. If you're installing from a network directory, the path is generally PUBLIC\CLIENT\DOSWIN32\IBM. If you're installing from the CD-ROM, the directory is PRODUCTS\DOSWIN32\IBM.
4. Type **INSTALL**.
5. Press Enter to accept the license agreement.
6. Select the clients you want to install and press F10.
7. Specify if you want to use more country codes than the one currently installed on this machine (in most cases, answer No).
8. Network administrators are asked if they want to set the shared Windows path (in most cases, answer No unless you are an administrator who does want to set up a shared Windows path). Then press F10 to continue.
9. Choose whether you want to install a 16-bit or 32-bit driver. Select a 32-bit driver if one is available for your network board.
10. Allow the installation program to edit the AUTOEXEC.BAT and CONFIG.SYS files on the workstation.
11. Accept the default client directory (the location on the workstation where the client files should be installed) and the workstation's Windows directory.
12. Select your LAN driver and then press F10. If the driver you need isn't on the CD-ROM, you must have it on a diskette. (Drivers are available from the network board's manufacturer.)
13. After the installation is complete, restart the computer to make the new client take effect.

INSTALLING CLIENT32 FROM WINDOWS 95

You can install Client32 for Windows 95 on a workstation that is already running Windows 95. If you are installing several workstations that do not already have Windows 95 installed, and if you've set up a batch process in a network directory, you can install both Windows 95 and Client32 at the same time.

Installing Client32 on a Windows 95 Workstation

To install Client32 on a workstation that already has Windows 95 installed, complete the steps in the following checklist.

1. Install a network board in the workstation according to the manufacturer's documentation. Be sure to record the board's configuration settings, such as its interrupt and port address. (You may want to use a worksheet such as the "Workstation Installation and Configuration" worksheet in Appendix D.)
2. Cable the network board to the network, using the correct cabling hardware, including terminators, hubs, or any other hardware required by your topology. See Chapter 1 and your hardware manufacturer's documentation for more information about limitations and guidelines for installing network hardware.
3. Go to the installation directory on the network or the CD-ROM. If you're installing from a network directory, the path is generally PUBLIC\CLIENT\WIN95\IBM_ENU. If you're installing from the CD-ROM, the directory is PRODUCTS\WIN95\IBM_ENU.
4. Choose Yes to accept the license agreement.
5. Decide whether you want to use Microsoft's NDIS (Network Driver Interface Specification) LAN driver for your network board or Novell's ODI (Open Data-link Interface) LAN driver. By default, the box on the welcome screen is checked, indicating that the installation program will use an ODI driver instead of an NDIS driver if an ODI driver is available. ODI drivers generally perform better than NDIS drivers. The order of preference that the install program uses when automatically detecting LAN drivers is:
   - 32-bit ODI drivers
   - NDIS drivers (written to the version 3.3 specifications)
   - 16-bit ODI drivers
   - NDIS drivers (written to the version 2.x specifications)
6. Choose Start.
7. Client32 detects and will automatically load many LAN drivers. If it cannot detect your network board, it will prompt you to select a board.
8. If you want to install optional features or configure the workstation, choose Customize. This brings up the standard Network Neighborhood property pages. NetWare Client32 adds information to the Network Neighborhood for NetWare servers, NDS trees, volumes, print queues, users, and so on.

On the Configuration page, the heading "The Following Network Components Are Installed" lists several NetWare Client32 services and components that are now installed on this workstation. You can select one of these services or components and click the Properties button to configure that item, or you can click Add or Remove to add additional services (such as SNMP management services), adapters (network boards), protocols, or client software.

9. Highlight Novell NetWare Client32 and click the Properties button. Four pages appear, which you can use to configure the client: Client32, Login, Default Capture, and Advanced Settings. (When you are finished configuring the Client32, click OK to save your settings and continue.)

   a. On the Client32 page, you can specify a preferred server or preferred tree (the server or tree you want the workstation to log in to by default), a name context for the user, and the first network drive.

   b. On the Login page, you can set the NetWare GUI Login program to automatically display its Connection screen when the user starts NetWare Client32. It also lets you specify what information the user can type or change in the Connection screen.

   c. The Default Capture page lets you capture a port to a printer.

   d. The Advanced Settings page lets you set configuration parameters. These parameters are primarily the same ones you can set in NET.CFG for other workstation platforms. However, in Windows 95, these parameters are set in Microsoft's Windows 95 Registry.

10. Choose Reboot to restart the workstation so that the Client32 files can take effect.

Installing Windows 95 and Client32 Simultaneously

If you want to install both Windows 95 and Client32 on workstations that are currently running DOS or Windows 3.1, you can create a batch process to simplify the process. To do this, complete the steps in the following checklist.

1. Install a network board in the workstation according to the manufacturer's documentation. Be sure to record the board's configuration settings, such as its interrupt and port address. (You may want to use a worksheet such as the "Workstation Installation and Configuration" worksheet in Appendix D.)

2. Cable the network board to the network, using the correct cabling hardware, including terminators, hubs, or any other hardware required by your topology. See Chapter 1 and your hardware manufacturer's documentation for more information about limitations and guidelines for installing network hardware.
3. Map a drive to SYS:PUBLIC\CLIENT\WIN95\IBM_ENU on the network.
4. Go to the Windows 95 CD-ROM and run NETSETUP.EXE from the ADMIN\NETTOOLS\NETSETUP folder.
5. Choose Set Path, enter the path to the MSBATCH Setup install folder (such as F:\WIN95), and then choose OK.
6. Choose Install to install the Windows 95 source files to the server install path and then select Local Hard Drive. For Path to Install From, enter the path to the folder that contains the Windows 95 cabinet files (these files have the extension .CAB), such as F:\WIN95CAB.
7. When the installation is finished, choose Exit.
8. Insert the *NetWare 4.11 Operating System* CD-ROM and copy all the files from the PRODUCTS\WIN95\IBM_ENU directory to a new directory on the workstation.
9. In this new directory, remove or rename all files that have the extension .INF.
10. From the NetWare 4.11 CD-ROM, copy all .INF files from the PRODUCTS\ADM32\IBM_ENU\BATCH95\NLS\ENGLISH directory to the same directory you used in Steps 8 and 9.
11. To integrate Client32 help files with the Windows 95 help files, edit the NWCLIENT.INF file to remove the semicolon (;) from the line that has OEM.CNT.
12. Run BATCH.EXE on the workstation and fill in the setup information.
13. Choose Network Options and uncheck any protocols, services, clients, or other options.
14. Under Available Protocols, check IPX/SPX Compatible Protocol and then choose OK.
15. Choose Installation Options and specify the installation options you want. Specifying options here prevents users from having to make too many decisions when they install Windows 95 and Client32 from the server. Choose OK when you're finished.

16. Select Optional Components if necessary.
17. When finished, choose Done.
18. Save the file and give it a unique file name in the MSBATCH Setup installation folder (F:\WIN95).
19. Locate the MSBATCH.INF file, remove the Read-Only attribute from that file, and rename it to something else.
20. Rename the file you saved in Step 18 to MSBATCH.INF.
21. Log in to the network and map a drive to the MSBATCH Setup installation folder that contains the NETSETUP.EXE file.
22. Run the INF Installer (INFINST.EXE), choose Set Path, and specify the MSBATCH Setup installation folder (F:\WIN95).
23. Choose Install INF and select NECLIENT.INF. Then choose OK.
24. Follow any messages on the screen. If you receive a message that the existing NETWARE.DRV file is newer than the Client32 file you're trying to install, overwrite it with the Client32 version anyway. If you receive a message that a file couldn't be found, don't skip the file; enter a path where you think the file may be, such as the directory you created in Step 8.
25. When finished, choose Exit.
26. From the BATCH95 directory on the NetWare 4.11 CD-ROM, copy NETDEF.INF to the MSBATCH Setup installation folder on the server and to its INF and SUWIN subdirectories.

When you finish creating the batch process, you can run the process to install both Windows 95 and Client32 on each workstation. To do this, go to the workstation you want to upgrade and complete the steps in the following checklist.

1. Map a network drive to the volume that contains the Windows 95 and Client32 files.
2. Run SETUP.EXE with MSBATCH.INF as the first parameter by typing a command similar to the following (substituting your drive and path):

```
SETUP F:\WIN95\MSBATCH.INF
```

NOTE

You can set up the Windows 95 workstation for "deviceless printing," which means that the workstation can send print jobs to a network printer without having to capture a port to a queue. To do this, select the Network Neighborhood, browse for the printer you want to use, right-click on the printer, and select Install.

SIMPLIFYING THE UPGRADE PROCESS

If you are upgrading many existing NetWare workstations to NetWare Client32, you can use the Automatic Client Upgrade (ACU) feature to automate this process. With the ACU, you place ACU commands in a profile or system login script to detect if the Client32 software needs to be installed, and then the ACU updates the workstation automatically.

NOTE

Another way to simplify the upgrading process is to use the NetWare Application Launcher to set up an icon on each workstation to point to the Client32 Setup program. See Chapter 6 for more information about using the NetWare Application Launcher.

The ACU feature works best in situations where you have many workstations with similar configurations, since you define a common set of instructions for updating all the workstations in the same way.

Six utilities are involved in the ACU process:

- NWDETECT.EXE starts the update by searching the workstation's NET.CFG file for an Install Stamp.
- NWSTAMP.EXE creates the Install Stamp in the workstation's NET.CFG file. The Install Stamp is a set of four parameters in the NET.CFG file that indicate the version of client software currently installed on the workstation. The network administrator sets new parameters in the login script, and NWDETECT.EXE compares the workstation's parameters with those in the login script. The Install Stamp in a NET.CFG file may look similar to the following:

```
INSTALL STAMP
    NAME = Novell_Client_32
    MAJOR VERSION = 4
    MINOR VERSION = 1
    REVISION VERSION = 0
```

- NWLOG.EXE creates a log file that lists all upgraded workstations, along with the date and time, user name, and IPX external network number of each upgraded workstation.
- INSTALL.EXE is the regular DOS-based NetWare Client32 installation program, which is launched automatically if NWDETECT.EXE determines that the workstation needs to be upgraded.
- INSTALL.CFG is the configuration file that lists all of the client files and configuration parameters that will be copied to the workstation during the update. A default INSTALL.CFG file is available, but you can edit it to specify only the files you want.
- REBOOT.COM reboots the workstation automatically after the update.

To set up the ACU process, complete the steps in the following checklist.

1. Make sure the Client32 installation files are located in a network directory. (If you haven't already installed the Client32 files on the server, load INSTALL.NLM on the server, choose Product Options, and then choose Create Client Installation Directories on Server.)
2. Copy the ACU files from the *NetWare 4.11 Operating System* CD-ROM to the server.

   a. First, go to the PRODUCTS\ADM32\IBM_ENU\DOS_ACU on the CD-ROM. Then copy the following files from that directory to the SYS:PUBLIC directory on the server:
      - NWDETECT.EXE
      - NWLOG.EXE
      - NWSTAMP.EXE
      - REBOOT.COM

   b. Next, go to PRODUCTS\ADM32\IBM_ENU\DOS_ACU\NLS\ENGLISH on the CD-ROM. Then copy the following files (the readme file and the files that hold the English messages for the executables you copied in the previous step) from that directory to the SYS:PUBLIC\NLS\ENGLISH directory:
      - ACU.TXT
      - NWDETECT.MSG
      - NWLOG.MSG
      - NWSTAMP.MSG
3. Print out the ACU.TXT file. This file, which can be read and printed from any text editor, contains detailed instructions, an example

INSTALL.CFG file, and example login script commands for using ACU.

4. Locate the INSTALL.CFG file in the SYS:PUBLIC\CLIENT\DOSWIN32\IBM_6\NLS\ENGLISH directory. Using a text editor, open this file and review its contents. This file dictates which files get copied to the workstation during installation and which parameters get set.

5. If you would like to edit the file to change which files get installed or to change some of the parameters, save the existing INSTALL.CFG in a safe place before editing it.

6. Edit the file to fit your workstations' needs. You can edit commands under the FILES, REQUESTER, TCP/IP, NWIP, SNMP, HOSTMIB, RSA, SETUP, and DriverTranslationTable sections of INSTALL.CFG. See the ACU.TXT documentation for detailed explanations of the settings you can change.

7. Using the NetWare Administrator utility (or SYSCON for bindery-based clients running NETX), open the profile or system (container) login script that will execute for the appropriate users.

8. In the login script, add the following command:

   `#NWDETECT` *`name version1 version2 options`*

   Replace *name* with the name you assign to this group of users (such as Novell_Client32 or Marketing). Replace *version1* with the beginning version number you want the program to detect. Replace *version2* with the ending version number you want the program to detect. Replace *options* with one of the following:

   - /T *type* — Replace *type* with the type of client loaded — NETX, VLM, or NIOS (for Client32).
   - /P "*prompt text*" — Lets you prompt the user as to whether to run the ACU. Replace *prompt text* with the prompt to ask the user to proceed with the ACU if the /T option returns "True" (or a 0 error code, meaning the client type matched that was specified in the login script). The user must respond with a Y or N. If the user responds with Y, the ACU process runs. If the user responds with N, the ACU does not run.

- /C *path\filename* — Specifies the full path and name of the configuration file that contains the Install Stamp. This is usually NET.CFG, so this option is generally not required.
- /NS — Detects whether there is an Install Stamp in the NET.CFG file. This returns an error code of 0 if no Install Stamp is found, which causes the ACU process to run.
- The following command detects any workstation, used by Marketing personnel, that is running Client32 software between versions 1.0.0 and 2.0.0:

```
#NWDETECT MARKETING 1.0.0 2.0.0 /T NIOS
```

9. Next, in the same login script, insert the following command:

```
#NWSTAMP name version options
```

Replace *name* with the name you assign in the STAMP section of the NET.CFG file (such as Novell_Client32). Replace *version* with the version number you want placed in the STAMP section of the NET.CFG file (the version number must be in *x.x.x* format). Replace *options* with one of the following:

- /B *backupname* — Makes a copy of the original NET.CFG file and names it with the path and name you specify in *backupname*.
- /C *path\filename* — Specifies the full path and name of the configuration file that contains the Install Stamp. This is usually NET.CFG, so this option is generally not required.

For example, the following command:

```
#NWSTAMP Novell_Client32 1.0.1
```

will cause the following commands to be added to the workstation's NET.CFG file:

```
Install Stamp
   Name = Novell_Client32
   Major Version = 1
   Minor Version = 0
   Revision Version = 1
```

10. In the same login script, insert the following command:

```
NWLOG /F path\filename /M "message"
```

Replace *path\filename* with the path and name of the file you want to store the logged information. The /M "*message*" parameter is optional; use it if you want to display an additional message with the log entry.

11. (Optional) In the same login script, insert the following command if you want the workstation to reboot automatically after the files have been updated:

    ```
    #REBOOT
    ```

12. Try running the ACU on a test workstation to see if it upgrades the files in the manner you were expecting. When you are satisfied that the right files are being upgraded, you can begin implementing ACU for all the workstations that use that login script.

Installing NetWare DOS Requester for DOS or Windows 3.1x

The NetWare DOS Requester consists of several files, which together regulate how the workstation communicates with the network and how tasks are accomplished. Each of these files, called *Virtual Loadable Modules* (VLMs), controls a different aspect of the workstation's activities, such as the workstation's connections to servers, user authentication, backward compatibility with older client software, and so on. The VLMs are all managed by a single executable file, called VLM.EXE.

Along with the NetWare DOS Requester, the workstation also needs additional files to boot the machine and connect it with the network. Some of these files are regular DOS boot files that the workstation already has but which need to be edited to provide NetWare support. Other files are provided by NetWare, such as the protocol files and LAN drivers for network boards.

The NetWare DOS Requester installation program copies all necessary NetWare files to the workstation automatically and edits any DOS or Windows files that require modifications. In addition, the NetWare DOS Requester also installs User Tools (a NetWare utility that users can use to work with the network) on the workstation automatically.

PREPARING TO INSTALL THE NETWARE DOS REQUESTER

Before you can install a new workstation, you must decide how you will install the client software. You can choose one of the following three methods for installing the NetWare DOS Requester on your workstation:

- You can install directly from the *NetWare 4.11 Operating System* CD-ROM.
- You can install from installation diskettes you create from the CD-ROM. To create installation diskettes, load INSTALL.NLM on the server, choose Product Options, and then choose Make Diskettes. You'll need six blank diskettes.
- If you are upgrading an existing NetWare workstation to the NetWare DOS Requester, you can install it from the CD-ROM, from diskettes, or from a network directory on the server. To use the network directory method, you must put the client installation files into a directory on the server. Load INSTALL.NLM on the server, choose Product Options, and then choose Create Client Installation Directories on Server.

INSTALLING THE NETWARE DOS REQUESTER

To install the NetWare client software on a DOS or Windows workstation, complete the steps in the following checklist.

1. Install a network board in the workstation according to the manufacturer's documentation. Be sure to record the board's configuration settings, such as its interrupt and port address. (You may want to use a worksheet such as the "Workstation Installation and Configuration" worksheet in Appendix D.)
2. Cable the network board to the network, using the correct cabling hardware, including terminators, hubs, or any other hardware required by your topology. See Chapter 1 and your hardware manufacturer's documentation for more information about limitations and guidelines for installing network hardware.
3. Boot DOS. If the workstation has Windows, make sure Windows is installed but is not running.
4. Move to the directory from which you will install the client software and start INSTALL:

   a. If you are installing from diskettes, insert Disk 1 into the workstation's floppy disk drive, change to that drive letter, and enter the following:

   ```
   INSTALL
   ```

b. If you are installing from the CD-ROM, insert the *NetWare 4.11 Operating System* CD-ROM in the workstation's CD-ROM drive, change to the CD-ROM's drive letter, and enter the following:

```
INSTALL
```

Then select the language as prompted and then choose the DOS/Windows Client Installation option.

c. If you are upgrading an existing workstation with older NetWare client software on it, map a drive to the network directory SYS:PUBLIC\CLIENT\DOSWIN and enter the following:

```
INSTALL
```

5. Accept the default directory (C:\NWCLIENT).
6. Allow the installation to modify the CONFIG.SYS and AUTOEXEC.BAT files.
7. Specify whether or not to support Windows.
8. Select the LAN driver that matches this workstation's network board. If you are installing from diskettes, insert the LAN driver diskette (Disk 5) and press Enter. If the driver you need isn't listed, press Esc, insert the manufacturer's diskette, and press Enter.
9. When all the information on the screen is correct, press Enter.
10. When the installation is complete, press Enter to quit the program. (If you were installing from diskettes, you will be asked to "Insert the disk with batch file." Insert Disk 1 at this point because the program is looking for the INSTALL file. Then the program will quit normally.)
11. If this workstation previously had NETX installed on it, edit AUTOEXEC.BAT and remove any commands that loaded IPX, IPXODI, LSL, and NETX. The NetWare DOS Requester places commands similar to these in the STARTNET.BAT file instead.

VLMs (Virtual Loadable Modules) are placed in the NWCLIENT directory by the NetWare DOS Requester installation. They control the workstation's communication and activities on the network.

After the NetWare DOS Requester has been installed on a workstation, the workstation's AUTOEXEC.BAT file contains a line that calls the STARTNET.BAT file from the NWCLIENT directory. STARTNET loads the LSL driver, the LAN driver, the protocol driver (such as IPXODI), and VLM.EXE.

VLM.EXE, by default, automatically loads twelve VLMs. Most of these VLMs are required but a few are optional. In addition, there are eleven more

VLMs that are not loaded by default but which you can add.

Table 4.1 lists the twelve default VLMs in the order in which they execute.

TABLE 4.1 *The Twelve Default VLMs*

VLM	REQUIRED/OPTIONAL	FUNCTION
CONN.VLM	Required	Allows the workstation to connect to a specified number of servers.
IPXNCP.VLM	Required	Builds and transmits IPX packets using the IPX protocol.
TRAN.VLM	Required	Handles protocols and manages IPXNCP.VLM.
SECURITY.VLM	Optional	Helps provide security at the transport level.
NDS.VLM	Required	Allows the workstation to form an NDS-based connection with an IntranetWare server.
BIND.VLM	Optional	Allows the workstation to form a bindery-based connection with a NetWare server. This provides backward compatibility for applications that are still using bindery-specific information to access the network.
NWP.VLM	Required	(NetWare Protocol Multiplexor) Allows other modules to log in and log out and to connect to network services.
FIO.VLM	Required	Controls file input and output (I/O) and provides file-caching support, Large Internet Packet (LIP) support, and packet burst support.
GENERAL.VLM	Required	Provides general services to other VLMs, such as server and queue information and the handling of search drives.

TABLE 4.1 *The Twelve Default VLMs (continued)*

VLM	REQUIRED/OPTIONAL	FUNCTION
REDIR.VLM	Required	(DOS Redirector) Redirects appropriate requests to the network.
PRINT.VLM	Optional	Provides printing redirection services using FIO.VLM.
NETX.VLM	Optional	Provides backward compatibility for applications that require APIs that were available in NETX.

Table 4.2 shows the additional VLMs that are also available but aren't loaded by default.

TABLE 4.2 *The Eleven Additional VLMs*

VLM	FUNCTION
AUTO.VLM	Tries to reconnect the workstation automatically if the connection to the server is temporarily broken.
MIB2IF.VLM	Provides support for MIB-II interface groups.
MIB2PROT.VLM	Provides MIB-II support for TCP/IP groups.
NMR.VLM	(NetWare Management Responder) Provides management information about the workstation to a network management program.
PNW.VLM	Implements NetWare protocol support for Personal NetWare.
RSA.VLM	Uses the RSA security encryption system to provide system-level background authentication for the workstation.
WSASN1.VLM	Provides SNMP ASN.1 translation.
WSDRVPRN.VLM	Gathers information about print mappings and captured printers.
WSREG.VLM	Provides SNMP MIB registration.
WSSNMP.VLM	Provides desktop SNMP support.
WSTRAP.VLM	Provides SNMP trap support.

To make one of these VLMs execute, you must add a command to the NET.CFG file under the NetWare DOS Requester heading, in the following format:

```
VLM=xxxx.VLM
```

where *xxxx* is the type of VLM. For example, to load AUTO.VLM, the command would appear under the NetWare DOS Requester heading in a fashion similar to the following:

```
NETWARE DOS REQUESTER

     FIRST NETWORK DRIVE = F

     NETWARE PROTOCOL = NDS,BIND

     VLM=AUTO.VLM
```

If you want to prevent one or more of the default VLMs from loading, you can add a new heading to NET.CFG, called USE DEFAULTS=OFF.

Then, under that heading, list all the default VLMs you want to load, excluding the unwanted ones from the list. For example, if you don't want to load BIND.VLM or NETX.VLM, this section of the NET.CFG file would look like this:

```
USE DEFAULTS=OFF

     VLM=CONN.VLM

     VLM=IPXNCP.VLM

     VLM=TRAN.VLM

     VLM=SECURITY.VLM

     VLM=NDS.VLM

     VLM=NWP.VLM

     VLM=FIO.VLM

     VLM=GENERAL.VLM

     VLM=REDIR.VLM

     VLM=PRINT.VLM
```

Boot and NetWare Files on Workstations

The following files are either copied to the workstation or modified during the NetWare client installation (both Client32 and NetWare DOS Requester). Some of these files can be edited later to add or change the workstation's functionality:

- CONFIG.SYS
- AUTOEXEC.BAT
- STARTNET.BAT
- LSL.COM or LSLC32.NLM
- LAN drivers
- Protocol drivers
- NET.CFG
- Unicode files
- Windows 3.1x configuration files (SYSTEM.INI, WIN.INI, PROGMAN.INI), or the Windows 95 Registry

In addition to the files listed here, the NetWare client installs the NetWare client files themselves, plus many support files, such as .DLL files, message files, and help files.

The main files affected are explained in the following sections.

CONFIG.SYS

CONFIG.SYS is a configuration file that is created at the root of the workstation's boot disk during the operating system's installation. It can also be created or edited with a text editor. CONFIG.SYS configures the workstation's DOS environment.

CONFIG.SYS is automatically modified by the NetWare client installation. The following is an example of a CONFIG.SYS file:

```
DEVICE=C:\DOS\SETVER.EXE

DEVICE=C:\WINDOWS\HIMEM.SYS

DEVICE=C:\WINDOWS\EMM386.EXE NOEMS

DOS=HIGH,UMB
```

```
SHELL=C:\COMMAND.COM /P C:\ /E:4096
DEVICE=C:\DOS\POWER.EXE
FILES=40
LASTDRIVE=Z
DEVICE=C:\WINDOWS\SMARTDRV.EXE /DOUBLE_BUFFER
STACKS=9,256
```

AUTOEXEC.BAT

AUTOEXEC.BAT is a batch file created at the root of the disk during DOS installation for most recent versions of DOS. It can also be created or edited with a text editor. It automatically executes when the workstation boots. It can be used to load TSRs (Terminate and Stay Resident programs) that provide added functionality for the workstation, such as CD-ROM support, DOS key buffering, network support, and so on. It can also be used to log the user into the network.

AUTOEXEC.BAT is automatically modified by the NetWare client installation to add a line that executes the STARTNET.BAT file.

The installation program also adds a DOS search path in AUTOEXEC.BAT to the new client directory.

After installation, you may want to add lines to set the user's variables for applications and automatically log the user into the network. (If you want to use the NetWare GUI Login with Client32, you don't need to add the LOGIN command to this file.) The following is an example of an AUTOEXEC.BAT file:

```
PATH C:\NWCLIENT\;C:\WINDOWS;C:\DOS;C:\NOTEUT;C:\
C:\DOS\SHARE.EXE /L:500 /F:5100
C:\WINDOWS\SMARTDRV.EXE /L
PROMPT $P$G
SET TEMP=C:\DOS
SET NOTEUT=C:\NOTEUT
C:\DOS\DOSKEY
```

```
C:\NOTEUT\HK.COM
SET NWLANGUAGE=ENGLISH
SET EMAILUSER=LSNOW
SET WP=/U-LKS
ECHO ON
CALL C:\NWCLIENT\STARTNET
F:
LOGIN .LSNOW.MKTG.WEST.OUTVIEW
```

STARTNET.BAT

STARTNET.BAT is a batch file created by the NetWare client installation. It is located in the new client directory on the workstation. It can be edited with a text editor.

STARTNET.BAT specifies the workstation's language by setting the NWLANGUAGE environment variable, and then it loads LSL.COM or LSLC32.NLM, the LAN driver, and protocol support files. It then executes either VLM.EXE, which loads all necessary VLMs for NetWare DOS Requester, or CLIENT32.NLM for Client32.

In older versions of NetWare client software, called NETX, the commands to load these files were located in the AUTOEXEC.BAT file (instead of in STARTNET.BAT), so if you upgrade a workstation from NETX, you'll need to edit the AUTOEXEC.BAT file to remove those lines.

The following is an example of a STARTNET.BAT file for NetWare DOS Requester:

```
SET NWLANGUAGE=ENGLISH
C:\NWCLIENT\LSL.COM
C:\NWCLIENT\3C523.COM
C:\NWCLIENT\IPXODI.COM
C:\NWCLIENT\TCPIP.EXE
C:\NWCLIENT\VLM.EXE
```

The following is an example of a STARTNET.BAT file for Client32, using 16-bit drivers:

```
SET NWLANGUAGE=ENGLISH

C:\NOVELL\CLIENT32\NIOS.EXE

C:\NOVELL\CLIENT32\LSL.COM

C:\NOVELL\CLIENT32\N16ODI.COM

C:\NOVELL\CLIENT32\NESL.COM

C:\NOVELL\CLIENT32\CPQETHNW.COM

LOAD C:\NOVELL\CLIENT32\LSLC32.NLM

LOAD C:\NOVELL\CLIENT32\PC32MLID.LAN

LOAD C:\NOVELL\CLIENT32\IPX.NLM

LOAD C:\NOVELL\CLIENT32\CLIENT32.NLM
```

The following is an example of a STARTNET.BAT file for Client32, using 32-bit ODI drivers. Although configuration parameters for 16-bit LAN drivers are specified in the NET.CFG file, the configuration parameters for 32-bit LAN drivers are not. Instead, you must specify parameters for 32-bit drivers in the STARTNET.BAT file, as shown below. (Note that the command that loads the LAN driver and specifies its settings should appear on a single line in the file. It's shown on two lines here because of spacing constraints.)

```
SET NWLANGUAGE=ENGLISH

C:\NOVELL\CLIENT32\NIOS.EXE

LOAD C:\NOVELL\CLIENT32\LSLC32.NLM

LOAD C:\NOVELL\CLIENT32\CMSM.NLM

LOAD C:\NOVELL\CLIENT32\ETHERTSM.NLM

LOAD C:\NOVELL\CLIENT32\CNE2000.LAN INT=5 PORT=300
    FRAME=ETHERNET_802.2

LOAD C:\NOVELL\CLIENT32\IPX.NLM

LOAD C:\NOVELL\CLIENT32\CLIENT32.NLM
```

LSL.COM and LSLC32.NLM

LSL.COM (for 16-bit drivers) and LSLC32.NLM (for 32-bit drivers) are Link Support Layer files. These files enable the workstation to communicate with different protocols. The appropriate version of the LSL-related file is placed in the client directory by the NetWare client installation.

LAN DRIVERS

A *LAN driver* is the software module that allows the network board in a workstation (or server) to communicate with the network. You select and install the LAN driver during the NetWare client installation. Novell ships several LAN drivers with IntranetWare, so the LAN driver you need may be on the CD-ROM or in the client installation directory. If the driver you need does not come with IntranetWare, you'll have to obtain it from the board manufacturer.

The NetWare client installation automatically places the LAN driver in the client directory.

PROTOCOL DRIVERS

The *protocol driver* is placed in the client directory by the NetWare client installation. It enables the LAN driver to communicate with a protocol, such as IPX (the default) or TCP/IP.

NET.CFG

NET.CFG is created by the NetWare client installation. It is located in the client directory and can be edited with a text editor.

NET.CFG configures the NetWare client and 16-bit ODI LAN drivers for the workstation's needs. Because NET.CFG is used to configure a variety of different aspects of your workstation, NET.CFG can be quite simple or fairly involved.

The following is a sample NET.CFG file that was created automatically during NetWare DOS Requester installation to configure an NE2000 network board to use port 300, interrupt 3, and the Ethernet 802.2 frame type. Notice that the file is divided by headings. The Link Driver NE2000 heading contains indented lines that specify the information for that driver. The NetWare DOS Requester heading contains indented lines that specify general items for the Requester.

```
LINK DRIVER NE2000

     PORT 300
```

```
        INT 3
        FRAME ETHERNET_802.2

    NETWARE DOS REQUESTER
        NETWARE PROTOCOL=NDS, BIND
        FIRST NETWORK DRIVE=F
```

The following is a more complex NET.CFG file created for a NetWare DOS Requester client. In this file, there are two different boards loaded in the workstation, so there are two different Link Driver headings. Both boards are linked to more than one Ethernet frame type. Also, additional commands have been added beneath the NetWare DOS Requester heading to indicate a preferred Directory tree and a preferred server. Two of the optional VLMs are called out under this heading as well. Finally, because this workstation is using TCP/IP, a final section is added to the file to configure the TCP/IP support.

```
    LINK DRIVER PE3ODI
        FRAME ETHERNET_802.2
        FRAME ETHERNET_II
        PROTOCOL IPX E0 ETHERNET_802.2

    LINK DRIVER 3C523
        FRAME ETHERNET_802.2
        FRAME ETHERNET_II
        INT 3
        PORT 300
        MEM C0000
        PROTOCOL IPX E0 ETHERNET_802.2
        PROTOCOL IP 800 ETHERNET_II

    NETWARE DOS REQUESTER
```

```
    FIRST NETWORK DRIVE = F
    NETWARE PROTOCOL = NDS,BIND
    PREFERRED TREE = OUTVIEW_INC
    PREFERRED SERVER =PHOTO1
    NAME CONTEXT = "MKTG.WEST.OUTVIEW"
    NETWORK PRINTERS = 1
    PRINT HEADER =100
    PRINT TAIL = 100
    SHOW DOTS = ON
    AUTO RECONNECT = ON
    BIND RECONNECT = ON
    AUTO RETRY = 1
    VLM = AUTO.VLM
    VLM = RSA.VLM
    CONNECTIONS=10
LINK SUPPORT
    BUFFERS 8 1500
    MEMPOOL 4096
    MAX STACKS 8
PROTOCOL TCPIP
    PATH SCRIPT     C:\NET\SCRIPT
    PATH PROFILE      C:\NET\PROFILE
    PATH LWP_CFG      C:\NET\HSTACC
```

```
        PATH TCP_CFG        C:\NET\TCP
        IP_ADDRESS        135.26.101.26
        IP_ROUTER         135.26.101.254
        IP_NETMASK        254.254.254.0
        TCP_SOCKETS       8
        UDP_SOCKETS       8
        RAW_SOCKETS       1
        NB_SESSIONS       4
        NB_COMMANDS       8
        NB_ADAPTER        0
        NB_DOMAIN         DENVER.WEST.OUTVIEW.COM
```

The following is an example of a NET.CFG file for a Client32 workstation using 16-bit ODI drivers. The NIOS heading is specific to Client32.

```
LINK DRIVER CPQETHNW
    SLOT 1
    FRAME Ethernet_802.2
NetWare DOS Requester
    FIRST NETWORK DRIVE = G
    SHORT MACHINE TYPE = IBM
    NETWARE PROTOCOL NDS BIND
NIOS
    LINE DRAW CHARS = "┌┐└┘│─"
Protocol IPX
    IPX SOCKETS 40
```

There are numerous parameters that can be set in NET.CFG. Appendix A explains each of the commands you can enter in NET.CFG for NetWare DOS Requester. Client32 supports most of the commands in Appendix A plus some additional NET.CFG parameters, which are described in the Client32 help file.

UNICODE FILES

Unicode files are used to help the NetWare client software run on machines that use different country-specific keyboards and language-specific versions of DOS. During the NetWare client installation, the Unicode files specific to the country setting of your workstation are installed in a directory called NLS.

WINDOWS 3.1x AND WINDOWS 95 CONFIGURATION FILES

Windows configuration files help define how Windows 3.1x, Windows 95, and their applications run. Some of the regular Windows 3.1x configuration files — SYSTEM.INI, WIN.INI, and PROGMAN.INI — are modified during the NetWare client installation to add support for the NetWare client software. For Windows 95, the Windows 95 Registry is modified to add support for NetWare Client32.

Installing NetWare Client Software on an OS/2 Workstation

To make an OS/2 computer function as a workstation on a NetWare 4.11 network, you must install NetWare client software on the workstation. The NetWare client software for OS/2-based computers is called the NetWare Client for OS/2.

The NetWare Client for OS/2 consists of several files, which together regulate how the workstation communicates with the network and how tasks are accomplished.

Along with the NetWare Client for OS/2 files, the workstation also needs additional files to boot the machine and connect it with the network. Some of these files are regular OS/2 boot files that the workstation already has but which need to be edited to provide NetWare support. Other files are provided by NetWare, such as the protocol drivers.

The NetWare Client for OS/2 installation program automatically copies all necessary NetWare files to the workstation and edits any OS/2 files that require modifications. In addition, NetWare Tools (a NetWare utility that users can use to work with the network) is also installed automatically on the workstation.

PREPARING TO INSTALL THE NETWARE CLIENT FOR OS/2

Before you can install a new OS/2 workstation, you must decide how you will install the client software. You have two choices: You can install the software from diskettes or from a network directory (only if you're upgrading the workstation).

To use diskettes, you must make client installation diskettes from the *NetWare 4.11 Operating System* CD-ROM. To make the diskettes, format six high-density diskettes and label them Disk 1 through Disk 6. Then run INSTALL.NLM at the server and select the Create DOS/MS Windows/OS2 Client Install Diskettes option. Choose the set of diskettes you want to create (3.5-inch OS/2 Client Install) by making sure its check box is marked with an "X," and then press F10. This process automatically copies the needed files to the diskettes, prompting you when to swap diskettes.

If you are updating a workstation that already has an older version of NetWare client software installed on it and if you selected the Set up a Network Directory for Client Install option during the installation of the IntranetWare server, you can run the client installation program from a network directory instead of from diskettes.

INSTALLING THE NETWARE CLIENT FOR OS/2

To install the NetWare client software on an OS/2 workstation, complete the steps in the following checklist.

1. Install a network board in the workstation according to the manufacturer's documentation. Be sure to record the board's configuration settings, such as its interrupt and port address. (You may want to use a worksheet such as the "Workstation Installation and Configuration" worksheet in Appendix D.)
2. Cable the board to the network, using the correct cabling hardware, including terminators, hubs, or any other hardware required by your topology. See Chapter 1 and your hardware manufacturer's documentation for more information about limitations and guidelines for installing network hardware.
3. Boot the workstation.

4. Move to the appropriate directory from which you will install the client software and start INSTALL:
   a. If you are installing from diskettes, go to the OS/2 desktop, insert Disk 1 into the workstation's floppy disk drive, and select the Drive A icon. Then, from the Tree View window, select the drive A icon, and then select the INSTALL.EXE icon.
   b. If you are upgrading an existing workstation with older NetWare client software on it, map a drive to the network directory SYS:PUBLIC\CLIENT\OS2 and enter the following command:

   ```
   INSTALL
   ```
5. From the Installation menu, select Requester on Workstation.
6. Accept the default directory (C:\NETWARE) and specify the source drive.
7. Allow the installation to modify the CONFIG.SYS file and copy all files to the workstation.
8. Select the LAN driver that matches this workstation's network board. If you are installing from diskettes, insert the LAN driver diskette (WSDRV_1) or a diskette from another manufacturer, and choose OK.
9. Select the LAN driver you need and choose Continue.
10. Turn on IPX Support for DOS and Windows and Private NetWare ShellSupport by clicking on their respective buttons and then choose Continue.
11. Accept the default settings for AUTOEXEC.BAT by choosing Save.
12. Answer No when asked if you want to add files to another batch file.
13. If asked if you want to change the DOS_LASTDRIVE setting, choose OK.
14. Accept the default optional protocols by choosing Save.
15. Save the CONFIG.SYS file by choosing OK.
16. Choose the appropriate responses to let the installation program copy the ODI LAN driver files and requester files and finish the installation.
17. From the Configuration menu, select This Workstation.
18. Enter the path to your NET.CFG file (C:\NETWARE) and select Edit.
19. Enter the NET.CFG commands this workstation needs by selecting the commands from the window on the left and editing them in the window on the right. The bottom window displays help for each

command or parameter. (NET.CFG parameters are explained in Appendix A.)

20. When you are finished, select Save and exit the installation program.
21. Reboot the workstation to make the NetWare Client for OS/2 take effect.

INSTALLING NETWARE CLIENT SOFTWARE ON A WINDOWS NT WORKSTATION

To make a Windows NT computer function as a workstation on an IntranetWare network, you must install special NetWare software, called the NetWare Client for Windows NT, on it. This client software is not included in the IntranetWare box, but is available on Novell's Support Connection forums on CompuServe and on Novell's Internet site (http://www.novell.com). To make diskettes for the NetWare Client for Windows NT installation, download the necessary files from either online location onto your workstation's local hard disk, and then follow the readme instructions for creating the diskettes.

The NetWare Client for Windows NT consists of several files, which together regulate how the workstation communicates with the network and how tasks are accomplished.

Along with the NetWare Client for Windows NT files, the workstation also needs additional files to boot the machine and connect it to the network. Some of these files are regular Windows NT boot files that the workstation already has but which need to be edited to provide NetWare support. Other files are provided by NetWare.

The NetWare Client for Windows NT installation program automatically copies all necessary NetWare files to the workstation and edits any Windows NT files that require modifications. In addition, NetWare Tools (a NetWare utility that users can use to work with the network) is also installed automatically on the workstation. The Windows NT client software also includes the NetWare Administrator utility for the Windows NT platform.

If you plan to use the long file name formats that are allowed by Windows NT, you must also load the LONG.NAM name space on the volume that will store the Windows NT files. If you intend to use only DOS-type file names (eight-character names with a three-character extension), you do not need to load the LONG name space.

CHAPTER 5

Managing Novell Directory Services

Instant Access

Managing NDS Objects

- To create NDS objects, use the NetWare Administrator utility (which runs in Windows 3.1, OS/2, and Windows 95).
- To change a name context, use the CX command-line utility.

Managing Replicas and Partitions

- To manage replicas and partitions, use the NDS Manager utility (which can be run stand-alone or as a feature of the NetWare Administrator utility) or the PARTMGR menu utility (which runs in DOS).

Managing Bindery Services

- To set a bindery context, use the SET BINDERY CONTEXT parameter, which you can execute as a SET command at the console or choose from the SERVMAN.NLM menu.
- To display the bindery context, use the CONFIG console utility.

Managing NetWare 3.1x Users

- To synchronize NetWare 3.1x servers' binderies with NDS, install NetSync. To install NetSync, load NETSYNC4.NLM on the IntranetWare host server and load NETSYNC3.NLM and REMAPID.NLM on each NetWare 3.1x server.
- To manage users in a NetSync network, use the NetWare Administrator utility.
- To manage merged print servers in a NetSync network, use the NetWare Administrator utility or the PCONSOLE menu utility (which runs in DOS).

Merging NDS Trees

- To merge NDS trees, use DSMERGE.NLM.

Troubleshooting

- To monitor NDS messages, use the NDS TRACE commands.
- To repair the NDS tree, use DSREPAIR.NLM or the NDS Manager feature of the NetWare Administrator utility, which executes DSREPAIR remotely when necessary.

Novell Directory Services (NDS), in simplest terms, is a distributed database of network information. It contains information that defines every object on the network. *Objects* include network resources such as users, groups, printers, print queues, servers, and volumes.

In NetWare 3.1x and 2.x, this network information was stored in a database called the bindery. Each server had its own unique bindery. If you wanted a user to access more than one server, you had to create a separate account for that user on each server because the different binderies couldn't talk to each other to see which users were valid across multiple servers.

With NetWare 4, NDS replaced the bindery. The NDS database is not confined to a single server, as binderies are. Instead, all the NetWare 4 servers in a network tree share a single, distributed database. This way, you only have to create a user or other object once in the network tree; each server will recognize that same user or object. You can allow that user to access different servers simply by granting him or her the appropriate rights to the necessary volumes on each server.

Another difference between binderies and NDS is how the network information can be organized. Binderies use a *flat database structure,* which means all network objects — users, groups, print queues, and so on — exist at the same level. NDS uses a *hierarchical database structure*. With this type of structure, you can group objects together under categories and subcategories. This makes it easier to find the object you're looking for. It also enables you to control objects as a group, such as when you're modifying those objects' security levels.

The NDS database is called the Directory tree because it can be easily represented as an upside-down tree, with a root at the top and branches and subbranches fanning out below it. (See Figure 5.1.)

FIGURE 5.1 A Directory Tree

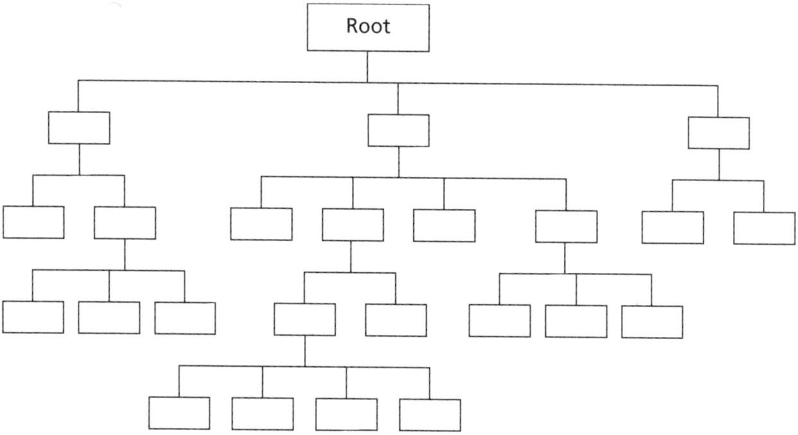

NDS Objects

For each type of network entity that will operate on the network, you will create an NDS object. This object may represent the real entity, such as a user, or it may represent a service, such as a print server. Each NDS object contains several properties, which are the pieces of information that define the object. For example, a User object contains properties that define the user's full name, his or her ID number, an e-mail address, group memberships, and so on. (Properties are also called attributes.) Each type of object, such as a Server or Printer object, may have different properties than another type of object.

Each type of object, such as User, Print Queue, or Server, is referred to as an *object class.*

CATEGORIES OF OBJECT CLASSES

Object classes fall into three basic categories:

- *Root object.* The Root object is unique and is situated at the very top of the Directory tree.
- *Container objects.* These are objects that contain other objects. Four container object classes are available: Country, Locality, Organization, and Organizational Unit. Country and Locality objects are used pri-

marily for compliance with X.500 naming specifications, but are seldom used in Novell Directory Services trees. (Some NetWare utilities don't recognize the Locality object.) In most cases, Organization and Organizational Unit objects are all you need to organize your NDS tree.

You can have only one level of Country objects (if you use it at all), which falls immediately below the Root object. (The Locality object, if used, can be located under any of the other container objects.) You also can have only one level of Organization objects, which falls below the Country object if there is one, or the Root object if there isn't. You need at least one Organization object. Finally, you can have multiple levels of Organizational Unit objects, which fall below the Organization objects.

NOTE

A fifth container object, the Licensed Product object, is used only if you install a license certificate or create a metering certificate using NetWare Licensing Services (NLS) technology. This container object contains those certificates, which are leaf objects.

- *Leaf objects*. These objects represent the entities on the network. Leaf objects, such as users, servers, and volumes, cannot contain other objects.

Figure 5.2 shows how these three categories of object classes appear in the Directory tree.

FIGURE 5.2 *Root, Container, and Leaf Objects in a Directory Tree*

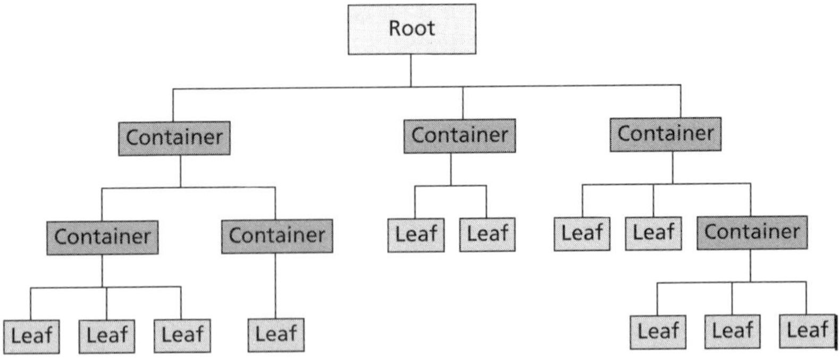

THE NDS SCHEMA

The types of NDS objects, their properties, and the rules that govern their creation and existence are called the *NDS schema*. The schema defines which objects and properties are allowed in the NDS database and determines how those objects can inherit properties and trustee rights of other container objects above it. The schema also defines how the Directory tree is structured and how objects in it are named.

Software developers can expand or change the schema by identifying new classes of objects (say, for example, a database server) or adding additional properties to existing object classes (such as adding a property called Pager Number to a User object).

NOTE

When you install IntranetWare, you may notice messages indicating that the NDS schema is being extended. This is to support some of the features of IntranetWare that require additional objects in the schema.

NDS OBJECT CLASSES

In IntranetWare, a wide variety of object classes is available. Table 5.1 lists the object classes that are available.

TABLE 5.1 *Object Classes Available by Default*

OBJECT CLASS	DESCRIPTION
AFP Server	An AppleTalk File Protocol (AFP) server that is a node on the network.
Alias	A representation of an object that is really located in another part of the Directory tree.
Application	A pointer to an application installed on the network. There are different variations of this object, depending on the type of application: DOS, Windows 3.x, Windows 95, and Windows NT. An Application object can be "associated" with users or groups. Then that application can easily be executed from each user's NetWare Application Launcher.
Auditing File	An object that manages an audit trail's configuration and access rights; used only if the Auditing feature is used.

(continued)

TABLE 5.1 *Object Classes Available by Default (continued)*

OBJECT CLASS	DESCRIPTION
Bindery Object	An object that was upgraded from a bindery-based server but which could not be converted into a corresponding NDS object.
Bindery Queue	An object that represents a print queue that exists outside the NDS tree (either on a NetWare 3.x server or in another NetWare 4 tree). This object lets you manage this queue, even though it's outside your current NDS tree.
Computer	A computer.
Country	An optional container object representing the country where a portion of your company is located.
Directory Map	A representation of a directory path, which typically points to an application or directory.
Distribution List	A list of e-mail recipients; used if Message Handling Services (MHS) is installed.
External Entity	An object that stores information about non-NDS entities for other applications or services; used if Message Handling Services (MHS) is installed.
Group	A list of users who have at least some identical characteristics, such as the need for access rights to the same application. Users listed as group members receive a security equivalence to the group.
Locality	An optional container object that represents a location.
License Certificate	An object that represents a product license certificate. When an application that uses NetWare Licensing Services is installed, that product's license certificate is added as an object in the License Product container object.
List	A list of objects. Objects that are list members do not have a security equivalence to the List object.
LSP Server	An object that represents a License Service Provider server; used only if NetWare Licensing Service is used.

TABLE 5.1 *Object Classes Available by Default (continued)*

OBJECT CLASS	DESCRIPTION
Message Routing Group	Messaging servers that are connected directly to each other so that e-mail messages can be routed between them; used if Message Handling Services (MHS) is installed.
Messaging Server	A server that receives and transfers e-mail messages.
NetWare Server	A NetWare server.
Organization	An organization's name (such as a company name).
Organizational Role	A position (such as director, project leader, or recreation coordinator) that various users can occupy (allows you to assign rights to the position rather than to specific users).
Organizational Unit	A container object that can form a subdivision under an Organization, such as a division, department, project team, or workgroup.
Print Server	A NetWare print server, which provides print services.
Printer	A printer attached to the network.
Profile	An object whose sole function is to provide a login script that can be used by several users, all of whom do not need to be in the same container.
Queue	A print queue.
Root	The highest point (starting point) of the Directory tree (it contains no information).
Unknown	An object that was created by the server in an effort to restore an object whose class is no longer defined in the current schema.
User	A network user.
Volume	A volume on a NetWare server.

NDS OBJECT SECURITY

If you have used previous versions of NetWare, you know that NetWare uses a set of trustee rights that can be granted to and revoked from users to control what those users can do within specific files and directories.

NetWare 4 uses a similar set of trustee rights to control how NDS objects can work with each other. These NDS object rights are separate from the file system rights, but they operate in a similar fashion. Using NDS object rights, you can allow users to see and manipulate other NDS objects.

NDS object rights are explained in Chapter 7.

WORKING WITH NDS OBJECTS

The primary tool for creating or modifying NDS objects is the NetWare utility called *NetWare Administrator* (sometimes referred to as NWAdmin), which runs in Windows 3.1, OS/2, or Windows 95.

NOTE

There is a DOS-based utility, called NETADMIN, which can also be used to work with NDS objects. However, NetWare Administrator has more features than NETADMIN, and because of its graphical interface, NetWare Administrator is easier to use in some situations. In addition, because of conventional memory limitations, NETADMIN may have difficulty working with NDS Directories that contain several thousand objects in a single context. Therefore, most people prefer to use the NetWare Administrator instead. For this reason, NETADMIN is not discussed in this book.

Typical tasks you can do with NetWare Administrator are:

- Create new NDS objects
- Delete objects
- Move objects
- Search for objects by particular properties (such as all users in a given department)
- Change an object's properties
- Rename objects

The Windows 3.1 version of NetWare Administrator (which can also run on OS/2) is called NWADMN3X.EXE; it is located in SYS:PUBLIC. The Windows 95 version is called NWADMN95.EXE; it can be found in SYS:PUBLIC\WIN95.

NOTE

If you have upgraded your network from NetWare 4.1 to IntranetWare, you will discover that the old version of NetWare Administrator, called NWADMIN.EXE, is still in your SYS:PUBLIC directory. If you want to use the new NetWare Administrator utility that comes with IntranetWare, you must first upgrade your workstation to the client software that comes with IntranetWare (either VLMs or Client32). The new version of NetWare Administrator requires new .DLL files that will be installed with the new client software. If you don't upgrade your client software, you will have to continue using the older NetWare Administrator utility.

To use NetWare Administrator, you must install it on your workstation and add its program icon to your workstation's desktop, as explained in the following sections.

Setting up the NetWare Administrator Utility for Windows 3.1

To set up NetWare Administrator on a Windows 3.1 workstation, complete the following steps.

1. From a Windows 3.1 workstation, start Windows and highlight the program group in which you want NetWare Administrator to appear. (The NetWare Tools program group was created during the workstation installation, so you can use that group.)
2. From the File menu, choose New, and then select Program Item.
3. For the Description, enter the name you want to use, such as NetWare Administrator or NWAdmin.
4. Use the Browse button to specify the location of the NWADMN3X.EXE file (SYS:\PUBLIC\NWADMN3X.EXE) and the working directory (SYS:\PUBLIC).
5. Click OK. The NetWare Administrator icon appears on the desktop.

Setting up the NetWare Administrator Utility for Windows 95

To set up NetWare Administrator on a Windows 95 workstation, complete the following steps.

1. From the Windows 95 desktop, right-click your mouse and choose New.
2. Select Shortcut.
3. Choose Browse, and then locate the SYS:PUBLIC\WIN95 drive and choose NWADMN95.EXE.
4. Choose Open, and then Finish. NetWare Administrator appears as a shortcut icon on the desktop.

Now you can use NetWare Administrator to create and manage all NDS objects, including users and groups.

Planning the NDS Directory Tree

To plan your Directory tree, take advantage of the container objects to make the tree resemble your company's organization. For example, if your company is quite large, with many divisions and departments, you can use a single Organization object to represent the company's name and multiple Organizational Unit objects to represent the various divisions and departments.

Individual users, printers, and so on can be placed inside the Organizational Unit that corresponds to their department. (These individual objects are all leaf objects.) Figure 5.3 shows how a large company, named RedHawk AeroSpace, Inc., might set up its Directory tree.

If your company is small, you may not need to break up your network into Organizational Units. You may want to just have a single Organization object representing your company, and then place all leaf objects directly beneath that container. This is how the Simple Installation feature of the NetWare INSTALL utility works. Figure 5.4 shows how a tree for a small company, named Rise 'n Shine Clockworks, might look.

FIGURE 5.3 *A Sample Directory Tree for a Large Company*

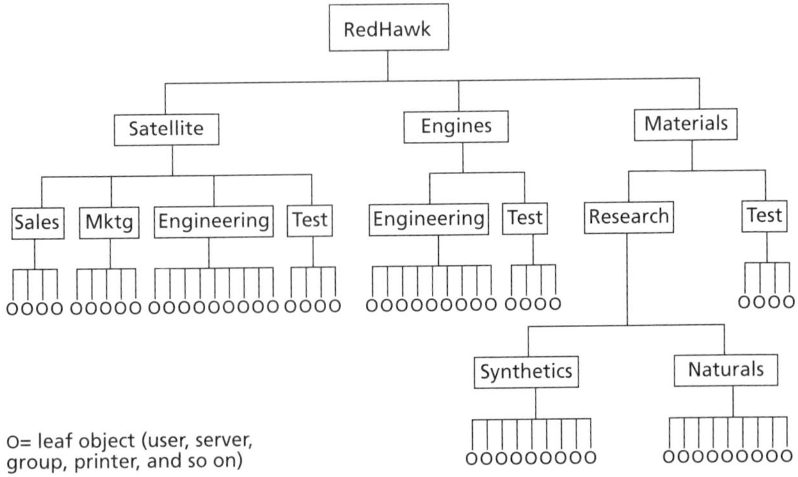

FIGURE 5.4 *A Sample Directory Tree for a Small Company*

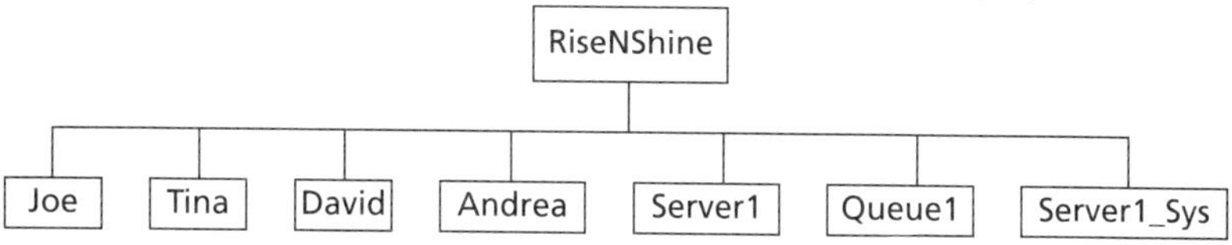

Name Context — Your Location in the Tree

Each object in the Directory tree exists in a specific location of the tree, which is called the object's *name context.* The name context is really a sort of "address" for that object's location, consisting of the names of any container objects over that object. An object's *full name* (or *full distinguished name*) consists of the object's name plus the list of container names, with the names separated by periods. The name of the object by itself (without the rest of the container names listed) is called its *relative distinguished name*, although it is also often referred to as an object's *common name* (CN).

Within any container, all object names must be unique. For example, you can have only one user with the common name Eric within the container called Mktg. However, there can be other users named Eric on the tree if they are within other containers. Say there's an Eric in Mktg and another Eric in Sales, both of whom work in the Satellite division of RedHawk AeroSpace, Inc.

The Marketing Eric's full name would be Eric.Mktg.Satellite.RedHawk. Each container name is added to Eric's common name (separated by periods) to spell out his address in the Directory tree, clear back to the Organization's name. His name context, or location in the tree, is Mktg.Satellite.RedHawk.

The Sales Eric's full name would be Eric.Sales.Satellite.RedHawk. Because his full name is different from the other Eric's full name, NDS can keep them both straight.

Specifying objects in the Directory tree is very similar to specifying subdirectories in a DOS file system. In the file system, if you are at the root of the volume or disk or in a completely separate directory path, you have to specify a full directory path to get to the subdirectory you want. If you are at the root of the Directory tree or in a completely different branch of the tree, you have to specify an object's full name to find it.

However, if you are somewhere in the subdirectory's directory path already, you only need to specify the portion of the path that will get you to the desired subdirectory. You don't need to specify the subdirectory's full path. Similarly, if you are already within a container over an object's location, you only need to specify the portion of the Directory tree address that exists between you and the object. You don't need to specify the object's full name, back to the root. This is called specifying a *partial name* (or a *relative distinguished name*).

If you want to specify an object's full name back to the root, place a period at the beginning of the object's name (in any commands you type) to indicate to the utility you're using that this is a full name and shouldn't be interpreted as a partial name. For example, you would type .Eric.Mktg.Satellite.RedHawk to indicate that this is Eric's full name.

To move around in the Directory tree's context, moving up and down through containers, you can use a NetWare command-line utility called CX. This utility is similar to DOS's CD utility, which lets you move around in the file system's subdirectory structure. More often, however, you will navigate through the levels of the Directory tree by using the NetWare Administrator utility.

NDS Replicas and Partitions

Because the NDS database is common to all servers on the network, the entire network would be disabled if the database were stored on only one server (with all other servers accessing the database from that server) and that server went down.

To prevent this single point of failure, IntranetWare can create *replicas* of the NDS database and store those replicas on different servers. Then, if one server goes down, all the other servers can still access the NDS database from another replica of the database.

If your NDS database is large enough, you may not want to store the entire database on multiple servers. In this case, you can create Directory *partitions*, which are portions of the database that can be replicated on different servers. A Directory partition is a branch of the Directory tree, beginning with any container object you choose. Partitions can also hold subpartitions beneath them (called *child partitions*). If you have a smaller NDS database, the whole database can reside in a single partition. Using partitions can improve network performance, especially if the network spans across a WAN (wide area network). Partitions also can make it easier to manage portions of the tree separately.

TYPES OF NDS REPLICAS

There are four types of replicas that can be created and stored on servers:

- *Master replica.* The master replica is the only replica that can make changes to the Directory partition, such as adding, merging, or deleting replicas. There is only one master replica per partition.
- *Read-write replica.* Read-write replicas will accept requests to modify NDS objects. Any number of read-write replicas can exist on a network.
- *Read-only replica.* The information in a read-only replica can be read, but not modified. Any number of these replicas can exist on a network.
- *Subordinate reference replica.* A subordinate reference replica exists on a server if that server holds a replica of a parent partition, but does not hold a replica of the child partition. The subordinate reference replica basically provides pointers to the objects in the real child partition. These replicas are created automatically if necessary; you cannot create them manually.

Novell Directory Services handles the locations of any modifications to the NDS Directory in the background, so that you and other network administrators do not need to know which replica to use to make changes to the Directory. Whenever a change is made to a replica, the change is synchronized automatically with all other replicas on the network.

To keep NDS performance optimal, you should have between three and six replicas of a partition. The more replicas of a partition you have, the more synchronization traffic occurs on the network, so you may not want to have more replicas than necessary.

When you install a new server into an existing NDS tree, the installation program determines how many replicas of the partition into which you are installing the server already exist. If there are three or more replicas, the installation program will not create a new replica on the new server by default.

WORKING WITH NDS PARTITIONS AND REPLICAS

To create, delete, or merge partitions, you can use the NDS Manager utility. This utility can be executed by itself or as a feature of the NetWare Administrator utility under the Tools option.

NOTE

There is also a DOS-based utility, called PARTMGR, which you can use to perform some of the same tasks, but because most administrators prefer the NetWare Administrator utility, PARTMGR is not discussed here. (For the most part, NetWare Administrator is easier to use because of its graphical interface, while the DOS-based menu utilities such as PARTMGR are less user-friendly.)

If problems occur with Directory partitions and replicas, you can use the DSREPAIR utility to analyze them and repair them if necessary. (The NDS Manager utility automatically executes DSREPAIR for repair options, so you may prefer to use NDS Manager from a workstation instead of using DSREPAIR from the console.) DSREPAIR is explained in the section "DSREPAIR.NLM" later in this chapter.

By default, NDS Manager is not part of NetWare Administrator, but you can easily add it. If you don't want to add it to NetWare Administrator, you must add NDS Manager to your workstation desktop as its own icon. The following sections describe how to add NDS Manager to NetWare Administrator and how to set up NDS Manager to execute from the desktop.

Adding NDS Manager to NetWare Administrator

To add the NDS Manager feature to the NetWare Administrator utility on a Windows 3.1 workstation, complete the following steps.

1. If you haven't yet opened the NetWare Administrator utility, open it and close it.
2. From the Windows File Manager on your workstation, double-click on the NWADMN3X.INI file (located in the WINDOWS directory) to open it for editing.
3. Under the heading [Snapin Object DLLs WIN3X], add the following line:

   ```
   NDSMGR=NMSNAP16.DLL
   ```

4. Save and close the file. Now, when you open the NetWare Administrator utility, NDS Manager appears as an option under the Tools menu.

To add the NDS Manager feature to the NetWare Administrator utility on a Windows 95 workstation, complete the following steps.

1. From your workstation, open the NetWare Administrator utility.
2. From the Options menu, select Save Settings on Exit, and then close NetWare Administrator.
3. Run REGEDIT.EXE (the Windows 95 editor), and choose the following path:

   ```
   HKEY_CURRENT_USER\SOFTWARE\NETWARE\
   PARAMETERS\NETWARE
   ```
4. Highlight Snapin Object DLLs WIN95.
5. From the Edit menu, choose New, and then String Value.
6. Type NDSMGR and press Enter.
7. Highlight NDSMGR, and then choose Modify from the Edit menu.
8. Type NMSNAP32.DLL in the Value Data field.
9. Choose OK. Now, when you open the NetWare Administrator utility, NDS Manager appears as an option under the Tools menu.

Adding NDS Manager Directly to the Desktop

To set up NDS Manager on a Windows 3.1 workstation, complete the following steps.

1. From a Windows 3.1 workstation, start Windows and highlight the program group, such as NetWare Tools, in which you want NDS Manager to appear.
2. From the File menu, choose New, and then select Program Item.
3. For the Description, enter NDS Manager.
4. Use the Browse button to specify the location of the NDSMGR16.EXE file (SYS:\PUBLIC\NDSMGR16.EXE) and the working directory (SYS:\PUBLIC).
5. Click OK. The NDS Manager icon appears on the desktop.

To set up NDS Manager on a Windows 95 workstation, complete the following steps.

1. From the Windows 95 desktop, right-click your mouse and choose New.
2. Select Shortcut.
3. Choose Browse, locate the SYS:PUBLIC\WIN95 drive, and then choose NDSMGR32.EXE.
4. Choose Open, and then Finish NDS Manager appears as a shortcut icon on the desktop.

Using NDS Manager

To use NDS Manager from the NetWare Administrator utility to work with partitions, select NDS Manager from the Tools menu. To execute NDS Manager in stand-alone mode, double-click on its icon on your workstation's desktop. You can access most NDS Manager options through the menu bar, the button bar, or by right-clicking on objects you want to work with.

NOTE

All of the documentation for NDS Manager is located in the help file. Open the help file to see a description of all the tasks you can do with NDS Manager.

NDS Manager displays three main views of the NDS information. The Tree view shows the containers and servers in the tree and displays information about the tree's partitions. The Partitions and Servers view is a different way to look at the partitioning information. The Partition Continuity view lets you see any synchronization errors that may be occurring in a partition's replicas. You can see these views by clicking on their respective buttons in the button bar.

Here are some of the partitioning and replication tasks you can do with NDS Manager:

- See the partitions on a server. From the Tree view or the Partitions and Servers view, select a server to display a list of the partitions it holds.
- See a partition's replicas. From the Tree view or the Partitions and Servers view, select a partition (a container with the partition icon next to it) to display its replicas and the servers those replicas are on.
- See information about a server or partition. From the Tree view or the Partitions and Servers view, select the server or partition, right-click, and then choose Information.
- Create a partition. You must create new partitions at the container level. Select the container you want to be the root of the partition, and then choose Create Partition.
- Merge two partitions. You can merge a child partition into its parent partition. The end result is a single partition that includes all objects from both of the original partitions. To merge partitions, select the container that is the root of the child partition, and then choose Merge Partition.
- Move a partition. You can move a partition and its container object only if it does not have any child partitions. (If you want to move a partition that has a child partition, you can merge the two before you try to move the parent partition.) To move a partition, select the icon for the

partition you want to move, and then choose Move Partition. Specify a destination by clicking the Browser button, browsing through the directory, and selecting a container. Then check Create an Alias for this Container Object. By creating an alias, users will be able to find the partition in the location they're used to. Otherwise, you may have users unable to log in because their NET.CFG files specify the wrong name context. To update NET.CFG files with a new context, use the NCUPDATE utility. Finally, choose Yes, and the partition will be moved.

- Stop a partition operation. If you need to stop a creation, deletion, or merge of a partition, you can do so as long as at least one of the replicas involved has not yet completed the operation (as indicated by the State box). To stop an operation, select the partition that is being affected, right-click, and choose Abort Operation.
- See information about a replica. To see information about a replica, select the partition or server. Right-click on a replica and select Information.
- Create a replica. To create a replica of a partition, select the partition you want to replicate, and then choose Add Replica. Select the server you want to store the replica on, and choose OK. Next, choose the type of replica you want this to be (read-write replica or read-only replica), and then click OK.
- Delete a replica. To delete a replica, select the partition whose replica you want to delete, choose the replica you want to delete, right-click, and then choose Delete. Master replicas cannot be deleted. If you want to delete a master replica, you must first designate another replica as master. This will automatically change the original master to a read-write replica, which you can then delete.
- Change a replica's type. To change a replica to a different type (read-write, master, or read-only), select the partition whose replica you want to change, select the replica you want to change, and then choose Change Replica Type. Select the type you want, and then choose OK.
- Delete a server. To delete a server from the Directory tree, you can select the server object, right-click, and choose Delete. However, in most circumstances, the recommended way to remove a NetWare 4 server from the NDS tree is to "uninstall" NDS instead of deleting the server object.
- See the version of NDS on servers. Select the container that holds the servers you want to see. From the Object menu, select NDS Version,

and then choose View. Bindery-based servers (NetWare 3.x and 2.x) will be displayed as Unknown.

- Update the version of NDS on a server. Ideally, all replicas of a partition should be stored on servers running the same version of DS.NLM (the NDS database). Periodically, Novell releases an updated DS.NLM on NetWire (Novell's online service). If you install a new version of DS.NLM on a server, update that same version onto other IntranetWare servers by selecting the updated server object (the server you want to be the source for updating other servers). From the Object menu, select NDS Version, and then select Update. Select the servers you want to update and click on the right arrow to move them under the heading Target Servers to be Updated. Then choose OK. It may take 15 to 30 minutes to update the servers.
- Check partition continuity. To verify that all of a partition's replicas (called a replica ring) are synchronizing correctly, select the partition whose replicas you want to view, and then choose Partition Continuity. If any replica listed has an exclamation point (!), that replica has experienced synchronization errors. Double-click on the replica with the error. Then, from the Replica Information screen, click the help button beside Current Sync Error.
- Synchronize replicas. Partition replicas synchronize automatically. However, if you don't want to wait for the automatic synchronization, you can force an immediate synchronization by choosing the partition you want synchronized. Select Partition Continuity, and then select Synchronize Immediately.
- Send updates to other replicas. To send updates from one replica to other replicas (including the master), choose the server whose replica has the information you want to send out, and then select Send Updates.
- Receive updates from the master replica. If only one replica is out of sync, you can manually request an update from the master replica. Select the partition whose replica you want to update, and choose Receive Updates.
- Repair partition and replica problems. From the Partition Continuity view, you can repair several types of problems with your NDS database, such as replica problems, network address problems, and so on. Most of these operations load and run DSREPAIR.NLM on the server automatically.

- Print NDS Manager information. You can print out information displayed by NDS Manager. To print from the Tree view or Partitions and Servers view, choose Print from the Object menu. To print from the Partition Continuity view, choose Print from the File menu.

Bindery Services

Some applications and network services do not take advantage of NDS's hierarchical database structure. Instead, those applications make requests to a version of NetWare that uses a bindery.

To allow those applications to function with NDS, you can use a feature called *bindery services*. Bindery services makes the objects within a container appear as a bindery located on a particular server. That way, both bindery-based applications and NDS-aware applications can find the objects they need.

Bindery services also enables NetWare 3.x users to log in to a NetWare 4 server and use its resources.

SETTING UP A BINDERY CONTEXT

If you want to set up bindery services on a NetWare 4 server, you have to tell the server which *portion* of the tree you want to appear as its bindery. By default, the server installation process sets the container that the server was installed in as the bindery context for the server. This portion of the tree consists of any container you choose and its objects. You can specify up to 16 different containers to look like a single bindery on a server. To the bindery-based application, the objects in all 16 containers will look like objects in a single flat database. By specifying these containers, you are setting the server's *bindery context*.

To set a server's bindery context, you use the SET command. To set a server's bindery context to be a single container, for example Sales.Satellite.RedHawk, you would type the following command at the server's console:

```
SET BINDERY CONTEXT=Sales.Satellite.RedHawk
```

To set the bindery context to consist of two or more different containers, use the same command and separate the name of each container by a semicolon, as follows:

```
SET BINDERY
CONTEXT=Sales.Satellite.RedHawk;Mktg.Satellite.
RedHawk
```

For a server to be able to use bindery services after you've set its bindery context to a container, you need to make sure the server has a read-write replica of the partition that holds that container. If the container specified in the bindery context is not in a replica on the given server, IntranetWare still allows the container to be specified. However, the objects in that container will not be available for bindery services on that server until a replica of the container's partition is created on the server.

To view the current bindery context that you have specified for a server, type SET BINDERY CONTEXT at the server console. This displays the string of containers that you've assigned to this server's bindery context, but will not show you if any of the containers are invalid.

To see the "effective" bindery context for a server, use the CONFIG console utility. This utility displays the containers that are currently valid and being used by that server as its bindery context. It does not display any container that may have been specified to be part of the bindery context, but whose partition replica doesn't exist on the server.

To set the bindery context to "nothing" (effectively preventing any objects from being available for bindery services on that server), type SET BINDERY CONTEXT=. (Don't put anything after the equal sign.)

Managing NetWare 3.1x Servers from IntranetWare

If you are planning to manage both IntranetWare servers and NetWare 3.1x servers on the same network, NetSync can help. *NetSync* is a tool that lets you manage NetWare 3.1x users and groups from the NetWare Administrator utility.

Without NetSync, you would have to log in to each NetWare 3.1x server individually and use NetWare 3.1x utilities, such as SYSCON, to change each user's account. In addition, if the user has an account on more than one server, you would have to change each account; you couldn't just change it once and have it affect all of the user's entities.

NetSync eliminates this extra work. With NetSync, you can synchronize all of the users and groups on up to 12 NetWare 3.1x servers with the Directory database on a single IntranetWare server.

This feature is ideally suited to people who have to manage a mixed environment of NetWare 3.1x and 4.11 servers. However, if you have several people who are administrators of only the NetWare 3.1x servers, and you don't want to centralize management, you probably do not need to synchronize those servers.

HOW NETSYNC WORKS

To make NetSync work, you first load NETSYNC4.NLM on the host IntranetWare server, and then you load NETSYNC3.NLM on each of the NetWare 3.1x servers. Then, all of the user and group information from the binderies on those servers is automatically uploaded into the NDS database on the IntranetWare server. When the IntranetWare server receives the information about the bindery-based users and groups, it converts them into NDS objects and places them all in a single bindery context, or container. Then, it downloads the new information about these users and groups to each of the NetWare 3.1x servers.

In essence, the 12 individual binderies have now been combined into what appears to be a single *super-bindery.* When this super-bindery is downloaded onto the NetWare 3.1x servers, each server ends up with an identical copy. Now, any user that existed on server A will also exist on server B, server C, and so on. The user will retain the same file system trustee rights as before, so that user will not suddenly have rights to files on servers that he or she didn't have before.

If you want to synchronize more than 12 NetWare 3.1x servers, you will need to install more than one IntranetWare host server. If you set each IntranetWare host server to the same bindery context, and then attach up to 12 NetWare 3.1x servers to each of those IntranetWare servers, all of the 3.1x servers' bindery information will go into the same bindery context. In other words, if you have two IntranetWare host servers and each has 12 NetWare 3.1x servers attached, the super-bindery will contain all 24 servers' bindery information. The only problem is that the increased number of objects in the super-bindery could overtax your servers' memory capabilities during uploads and downloads.

If a user has accounts on more than one NetWare 3.1x server, those accounts are merged together so that only one account exists for that user. (For this reason, be sure that you verify that all users have unique names on any servers that will be synchronized together. Otherwise you may accidentally merge two different users named Debbie, for example.)

Also during NetSync installation, your NetWare 3.1x printing services are upgraded to IntranetWare printing services. All printing utilities are upgraded, and the PRINTCON and PRINTDEF databases are upgraded to the IntranetWare format and duplicated in the IntranetWare database.

You have the option of merging all of your NetWare 3.1x print servers into a single print server on the IntranetWare host server. This also places your printers into the NDS tree so that you can manage them from a IntranetWare print server.

LEAVING SYSCON BEHIND

Once the servers are all synchronized, you can use NetWare Administrator to make changes or add new users in the IntranetWare NDS tree. Whenever you change or add a user from the NetWare Administrator, that change is automatically downloaded to all the NetWare 3.1x servers.

Note, however, that you cannot use SYSCON to make a change at the NetWare 3.1x level. After the initial installation, information is not uploaded from the NetWare 3.1x servers anymore. If you make a change using SYSCON, that change will affect only the single NetWare 3.1x server from which you executed SYSCON. The NDS database will not be updated, and the other servers will not receive that change, so this NetWare 3.1x server will be out of synchronization with the other servers. You can force a manual upload if this happens by reloading NETSYNC3. However, it's much easier to simply turn on NetSync once, let it run continuously, and make all your changes via the NetWare Administrator.

The only user change you can make at the NetWare 3.1x server using NetWare 3.1x utilities is a user's password. Password changes are synchronized from either the IntranetWare or the NetWare 3.1x side.

HOW LOGIN SCRIPTS ARE SYNCHRONIZED

In NDS, server-specific system login scripts, such as those used in NetWare 3.1x, are not used. Instead, NDS container objects have login scripts, which apply drive mappings and other settings to all users in that container. This eliminates the need to have a different system login script on each server. Because of the difference between server-specific login scripts in NetWare 3.1x and container-specific login scripts in IntranetWare, system login scripts are not synchronized between the servers when NetSync is installed.

User login scripts, however, are synchronized between the IntranetWare host server and the NetWare 3.1x server when you install NetSync. On the 3.1x server, the user login scripts are stored as files in the users' MAIL directories. On the IntranetWare server, user login scripts are properties of the user object.

During NetSync synchronization, a user's NetWare 3.1x login script is automatically copied into two places:

- The login script property of the user's new NDS user object
- The user's MAIL directory on the IntranetWare server

By putting a copy of the NetWare 3.1x login script file in the user's MAIL directory on the IntranetWare server, the user will be able to log in to the IntranetWare server using a bindery services connection.

After synchronization, you should make any login script changes to the user's NDS object property. Those changes will be automatically downloaded to both the NetWare 3.1x and the IntranetWare MAIL directories. If you use SYSCON to change the user's login script file, the change is made only in the NetWare 3.1x MAIL directory. The changes will not be uploaded to the IntranetWare MAIL directory or to the User object's login script property, and the login scripts will be out of sync.

NOTE

If your NetWare 3.1x server contains users running OS/2 workstations, their user directories will contain both DOS and OS/2 login scripts. NetSync combines them into one script, adding appropriate conditional commands to execute only the portion of the script that applies to the workstation from which the user logs in.

The NetWare 3.1x system login script, which is a file on the NetWare 3.1x server, is not synchronized at all. It remains intact on the specific server for which it was created, so that when users log in to that server, they will get the drive mappings they need for that server alone.

For more information about login scripts, see Chapter 6.

INSTALLING NETSYNC

During the original IntranetWare installation procedure, a NETSYNC directory is created beneath SYS:SYSTEM on the IntranetWare server. This directory contains the NetSync files that have to be copied to each NetWare 3.1x server. This directory also contains the NetSync log file for this server. NETSYNC4.NLM appears directly in SYS:SYSTEM.

After you've set up the IntranetWare server as usual, you can install NetSync.

To install NetSync on the IntranetWare and NetWare 3.1x servers, complete the following steps.

1. On the IntranetWare server, load NETSYNC4. (You must load NETSYNC4 before you can connect the NetWare 3.1x servers.)
2. A blank list of authorized NetWare 3.1x servers appears. Press Enter. On a blank line in the authorized servers list, press Enter or Insert, and enter the name of the first NetWare 3.1x server you want to synchronize.
3. Make up a password and enter it. Make a note of the password because you must enter this same password once at each NetWare 3.1x server as you connect it to the NetSync network. After that, NetSync will automatically change the password to a randomly generated one for security. Even you won't know what it is. If you forget the password you just entered before you bring up the NetWare 3.1x server for the first time, you'll have to remove the server from this Authorized 3.1x Servers list and reauthorize it by giving it a brand-new password.
4. Accept the default (Yes) to copy the NetSync files to the NetWare 3.1x server.
5. To upload the bindery information from the NetWare 3.1x server to the IntranetWare host server, accept the default (Yes).
6. Press Esc, and then press Enter to save your responses.
7. When asked for a NetWare 3.1x username, enter SUPERVISOR or the name of another user that has Read, Write, Modify, and Delete rights to the SYS:SYSTEM directory on the NetWare 3.1x server. Then enter that user's password.
8. Press Enter, and the server will be added to the Authorized 3.1x Servers list.
9. Allow the AUTOEXEC.NCF files on the IntranetWare server and the 3.1x servers to be edited so that they load the appropriate NetSync files automatically.
10. Now that the NetSync files have been copied to the NetWare 3.1x server, restart the server to load the newer NLMs. (Type DOWN, type EXIT, and then type SERVER to restart it.) When the server reboots, its AUTOEXEC.NCF file will load NETSYNC3.NLM (which will automatically load other NLMs).
11. Enter the name of the IntranetWare host server if necessary and the NetSync password you entered earlier.

12. If you have printers connected to workstations on the NetWare 3.1x network, replace the RPRINTER.EXE file on those workstations with the new NPRINTER.EXE file. NPRINTER.EXE was copied to your NetWare 3.1x server during NetSync installation.

Now the servers are synchronized with each other. If you use NetWare Administrator to make changes to a user on the IntranetWare server, those changes will be automatically and immediately downloaded to the NetWare 3.1x server.

MERGING PRINT SERVERS

After you have synchronized the servers, you may want to move your NetWare 3.1x print servers to the IntranetWare host server. This step is optional. If you have only a few printers, you probably don't need to merge your printers. You will still be able to manage them as you have in the past, with the NetWare 3.1x utilities. The NetWare 3.1x print servers and printers will not be synchronized with each other.

However, if you want to combine all print servers and merge them into a single print server on the IntranetWare host server, you can do that with NetSync.

On a IntranetWare server, only one PSERVER.NLM can be loaded, and it can support up to 255 printers. Therefore, if you have more than one print server on your NetWare 3.1x network, they will all have to be merged into a single print server on the IntranetWare server or into different print servers on separate IntranetWare servers.

Merging print servers and moving printers into the NDS tree will probably require some manual adjustments to printer configurations, such as changing printer numbers. The first print server you move to IntranetWare will retain its configuration, including printer numbers. Any subsequent print servers you move will probably end up with printer number conflicts, so NetSync will automatically renumber those printers.

To move the print servers, complete the following steps.

1. Make sure NETSYNC3 and NETSYNC4 are already loaded on their respective servers.
2. From the Options menu, select Move a Print Server.
3. If more than one print server is available, select the one you want to move.
4. At the prompt, enter a name for the print server you are moving. If you want to merge this print server into one that already exists on the

IntranetWare network, enter the IntranetWare print server's name. If you give this print server a name that doesn't already exist on the IntranetWare network, a new IntranetWare print server object with that name will be created in the NDS database.

5. If you have printers connected directly to your NetWare 3.1x server, unload the PSERVER.NLM from the NetWare 3.1x server. Then load PSERVER.NLM on the IntranetWare host server. Finally, load the new file NPRINTER.NLM on the NetWare 3.1x servers.

The print server is now moved to the IntranetWare server.

Printers are moved into the NDS tree along with their print servers, and they will continue to service the same print queues they did before. New printer NDS objects are created for these printers.

Because printer numbers may have been changed if you merged more than one print server into the NDS tree, use PCONSOLE or NetWare Administrator to discover the new printer numbers. Then you may need to update the printer number at workstations that will load NPRINTER.EXE.

After the print servers are merged into IntranetWare, manage the IntranetWare print server and queues using NetWare Administrator or the IntranetWare PCONSOLE.

If you moved a print server to IntranetWare and changed its name, a reference print server of that new name is created on the NetWare 3.1x server. The *reference print server* is a new bindery object located in the NetWare 3.1x bindery. The IntranetWare print server will use it to attach to the NetWare 3.1x server so that it can service the NetWare 3.1x print queues. Therefore, do not delete the reference print servers.

AFTER THE INITIAL INSTALLATION OF NETSYNC

After the initial installation and synchronization of NetSync, you can just let the servers run. Any changes made on the IntranetWare host server are automatically downloaded to the NetWare 3.1x server without intervention from you.

If a NetWare 3.1x server goes down and then comes back up, the IntranetWare host will automatically download the super-bindery to it again, so that the NetWare 3.1x server will get any changes it might have missed.

If you want to unload NetSync from the NetWare 3.1x server to remove the server from the synchronizing cluster of servers, simply unload NETSYNC3. However, do not unload REMAPID.NLM. This NLM is automatically loaded by NETSYNC3. It controls how passwords are synchronized, so once it is loaded, you shouldn't unload it, or you will have to change every user's password on the server. (Make sure REMAPID.NLM is loaded by the AUTOEXEC.NCF file. This command should have been added to the file during NetSync installation.)

To see the NetWare 3.1x server's log file of the NetSync messages that are generated during uploads and downloads, you can use a text editor or EDIT.NLM. To read the log file on the IntranetWare server, you can use a text editor or EDIT.NLM, or you can use the NETSYNC4.NLM and choose View Active Log from the main menu. Both the NetWare 3.1x server's log files and the IntranetWare server's log files are named NETSYNC.LOG.

By default, the log file will grow to 0.5MB in size. At that point, NetSync renames the file to NETSYNC.OLD and starts a new NETSYNC.LOG. Only two log files are retained at a time. Older log files are automatically deleted. You can change the default size of the log file by using the Log File Options item in NetSync's main window.

If you decide to upgrade a NetWare 3.1x server (which has been synchronized in the NetSync group of servers) to IntranetWare, simply unload NETSYNC3, and then remove the NetWare 3.1x server's name from the Authorized 3.1x Servers list. Then use the normal upgrade feature of IntranetWare's INSTALL.NLM (see Chapter 2) to upgrade the server to IntranetWare.

Merging Multiple NDS Trees into One Tree

If you have two or more NDS trees, you can merge them into a single tree by using DSMERGE.NLM. (Do not use this utility to merge Directory partitions. This utility should be used only for merging two Directory trees.) You can also use this utility to rename a tree.

DSMERGE merges both trees at their roots. The tree from which you are running DSMERGE is the *local source tree*. The tree into which you are merging your source tree is called the *target tree*. The target tree's Root object will become the Root object for the new merged tree, and the target tree's name is the new tree's name as well. Objects that were located immediately under the root of the source tree will be located immediately under the new tree's root.

Merging two trees doesn't change any contexts or NDS names. All containers in the original two trees are retained, along with their respective objects.

During the merge, all replicas of the source tree's root partition are removed from all servers. Then the server that contained the master replica of the source tree will receive a read-write replica of the new tree's root partition. In addition, DSMERGE will create new partitions for each container below the source tree's root.

The following is a checklist of the preliminary steps you must take to merge two trees.

1. Remove any leaf objects or alias objects from the root of the source tree. Either move these objects to a container, or delete them for now and re-create them later. If you've enabled auditing at the root level, you must disable it and remove any auditing objects that were created at the root before starting the merge process.
2. Make sure there are no similar names between the two trees. For example, if each tree has a container called Mktg immediately beneath the root, those two names will conflict. Rename one or the other before trying to merge them.
3. Make sure all users are logged out of both trees, and close all connections.
4. Verify that both trees are running the same version of NDS and are using the same NDS schema. (DSMERGE.NLM will check this for you, too.)
5. Make sure all servers that have a replica of either tree's root partition are up and running.
6. After the merge, only one Reference or Single Reference time server can exist. Therefore, before the merge, make sure only one of the trees has such a server. Convert the other tree's server to a Primary time server, if necessary. Ensure that all servers in both trees are synchronized to within two seconds of each other and that they are using only one time source. You can view the time synchronization information with DSMERGE before you begin the merge process.
7. From a server on the source tree, load DSMERGE.NLM.
8. If both trees have the same tree name, use the Rename this tree option to change the source tree's name.
9. Use the Check servers in this tree option to verify that each server's status is listed as Up.
10. When you are satisfied that you can safely merge the trees, choose Merge Two trees.
11. Enter the administrator's name and password for the source tree.
12. Choose Target Tree and select the target tree from the list.
13. Enter the administrator's name and password for the target tree.
14. Press F10 to start the merge process.

15. Evaluate the new partitions and replicas that exist. You may want to merge some or split others to make the partitions more useful in the new tree.
16. If necessary, re-create any leaf or Alias objects you deleted from the source tree's root, reenable auditing, and re-create auditing objects.

NDS Troubleshooting

There are two utilities and some SET parameters you can use to diagnose and repair any suspected problems with your NDS database: DSREPAIR.NLM, NDS Manager, and the NDS TRACE commands. (Most of NDS Manager's repair features execute DSREPAIR.NLM. Because NDS Manager can execute from a workstation, you may prefer to use it rather than DSREPAIR.NLM. NDS Manager was discussed earlier in this chapter.)

NDS TRACE

NDS TRACE is a set of server SET commands that lets you monitor NDS status and error messages. To turn on the NDS TRACE screen, type the following command at the server console:

```
SET NDS TRACE TO SCREEN = ON
```

You can also use the following command to do the same thing:

```
SET DSTRACE = ON
```

If you want to send the messages to a file so that they are saved for later reference, type:

```
SET NDS TRACE TO FILE = ON
```

You can also use the following shorter command:

```
SET TTF = ON
```

The file that will receive these messages is called DSTRACE.DBG, and it is located in the SYS:SYSTEM directory. This file will grow to a maximum size of 1MB by default. When the file reaches its maximum size, it will wrap to the beginning of the file and overwrite older information. You should only need to send the information to a file if you are trying to capture an error condition for diagnostic purposes. There's no need to save this information on a routine basis.

If you see the following message as you read the information displayed by NDS TRACE:

```
All processed = YES
```

it means that all of the pending NDS activities have been successfully completed for the specified partition.

Messages with the numbers -601 through -716 and F966 through F9FE indicate NDS status or error messages. Not all messages will be errors. Many will simply indicate the current status of NDS. Therefore, you need to look up the messages in the System Messages manual (located online) to see if any of the messages require an action on your part.

To turn off the NDS tracing feature, type one of the following commands:

```
SET NDS TRACE TO SCREEN = OFF
```

or

```
SET DSTRACE = OFF
```

If you sent the NDS Trace information to a file, be sure you turn it off when you're finished with it by typing one of the following commands:

```
SET NDS TRACE TO FILE = OFF
```

or

```
SET TTF = OFF
```

DSREPAIR.NLM

If you discover a problem with your NDS database, you may be able to fix it using DSREPAIR.NLM.

You use DSREPAIR.NLM to repair the NDS database on individual servers. You have to run it on each server that has a problem. Most DSREPAIR.NLM features are specific to the local server. DSREPAIR will also perform replica synchronization operations and enable you to see the current status of this server's view of the network or Directory. For example, DSREPAIR.NLM lets you see a list of servers known to the given server. Not all DSREPAIR features are necessarily repair functions, but they can be used to help diagnose or verify the health of your NDS Directory.

With DSREPAIR.NLM, you can do tasks such as:

- Check the local Directory database records for consistency and repair them if necessary
- View the structure of the local NDS tree
- View file system trustees
- Update the NDS schema
- View the status of the Directory tree's replica synchronization and repair replicas
- Verify external references to objects in subordinate reference replicas
- View information about the network's time synchronization
- View NDS object and property information

DSREPAIR also lets you create a log file of DSREPAIR operations. If necessary, you can use DSREPAIR to create a *dump file* of a damaged NDS database that you can send to Novell Technical Support technicians for use in diagnosing a problem.

To use DSREPAIR, load the NLM on the server whose database you want to examine or repair. The options described in Table 5.2 are available for DSREPAIR.

TABLE 5.2 *DSREPAIR.NLM Options*

OPTION	DESCRIPTION
Unattended Full Repair	Repairs everything it can in the database without asking for user intervention.
Time Synchronization	Contacts all servers in this server's partition to display time synchronization information.
Replica Synchronization	Displays the status of each replica's synchronization.
View Repair Log File	Sends messages about DSREPAIR activities to a log file and lets you view the file.
Advanced Options	Lets you manually perform repair options on the NDS tree (rather than choosing the Unattended Full Repair option). It can also display diagnostic information about the NDS database, let you configure the log file, create a database dump file, and so on.

Keeping Up to Date

Periodically, Novell releases updated versions of DS.NLM (the NDS database program) and its management utilities on NetWire, Novell's online service. These updates may add minor features or fix problems. You should try to keep your network updated with these new versions whenever possible.

If you obtain an updated version of DS.NLM, install it on all of the IntranetWare servers in your network. All servers in a partition's replica ring must be running the same version of DS.NLM in order to use any new features of DS.NLM. Keeping all of your servers running the same version will help simplify your support of the Directory tree.

For more information about NetWire, see Appendix C.

CHAPTER 6

Managing Users and Groups

Creating Users and Groups

- To create User objects and Group objects, use the NetWare Administrator utility (which runs in Windows, OS/2, or Windows 95).
- To set up a template so all users you create and receive a set of common characteristics, use the NetWare Administrator utility to create a Template object.

User Tasks

- To log in, users can use the LOGIN command-line utility, the Windows-based Login program, the NETUSER menu utility (which runs in DOS), or the NetWare User Tools utility (which runs in Windows).
- To log out, users can use the LOGOUT command-line utility, the NETUSER menu utility, or the NetWare User Tools utility.
- To specify a default name context (location in the NDS tree) for logging in, users can put the NAME CONTEXT command in their NET.CFG files.
- To change the name context after they are logged in, users can use the NetWare User Tools utility, the CX command-line utility, or the NETUSER menu utility.
- To control print jobs, users can use the NetWare User Tools utility or the NETUSER menu utility.
- To send brief messages to other network users, users can use the NetWare User Tools utility, the SEND command-line utility, or the NETUSER menu utility.
- To map drives to network directories, users can put MAP commands in their login scripts, or they can use the NetWare User Tools utility, the MAP command-line utility, or the NETUSER menu utility.
- To change their passwords, users can use the NetWare User Tools utility, the NETUSER menu utility, or the SETPASS command-line utility.
- To complete many of these same network tasks, Windows 95 users can use the Windows Explorer or the Network Neighborhood.

Managing Users' Work Environments

- To create login scripts, use the NetWare Administrator, select a container object, Profile object, or User object (depending on the type of login script you want to create), select Details from the Object menu, and then open the Login Script page.
- To enable users to launch applications from their desktops without having to know what drives to map or where to find the application, use the NetWare Administrator utility to create an Application object, and then set up the NetWare Application Launcher on the user's desktop.
- To create a menu program, use a text editor to create a source file, and then use the MENUMAKE command-line utility to compile it.
- To execute a menu program, use the NMENU command-line utility.
- To upgrade old menus from previous versions of NetWare, use the MENUCNVT command-line utility.

Once you've set up the hardware and software, it's time to start managing the human elements of your network: users. After a brand-new installation, the only User objects that will exist in the tree are as follows:

- The Admin User object
- The Supervisor User object (which is used for bindery services only and can be accessed only from NetWare 3.1x or 2.x utilities)

Before your users can begin using the network, you have to create user accounts for each of them. In addition, you may want to organize the users into groups to more easily manage security, printer assignments, and other issues that may affect many or all of the users in the same way.

To make the network easier to use, you can also create login scripts and menus. Login scripts can automatically set up the users' workstation environments with necessary drive mappings and other types of useful environmental settings. Menus can shield the user from having to see or use commands at the DOS prompt. Menus can also be used to restrict the user to selecting common tasks from a menu that you design.

In addition, you can use the NetWare Application Manager feature of the NetWare Administrator utility to set up an icon on users' desktops that points directly to network applications. Then the users can simply launch the application from their desktops without having to know where the application is, which drives to map, and so on.

After the user has logged in to the network, there are a few common tasks that the user may want to perform, such as logging in and out, redirecting the workstation's printer port to a network print queue, or mapping a drive to a directory. NetWare User Tools is a Windows-based NetWare utility that is geared toward end users. They can use this utility to perform most of these common tasks.

What Do Users Need?

Creating a user's account involves more than just creating a new object for the user in the NDS tree. Before a user can really work on the network, you need to set up many of the following tools or characteristics (some are optional, depending on your situation):

- The user's NDS account (which is an object for the user with its associated properties filled in, such as the user's last name, full name, telephone number, and so on)

- The user's group memberships
- A home directory for the user's individual files
- A login script that maps drives to the directories and applications to which the user will need access
- NDS trustee rights (to control how the user can see and use other NDS objects in the tree)
- File system trustee rights to the files and directories the user needs to work with (to regulate the user's access and activities in those files and directories)
- Account restrictions, if necessary, to control when the user logs in, how often the user must change passwords, and so on
- An e-mail account, if necessary
- Access to the network printers
- A menu program to prevent the user from having to use commands at the DOS prompt

The following section describes how to create user and group accounts on the network.

Creating Users and Groups

Users, of course, are the individual people who have accounts on the network. You can assign users to groups, so that you can manage things such as security and login script commands for many people simultaneously, rather than one-by-one. A group is really a Group object, which contains a list of users assigned to that group.

NOTE

Because you can use container objects to assign rights and login scripts to all the users in those containers, you may find that you don't need to use as many groups as you may have in previous versions of NetWare. For example, users in a container gain a security equivalence to that container by default. Therefore, granting rights at the container level is a quick way to grant identical rights to all users in the container, eliminating the need to create a separate group object to grant those same users the same rights.

To create a new user or group on the network, you use the NetWare Administrator utility from a workstation. The NetWare Administrator is a NetWare utility that can run on either Windows 3.1, OS/2, or Windows 95. (If you have not yet installed the NetWare Administrator on your workstation, see Chapter 5 for instructions.)

CREATING A USER

To create a user, complete the steps in the following checklist.

1. Create a directory for all users' home directories. For example, you might want to create a network directory called Users on volume VOL1.
2. Start up NetWare Administrator.
3. Select the container object that will hold the new user.
4. From the Object menu, choose Create.
5. From the New Object dialog box that appears, choose User, and then choose OK.
6. In the Create User dialog box, enter the user's login name and last name. The login name is the name you want this user to type when he or she logs in.
7. Create a home directory for this user.
   a. Mark the check box next to Create Home Directory.
   b. Click the Browse button.
   c. From the Directory Contents panel on the right, double-click on the container and then the volume that will hold the user directories.
   d. When the directory you created in Step 1 appears in the left panel (under Files and Directories), select that directory and click OK. The path to that directory should now appear in the Create User dialog box.
8. To specify additional optional properties, mark the Define Additional Properties check box.
9. Choose Create. The user's Identification page appears. The Identification page will appear every time you look at this object in the future. Along the right side of the screen are large rectangular buttons with turned-down corners. Each of these buttons represents a different page of information about the user. You can fill in some, none, or all of the information on these pages, depending on your

needs. If you have entered new information in one of these pages that needs to be saved, the turned-down corner will appear black. Choose OK when finished.

10. Create another user by following these same steps.

USING A USER TEMPLATE

If you plan to assign many of your users some identical properties, you can use a user template. The template will automatically apply default properties to any new user you create using the template. (It will not, however, apply those properties to any users that existed before you created the user template.) Network administrators often use a template to grant default NDS and file system rights to users automatically.

To create a user template, complete the steps in the following checklist.

1. Create a directory for all users' home directories. For example, you might want to create a directory called Users.
2. Start up NetWare Administrator.
3. Select the container object that will hold the new user template.
4. From the Object menu, choose Create.
5. From the New Object dialog box that appears, choose Template, and then choose OK.
6. When the Template object's dialog box appears, enter a name for the template.
7. If you want this template to specify some or all of the same information that appears in another Template object or User object, check the Use Template or User box and use the Browser button to select the Template or User object.
8. Check the Define Additional Properties box, and then click Create.
9. Enter any additional information (or edit existing information) that you want assigned to each user, and then click OK when you're finished.
10. Next time you create a new user and want to use the information in this template, mark the Use Template check box and select the Template object from the Browser button.

EDITING INFORMATION FOR SEVERAL USERS AT ONCE

With NetWare 4.11, it's easy to edit the same information for several users simultaneously. For example, suppose a whole department moves to a different floor in the building. If you've entered the Location or Address information in those users' Details pages, you can update the information quickly.

From the NetWare Administrator Browser, select all of the user objects you want to update, and then choose Details on Multiple Users from the Object menu. Any information you enter in this screen will be applied to all the users you selected.

NOTE

To select multiple objects at once from the Browser, use Shift-Click or Ctrl-Click.

CREATING GROUPS AND ASSIGNING GROUP MEMBERSHIP TO A USER

Creating a group is very similar to creating a user. The following checklist outlines the steps to create a group and assign group membership to a user.

1. Start up NetWare Administrator.
2. Select the container object that will hold the new group.
3. From the Object menu, choose Create.
4. From the New Object dialog box that appears, choose Group, and then choose OK.
5. Enter the group's name.
6. Mark the check box next to Define Other Properties.
7. Choose Create. The group's Identification page appears. Enter any information you desire under the Identification page.
8. Choose the Members page and click Add.
9. Specify any existing users who should be members of this group. From the right panel, open the container that holds the user you want. From the left panel, select the user, and then choose OK. The user's name now appears as a member of the group. (To select multiple users, use Shift-Click or Ctrl-Click.)

If the group already exists, you can also assign a user to that group by selecting the User object, opening the user's Group Membership page, and adding the group.

User Network Activities

Once users have been created, they can begin working on the network. In most cases, users on a network will notice very little difference from working on a stand-alone computer. They still use the applications they used before. They still open, save, and delete files the same way. They can still play the same games — if they can get away with it.

The primary differences for most users are that they have to enter a login name and password; they have more drives and directories available to them; there are some files that are restricted to them; and their print jobs go to the same printer as everyone else's. Whether you want them to be able to control most of these network activities themselves is up to you.

For most users, three NetWare utilities will take care of their networking tasks:

- LOGIN (from either the DOS command line or from Windows)
- LOGOUT
- NetWare User Tools

LOGGING IN AND OUT

To log in to the network, the user uses the LOGIN utility at the DOS prompt or the NetWare GUI Login program from Windows 3.1 and specifies a login name and a password. (The NetWare GUI Login program for Windows 3.1 is installed as part of the Client32 software for DOS and Windows.) From Windows 95, the user can right-click the desired server or tree, click Authenticate, and then enter a login name and password.

Which login name the user enters depends on whether you've modified the user's NET.CFG file to specify the user's name context.

If you are using the default NET.CFG file that was created when you installed the workstation, the Login utility doesn't know the context in which the user was created. It assumes the default context is at the root of the tree. If you've created the user in a container beneath the root, which is most likely the case, Login won't find the user in the tree if the user enters only his or her common name and will deny the user access to the network.

There are two ways to make sure Login finds the user's correct name context. The first way is for the user to specify a complete name, all the way back to the root of the tree. Obviously, this can be a little cumbersome for the user. For example, Eric would have to log in using the following command:

```
LOGIN .Eric.Mktg.Satellite.RedHawk
```

The period at the beginning of Eric's full name indicates that this name goes clear back to the root of the tree.

The other way to make sure Login finds the user's context is to specify the context in the NET.CFG file under the NetWare DOS Requester heading. For example, to specify Eric's context, put the following command in the NET.CFG file:

```
NAME CONTEXT = "Mktg.Satellite.RedHawk"
```

Then, Eric can just log in using his common name, Eric, which is obviously going to be easier for him to remember.

To simplify the user's life even more, you may also want to put the Login command in the user's AUTOEXEC.BAT file so that it executes every time the user boots the workstation.

To log out, the user simply enters the command:

```
LOGOUT
```

USING NETWARE USER TOOLS

IntranetWare includes a special utility, called NetWare User Tools, that allows users to perform their most common network tasks. There is both a DOS-based version and a Windows-based version of this utility. With this utility, users can do the following:

- Set up print queues and control how their print jobs are printed on the network
- Send short messages to other network users
- Map drive letters to network directories
- Change passwords
- Log in and out of Directory trees and network servers (but without a login script executing)
- Change their own name context in the Directory tree
- Edit user login scripts (DOS version only)

NOTE

Most Windows 95 users will use the Windows Explorer and Network Neighborhood instead of the NetWare User Tools to complete network tasks.

NetWare User Tools for DOS

To execute the DOS-based version of NetWare User Tools, called NETUSER.EXE, simply enter the command

```
NETUSER
```

at the DOS prompt. NETUSER allows you to modify a user login script, so that you can make drive mappings and other aspects of the workstation environment "permanent" (which means they are in effect each time the user logs in to the network, until the user decides to change them). Use the F1 key to read help screens about the different tasks you can perform with this utility.

NetWare User Tools for Windows

To use the Windows-based version of NetWare User Tools, double-click on the NetWare User Tools icon, which is automatically placed in the NetWare Tools program group when the NetWare client software is installed.

The Windows-based version of this utility doesn't allow you to edit a login script. Instead, you can set up drive mappings and printer port redirection right in the utility, and then click the Permanent button to make those assignments permanent. This has the same effect as placing the corresponding commands in a login script. Every time you log in, NetWare User Tools will automatically map the drives and capture printer ports the way you specified. Use the Help button to read about the tasks you can perform with this utility.

Making Applications Easy to Access

One of the best new features of IntranetWare, as far as users are concerned, is the NetWare Application Launcher. Once you have the NetWare Application Launcher set up on each user's workstation, you can use NetWare Administrator to make an application become an object in the NDS tree. Then, the icon for the Application object will appear automatically on the desktop of each user you assign to that application.

The users don't need to know where the application is; they don't need to map drives or enter launch parameters; and you don't need to update login scripts. When you update the application, the icons in all the desktops will continue to point to the new application.

To set up the NetWare Application Launcher on a Windows 3.1 workstation, complete the steps in the following checklist.

✓ 1. Start Windows and highlight the program group in which you want NetWare Application Launcher to appear. The NetWare Tools program group was already created during the workstation installation, so you can use that group.
2. From the File menu, choose New, and then select Program Item.
3. For the Description, enter the name you want to use, such as NetWare App Launcher or NAL.
4. Use the Browse button to specify the location of the NAL.EXE file (SYS:\PUBLIC\NAL.EXE) and the working directory (SYS:\PUBLIC).
5. Click OK. The NetWare Application Launcher icon appears on the desktop. Now, any Application object you create and "associate" with this user will automatically appear in this user's Application Launcher window.

To set up the NetWare Application Launcher on a Windows 95 workstation, complete the steps in the following checklist.

✓ 1. From the Windows 95 desktop, right-click the mouse and choose New.
2. Select Shortcut.
3. Choose Browse, locate the SYS:PUBLIC drive, and choose NAL.EXE.
4. Choose Open, and then Finish. The NetWare Application Launcher appears as a shortcut icon on the desktop.

To create an Application object for a network application, complete the steps in the following checklist.

✓ 1. Start up NetWare Administrator.
2. Select the container object that will hold the Application object.
3. From the Object menu, choose Create.
4. From the New Object dialog box that appears, choose the Application object for the appropriate operating system (DOS, Windows 3.x, Windows 95, or Windows NT), and then choose OK.
5. When the Application object's dialog box appears, enter its name and path.
6. Check the Define Additional Properties box, and then click Create.
7. Enter any additional information necessary for this application, such as its command line parameters, working directory, drives or ports, a description of the application, and so on.

8. In the Associations page, add the users or groups who should be able to use this application.
9. Click OK when you're finished.

Login Scripts

Login scripts are tools similar to batch files that you can use to automatically set up users' workstation environments. Each time a user logs in, the LOGIN utility executes the login scripts, which can set up frequently used drive mappings, capture the workstation's printer port to a network print queue, display connection information or messages on the screen, or perform other types of tasks for the user.

In previous versions of NetWare (3.1x and 2.x), there were two types of login scripts: user login scripts and system login scripts. The system login script was a file on the server. It executed for every user who logged in to that server, so it was a good place to store drive mappings or other information that was common to all users. The user login script was a separate file for each user, stored in users' MAIL subdirectories. In the user login script, you could create drive mappings or other items that were specific to only that user.

In IntranetWare, there are three types of login scripts:

- **User Login Scripts.** User login scripts in IntranetWare are the same as in previous versions, except that they are not stored as text files. Instead, they are actual properties of the User object. You still store user-specific drive mappings in the user login script. If the user does not have a specific user login script, a default login script will execute instead, setting up the most basic drive mappings.
- **System Login Scripts.** Instead of belonging to a server, a system login script belongs to a container object. Because users no longer log in to a server, and because all the users in a container may access different servers for files, keeping a server-specific login script seems useless. However, a script that applies to all users within a given container makes much more sense. Therefore, the system login script (also called a container login script) is a property of a container object. It applies to every user in that container.
- **Profile Login Scripts.** With a profile script, you can create a script that will apply to several users who don't necessarily have to be in the same container. It's kind of a group login script. The profile login script is a

property of a Profile object, which defines a list of users belonging to the Profile. A user can have only one profile login script execute upon login.

These three types of login scripts work together to set up each user's environment upon login. They execute in the following order:

- System (container) login script
- Profile login script
- User login script (or default login script if a user login script doesn't exist)

All three are optional. If you don't create one of them, LOGIN will skip to the next login script in the list.

Because up to three different login scripts can execute for a given user, conflicts between the login scripts may occur. If they do, the final login script to execute wins. Therefore, if the system login script maps a directory to drive letter G, and then the user script maps a different directory to drive letter G, the user script's mapping overwrites the system script's mapping.

System login scripts apply only to the users immediately within that container. They don't apply to users in a child container. If the container that holds user Andrea doesn't have a login script, no system login script will execute when Andrea logs in, even if a container higher up in the tree has a login script.

To simplify the administration of login scripts, try to put as much common information as possible, such as drive mappings to application directories, in the container and profile login scripts. It's much easier to change a drive mapping in one script and have it apply to all your users than to make the same change dozens or hundreds of times for every user script.

If you upgrade NetWare 2.x or 3.x to IntranetWare, the user login scripts are automatically transferred into the Login Script property of each User object. Server-specific system login scripts, however, are not upgraded. You will need to re-create the system login script, if needed, as a property of a container object. (The server-specific system login script in previous versions of NetWare is a text file in the SYS:PUBLIC directory called NET$LOG.DAT. You can print out this file to refer to while creating a container system login script.)

TIP

If you want to log in to the network without executing a login script, add the /NS option to the login command. For example, user Lauren would type LOGIN LAUREN/NS.

CREATING A LOGIN SCRIPT

You use the NetWare Administrator utility to create login scripts, just as you assign any other properties to NDS objects. Open the object's Details page, and then click on the button for the Login Script page.

When you open up the Login Script property for a User, Profile, or container object, you are presented with a blank screen (or the previous login script, if one already exists). In this screen, you type any commands you want the login script to hold: drive mappings, printer port captures, messages, environment settings, and so on.

To create or edit a login script, you must have the Write NDS right to the object that will contain the script.

When creating login scripts, keep the following conventions and rules in mind. (Login script commands mentioned here are explained in the next section.)

- Begin each command in the login script on its own line. (Commands that wrap automatically to another line are considered a single line. Commands are limited to 150 characters per line.)
- To make multiline WRITE commands display better and to avoid having a line misinterpreted by LOGIN, begin each line of the displayed message with the word WRITE.
- If you use the pound sign (#) to execute an external program, note that some programs may require that the user have drives mapped to particular directories. If so, make sure the MAP commands that map drives to those directories are placed in the login script ahead of the command that executes the external program.
- Enter commands in the general order in which you want them to execute. If order isn't important, group similar commands together (such as MAP and CAPTURE commands) to make the login script easier to read.
- Remember that most commands are case insensitive. The only exception is identifier variables enclosed in quotation marks and preceded by a percent sign (%); they must be uppercase.
- Use identifier variables to make generic commands useful to specific users. When a user logs in, his or her specific information is substituted for the identifier variable in the generic command. Identifier variables (explained later in the "Using Identifier Variables" section) make it possible to put most necessary commands in the system or profile script, rather than in a user login script.

- Use blank lines to separate groups of commands in the script if it makes it easier to read. Blank lines don't affect the execution of the login script.
- For future reference, use remarks in the login script to explain what commands in the script are doing. Lines in the login script beginning with the word REM, an asterisk, or a semicolon are remarks, and they don't display when the login script executes.
- Copy portions of a login script by using the mouse to highlight the desired text and pressing Ctrl-C. To paste the text, either elsewhere in the script or in another object's script, press Ctrl-V.

ASSIGNING PROFILE LOGIN SCRIPTS TO USERS

To create a profile login script, you create a Profile object just as you create any other NDS object. Create its script in the Profile object's Login Script property. After you've created the script, you must assign it to individual users. To do this, complete the steps in the following checklist.

1. Use the Browser to select a User object.
2. Choose Details from the Object menu, and then open the Login Script page.
3. Enter the name of the Profile object in the Profile field beneath the login script text window.
4. Save the information and return to the Browser.
5. From the Browser, select the Profile object.
6. From the Object menu, choose Trustees of This Object.
7. Click the Add Trustee button and enter the name of the user who will use this profile login script.
8. Make sure the Browse object right and Read property right are checked, and then choose OK to assign those rights to the user.

LOGIN SCRIPT COMMANDS

The many commands you can use in NetWare login scripts are explained in the following sections. Many of these commands are unique to NetWare login scripts. Some commands may work similarly to DOS commands or may actually execute DOS commands you might be familiar with, such as the SET and DOS BREAK ON commands. All of them are optional. You only need to use the commands that accomplish tasks you want performed for the user.

Command

This command executes an external command or program, such as a NetWare utility, from the login script. To execute the program, use the pound (#) symbol at the beginning of the command. When the program is finished executing, the login script will take over again and continue running.

When this command is used to execute another program, the LOGIN utility may be swapped out of conventional memory and into extended or expanded memory (if available) or onto the hard disk, enabling both LOGIN and the program to execute at the same time. If you do not want LOGIN to be moved out of conventional memory, use the NOSWAP login script command, covered later in this chapter.

The # command is commonly used with the CAPTURE utility (explained in Chapter 6). For example, to capture a user's LPT1 port to use a network print queue named LaserQ, you might put the following command in the login script:

```
#CAPTURE L=1 Q=.LaserQ.Sales.Satellite.RedHawk NB
NT NFF TI=5
```

ATTACH Command

This command attaches the user to a IntranetWare server using bindery services. It can also be used to attach the user to a NetWare 3.1x or 2.x server. ATTACH doesn't execute a login script for that server; it simply attaches you to the server so you can access its resources. Do not use ATTACH if you want to use Novell Directory Services on a IntranetWare server (there is no need to attach to a IntranetWare server if you're already logged in to the NDS tree).

To use ATTACH, put the following command in the login script, replacing *server* with the server's name and *username* with the user's login name:

```
ATTACH server/username
```

BREAK ON Command

BREAK OFF is the default. This command lets you abort the login script while it is executing by pressing Ctrl-C or Ctrl-Break.

BREAK ON only lets you break out of the login script. To break out of programs other than the login script, use the DOS BREAK ON command, explained later in this chapter.

To use BREAK ON, put the following command in the login script:

```
BREAK ON
```

CLS Command

Use this command to clear the workstation's screen of any commands that have been displayed by the login script up to the point where this CLS command occurs.

To use CLS, put the following command in the login script:

```
CLS
```

COMSPEC Command

If you have set up your workstations to run DOS from a network directory instead of from a local disk, use this command. The COMSPEC command lets you tell the workstation that the DOS command processor (COMMAND.COM) is located on the network. If your workstations are running DOS locally, don't use this command.

OS/2 users who run virtual DOS sessions can't use this command in the login script. Instead, they must put it in the CONFIG.SYS file to indicate that DOS is on the local disk.

To use COMSPEC, put the following command in the login script:

```
COMSPEC=path COMMAND.COM
```

For example, if DOS is located in the directory SYS:PUBLIC\%MACHINE\%OS\%OS_VERSION, and you have mapped search drive S2 to that directory, you would enter the following command in the login script:

```
COMSPEC=S2:COMMAND.COM
```

CONTEXT Command

Use this command to set the user's name context. CONTEXT works in the login script similarly to how the CX workstation utility works when typed at the workstation's DOS prompt. This command will change the context the user sees after he or she logs in. To change the context before the user logs in, use the NET.CFG file instead of the login script.

To use CONTEXT, put the following command in the login script:

```
CONTEXT context
```

Replace *context* with the user's new name context, such as .Satellite.RedHawk.

DISPLAY Command

This command displays an ASCII text file on the workstation screen during login. If you want to display a word-processed file that has word-processing and printer codes embedded in it, use FDISPLAY instead. (FDISPLAY is covered later in this chapter.)

To use DISPLAY, put the following command in the login script, replacing *path\filename* with the directory path and name of the file you want to display:

```
DISPLAY path\filename
```

DOS BREAK ON Command

This command lets you abort a program (other than the login script) while it is executing by pressing Ctrl-C or Ctrl-Break. DOS BREAK OFF is the default. (This command does not apply to OS/2 workstations.)

To break out of the login script, use the BREAK ON command instead (explained earlier in this chapter).

To use DOS BREAK ON, put the following command in the login script:

```
DOS BREAK ON
```

DOS VERIFY ON Command

Use this command to make DOS's COPY command verify that files can be read after they are copied. You do not need to use this command if you use only the NetWare NCOPY utility because NCOPY verifies the copies automatically.

The default is DOS VERIFY OFF.

To use DOS VERIFY ON, put the following command in the login script:

```
DOS VERIFY ON
```

DRIVE Command

This command lets you change to a different default network drive while the login script is executing. Be sure to place this command in the login script after the MAP command that maps a drive to the desired directory.

For example, to map drive H to SYS:USERS\PAULINE\STATUS, and then make drive H the default drive, put the following commands in the login script:

```
MAP H:=SYS:USERS\PAULINE\STATUS

DRIVE H:
```

(On OS/2 workstations, DRIVE changes only the default directory while the login script is running. After the login script finishes, the default drive returns to the drive in effect when you executed the LOGIN utility.)

EXIT Command

Use this command at the end of a login script to stop the script and go immediately into another program, such as a menu program or an application, instead of returning to the DOS prompt.

This command does not apply to OS/2 workstations.

EXIT stops the current login script, which is why you must place it at the end of the script. In addition, it prevents any other login scripts from executing. If you put an EXIT command at the end of the container system login script, the profile and user scripts will not execute, so be sure you place the EXIT command at the end of any scripts you want to execute.

To use EXIT, put the following command in the login script:

```
EXIT "program"
```

Inside the quotation marks, replace *program* with the command that executes the program you want the user to enter. The command inside the quotation marks can't exceed the number of the workstation's keyboard buffer length (typically 15) minus 1. (In other words, most workstations are limited to 14 characters inside the quotation marks.)

For example, to exit to a menu program called DATA, use the following command at the end of the login script:

```
EXIT "NMENU DATA"
```

If you have changed the workstation's long machine name in the NET.CFG file, you need to execute the PCCOMPATIBLE login script command before the EXIT command.

FDISPLAY Command

This command displays a word-processed file that has word-processing and printer codes embedded in it on the workstation screen during login. It removes these embedded codes and displays just the text of the file. If you want to display an ASCII text file, you can use DISPLAY instead (covered earlier in this chapter).

To use FDISPLAY, put the following command in the login script, replacing *path\filename* with the directory path and name of the file you want to display:

```
FDISPLAY path\filename
```

FIRE PHASERS Command

This command makes the workstation emit a phaser sound. You can specify how many times (up to nine) the phaser sound occurs. You can use this command to draw attention to a displayed message during login.

To use FIRE PHASERS, put the following command in the login script:

```
FIRE PHASERS x TIMES
```

where *x* is a number from 1 to 9.

GOTO Command

Use this command to make the login script skip to another portion of the script. To use this command, label the part of the login script you want to execute with a single word of your choice, and then put the following command in the login script, substituting the word you used in the script for *label*.

```
GOTO label
```

IF...THEN Command

Use this command to indicate that a command should execute only if certain conditions are met. For example, you could use IF...THEN to make a message display only on a particular day of the week.

The IF...THEN command uses this basic format:

```
IF something is true THEN

execute this command

ELSE execute this command

END
```

The ELSE portion of the command is optional. You use it only when you have two or more commands that you want to execute at different times, based on different circumstances.

For example, to display the message "Friday's here at last!" on Fridays, you would use the following commands:

```
IF DAY_OF_WEEK="Friday" THEN

WRITE "Friday's here at last!"

END
```

No message will appear on any other day of the week.

Suppose you want to make the same message appear on Fridays, and on all other days you want to display the message "Customers are our first priority." To do this, use the same command, but add an ELSE portion:

```
IF DAY_OF_WEEK="Friday" THEN
WRITE "Friday's here at last!"
ELSE
WRITE "Customers are our first priority."
END
```

The first line of the IF...THEN command (IF *something is true*) is called a conditional statement because this is the condition that makes the rest of the command execute. To use a conditional statement, you use a variable, and you indicate what value that variable has to have before it can execute the command.

These variables are called *identifier variables*. The identifier variables you can use in login scripts are explained in the "Using Identifier Variables" section later in this chapter.

For example, if you specify the DAY_OF_WEEK variable, you can also indicate the value you need the variable to have, such as "Friday." Then, whenever the day's value matches the one you indicated in the command, the command will execute. (In other words, on every Friday the command will execute.)

In conditional statements, the value must be enclosed in quotation marks.

INCLUDE Command

This command lets you execute another text file or another object's login script as part of the login script currently executing. The other file or login script, called a *subscript*, must contain regular login script commands.

To call a subscript, put one of the following commands in the main login script at the point where you want the subscript to execute:

```
INCLUDE path\filename
```

or

```
INCLUDE object
```

Replace *path\filename* with the directory path and name of the text file that contains the login script commands, or replace *object* with the name of the object whose login script you want to execute.

LASTLOGINTIME Command

This command simply displays the time of the user's last login on the workstation screen.

To use LASTLOGINTIME, put the following command in the login script:

```
LASTLOGINTIME
```

MACHINE Command

Use this command to set the workstation's DOS machine name. The default is IBM_PC. Some programs, such as NetBIOS, may need this command if they were written to run under PC DOS, but in most cases you shouldn't have to use this command. It does not apply to OS/2 workstations.

This command is different from the MACHINE identifier variable. That variable, which can be used in MAP and WRITE login script commands, gets its value from the NET.CFG file.

The machine name can be up to 15 characters long.

To use MACHINE, put the following command in the login script, replacing *name* with the machine name:

```
MACHINE=name
```

MAP Command

Use this command to map drive letters to network directories. When you put a MAP command in a login script, that command will be executed every time the user logs in.

Use the MAP login script command just as you use the MAP utility at the DOS prompt, with the following command format:

```
MAP letter:=path
```

For example, to map drive L to VOL1:APPS\WP, the command would be as follows:

```
MAP L:=VOL1:APPS\WP
```

Because your users probably have home directories in which they store their individual files, you may want to map a drive to the user's home directory. You can do that generically in a system or profile script by using the LOGIN_NAME identifier variable. For example, if all your users have a subdirectory under the directory USERS, and you want the first available drive to be mapped to this subdirectory, you can put the following mapping in the system or profile login script:

```
MAP N VOL1:USERS\%LOGIN_NAME
```

%LOGIN_NAME is the identifier variable. When user Tina logs in, her name will automatically be substituted for this variable, and the first available network drive will be mapped to VOL1:USERS\TINA.

For OS/2 workstations, map drive P to SYS:PUBLIC.

If users are running Windows from the network instead of from their own local hard disk, map drives to the users' directories that contain their individual files.

You can also use MAP to map search drives. Search drives are used to indicate directories that contain applications or utilities. Search drives let users execute an application without having to know where the application is; the network searches through the designated search drives for the application's executable file when the user types the program's execution command.

To map a search drive, you use the letter S, followed by a number, rather than designating a drive letter. The search drive will assign its own letters in reverse order, starting with the letter Z. (You can have up to 16 search drives mapped.) For example, to map the first search drive to the SYS:PUBLIC directory, enter the following line in the login script:

```
MAP S1:=SYS:PUBLIC
```

Search drive mappings are added to the workstation's DOS PATH environment variable. This means that if you specify that a search drive is S1, as in the preceding example, the mapping to SYS:PUBLIC will overwrite the first DOS path that had already been set. To avoid overwriting a path setting, use the INS option. By entering

```
MAP INS S1
```

instead of

```
MAP S1
```

the search drive mapping will be inserted at the beginning of the DOS path settings, moving the path setting that was previously first to the second position.

In login scripts, some drives should be mapped in a particular order. In the system login script, the following search drives should be mapped first:

```
MAP INS S1:=SYS:PUBLIC
MAP INS S2:=SYS:PUBLIC\%MACHINE\%OS\%OS_VERSION
```

The SYS:PUBLIC directory contains the NetWare utilities and other NetWare files that users need. The second mapping maps a search drive to the DOS directories. If you want your users to run DOS from the network instead of from their local disks, use this command, which points to the network directories that contain DOS. (This command uses identifier variables for some directory names. For example, the identifier variable %OS represents the workstation's operating system. Therefore, if a workstation requires MS-DOS version 5.0, the search drive would be mapped to SYS:PUBLIC\IBM_PC\MSDOS\50.)

After these two search drives, you can map additional search drives in any order you want.

TIP

Instead of mapping search drives in order (S3, S4, S5, and so on), use MAP S16 for all subsequent mappings that don't require an exact position (as do the first two mappings, mentioned above). Each MAP S16 command will insert its drive mapping at the end of the list, pushing up the previous mappings. This just makes the list of search drives more flexible, so that if you delete one the others will reorder themselves automatically. Also, you don't run the risk of overwriting a search drive that may have been specified in another login script.

There are several variations of the MAP command you can use to accomplish different tasks, as shown in Table 6.1.

TABLE 6.1 *MAP Command Options*

TASK	DESCRIPTION
Map drives in order without specifying drive letters	If you don't want to specify exact drive letters, you can map each available drive in order. This is useful if you don't know what drive letters have already been mapped in a system or profile login script. To assign drive letters this way, use an asterisk, followed by a number. For example, to get the first and second available drives, you could use the following commands:
	MAP *1:=VOL1:APPS\WP
	MAP *2:=VOL1:DATA\REPORTS
Map the next available drive	To map the next available drive, use the letter N (without a colon), as in the following command:
	MAP N=VOL1:APPS\WP
Delete a drive mapping	To delete a mapping for drive G, for example, use the following command:

(continued)

MAP DEL G:

TABLE 6.1 *MAP Command Options (continued)*

TASK	DESCRIPTION
Turn off MAP's display	Whenever a MAP command is executed in the login script, it will display the new drive mapping on the workstation screen unless you specify otherwise. To turn off this display, use the following command: MAP DISPLAY OFF
Turn on MAP's display	At the end of the login script, you may want to turn MAP's display back on and show a listing of all the completed drive mappings. To do this, put the following command at or near the end of the login script: MAP DISPLAY ON MAP
Map a fake root	Some applications must be installed at the root of a volume or hard disk. If you would rather install the application in a subdirectory, you can do that, and then map a fake root to the application's subdirectory. You can map a fake root in a regular drive mapping or in a search drive mapping. To map drive H as a fake root to the VOL1:APPS\CAD subdirectory, use the following command: MAP ROOT H:=VOL1:APPS\CAD
Map a drive to a Directory Map object	You can create an NDS object, called a Directory Map object, that points to a particular directory. Then, you can map drives to that object instead of to the actual directory path. This way, if you later move the directory to another part of the file system, you can just change the Directory Map object's description instead of updating all the affected login scripts. Preferably, use Directory Map objects in the user's current context. If the Directory Map object is in another part of the NDS tree, create an Alias object for the Directory Map object in the user's current context. To map a search drive to a Directory Map object named Database, use the following command: MAP S16:=DATABASE

NO_DEFAULT Command

Use this command at the end of a system or profile login script if you do not want the default script to execute for a user who doesn't have a user login script.

To use NO_DEFAULT, put the following command in the login script:

```
NO_DEFAULT
```

NOSWAP Command

Use this command to keep LOGIN from being moved out of conventional memory into higher memory.

When the # command is used to execute another program, the LOGIN utility may be swapped out of conventional memory and into extended or expanded memory (if available) or onto the hard disk to allow both LOGIN and the program to execute at the same time. This happens by default. If you do not want LOGIN to be moved out of conventional memory, use the NOSWAP login script command. If the workstation doesn't have enough memory to run both LOGIN and the external program, the external program will fail, but the rest of the login script will execute.

To use NOSWAP, put the following command in the login script:

```
NOSWAP
```

PAUSE Command

This command makes the login script pause in its execution. The message "Strike any key when ready . . ." appears on the workstation's screen. When the user presses a key, the login script continues executing.

To use PAUSE, put the following command in a login script, wherever you want the pause to occur:

```
PAUSE
```

PCCOMPATIBLE Command

Use this command only if you are using the EXIT command and have changed the workstation's long machine name in the NET.CFG file to something other than IBM_PC.

This command doesn't apply to OS/2 workstations.

To use this command, place it before the EXIT command, as in the following example (which exits the login script and goes into a program called CAD):

```
PCCOMPATIBLE
EXIT "CAD"
```

PROFILE Command

Use this command in a system login script to set or override a user's assigned profile script. To use this command, replace *name* in the command shown here with the Profile object's name:

```
PROFILE name
```

REMARK Command

Use REMARK — or its equivalents REM, an asterisk (*), or a semicolon (;) — to indicate that the rest of the line in the login script is a comment and should not be displayed or executed. Use comments to describe commands in the login script so that you or others will recall why certain commands are there when you read the script later.

For example, the following line in the login script indicates that a map command follows it:

```
REM The next drive mapping is for students' tem-
porary use. Delete at end of quarter.
```

SCRIPT_SERVER Command

This command specifies a home server from which the workstation can read a bindery login script. This command does not apply to IntranetWare servers.

To use SCRIPT_SERVER, put the following command in a login script, replacing *server* with the bindery server's name:

```
SCRIPT_SERVER server
```

SET Command

Use SET to set DOS and OS/2 environment variables. For OS/2 workstations, these variables are in effect only while the login script is running. For DOS workstations, the variables remain in effect after the login script is finished (unless you change them from the DOS command line at some point after login — but then the variables will be reset when the login script is executed again). You can use any of the regular DOS or OS/2 variables in this command.

Use the SET login script command just as you would use regular DOS SET variables, with one exception: For a login script command, you must enclose the value you are setting in quotation marks.

For example, to set the prompt to display the current directory, add the following command to the login script:

```
SET PROMPT= "$P$G"
```

If you use SET PATH, the path will overwrite any previous path settings established in AUTOEXEC.BAT or earlier in the login script.

To use a SET variable as an identifier variable in another login script command, enclose the variable in angle brackets, such as <path>. For example, the following MAP login script command uses the path variable:

```
MAP S16:=%<PATH>
```

If you want the variable to be set for a DOS workstation only while the login script is executing, and you want it to return to its original state after execution, add the word TEMP to the beginning of the SET command, as in the following example:

```
TEMP SET PROMPT= "$P$G"
```

SET_TIME OFF Command

By default, when a workstation logs in, it sets its time to the time of the first server it connects to. To prevent the workstation from adopting the server's time, use the command SET_TIME OFF. To allow the workstation to adopt its time from the server after all, use SET_TIME ON (the default).

To use SET_TIME OFF, put the following command in the login script:

```
SET_TIME OFF
```

SHIFT Command

This command changes the order in which variables entered at the LOGIN command line are interpreted. You can use special variables, called %*n* variables, as placeholders in a login script command. Then, when a user logs in, the values the user enters at the command line are substituted for the %*n* variable.

The SHIFT command lets you change the order in which the %*n* variables are executed. In the SHIFT command, specify a positive or negative number to indicate that you want to shift the variables one direction or the other. For example, the following command moves each %*n* variable one position to the right:

```
SHIFT +1
```

Using *%n* variables is described later in this chapter.

SWAP Command

Use this command to move LOGIN out of conventional memory into higher memory.

When the # command is used to execute another program, the LOGIN utility may be swapped out of conventional memory and into extended or expanded memory (if available) or onto the hard disk to allow both LOGIN and the program to execute at the same time. This happens by default. However, if you do not want LOGIN to be moved out of conventional memory, you can use the NOSWAP login script command. If NOSWAP has been used earlier in the login script, you can use SWAP to again enable LOGIN to swap into higher memory.

To use SWAP, put the following command in the login script:

```
SWAP
```

WRITE Command

Use WRITE to display short messages on the workstation screen during login. To use WRITE, enter the command

```
WRITE
```

followed by quotation marks enclosing the text you want to appear on the user's screen. For example, to display the message "Have a nice day" enter the following command:

```
WRITE "Have a nice day"
```

To display a message that is too long for a single line, use the word WRITE at the beginning of each line. For example, suppose you want to display the following message:

```
Please attend today's weekly staff meeting
in Conference Room B.

Be prepared to discuss your client call
status and success stories.

Remember to bring your expense reports.
```

To get these sentences to appear correctly on five lines, you should enter the following commands:

```
WRITE "Please attend today's weekly staff meeting"
WRITE "in Conference Room B."

WRITE "Be prepared to discuss your client call"
WRITE "status and success stories."

WRITE "Remember to bring your expense reports."
```

For information about using identifier variables in WRITE commands, see the next section "Using Identifier Variables."

There are a few special characters you can enter in a WRITE command to make the command appear as you want. These are shown in Table 6.2.

TABLE 6.2 *Special Characters for the WRITE command*

CHARACTER	DESCRIPTION
;	Links two WRITE commands together so they appear as a continuous sentence or paragraph. Can also be used to link text within quotation marks to an identifier variable that isn't included in the quotation marks.
\r	Causes a carriage return when used inside the text string.
\n	Begins a new line of text when used inside the text string.
\"	Makes a quotation mark display inside the text message when used inside the text string.
\7	Causes a beep sound to occur when used inside the text string.

USING IDENTIFIER VARIABLES

Using identifier variables in login scripts is effective for two reasons:

- It's an efficient way to make generic commands work for most users.
- It allows you to make different commands execute only at certain times or in particular situations.

An identifier variable is simply a placeholder for information that is substituted whenever a user logs in. An identifier variable might be replaced by specific user information, such as the user's login name or full name, or it might be replaced by information about the user's workstation, such as its address or machine type. It might also be replaced by general information that has nothing to do with the user, such as the day of the week, time, or network address.

You can use identifier variables in many different login script commands. You can use them in WRITE commands to display the value that is provided. For example, suppose you add the following command to the system login script:

```
WRITE "GOOD %GREETING_TIME, %LOGIN_NAME."
```

When user Eric logs in at 8:00 a.m., the following message displays on his screen:

```
Good MORNING, ERIC.
```

When user Maude logs in at 1:30 p.m., she receives this message:

```
Good AFTERNOON, MAUDE.
```

You can also use identifier variables in other types of commands, such as IF...THEN commands, to allow a particular command to execute only under certain conditions. For example, the following IF...THEN command will execute a WRITE command only on Wednesdays:

```
IF DAY_OF_WEEK="Wednesday" THEN

WRITE "Don't forget staff meeting today at 3:00."

END
```

For more about the IF...THEN command, see the section in this chapter called "IF...THEN Command."

Syntax for Using Identifier Variables

In the examples given above, you may have noticed that sometimes a percent sign (%) is added to the beginning of the variable and sometimes it isn't. Ordinarily, in a WRITE command, everything inside the quotation marks is displayed. However, the percent sign indicates that the following word is not to be displayed as is; rather, it is an identifier variable, and the variable's value should be displayed instead.

In other commands, when the identifier variable is not enclosed in quotation marks, do not use the percent sign.

The basic syntax rules for identifier variables are as follows:

- Identifier variables should be typed in uppercase.

- If you want the variable's value to be displayed in a WRITE command, precede the variable with a percent sign and enclose it in quotation marks.
- To use a variable in any other command, do not use a percent sign.
- If you specify a desired value for the variable in an IF...THEN command, enclose the value in quotation marks, such as IF DAY_OF_WEEK="Monday".

You can specify how an identifier variable matches a particular value in six different ways, as shown in Table 6.3.

TABLE 6.3 *Operators for Assigning Values to Identifier Variables*

OPERATOR	EXAMPLE
= (equals)	IF LOGIN_NAME = "David" means *If the user is David*
<> (doesn't equal)	IF LOGIN_NAME <> "Admin" means *If the user isn't Admin*
> (is greater than)	IF HOUR > "9" means *If the hour is 10:00 or later*
>= (is greater than or equal to)	IF HOUR >= "9:00" means *If the hour is 9:00 or later*
< (is less than)	IF HOUR < "5" means *If the hour is 4:00 or earlier*
<= (is less than or equal to)	IF HOUR <= "5" means *If the hour is 5:00 or earlier*

Using the %*n* Identifier Variable

When users log in, they type a LOGIN command that usually includes at least two parameters: their login names and either a tree name or a server name. If there is only one tree or server available, a user may have to only specify the login name parameter, but the other parameter is implied.

In addition, a user can add additional parameters to the LOGIN command, such as an application name or other keyword he or she wants to use. This can allow the user to have different login script commands execute depending on the parameter the user specifies in the LOGIN command.

In login scripts, you can insert a special type of identifier variable to use and display these LOGIN parameters. It is called the %*n* variable (where *n* is a number, such as 0, 1, and so on).

To use a %*n* variable, you insert it into a command just like any other identifier variable, except that it is always preceded by a percent sign and enclosed in quotation marks. Then, whenever a user logs in, the parameters he or she enters are substituted for the %*n* variable in the login script command.

The first two variables, %0 and %1, must always have the following values:

- %0 — The server or tree name, depending on how the user logs in
- %1 — The user's login name

Subsequent numbers, such as %2 and %3, can be fulfilled by whatever additional parameters the user enters with the LOGIN command.

The following is an example of how %*n* variables can be used in login script commands:

```
IF "%1"="Jessica" THEN

MAP *3:=VOL1:APPS\DB

IF "%2"="wp" THEN

MAP *4:=VOL1:APPS\WP

END
```

In this example, two %*n* variables are used: %1 and %2. Because %1 is always a user login name, the first line of the command is specifying that the following commands execute only if the login name is Jessica.

The second variable, %2, will be whatever variable user Jessica enters after her login name. If she enters

```
WP
```

after her login name, she will get an additional drive mapping to the WP subdirectory. She would enter the following command when she logs in:

```
LOGIN JESSICA WP
```

In this command the first variable, %0, wasn't supplied but is implied to be the server to which she attaches, since %0 is always the server. The second variable, %1, is the user login name (Jessica in this case). The third variable, %2, is the WP parameter she entered after her login name. Whenever she uses this command to log in, Jessica will receive two drive mappings — one to the DB subdirectory and one to the WP subdirectory.

If Jessica logs in using the following command

```
LOGIN JESSICA
```

she will receive only a drive mapping to the DB subdirectory.

If anyone other than Jessica logs in, they will not receive either drive mapping.

The SHIFT login command lets you actually shift the position of the parameters to the right or left, depending on whether you enter a positive or negative number. (See the description of the SHIFT login script command earlier in this chapter.)

Identifier Variables

The identifier variables can be grouped into the following categories:

- User
- Workstation
- Network
- Date
- Time
- Miscellaneous

Table 6.4 lists each of the available user identifier variables.

TABLE 6.4 *User Identifier Variables*

IDENTIFIER VARIABLE	DESCRIPTION	EXAMPLE
CN	Common name of the User object.	Eric
ALIAS_CONTEXT	Displays "Y" if the requester context is an alias.	
FULL_NAME	The user's full name, if defined in the User object's properties.	Eric V. McCloud
LAST_NAME	The user's last name in NDS (or full name on the bindery servers).	McCloud
LOGIN_CONTEXT	The user's name context in the NDS tree.	Mktg.Satellite.RedHawk
LOGIN_NAME	The user's login name (same as common name).	Eric

(continued)

TABLE 6.4 *User Identifier Variables (continued)*

IDENTIFIER VARIABLE	DESCRIPTION	EXAMPLE
MEMBER OF "*group*"	The group a user might belong to. Can also use the word NOT with this variable.	IF MEMBER OF "Design" THEN . . . IF NOT MEMBER OF "Design" THEN. . .
PASSWORD_EXPIRES	Displays how many days before the user's password expires.	WRITE "Your password expires in %PASSWORD_EXPIRES days."
REQUESTER_CONTEXT	The context from which LOGIN was started. This may not necessarily be the same context the user will be in after login.	IF REQUESTER_CONTEXT = "RedHawk" THEN . . .
USER_ID	Unique number assigned to each user.	12345678

Table 6.5 lists each of the available workstation identifier variables.

TABLE 6.5 *Workstation Identifier Variables*

IDENTIFIER VARIABLE	DESCRIPTION	EXAMPLE
MACHINE	The workstation's computer type	IBM_PC (This is the default.)
NETWARE_REQUESTER	Version of the NetWare client software for OS/2 or DOS and Windows	V1.20
OS	The workstation's type of operating system	MDOS
OS_VERSION	The version of the workstation's operating system	V6.20
P_STATION	The workstation's node address	000106FFACDE (12-digit hexadecimal number)
SHELL_TYPE	The version of the workstation's DOS shell	V4.20A

(continued)

TABLE 6.5 *Workstation Identifier Variables (continued)*

IDENTIFIER VARIABLE	DESCRIPTION	EXAMPLE
SMACHINE	The workstation's short machine name	IBM (This is the default.)
STATION	The workstation's connection number	14

Table 6.6 lists each of the available network identifier variables.

TABLE 6.6 *Network Identifier Variables*

IDENTIFIER VARIABLE	DESCRIPTION	EXAMPLE
FILE_SERVER	The NetWare server name	Sales1
NETWORK_ADDRESS	The IPX external number of the cabling system attached to the server's network board	00120FED (eight-digit network hexadecimal number)

Table 6.7 lists each of the available date identifier variables.

TABLE 6.7 *Date Identifier Variables*

IDENTIFIER VARIABLE	DESCRIPTION	EXAMPLE OR VALUES
DAY	The day's date	Values: 01 through 31
DAY_OF_WEEK	The day's name	Example: Tuesday
MONTH	The month's number	Values: 01 through 12
MONTH_NAME	The month's name	Example: October
NDAY_OF_WEEK	The number of the day of the week	Values: 1 through 7 (1=Sunday)
SHORT_YEAR	The last two digits of the year	Example: 96
YEAR	All four digits of the year	Example: 1996

Table 6.8 lists each of the available time identifier variables.

TABLE 6.8 *Time Identifier Variables*

IDENTIFIER VARIABLE	DESCRIPTION	VALUES
AM_PM	Morning or afternoon	AM or PM
GREETING_TIME	General time of day	Morning, Afternoon, or Evening
HOUR	Hour on a 12-hour scale	1 through 12
HOUR24	Hour on a 24-hour scale	00 through 24 (00=Midnight)
MINUTE	Minute	00 through 59
SECOND	Second	00 through 59

Table 6.9 lists each of the miscellaneous identifier variables.

TABLE 6.9 *Miscellaneous Identifier Variables*

IDENTIFIER VARIABLE	DESCRIPTION	EXAMPLE OR VALUES
<DOS variable>	Any DOS variable, such as PATH, PROMPT, etc. Must be enclosed in angle brackets. If in a MAP command, this variable must also be preceded by a percent sign (%).	Example: MAP S16:=%<PATH>
%n	Variable for LOGIN parameters, such as server name and user name.	Example: IF %1 = "Joel" THEN...
ACCESS_SERVER	Displays whether the access server is online.	Values: TRUE (functioning) or FALSE (not functioning)
ERROR_LEVEL	An error number.	Values: Any error number (0=No errors)

LOGIN SCRIPT EXAMPLE

The following is an example of a system (container) login script.

```
MAP DISPLAY OFF

IF "%1"="ADMIN" THEN

MAP *1:=SERVER1_SYS:SYSTEM

ELSE MAP *1:=SERVER1_VOL1:USERS\%LOGIN_NAME

END


MAP INS S1:=SERVER1_SYS:PUBLIC

MAP INS S2:=SERVER1_SYS:PUBLIC\%MACHINE\%OS\%OS_
VERSION

COMSPEC=S2:COMMAND.COM

MAP S16:=VOL1:APPS\WORD

MAP S16:=VOL1:APPS\DATAB

IF MEMBER OF "Design" THEN

MAP ROOT S16:=VOL1:APPS\CAD

MAP *2:=VOL1:DESIGNS\PROJECTA

MAP *3:=VOL1:DESIGNS\PROJECTB

END

IF MEMBER OF "Field" THEN

MAP S16:=VOL1:APPS\CDBASE

MAP *4:=VOL1:REPORTS\CLIENTS\NEW

END
```

```
#CAPTURE L=1 Q=.LaserQ.RedHawk NB NT NFF TI=5


MAP DISPLAY ON

MAP

WRITE "Good %GREETING_TIME, %LOGIN_NAME."


IF DAY_OF_WEEK="Monday" THEN

WRITE "It's a great week to design satellites!"

FIRE PHASERS 3 TIMES

END
```

The first line in the script

```
MAP DISPLAY OFF
```

turns off the display of any MAP commands as they're being executed during the login process. This simply keeps the screen from looking too busy and distracting or concerning the user.

The next group of four lines

```
IF "%1"="ADMIN" THEN

MAP *1:=SERVER1_SYS:SYSTEM

ELSE MAP *1:=SERVER1_VOL1:USERS\%LOGIN_NAME

END
```

maps the first network drive to a network directory. If the user who logs in is user Admin, then the first drive mapping is to the SYS:SYSTEM directory on server SERVER1. All other users who log in will get a drive mapped to their home directories on volume VOL1 instead.

The next line

```
MAP INS S1:=SERVER1_SYS:PUBLIC
```

maps the first search drive to the SYS:PUBLIC directory for all users. This is the directory where all NetWare utilities are stored, so it's important for users to have access to it.

The next two lines

```
MAP INS S2:=SERVER1_SYS:PUBLIC\%MACHINE\%OS\%OS_
VERSION

COMSPEC=S2:COMMAND.COM
```

map a search drive to the directory that contains DOS so that users can run DOS from the network instead of from the local hard disk. For every version of DOS your users will run on their machines, you should create a unique DOS directory, named with the workstation's machine type, DOS type, and DOS version, and load that version of DOS in the version subdirectory. For example, if your user is running an IBM compatible computer with MS-DOS version 6.2 on it, the DOS directory would be

```
SYS:PUBLIC\IBM_PC\MSDOS\6.20
```

The login script command, which uses identifier variables in the directory path, will gather the workstation's particular information and map a drive to the correct directory.

The next two lines

```
MAP S16:=VOL1:APPS\WORD

MAP S16:=VOL1:APPS\DATAB
```

map search drives to two application directories so that users can access them.

The next five lines execute only if the user logging in is a member of the group called "Design." If so, then a fake root search drive is mapped to the CAD subdirectory, and regular network drives are mapped to two subdirectories: PROJECTA and PROJECTB.

```
IF MEMBER OF "Design" THEN

MAP ROOT S16:=VOL1:APPS\CAD

MAP *2:=VOL1:DESIGNS\PROJECTA

MAP *3:=VOL1:DESIGNS\PROJECTB

END
```

The next four lines

```
IF MEMBER OF "Field" THEN

MAP S16:=VOL1:APPS\CDBASE

MAP *4:=VOL1:REPORTS\CLIENTS\NEW

END
```

execute only if the user logging in is a member of the group called "Field." These users, who are field sales people, get a search drive mapped to their CDBASE application and a regular network drive mapped to the NEW subdirectory where they log new clients.

The next line

```
#CAPTURE L=1 Q=.LaserQ.RedHawk NB NT NFF TI=5
```

captures the workstation's LPT1 port to a network print queue named LaserQ. Its full NDS name is given in this case (.LaserQ.Sales.Satellite.RedHawk). The full name isn't necessary if the print queue is in the same context as the user logging in. The NB parameter means "No Banner," the NT parameter means "No Tabs," NFF means "No Form Feed," and TI=5 means that the capture will time out after five seconds, if necessary.

The next line turns MAP's display back on:

```
MAP DISPLAY ON
```

The next line displays a list of all the drive mappings that have been successfully mapped during the login process:

```
MAP
```

The next line displays a greeting to the user, such as "Good MORNING, ERIC."

```
WRITE "Good %GREETING_TIME, %LOGIN_NAME."
```

The final four lines

```
IF DAY_OF_WEEK="Monday" THEN

WRITE "It's a great week to design satellites!"
```

```
FIRE PHASERS 3 TIMES

END
```

execute only on Mondays. They display a supposedly inspirational message to the user and make the phaser sound three times as the login script ends.

Using Menus

Another way you can automate a user's working environment is to use a menu program. With a menu program, you can allow a user to choose items such as e-mail or word-processing programs from a menu. This way, the user does not ever have to see the DOS prompt or learn to execute commands.

NetWare allows you to create a simple menu program by using the NMENU utilities. NMENU is a pared-down version of Saber Software Corporation's Saber Menu System for DOS. If the menu programs you want to create are fairly simple, you can use the NMENU utilities. If you want to create more complex menu programs, you may want to get the complete Saber products or another third-party menu system.

You can use NMENU to create a new menu program for your users. In addition, if you are using a menu program you created with the older MENU utility included in NetWare 3.11 and earlier, NMENU can convert those old menu programs into the new NMENU format.

CREATING A NEW MENU PROGRAM

To create a new menu program, complete the steps in the following checklist:

1. Create a program directory on the network to hold the menu program files. You can name it anything you like. If you create the directory under SYS:PUBLIC, users' search drives will be able to find the directory, which can help simplify matters.
2. Create another directory that will hold the temporary files that the menu program will generate. This directory can be located either on the network or on each user's hard disk. It can be named anything you want.
3. Use a text editor to create a text file containing the appropriate menu commands. (Menu commands are explained in the "NMENU Program Commands" section.) You must save the file with the file name extension .SRC.

4. Use the MENUMAKE utility to compile the text file into a program file. If the file name of the text file is DESIGN.SRC, enter the following command (leave off the file's extension when you type its name):

```
MENUMAKE DESIGN
```

5. If necessary, set up drive mappings in login scripts to the program and temporary directories so that users can access them. (See the "MAP Command" section earlier in this chapter for more information about mapping drives.)
6. If the directory for the user's temporary files is in a network directory, add SET commands to the user or system login script to point to the directories and indicate the workstation's connection number. (You don't need to use SET login script commands if the files are on the local disk.) For example, if the directory is called MENUTEMP under SYS:PUBLIC, add the following commands to the login script:

```
SET S_FILEDIR="Z:\PUBLIC\MENUTEMP\"
SET S_FILE="%STATION"
```

7. To execute the menu program from the DOS command line, use the NMENU utility. For example, to execute the DESIGN menu program, enter the command:

```
NMENU DESIGN
```

8. If you want users to enter the menu program automatically when their login scripts finish executing, add the EXIT command to the end of the login script, as shown here (remember to enclose the execution command in quotation marks in the EXIT command):

```
EXIT "NMENU DESIGN"
```

UPGRADING AN OLD MENU PROGRAM

A different menu system was used in NetWare 3.11 and earlier versions. If you have a menu program you created using the older MENU utility (whose files have the extension .MNU), you can upgrade those programs to the new NMENU program.

To upgrade an older menu file, complete the steps in the following checklist:

1. Create a program directory on the network to hold the menu program files. You can name it anything you like. If you create the directory under SYS:PUBLIC, users' search drives will be able to find the directory,

which can help simplify matters. (If you already have a directory for your existing menu programs, you can use that directory.)

2. Create another directory that will hold the temporary files that the menu program will generate. This directory can be located either on the network or on each user's hard disk. It can be named anything you want. (If you already have a directory for your existing menu programs, you can use that directory.)
3. Use the MENUCNVT utility to convert the old menu file. The utility will create a new file with the file name extension .SRC and will leave the old .MNU file unchanged. To convert a menu file called ACCOUNT.MNU, for example, enter the following command (leave off the file's extension when you type its name):

   ```
   MENUCNVT ACCOUNT
   ```
4. If necessary, use a text editor to edit the new .SRC file to add any new commands or options.
5. Use the MENUMAKE utility to compile the .SRC file into a program file. For example, enter the following command:

   ```
   MENUMAKE ACCOUNT
   ```
6. If necessary, set up drive mappings in login scripts to the program and temporary directories so that users can access them. (See the "MAP Command" section earlier in this chapter for more information about mapping drives.)
7. If the directory for the user's temporary files is in a network directory, add SET commands to the user or system login script to point to the directories and indicate the workstation's connection number. (You don't need to use SET login script commands if the files are on the local disk.) For example, if the directory is called MENUTEMP under SYS:PUBLIC, add the following commands to the login script:

   ```
   SET S_FILEDIR="Z:\PUBLIC\MENUTEMP\"
   SET S_FILE="%STATION"
   ```
8. To execute the menu program from the DOS command line, use the NMENU utility. For example, to execute the ACCOUNT menu program, enter the following command:

   ```
   NMENU ACCOUNT
   ```

9. If you want users to enter the menu program automatically when their login scripts finish executing, add the EXIT command to the end of the login script, as shown here (remember to enclose the execution command in quotation marks in the EXIT command):

```
EXIT "NMENU ACCOUNT"
```

NMENU PROGRAM COMMANDS

The following sections describe several different commands you can use to create menu program files for your users.

MENU Command

Command Format MENU *number*, *name*

Description: Identifies the heading of a menu or submenu. The *number* is a unique number that is assigned to this menu or submenu so that other commands in the program file can reference it. The *name* is the title of the menu or submenu and can be up to 40 characters long. Type it as you want it to display on the user's screen.

Example: MENU 1, Design Group

ITEM Command

Command Format ITEM *name* {*option option* ...}

Description: Names an option that will be displayed in the menu. The *name* is the text that will actually appear on this line of the menu. Type it as you want it to display on the user's screen. You can include one or more *options* inside a single pair of braces, separating each option with a space. The following options are available:

- BATCH — Removes the menu program from the workstation's memory before executing the command or application called for by this option. BATCH automatically sets the CHDIR option. Do not use the EXEC DOS command with this option.
- CHDIR — Changes the workstation back to the menu's original drive and directory after the command or application executed by the ITEM command is finished.
- PAUSE — Pauses the executing command or application so that the user can read any messages displayed on the screen. The message "Press any key to continue" appears.
- SHOW — Displays the name of the DOS command being executed by this ITEM command.

Example: ITEM Spreadsheet {CHDIR}

EXEC Command

Command Format EXEC *command*

Description: Executes the commands necessary to run the command or application being called by the ITEM option. For *command*, use the regular executable command that normally executes the application, command, or utility, such as "WP" for WordPerfect for DOS.

You can also use three EXEC commands that are specific to the menu program:

- EXEC DOS — Temporarily takes users out of the menu program and sends them to the DOS prompt. When finished working in DOS, users type EXIT to return to the menu.
- EXEC EXIT — Exits the menu program and sends the users to DOS.
- EXEC LOGOUT — Logs the user out of the network.

Example: EXEC wp

SHOW Command

Command Format SHOW *number*

Description: Calls the submenu (identified by the *number*) to be displayed when the user chooses this option from the menu.

Example: SHOW 2

LOAD Command

Command Format LOAD *filename*

Description: Calls and displays a completely different menu program as a submenu. In the LOAD command, specify the *filename* of the NMENU file and make sure that the menu program being called is located in the workstation's current directory or in a directory that has a search drive mapped to it. (The following example calls the ACCOUNT menu file to be displayed.)

Example: LOAD ACCOUNT

GETx Command

Command Format GETx *text {prepend} length, default, {append}*

Description: Requests input from the user before continuing the execution of a menu option. There are three different variations of this command:

- GETR — Requests input that is required.
- GETO — Requests input that is optional. This command can also be used to allow the user to press any key to continue.

- GETP — Requests input and assigns a variable to it so that the input can be reused.

  For *text*, insert the text you want displayed (up to 40 characters long), such as

  ```
  Enter your password:
  ```

  For *prepend* and *append*, insert any values that should be automatically added by the menu program to the beginning and ending of the user's input. If no values are needed, put a space in between the braces.

  For *length*, insert the maximum number of characters that the user can input. Enter 0 if you want the user to press any key to continue.

  For *default*, insert any default response that will be displayed, which users can either select or replace with their own response. If you do not want to supply a default value, leave out the value but still use the separating commas, as shown in the example below.

Example: GETR Enter your password: { } 12,, { }

EXAMPLE OF AN NMENU MENU PROGRAM

Figure 6.1 shows a sample menu program that is executed whenever someone in the Design group logs in.

FIGURE 6.1

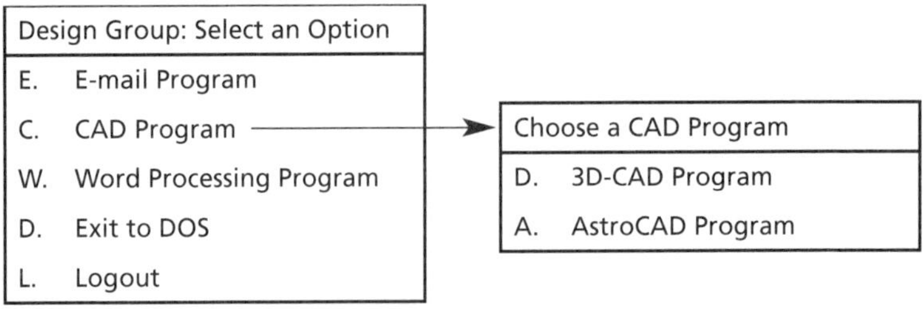

The source file to produce the menu program illustrated in Figure 6.1 would be as follows:

```
MENU 1, Design Group: Select an Option
     ITEM ^E-Email Program
     GETR Enter your e-mail name: { } 8,, { }
```

```
    EXEC mail
    ITEM ^CCAD Program
    SHOW 2
    ITEM ^WWord Processing Program
    EXEC WP
    ITEM ^DExit to DOS
    EXEC DOS
    ITEM ^LLogout
    EXEC LOGOUT

MENU 2, Choose a CAD Program
    ITEM ^D3D-CAD Program
    EXEC 3dcad
    ITEM ^AAstroCAD Program
    EXEC astro
```

In this menu source file, notice the formatting conventions:

- Each section of the file that pertains to a different menu or submenu is separated from the rest of the file by a blank line.
- Commands for each option in the menu are indented.
- Each ITEM command is followed by the EXEC command that executes that option. For example, for the imaginary CAD program called AstroCAD, the executable command is "astro," which is entered in the EXEC command.
- If you want users to be able to select an option by typing a single character (in addition to being able to use the up and down arrow keys to move to the option), add a caret (^) and the letter that should be typed to the beginning of the ITEM command. The caret will not appear on the screen.
- Under the E-mail Program option, the GETR command asks the user

to enter an e-mail name. The text "Enter your e-mail name:" appears on the screen. Because there are no values you need to add automatically to either the beginning or the end of the user's e-mail name, both pairs of braces contain only a single space. The maximum length for an e-mail name in this e-mail system is eight characters, so 8 is entered in the length field. Finally, because you do not need to specify a default user name, you enter a comma instead of a default value.

CHAPTER 7

Network Security

Using Login Security

- To create account restrictions, use the NetWare Administrator utility (which runs in Windows, OS/2, or Windows 95).
- To set or change passwords, use the NetWare Administrator utility, the LOGIN utility, or SETPASS (a command-line utility).

Using NDS Security

- To view or change NDS rights, use the NetWare Administrator utility.

Using Directory and File Security

- To view or change file system rights, use the NetWare Administrator utility or RIGHTS (a command-line utility).
- To view or change directory and file attributes, use the NetWare Administrator utility or FLAG (a command-line utility).

Securing the Network from Intruders

- To use NCP Packet Signature, use both the SET command on the server and the NET.CFG file on the workstation, or use the advanced parameters of the Network Neighborhood Client32 property page on Windows 95 workstations.
- To set Intruder Detection, use the NetWare Administrator utility.
- To lock the server console, use MONITOR.NLM.
- To remove DOS and prevent NLMs from being loaded from insecure areas, use the SECURE CONSOLE console utility.

One of the aspects of NetWare that sets it apart from other network operating systems is its high levels of security. How you implement this security is up to you. You can make your NetWare network as open as you need or as secure as Fort Knox.

NetWare uses several different types of security mechanisms that enable you to have control over your network's security. Those types of security are as follows:

- Login security, which ensures that only authorized users can log in to the network
- NDS security, which controls whether NDS objects, such as users, can see or manipulate other NDS objects and their properties
- File system security, which controls whether users can see and work with files and directories
- Intruder detection, which automatically detects someone trying to break into an account and locks them out
- NCP Packet Signature, which prevents fraudulent packets from being forged on a network
- Server protection, which includes ways to prevent unauthorized users from accessing the server

Each of these types of security is described in this chapter.

Login Security

Login security ensures that only authorized users can get into the network in the first place. Login security means that users are required to have valid user accounts and valid passwords. You can also use account restrictions to limit the number of times users can log in, the workstations they can use, and such things as the length of their passwords and how frequently they must change their passwords.

ACCOUNT RESTRICTIONS

With account restrictions, you can limit how a user can log in to the network. Table 7.1 shows the four different types of account restrictions you can implement.

TABLE 7.1 *Account Restrictions*

RESTRICTION	DESCRIPTION
Login Restrictions	Control whether the account has an expiration date (which might be useful in situations such as schools, where the authorized users will change with each semester) and whether the user can be logged in from multiple workstations simultaneously.
Password Restrictions	Control whether passwords are required, how often they must be changed, whether they must be unique so that users can't reuse them, and how many grace logins a user can have before being locked out of the account.
Login Time Restrictions	Control the times of day by which users must be logged out of the network. By default, users can be logged in at any time; there are no restrictions.
Network Address Restrictions	Control which network addresses (workstations) a user can use to log in. By default, there are no restrictions on addresses.

You can set each of these types of account restrictions for individual users, or you can set them in a user template so that they apply to all users you create in a particular container. If you set them up in a user template, the restrictions will apply to any new users you create from that point on. They aren't retrofitted to users that already exist. Managing account restrictions for all new users in a user template can save you time if all your users need the same types of restrictions.

To set account restrictions, use the NetWare Administrator utility. (For instructions on setting up the NetWare Administrator utility on a workstation, see Chapter 6.)

To set account restrictions for a single user, use the NetWare Administrator utility and select the User object. Then select Details from the Object menu, open the appropriate information pages, and specify the restrictions you want. (Each type of account restriction has its own Information page.)

To set account restrictions for all new users that you create, use the NetWare Administrator utility and select the appropriate Template object. Then select Details from the Object menu, open the appropriate restriction pages, and specify the correct restrictions. (Changes to the Template object apply only to users you create subsequently. These changes will not apply to users that already exist.) For more information about using Template objects, see Chapter 6.

PASSWORDS

If passwords are to be a useful form of security, you should ensure that they are being used, that users are changing them frequently, and that users aren't choosing easily guessed passwords.

The following tips can help preserve password security:

- Require passwords to be at least five characters long (seven or eight are better). Five characters is the default minimum.
- Require that passwords be changed every 30 days or less.
- Require unique passwords so that users can't reuse a password they've used before.
- Do not allow unlimited grace logins. Limit the number of grace logins to three.
- Tell users to avoid choosing passwords that can be easily guessed, such as birthdays, favorite hobbies or sports, family member names, pet names, and so on.
- Remind users not to tell others their passwords or allow others to use their accounts.
- Tell users to mix words and numbers together to form words that can't be found in a dictionary, such as BRAVO42 or STAR2CLOUD.

To set password restrictions for a user or a user template, use the NetWare Administrator utility and select the User (or User Template) object. Then open the Details screen, select the Password Restrictions page, and enter the restrictions you want to apply to the user or the template.

Users can change their own passwords by entering the command

```
SETPASS
```

at the DOS prompt or by using the Password Restrictions page in the NetWare Administrator utility. More often, however, users will change their passwords when the LOGIN utility informs them that their passwords have expired and offers them the opportunity to type in new passwords.

NDS Security

Once you've created your NDS tree, you've probably invested a fair amount of time in making sure that the objects you've created contain all the right information in their properties. Now you can decide who gets to see that information and who can change it.

To make the information about the objects in your tree secure, you can use NDS trustee rights to control how objects in the tree can work with other objects and their properties. *NDS trustee rights* are permissions that allow users or objects to perform tasks such as viewing other objects, changing their properties, deleting them, and so on.

When you assign a user enough NDS trustee rights to work with another object, you've made that user a *trustee* of the object. Each object contains a property called the Access Control List (ACL), which is a list of all the trustees of this particular object.

When the network is first installed, the user Admin has all NDS trustee rights to all objects in the tree. This means that when you log in as user Admin, Admin's NDS trustee rights let you create and delete other objects, see them, read and modify all their properties, and so on. Admin is the only user who has full NDS rights to everything in the network immediately after installation. However, while logged in as Admin, you can grant other users the same NDS rights, so that they can have the same privileges as Admin. By default, users are granted only a subset of NDS rights, so they have limited abilities to work with other objects. You can add to or remove these NDS rights to customize your users' abilities.

For security reasons, you should be frugal with NDS rights. NDS rights are a tool to protect your network objects from both accidental and intentional tampering. You may want to assign two users to have full NDS rights to the network, such as Admin and another user account that only you can use. This way, there is a backup account you can use if, for example, you forget the Admin's password or delete the Admin user.

There are two types of NDS trustee rights. *Object rights* control how the user works with the object. These are listed in Table 7.2.

Property rights control whether the user can see and work with an object's properties. These are listed in Table 7.3.

To change object or property rights, see the "Seeing and Changing an Object's NDS Rights" section later in this chapter.

TABLE 7.2 *NDS Object Rights*

NDS OBJECT RIGHT	DESCRIPTION
Supervisor	Grants the trustee all NDS rights to the object and all of its properties. It can be blocked by the Inherited Rights Filter (explained in the next section).

TABLE 7.2 *NDS Object Rights (continued)*

NDS OBJECT RIGHT	DESCRIPTION
Browse	Allows the trustee to see the object in the NDS tree.
Create	Allows the trustee to create a new object in this container. (This right appears only if you're looking at the trustee assignments for a container object.)
Delete	Allows the trustee to delete an object.
Rename	Allows the trustee to change the object's name.

TABLE 7.3 *NDS Property Rights*

NDS PROPERTY RIGHT	DESCRIPTION
Supervisor	Grants the trustee all NDS rights to the property. It can be blocked by the Inherited Rights Filter (explained in the next section).
Compare	Allows the trustee to compare the value of this property with a value the user specifies in a search. (For example, with the Compare right to the Department property, a user can search the tree for any object that has Marketing listed in its Department property.)
Read	Allows the trustee to see the value of this property. (The Read right automatically grants the Compare right, as well.)
Write	Allows the trustee to add, modify, or delete the value of this property. (The Write right automatically grants the Add or Delete Self right, as well.)
Add or Delete Self	Allows trustees to add or remove themselves as a value of this property. This right applies only to properties that list User objects as values, such as group membership lists or the Access Control List.

INHERITING NDS RIGHTS

NDS object and property rights can be inherited. This means that if you have NDS rights to a parent container, you can inherit those rights and exercise them in an object within that container, too. Inheritance keeps you from having to grant users NDS rights at every level of the Directory tree.

However, it is sometimes desirable to block inheritance. For example, you may want to allow a user to delete objects in a parent container, but not let that user delete any objects in a particular subcontainer. Inheritance can be blocked in two ways:

- By granting a new set of NDS rights to an object within the container. Any new assignment will cause the inherited NDS rights from a parent container to be ignored. You can grant a new set of rights using the NetWare Administrator utility, as explained later in this chapter.
- By removing the right from an object's Inherited Rights Filter (IRF). Every object has an Inherited Rights Filter that specifies which NDS rights can be inherited from a parent container. By default, an object's IRF allows all NDS rights to be inherited. You can change the IRF, however, to revoke one or more NDS rights. Any rights that are revoked from the IRF cannot be inherited.

NOTE

The NetWare Administrator utility prevents you from cutting off all supervisor access to a branch of the NDS tree accidentally. It does this by searching for an object with Supervisor rights to the given container. If an object with Supervisor rights isn't found, NetWare Administrator warns you and prevents you from blocking rights.

You can inherit an NDS right only if you've been assigned that right at a higher level. If you don't have the Supervisor right in the parent container, for example, you can't inherit it and use it in another object even though that right is allowed in the IRF. The IRF doesn't grant NDS rights; it just allows you to inherit them if they've already been assigned to you.

When you assign a user property rights to an object's properties (by using the NetWare Administrator utility), you can click the All Properties button, which is a quick way to give the user the same property rights to all the properties of that object. Alternatively, you can choose Selected Properties and give the user different property rights to each individual property. If you select All Properties, those property rights can be inherited. Property rights assigned to only specific properties cannot be inherited.

NDS SECURITY EQUIVALENCE

You can assign one object to have the same NDS rights as another object by using the Security Equal To property. With security equivalence, you can make user Lila have the same NDS rights to the same NDS objects as user Erica, for example. (In fact, Lila will also receive the same file system rights as Erica, too. File system rights are explained later in this chapter.)

When you add a user to a Group object's membership list or to an Organizational Role object's list, the user really becomes security equivalent to that Group or Organizational Role object.

When you are given *security equivalence* to another user, you receive only the same NDS rights that the other user was explicitly granted. You do not get equivalences to that other user's equivalences. In other words, security equivalence doesn't travel. If Lila is equivalent to Erica, and Erica is equivalent to Jess, Lila doesn't end up being equivalent to Jess, too. Lila receives only whatever rights Erica received explicitly.

EFFECTIVE NDS RIGHTS

Because a user can be given NDS rights to an object and its properties through a variety of methods (explicit assignment, security equivalence, and inheritance), it can be confusing to determine exactly what NDS rights the user really has. A user's *effective NDS rights* are the NDS rights that the user can ultimately execute. The user's effective rights to an object are determined in one of two ways.

- The user's inherited NDS rights from a parent container, minus any rights blocked by the object's IRF.
- The sum of all NDS rights granted to the user for that object through direct trustee assignments and security equivalences to other objects. The IRF does not affect direct trustee assignments and security equivalences.

For example, suppose user Joanna has been given the Browse right to a container object. Joanna has also been given a security equivalence to user Eric, who has Create, Delete, and Rename rights to the same container. This means Joanna's effective NDS rights to this container are now Browse, Create, Delete, and Rename. Even if the container's IRF blocks the Delete right, Joanna still has that right. This is because the IRF affects only inherited rights, and inherited rights are completely ignored if the user has explicit trustee assignments to an object or a security equivalence that gives her NDS rights to that object.

SEEING AND CHANGING AN OBJECT'S NDS RIGHTS

To see the trustees of an object, use the NetWare Administrator utility (which runs in Windows). From the NetWare Administrator's Browser, select the object whose list of trustees you want to see, and then choose Trustees of

This Object from the Object menu. (You can also click the right mouse button to bring up a menu that contains some of the more frequently used tasks, and select Trustees of This Object from that menu.)

The Trustees of This Object screen appears, and you can see all the trustees of this object, as shown in Figure 7.1. If you click on each trustee, you can see the specific NDS object and property rights belonging to that trustee. You can also add or delete NDS rights from that trustee by marking the check boxes next to each right.

FIGURE 7.1 *The Trustees of this Object Screen*

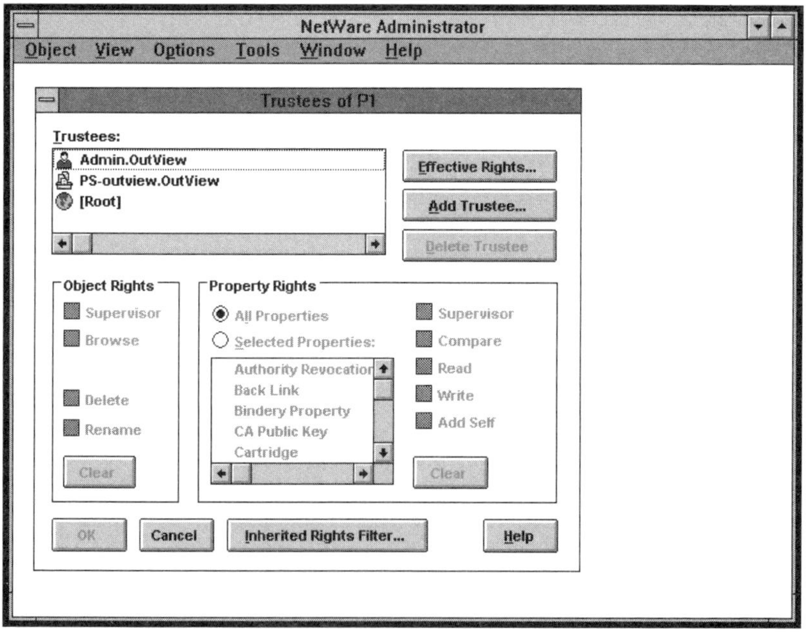

In addition, in this screen you can see the object's Inherited Rights Filter. By default, any object or property rights can be inherited from the parent object. If you want to block an NDS right from being inherited, click on the check box next to the right to clear its box.

If you want to see all the objects that a particular object has NDS rights to, use the NetWare Administrator's Browser and select the object. Then, from the Object menu, choose Rights to Other Objects (or click the right mouse button and select the same option from the menu that appears). Specify the name context (location in the NDS tree) that you want to search for other objects. Then, the Rights to Other Objects screen appears, as shown in Figure 7.2.

FIGURE 7.2 *The Rights to Other Objects Screen*

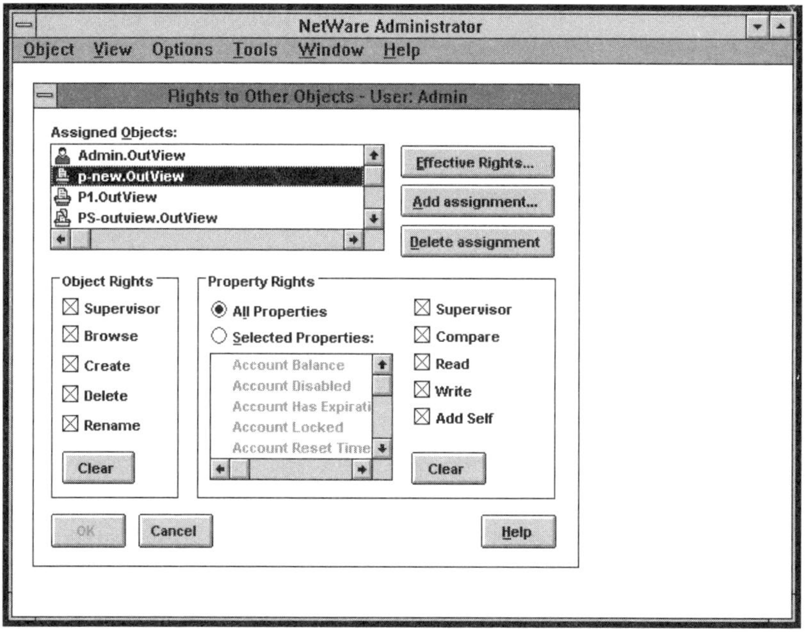

To see or change a user's security equivalence, use the NetWare Administrator's Browser and select the user. Then, from the Object menu, select Details, and then choose the Security Equal To page. There, you can add or delete other objects to which this user has a security equivalence.

File System Security

File system security ensures that users can access and use only the files and directories you want them to see and use. There are two different types of security tools you can implement in the file system, either together or separately, to protect your files:

- File system trustee rights, which you assign to users and groups. Just as NDS object rights and NDS property rights control what users can do with other objects, file system trustee rights control what each user or group can do with the file or directory.
- Attributes, which you can assign directly to files and directories. Unlike file system rights, which are specific to different users and groups, attributes belong to the file or directory, and they control the activities of all users, regardless of those users' file trustee rights.

The next few sections explain file system trustee rights. File and directory attributes are explained in the "File and Directory Attributes" section later in this chapter.

FILE SYSTEM TRUSTEE RIGHTS

File system trustee rights allow users and groups to work with files and directories in specific ways. Each right determines whether a user can do things such as see, read, change, rename, or delete the file or directory. When a file system right is assigned to a file, the right affects the user's allowable actions in only that file. When a file system right is assigned to a directory, the right affects the user's allowable actions on that particular directory and in all the files within that directory.

Although file system rights are similar in nature to the NDS rights for objects and properties (described earlier in this chapter), they are not the same thing. File system rights are separate from NDS rights. They affect only how users work with files and directories. NDS rights affect how users work with other NDS objects.

The only place where NDS rights and file system rights overlap is at the NetWare Server object. If a user is granted the Supervisor object right to a Server object, that user is also granted the Supervisor file system right to any volumes attached to that server. Therefore, because user Admin has full NDS rights to all objects in the tree after the installation (although you can limit Admin's rights later), user Admin has the Supervisor file system right to the entire file system, too.

There are eight different file system trustee rights. You can assign any combination of those file system rights to a user or group, depending on how you want that user or group to work.

Table 7.4 lists the available file system rights and explains what each right means when assigned for a directory and for a file.

TABLE 7.4 *File System Rights*

FILE SYSTEM RIGHT	ABBREVIATION	DESCRIPTION
Read	R	Directory: Allows the trustee to open and read files in the directory. File: Allows the trustee to open and read the file.
Write	W	Directory: Allows the trustee to open and write to (change) files in the directory. File: Allows the trustee to open and write to the file.
Create	C	Directory: Allows the trustee to create subdirectories and files in the directory. File: Allows the trustee to salvage the file if it was deleted.
Erase	E	Directory: Allows the trustee to delete the directory and its files and subdirectories. File: Allows the trustee to delete the file.
Modify	M	Directory: Allows the trustee to change the name, directory attributes, and file attributes of the directory and its files and subdirectories. File: Allows the trustee to change the file's name or file attributes.
File Scan	F	Directory: Allows the trustee to see the names of the files and subdirectories within the directory. File: Allows the trustee to see the name of the file.

(continued)

TABLE 7.4 *File System Rights (continued)*

FILE SYSTEM RIGHT	ABBREVIATION	DESCRIPTION
Access Control	A	Directory: Allows the trustee to change the directory's IRF and trustee assignments. File: Allows the trustee to change the file's IRF and trustee assignments.
Supervisor	S	Directory: Grants the trustee all rights to the directory, its files, and its subdirectories. It cannot be blocked by an IRF. File: Grants the trustee all rights to the file. It cannot be blocked by an IRF.

Inheriting File System Rights

Just like NDS rights, file system rights can be inherited. This means that if you have file system rights to a parent directory, you can inherit those rights and exercise them in any file and subdirectory within that directory, too. Inheritance keeps you from having to grant users file system rights at every level of the file system.

Inheritance can be blocked by granting a new set of file system rights to a subdirectory or file within the parent directory. Any new assignment will cause the inherited rights from a parent directory to be ignored.

You can also block inheritance by removing the right from a file or a subdirectory's Inherited Rights Filter. Every directory and file has an Inherited Rights Filter, which specifies which file system rights can be inherited from a parent directory. By default, a file or directory's IRF allows all rights to be inherited. You can change the IRF, however, to revoke one or more rights. Any file system rights that are revoked from the IRF cannot be inherited.

You can inherit a file system right only if you've been assigned that right at a higher level. If you don't have the Create right in the parent directory, for example, you can't inherit it and use it in another subdirectory even though that right is allowed in the IRF. The IRF doesn't grant rights; it just allows you to inherit file system rights if they've already been assigned to you at a higher level.

For instructions on assigning file system rights or changing the IRF, see the "Seeing and Changing a User's File System Rights" section later in this chapter.

File System Security Equivalence

Security equivalence for file system rights works the same way as security equivalence for NDS rights (explained earlier in this chapter). You can assign one user to have the same NDS rights and file system rights as another user by using the Security Equal To property. With security equivalence, you can make user Lila have the same rights to the same NDS objects, files, and directories as user Erica, for example.

When you add a user to a Group object's membership list or to an Organizational Role object's list, the user becomes security equivalent to that Group or Organizational Role object.

When you are given security equivalence to another user, you receive only the same rights that the other user was explicitly granted. You do not get equivalences to that user's other equivalences. Security equivalence doesn't travel. If Lila is equivalent to Erica, and Erica is equivalent to Jess, Lila doesn't end up being equivalent to Jess, too. Lila receives only whatever rights Erica received explicitly.

Effective File System Rights

Just as with NDS rights, determining which file system rights a user can actually exercise in a file or directory can be confusing at first. A user's *effective file system rights* are the file system rights that the user can ultimately execute in a given directory or file. The user's effective rights to a directory or file are determined in one of two ways.

- The user's inherited rights from a parent directory, minus any rights blocked by the subdirectory or file's IRF
- The sum of all rights granted to the user for that directory or file, through direct trustee assignment and security equivalences to other users

A file or directory's IRF does not affect direct trustee assignments and security equivalences. Therefore, if you have been given an explicit trustee assignment in a file or directory, any rights you might have inherited from a parent directory will be completely ignored. On the other hand, if you have not been given an explicit trustee assignment or security equivalence that specifically gives you rights in a file or directory, you will automatically inherit any rights you had in a parent directory, minus any rights blocked by the IRF.

Seeing and Changing a User's File System Rights

To see a user's file system rights, you can use either the NetWare Administrator utility (from Windows) or the RIGHTS command-line utility.

To use the NetWare Administrator utility, you can either select a user and see the user's trustee assignments (a list of the files and directories of which that user is a trustee), or you can select a file or directory and see a list of all its trustees.

To see or change a user's trustee assignments, complete the following checklist.

1. From the NetWare Administrator's Browser, select the user and choose Details from the Object menu.
2. Open the Rights to Files and Directories page.
3. To see the user's current file system rights, you must first select a volume that contains directories to which the user has rights. To do this, click on the Show button. Then, in the Directory Context panel on the right side, navigate through the Directory tree to locate the desired volume. Select the volume from the Volumes panel on the left side, and then click OK.
4. Now, under the Files and Directories panel, a list appears showing all of the files and directories of which the user is *currently* a trustee, as shown in Figure 7.3. To see the user's assigned file system rights to one of these directories or files, select the directory or file, and then look at the list of rights below. An "X" in the check box next to each right means that the user has rights to this file or directory. To change the user's rights, click on each desired check box to either mark it or clear it.
5. To see the user's effective file system rights to this file or directory, click on the Effective Rights button.
6. To assign the user file system rights to a new file or directory, click on the Add button. In the Directory Context panel on the right side, navigate through the Directory tree to locate the desired volume or directory. Then, select the volume, directory, or file from the left panel, and click OK. Now the newly selected file, directory, or volume appears under the Files and Directories panel. Make sure the new file, directory, or volume is selected, and then assign the appropriate file system rights by marking each desired check box.
7. To see or change a user's security equivalence, open the user's Security Equal To page. There, you can add or delete other objects to which this user has a security equivalence. Remember that security equivalence affects both NDS and file system rights.

FIGURE 7.3 *Rights to Files and Directories*

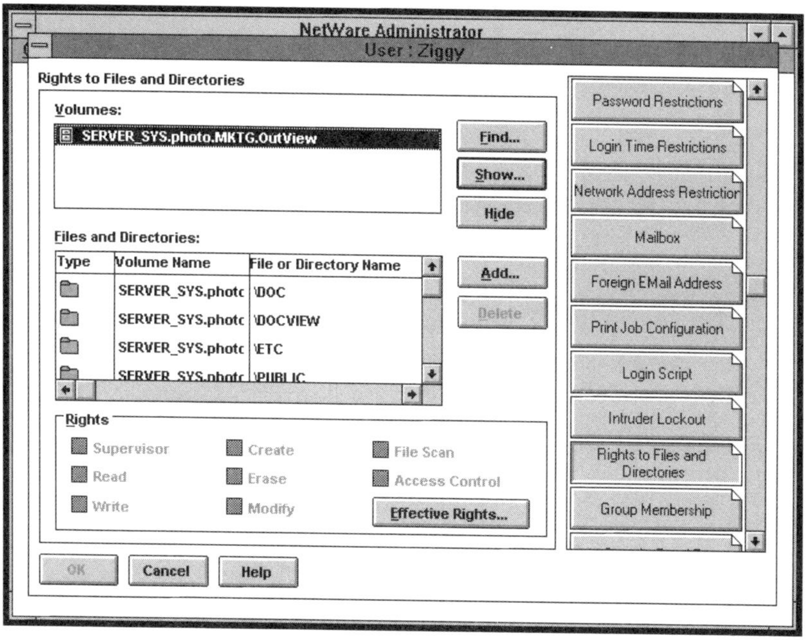

To use the NetWare Administrator utility to see all the trustees of a directory (or a file or volume), complete the following steps.

1. From the NetWare Administrator's Browser, select the directory and choose Details from the Object menu.
2. Open the Trustees of this Directory page. This page shows the containers and users that have trustee rights to this directory, as shown in Figure 7.4. This page also shows the directory's IRF. By default, the IRF allows any file system rights to be inherited from the parent directory.
3. To change the IRF to block a file system right from being inherited, click on the check box next to that right to clear its box.
4. To see a particular trustee's effective file system rights to the directory, click the Effective Rights button, and then select the trustee. (You can either type in the trustee's name or click the Browse button next to the Trustee field to navigate the NDS tree and select the trustee that way.) That trustee's effective rights will appear in bold type.

FIGURE 7.4 *Trustees of this Directory Page*

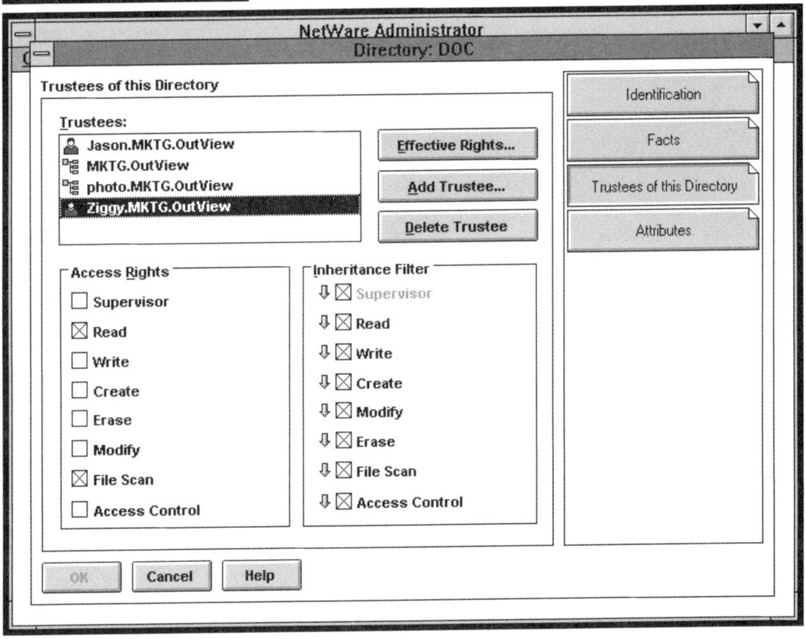

5. To add a trustee to the directory, click the Add Trustee button. Navigate through the Directory tree in the right panel, and then select the user you want from the Objects panel on the left side. That user now appears in the Trustees list. Select that user, and then mark the check boxes next to the file system rights you want the user to have.

To use the RIGHTS command-line utility to see a list of all the trustees with rights to a directory or file, use the following command format at the workstation's DOS prompt, replacing *path* with the path to the directory or file.

```
RIGHTS path /T
```

To use RIGHTS to see or change a user's current file system rights to a file or directory, use the following command:

```
RIGHTS path rights /option
```

For *path*, insert the path to the directory or file you want. To indicate the current directory, use a single period (.).

For *rights*, insert the list of rights you want to assign. (Use the rights' abbreviations and separate each one with a space.) If you want to add some rights to the existing rights already assigned, you can use the plus (+) sign in front of the abbreviation. To delete a right, leaving the others intact, use a minus (-) sign. To replace all existing rights with the ones you specify, don't use either sign. If you want to assign all available rights, use the word ALL instead of specifying individual attributes. If you want to revoke all rights from the specified trustee, use the letter N (for No Rights) instead of specifying individual attributes. To completely remove the trustee from the file or directory, use the word REM (for Remove).

For *options*, insert the options you want. The available options are listed in Table 7.5.

TABLE 7.5 *RIGHTS Options*

RIGHTS OPTION	DESCRIPTION
/C	Scrolls continuously through the display.
/F	Displays the IRF.
/I	Displays where the inherited rights are coming from.
/NAME=*name*	Displays or changes the rights for the specified user or group. (If the user or group is in a different name context in the NDS tree than the volume is, you will have to specify the user's complete NDS name.)
/S	Displays or changes all subdirectories below the current directory.
/T	Displays the trustee assignments for a directory.
/VER	Displays the version number of the RIGHTS utility.
/?	Displays help screens for the RIGHTS utility.

For example, if you want to see the list of trustees for the SYS:PUBLIC directory, which is mapped to search drive Z, you can use the following command:

```
RIGHTS Z: /T
```

at the workstation's DOS prompt.

To assign user Paul all available rights to the directory that is currently mapped to drive G (assuming Paul is in your own current name context), use the following command:

```
RIGHTS G: ALL /NAME=PAUL
```

To grant user Teresa (who is in a different name context than you) the Create, Erase, Modify, and File Scan rights to the REPORTS.2 file in the current directory, use the following command, specifying Teresa's full name:

```
RIGHTS G:REPORTS.2 CEMF /NAME=.TERESA.MKTG.OUTVIEW
```

For more examples of how to use RIGHTS, display the help screens for the utility with the following command:

```
RIGHTS /? ALL
```

FILE AND DIRECTORY ATTRIBUTES

Another important NetWare security tool for securing files and directories is attributes. *Attributes* are properties of files and directories that control what can happen to those files or directories. Attributes, which are also called *flags*, are different from trustee rights in several ways:

- Attributes are assigned directly to files and directories, while rights are assigned to users.
- Attributes override rights. In other words, if that directory has the Delete Inhibit attribute, you can't delete the directory even if you've been granted the Erase right.
- Likewise, attributes don't grant rights. Just because a file has the Read-Write attribute doesn't mean you can write to it if you don't have the Write right.
- Attributes affect all users, including the Admin user.
- Attributes affect some aspects of the file that rights do not, such as determining whether or not the files in a directory can be purged immediately upon deletion.

Kinds of File and Directory Attributes

There are eight attributes that apply to either files or directories. There are an additional eight that apply only to files. These attributes are listed in Table 7.6. The table also shows the abbreviations used for each attribute (when using the FLAG command) and whether the attribute applies to both directories and files or only to files. The FLAG command is discussed in the following section "Assigning File and Directory Attributes."

TABLE 7.6 *File and Directory Attributes*

ATTRIBUTE	ABBREVIATION	FILE	DIRECTORY	DESCRIPTION
Delete Inhibit	Di	X	X	Prevents users from deleting the file or directory.
Hidden	H	X	X	Hides the file or directory so it isn't listed by the DOS DIR command or in the Windows File Manager, and can't be copied or deleted.
Purge Immediate	P	X	X	Purges the file or directory immediately upon deletion. Purged files can't be salvaged.
Rename Inhibit	Ri	X	X	Prevents users from renaming the file or directory.
System	Sy	X	X	Indicates a system directory that may contain system files (such as DOS files). Prevents users from seeing, copying, or deleting the directory (however, does not assign the System attribute to the files in the directory).
Don't Migrate	Dm	X	X	Prevents a file or directory from being migrated to another storage device.

(continued)

TABLE 7.6 *File and Directory Attributes (continued)*

ATTRIBUTE	ABBREVIATION	FILE	DIRECTORY	DESCRIPTION
Immediate Compress	Ic	X	X	Compresses the file or directory immediately.
Don't Compress	Dc	X	X	Prevents the file or directory from being compressed.
Archive Needed	A	X		Indicates that the file has been changed since the last time it was backed up.
Execute Only	X	X		Prevents an executable file from being copied, modified, or deleted. Use with caution! Once assigned, it cannot be removed, so assign it only if you have a backup copy of the file. You may prefer to assign the Read-Only attribute instead of the Executable Only attribute.
Read-Write	Rw	X		Allows the file to be opened and modified. Most files are set to Read-Write by default.

TABLE 7.6 *File and Directory Attributes (continued)*

ATTRIBUTE	ABBREVIATION	FILE	DIRECTORY	DESCRIPTION
Read-Only	Ro	X		Allows the file to be opened and read, but not modified. All NetWare files in SYS:SYSTEM, SYS:PUBLIC, and SYS:LOGIN are Read-Only. Assigning the Read-Only attribute automatically assigns Delete Inhibit and Rename Inhibit.
Shareable	Sh	X		Allows the file to be used by more than one user simultaneously. Useful for utilities, commands, applications, and some database files. All NetWare files in SYS:SYSTEM, SYS:PUBLIC, and SYS:LOGIN are shareable. Most data and work files should not be shareable, so that users' changes do not conflict.
Transactional	T	X		When used on database files, allows NetWare's Transactional Tracking System (TTS) to protect the files from being corrupted if the transaction is interrupted.

(continued)

TABLE 7.6 *File and Directory Attributes (continued)*

ATTRIBUTE	ABBREVIATION	FILE	DIRECTORY	DESCRIPTION
Copy Inhibit	Ci	X		Prevents Macintosh files from being copied. (Does not apply to DOS files.)
Don't Suballocate	Ds	X		Prevents a file from being suballocated. Use on files, such as some database files, that may need to be enlarged or appended frequently. (See Chapter 8 for information on block suballocation.)

Assigning File and Directory Attributes

To assign attributes to a file or directory, you can use either the NetWare Administrator utility (which runs in Windows) or the FLAG command-line utility.

To use NetWare Administrator, select the file or directory and choose Details from the Object menu. Then select the Attributes page. The marked check boxes show which attributes have been assigned to the file or directory. To change the attributes, click on the check boxes to mark or unmark them.

To use the FLAG utility, use the following command format at the workstation's DOS prompt:

```
FLAG path attributes /options
```

For *path*, indicate the path to the directory or file whose attributes you're changing.

For *attributes*, insert the list of attributes you want to assign. Use the attributes' abbreviations and separate each one with a space. If you want to add an attribute to the existing attributes already assigned, you can use the plus (+) sign in front of the abbreviation. To delete an attribute from the file or directory, leaving the others intact, use a minus (-) sign. To replace all existing attributes with the ones you specify, don't use either sign. If you want to assign all available attributes, use the word ALL instead of specifying individual attributes. If you want to reset the attributes to the default settings, use the letter N (for Normal) instead of specifying individual attributes.

For *options*, insert the options you want. The available options are listed in Table 7.7.

TABLE 7.7 *FLAG Options*

FLAG OPTION	DESCRIPTION
/C	Scrolls continuously through the display.
/D	Displays details about the file or directory.
/DO	Displays or changes attributes for all subdirectories (no files) in the specified path.
/FO	Displays or changes attributes for all files (no subdirectories) in the specified path.
/M=*mode*	Changes the search mode for executable files. (Search modes are explained in Chapter 8.)
/NAME=*name*	Changes the owner of the file or directory.
/OWNER=*name*	Displays all files and directories owned by the specified user.
/S	Searches all subdirectories in the specified path.
/VER	Displays the version number of the FLAG utility.
/?	Displays help screens for the FLAG utility.

For example, to assign the Read-Only and Shareable attributes to the TEST.BAT file in the current directory, use the following command:

```
FLAG TEST.BAT RO SH
```

To add the Purge Immediate attribute to this same file, without removing the Read-Only and Shareable attributes, use the following command:

```
FLAG TEST.BAT +P
```

To reset the TEST.BAT file to its normal setting (the Read-Write attribute), use the following command:

```
FLAG TEST.BAT N
```

To see the attributes for the directory currently mapped to drive G, use the following command:

```
FLAG G: /DO
```

To see the help screens for FLAG (which contain more examples), use the following command:

```
FLAG /? ALL
```

Intruder Detection

NetWare can detect if a user is trying unsuccessfully to log in to the network. You can set the network so that users are locked out after a given number of failed login attempts. This helps ensure that users don't try to break into the network by simply guessing another user's password or by using programs that automatically generate passwords.

To set up intruder detection, you use the NetWare Administrator utility and assign intruder detection for a container. Then any user account within that container is subject to being locked if login attempts fail. To enable intruder detection, complete the steps in the following checklist.

1. From the NetWare Administrator's Browser, select the container for which you want to set up intruder detection and then choose Details from the Object menu.
2. Open the Intruder Detection page (shown in Figure 7.5).
3. To detect intruders, mark the Detect Intruders check box. Then specify the intruder detection limits. The Incorrect Login Attempts and Intruder Attempt Reset Interval let you to specify how many incorrect login attempts will be allowed in a given time. If you mark the Detect Intruders check box, the default values that appear allow seven incorrect attempts within a 30-minute interval. You may want to reduce the number of attempts to four or five, depending on how likely your network is to have such an intruder.
4. If you want the user's account to be locked after an intruder is detected, mark the Lock Account After Detection check box. Then specify how long you want the account to remain locked. The default locks the account for 15 minutes after the given number of failed login attempts. After 15 minutes, the account will be reopened automatically (intruder detection for that account will be reset). You may want to increase this time if you are concerned about intruders.

FIGURE 7.5 *Intruder Detection Page*

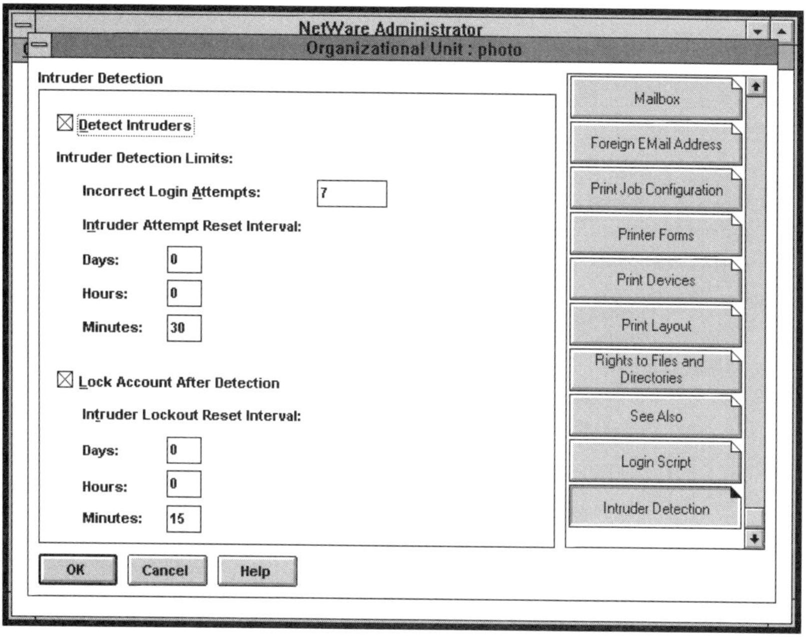

To see if a user's account has been locked, use the NetWare Administrator and select the user in question. Choose Details from the Object menu, and then open the user's Intruder Lockout page. This page shows whether the account is locked, as shown in Figure 7.6. If the Account Locked check box is marked, the account is locked. To unlock it, click the check box to clear it.

This page also shows the number of incorrect login attempts within the specified interval, when a user's account was locked, and the address of the workstation from which the failed login attempts were tried.

FIGURE 7.6 *Intruder Lockout Page*

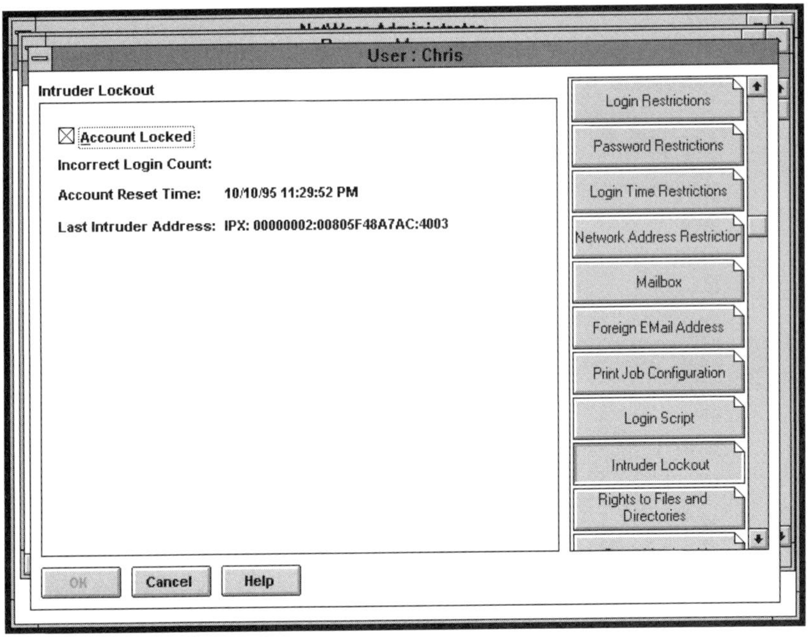

NCP Packet Signature

NCP Packet Signature is another feature designed to thwart intruders of a more persistent and knowledgeable type. NCP Packet Signature makes it impossible for someone to forge packets and access network resources through these forged packets. This feature requires workstations and servers to automatically "sign" each NCP packet with a signature and to change the signature for every packet.

NCP Packet Signature is an optional security feature. It can slow down network performance on busy networks, so you may prefer not to use packet signatures if your network is operating in a trusted environment with little threat of intruders stealing sensitive information.

There are four levels of NCP Packet Signature, which must be set on both workstations and servers. If the levels on the workstation and server don't form an allowable combination, the two computers will not be able to communicate with each other.

To set the signature level on a server, use SERVMAN.NLM to change the following SET command in the server's STARTUP.NCF or AUTOEXEC.NCF file.

```
SET NCP PACKET SIGNATURE OPTION=number
```

Replace *number* with the signature level (0 through 3) you want the server to use. After the server has been booted, you can execute the SET command at the server's console to increase the signature level. However, if you want to decrease the level, you have to add the SET command to the STARTUP.NCF or AUTOEXEC.NCF file (SERVMAN.NLM makes this easy to do) and reboot the server. Table 7.8 shows the NCP Packet Signature levels for servers.

TABLE 7.8 *Server Levels for NCP Packet Signature*

LEVEL	DESCRIPTION
0	Server does not sign packets.
1	Server signs packets only if workstation requests signature.
2	Server prefers to sign packets, but will allow access from workstations that cannot sign.
3	Server and workstation must both sign packets.

To set the signature level on DOS or Windows 3.1 workstations, add the following command to the NET.CFG file:

```
SIGNATURE LEVEL=number
```

Replace *number* with the signature level (0 through 3) you want the workstation to use. Table 7.9 shows the NCP Packet Signature levels for workstations.

For Windows 95 workstations running the NetWare Client32 software, set the signature level in the advanced parameters of the Client32 property page in the Network Neighborhood.

TABLE 7.9 *Workstation Levels for NCP Packet Signature*

LEVEL	DESCRIPTION
0	Workstation does not sign packets.
1	Workstation signs packets only if server requests signature.
2	Workstation prefers to sign packets, but will access a server that cannot sign.
3	Workstation and server must both sign packets.

Figure 7.7 shows how the signature levels on servers and workstations combine to either allow unsigned packets, force signed packets, or deny login.

FIGURE 7.7 *NCP Packet Signature Levels Combine to Allow or Deny Login*

Workstation Level

Server Level		0	1	2	3
	0	Unsigned	Unsigned	Unsigned	Log in Denied
	1	Unsigned	Unsigned	Signed	Signed
	2	Unsigned	Signed	Signed	Signed
	3	Log in Denied	Signed	Signed	Signed

Server Protection

An important aspect of network security is to make sure the server itself is secure from tampering. This is a simple task but is often overlooked, leaving the network vulnerable to either deliberate or accidental damage.

If the server is sitting in an area that is easily accessible and isn't protected with a keyboard lock or password, a malicious user can easily access the server and wreak havoc. Less dramatic, but potentially just as damaging, is the accidental tampering that could occur. A janitorial employee could unplug the server to plug in the vacuum cleaner; a helpful employee could try to load a virus-infected file directly on the server; another employee could try to "fix" a printing problem while you're not around and end up with a worse problem than the original one.

The following are some of the simple ways you can secure your server:

- Lock the server in a separate room. Just putting the server in a locked room can prevent much of the potential tampering that could occur.
- Lock the server's console with MONITOR.NLM. To do this, select Lock File Server Console from MONITOR's Available Options menu and type in a password to use to unlock the console (you'll have to type the password twice to verify it). Then, to unlock the console, you can either use the password you entered or the Admin user's password. (You may have to press any key to clear the screen saver first.) Use a different password each time you lock the console to ensure higher protection.
- Prevent loadable modules from being loaded from anywhere but SYS:SYSTEM by using the SECURE CONSOLE command at the server's console. Then make sure that only authorized users have rights to SYS:SYSTEM. Without SECURE CONSOLE enabled, an intruder could create an NLM that breaches security and load that NLM from the server's diskette drive or another directory where he or she has more rights than in SYS:SYSTEM. SECURE CONSOLE also prevents anyone from accessing the operating system's debugger and from changing the server's date and time. To remove SECURE CONSOLE, you must down the server and reboot it.
- Use a secure password for the Remote Console feature. When you load REMOTE.NLM, you're asked to enter a password (it can be any password you make up at this time). To use Remote Console, then, you have to enter that same password. Make sure the REMOTE.NLM password is secure, and change the password periodically by reloading REMOTE.NLM.
- Protect the server from electrical problems by installing an *uninterruptible power supply* (UPS). Because the UPS allows the server to close all its files safely before shutting itself down in the event of a power problem, the UPS can prevent excessive damage to the server's files.
- Use disk mirroring or disk duplexing to protect the network data in case one disk fails.
- Use SFT III to mirror two entire servers, so that a hardware failure in one server won't stop the network from functioning.

- Keep a regular, up-to-date series of backups, so that all server and network files are archived and can be readily restored.
- Maintain updated virus protection software and regularly scan for viruses.

Following these practices can help protect your server and, therefore, your entire network.

CHAPTER 8

File Management

Managing Disk Space

- To manage file compression, use SERVMAN.NLM to set file compression SET parameters.
- To manage data migration, install HCSS (see Chapter 3).
- To limit users' disk space, use the NetWare Administrator utility (which runs in Windows, OS/2, or Windows 95).

Managing Files

- To purge or salvage files that have been deleted, use the NetWare Administrator utility, FILER (a menu utility that runs in DOS), or PURGE (a command-line utility).
- To copy files, use NCOPY (a command-line utility).
- To display information about files and directories, use the NetWare Administrator utility, FILER, or NDIR (a command-line utility).
- To set the search mode for executable files, use FLAG (a command-line utility).
- To rename a directory, use RENDIR (a command-line utility).

Creating a Fake Root

- To create a fake root for an application that needs to be installed at the root of the volume, use MAP (a command-line utility).

Backing Up and Restoring Files

- To back up and restore network files, use SBACKUP.NLM or a third-party backup solution.

Managing Volumes

- To create, delete, or enlarge a volume, use INSTALL.NLM, and select Volume Options.
- To mount a volume, use INSTALL.NLM or MOUNT (a console utility).
- To dismount a volume, use INSTALL.NLM or DISMOUNT (a console utility).

- To add name space support to a volume, load the name space module on the server, and then use the ADD NAME SPACE *module* TO *volume* command at the server console.

Protecting Database Transactions

- To manage the NetWare Transaction Tracking System (TTS), use SERVMAN.NLM to change the appropriate SET parameters.
- To set thresholds for TTS operation, use SETTTS (a command-line utility).
- To flag a file with the Transactional file attribute, use the NetWare Administrator utility, FILER, or FLAG.
- To reenable TTS after it's been disabled, use the ENABLE TTS console utility.

NetWare enables you to manage files in many different ways. How you manage your files can contribute significantly to how well users can find files, how well your disk space is conserved, and how easy it is to restore the network files when something goes wrong with them.

This chapter describes some of the techniques and features you can use to manage your file system.

Planning the File System

When you first set up your server, you will need to take into account how your file system will be structured. There are several factors that can affect how you organize your network files and applications. Careful planning can make it easier to back up and restore needed files, and it can make it easier to assign trustee rights to large numbers of users.

The following list indicates some tips that may help you plan an accessible, easy-to-manage file system. Note, however, that if you use the simple installation option for installing your server, your server will have only the SYS volume. This is acceptable, but having separate volumes can help save time in backup and restore processes, as explained in the following tips.

- You may want to reserve volume SYS for NetWare files and utilities. Try to avoid putting other types of files in SYS, such as applications or users' daily work files.
- Plan a separate volume for storing Macintosh files. To store Macintosh files on a volume, you have to load the Macintosh name space module (called MAC.NAM) on the server and then add the name space to that particular volume. The name space allows the Macintosh file's resource fork, long file name, and other characteristics to be preserved, but causes all files on the volume to use two directory entries. The default DOS name space for DOS files requires only one directory entry per file. The same principle holds true for the NFS (UNIX) name space and the name space that supports OS/2, Windows NT, and Windows 95 formats (called LONG.NAM). LONG.NAM replaces the older OS2.NAM and NT.NAM modules, which will not work on IntranetWare. For more information about Macintosh and other name spaces, see the "Adding a Name Space to a Volume" section later in this chapter.
- To simplify backups, create a separate volume for applications and other non-NetWare utilities. That way, you only need to back up the volume containing applications occasionally, while you back up the

volume with the users' daily work files more frequently. If an application and users' work files need to be stored in the same volume, this strategy won't work, of course. In this case, try to store the applications and the users' work files in separate branches of subdirectories in the same volume. For more information about backing up files, see the "Backing Up and Restoring Files" section later in this chapter.

- If different applications will be available to different groups of users, try to organize the applications' directory structures so that you can assign comprehensive rights in a parent directory. This may help prevent you from having to create multiple individual rights assignments at lower-level subdirectories. For more information about file system rights, see Chapter 7.
- If you want to use file compression to compress less frequently used files, try to group those types of files into directories separate from other files that are used more often. That way, you can turn on compression for the less-used directories and leave it turned off for the frequently used directories. For more information about file compression, see the "File Compression" section later in this chapter.
- Determine if you want users to run DOS and Windows from their local drives or from a network directory. (If you use diskless workstations, those workstations will need to boot and run DOS from the network.) For more information about running DOS and Windows from the network, see the "DOS and Windows Directories" section later in this chapter.
- Decide where you want users' daily work files to reside: in personal directories, in project-specific directories, or in some other type of directory structure. Allow for ample network directory space for users to store their daily work files. Encourage your users to store their files on the network so that those files can be backed up regularly by the network backup process, and so that the files can be protected by NetWare security.
- Decide if you want users to have their own individual home directories. You can have home directories created automatically when you create a new user, as explained in Chapter 6.

DIRECTORIES THAT ARE CREATED AUTOMATICALLY

When you first install IntranetWare on the server, some directories are created automatically in the SYS volume. These directories contain the files needed to run and manage IntranetWare. You can create additional directories and subdirectories in volume SYS or, if you created additional volumes during installation, you can create directories for your users in the other volumes.

The following directories are created automatically on volume SYS:

- LOGIN contains a few files and utilities that will let users change their name context (location) in the NDS tree and log in to the network.
- SYSTEM contains NLMs that the network administrator can load to configure, manage, monitor, and add services on the NetWare server.
- PUBLIC contains all of the NetWare utilities and related files. It also contains .PDF files (printer definition files) if you choose to install them on the server. In addition, client subdirectories are located under PUBLIC. These client subdirectories contain the files required for installing NetWare client software on workstations.
- MAIL is empty when it is first created. It may be used by e-mail programs that are compatible with NetWare. In NetWare 3.1x and NetWare 2.x, the MAIL directory contained subdirectories for each individual user. Each of these subdirectories, named with the user's object ID number, contained the user's login script file. If you upgrade a NetWare 3.1x or 2.x server to IntranetWare, those existing users will retain their MAIL subdirectories in IntranetWare, but the login scripts will become properties of their User objects instead.
- ETC contains files used for managing protocols and routers.
- DOCVIEW contains the DynaText viewers, which are used for reading the online documentation. (This directory is created only if you install the online documentation on the server.)
- DOC contains the actual online documentation. (This directory is created only if you install the online documentation on the server.)

Because these directories contain the files required for running and managing your NetWare network, do not rename or delete any of them without making absolutely sure they're unnecessary in your particular network's situation.

APPLICATION DIRECTORIES

It may be easier to assign file system trustee rights if you group all multi-user applications on the network under a single volume or parent directory. By installing, for example, your word-processing, spreadsheet, and other programs into their own subdirectories under a parent directory named APPS, you can assign all of your users the minimum necessary rights to APPS, and then the users will inherit those rights in each individual application's subdirectory. For more information about file system rights, see Chapter 7.

If you install applications into subdirectories under a common parent directory, you can then usually designate that users' daily work files be stored in their own home directories elsewhere on the network.

When planning network subdirectories for your applications, follow any special instructions from the manufacturer for installing the application on a network. Some applications can be run either from a local hard disk on the workstation or from a network directory. Be sure to follow the instructions supplied by the manufacturer.

In some cases, the instructions may indicate that the application has to be installed at the root of a volume. If your application requires this, you can still install it in a subdirectory under the APPS directory if you want, and then map a "fake root" to the application's subdirectory. A fake root mapping makes a subdirectory appear to be a volume, so that the application runs correctly.

For example, suppose you want to install an application called ABC into a subdirectory under a directory called APPS on the volume called VOL1. However, the application's instructions say that ABC must be installed at the root of the volume. Create a subdirectory called ABC under VOL1:APPS and install the application into ABC. Then, you can map a fake root to the ABC subdirectory and assign it to be a search drive at the same time by using the following command:

```
MAP ROOT S16:=VOL1:APPS\ABC
```

You can type this command at the workstation's DOS prompt if you only need the mapping to be in effect until the user logs out. If you want it to be in effect each time the user logs in, put the command in a login script. For more information about login scripts, see Chapter 6.

When you install an application, you may want to flag the application's executable files (usually files with the extension .COM or .EXE) with the Shareable and Read-Only file attributes. This enables users to simultaneously use the applications, but prevents users from deleting or modifying them. (This is more typically controlled by assigning restrictive trustee rights to users in those applications' directories, however.) You can use either the NetWare Administrator utility or the FLAG utility to assign file attributes. File and directory attributes are covered at length in Chapter 7.

DOS AND WINDOWS DIRECTORIES

Although most workstations run their own operating system from a local hard disk, it is possible to set up workstations so that they boot and run DOS or Windows from a network directory instead of a local disk. (Mac OS workstations can't run the Mac OS from the network. The Mac OS must be run from the local hard disk.)

Setting up your workstations to run DOS and/or Windows from a network directory offers a few advantages:

- You can use diskless workstations on your network, which can help prevent virus infections and keep users from uploading or downloading their own files on the network.
- You can prevent users from accidentally deleting or modifying important DOS or Windows files.
- You can centrally manage common DOS and Windows files. For example, you can upgrade all workstations to a new version of DOS or Windows at the same time by updating the files in the network directory instead of having to change files on each individual workstation.

To enable workstations to run DOS or Windows from the network, you install DOS or Windows into network subdirectories under SYS:PUBLIC.

Planning DOS Network Directories

To install DOS onto the network, create a subdirectory under SYS:PUBLIC for each version of DOS and type of computer that you run, and then copy the DOS files into those subdirectories. If all of your workstations are running the same version of DOS and are the same type of computers (such as all IBM or all Compaq), you need only one DOS directory for the whole network.

However, if you have different brands of computers on your network, or if any of the computers are using different versions of DOS, you must create several DOS directories.

First, make a list of the types of computers on your network and the versions of DOS that each uses. For example, suppose you have the following workstations on your network:

- IBMs running DOS 5.1
- Compaqs running DOS 5.1

- Compaqs running DOS 6.0
- AT&Ts running DOS 5.0

From this list, you can see that you need four different DOS directories on your network to match the four different types of DOS running in various workstations.

Regardless of whether you need one DOS directory or several, you have to create a specific path to each one using the following format:

```
SYS:PUBLIC\machine type\OS type\OS version
```

Replace *machine type* with the type of computer, replace *OS type* with the name of DOS that the workstation is using (for example MSDOS), and replace *OS version* with the DOS version number. For the workstations listed above, you would create four different DOS directories:

- SYS:PUBLIC\IBM_PC\MSDOS\5.1
- SYS:PUBLIC\COMPAQ\MSDOS\5.1
- SYS:PUBLIC\COMPAQ\MSDOS\6.0
- SYS:PUBLIC\ATT\MSDOS\5.0

After you create the appropriate DOS directories, complete the steps in the following checklist to set up workstations to run DOS from the network.

1. Copy the DOS files into the subdirectory named with the appropriate version number, such as 5.1.
2. Protect the DOS files by assigning them the Read-Only and Shareable file attributes.
3. In the system or profile login script, map a search drive (usually the second search drive) to the DOS directories. See Chapter 6 for more information on mapping search drives and using login scripts. If you use identifier variables in the MAP command, you can put a single command in the login script and it will locate the correct DOS directory for each workstation that logs in. Use the following command:

   ```
   MAP INS S2:=SYS:PUBLIC\%MACHINE\%OS\%OS_VERSION
   ```

4. Use the COMSPEC command in the login script to tell the workstation where to find the DOS command processor (COMMAND.COM). If you mapped the second search drive (S2) to the DOS directory, use the following COMSPEC command:

   ```
   COMSPEC=S2:COMMAND.COM
   ```

5. If the workstation's machine name is something other than IBM_PC (such as COMPAQ or ATT), put the machine name in the workstation's NET.CFG file. This way, the workstation will find its machine name in the NET.CFG file and know which DOS directory it should look for on the network. (IBM_PC is the default.)

Planning Windows Network Directories

In general, if you want to run Windows from the network, the most efficient way is to store the Windows program files in a common network directory that can be accessed by all users, and then copy the Windows user files into a separate directory for each individual user. However, you should still use a permanent swap file on each workstation's hard disk. (A *permanent swap file* is a file created by Windows that enables Windows to temporarily store programs and parts of Windows itself that are not currently in use. This file, in effect, acts like virtual memory for the workstation.)

If you prefer, you can store only the Windows program files in a network directory and store both the users' files and the permanent swap file on each user's local disk. However, you may find that it's easier for you to manage the network if all the Windows files are in network directories.

Saving Disk Space

There are several features in IntranetWare that will help you to conserve disk space:

- File compression, which compresses less frequently used files, typically can conserve up to 63 percent of your hard disk space.
- Block suballocation enables several files to share a single block to avoid wasting space unnecessarily.
- Data migration lets you automatically move less frequently used files to an alternate storage device, such as an optical jukebox system.
- Restricting users' disk space enables you to decide how much disk space users can fill up on a volume.
- Purging files lets you free up disk space by removing files that have been deleted but were still retained in a salvageable state. (You can also salvage deleted files, instead of purging them, but of course that doesn't free up any disk space.)

The following sections explain each of these features.

FILE COMPRESSION

File compression typically can save up to 63 percent of the server's hard disk space by compressing unused files. Compressed files are automatically decompressed when a user accesses them, so the user doesn't necessarily know that the files were compressed.

There are only two steps to make file compression occur on the server:

- First, during installation, you choose whether to enable the volume for file compression, which simply means that the volume can handle file compression if needed. The default is to enable the volume, but you can choose not to enable it if you want to. (If you use the simple installation option of INSTALL, compression is automatically enabled.)
- Second, you must decide whether you want file compression turned on or off. By default, file compression is turned on, so that any volumes enabled for compression will use file compression. However, you can easily turn off compression by changing the SET Enable File Compression parameter to Off. This SET parameter will affect file compression for all enabled volumes on the server.

Disabling and Reenabling Compression

By default, all NetWare volumes are enabled for file compression. Because you can easily turn on and off file compression using a SET parameter, there is really no reason to disable compression for a particular volume, especially because the only way to disable the volume is to delete and re-create it.

If the volume was disabled for compression, and you want to reenable it, use INSTALL.NLM. Load INSTALL, select Volume Options, choose the volume you want, go to the File Compression field, and press the Enter key, which will toggle the field from On to Off. Press the Esc key twice to save the new setting.

Managing Compression

By default, once the volume is enabled and compression is turned on, files and directories are compressed automatically after they've been untouched for seven days.

However, you can change several aspects of file compression, such as how long the files wait before being compressed, the time of day the compression activity occurs, and which files don't ever get compressed. To control file compression, you can use two file and directory attributes and several SET parameters.

The two file and directory attributes that affect compression are as follows:

- The Immediate Compress attribute compresses the file or directory immediately, without waiting for the standard duration of inactivity.
- The Don't Compress attribute prevents the file or directory from ever being compressed, even if compression is turned on for a parent directory.

To assign one of these attributes to a file or directory, you can use the NetWare Administrator utility, the FLAG utility (covered in Chapter 7), or the FILER utility.

The SET parameters that affect file compression let you control characteristics such as when compression happens, how many files can be compressed at the same time, how many times a file must be accessed before it is decompressed, and so on. The easiest way to change these parameters is to use SERVMAN.NLM. If you change a SET parameter, the change will affect all files and directories in all volumes on the server that have been enabled for compression.

The SET parameters that affect compression are listed in Appendix B, under the "File System" section. To change the SET parameters, load SERVMAN and choose Server Parameters. Then, from the Select a Parameter Category menu, choose File System and change the parameters you want. When you are finished, press Esc twice to get to the Update Options menu, and then update the STARTUP.NCF or AUTOEXEC.NCF files (or both) to save the new values. You do not need to reboot the server because the values have already taken effect.

BLOCK SUBALLOCATION

A block is a unit that is allocated to store a file. A file may take up more space on the disk than its actual size because NetWare allocates the disk into uniformly sized blocks that are used to store pieces of files. The default block size depends on the volume's size, as shown in Table 8.1. In general, larger block sizes are better for large database records because they can help speed up access. Smaller block sizes require more server memory, but help prevent disk space from being wasted. In previous versions of NetWare, you couldn't do anything to prevent the inefficient use of disk space if you wanted to use larger block sizes. For example, if your block size was 32K, a 35K file would take two 32K blocks, using a total of 64K of disk space.

TABLE 8.1 *Default Block Sizes for Storing Files*

VOLUME SIZE	BLOCK SIZE
0 to 31MB	4K
32 to 149MB	8K
150 to 499MB	16K
500MB to 1999MB	32K
2000MB or more	64K

However, IntranetWare includes a feature called block suballocation. Block suballocation lets the file system break a block into suballocation blocks as small as 512 bytes, so that several files (or pieces of files) can share a single block. With block suballocation turned on, the 35K file will use up one 32K block, plus enough suballocation blocks required, for a total of only 35K of disk space.

Block suballocation is turned on by default when IntranetWare is installed. You do not need to do anything to use or manage block suballocation.

DATA MIGRATION

Data migration is an IntranetWare feature that lets you extend the storage capabilities of your server to include optical disks. With data migration, less frequently used files can be migrated seamlessly off of the server's hard disk onto an *optical storage system*, often called a *jukebox*.

Data migration is transparent to the user. The migrated files still appear to be available on the server's volume, just as they did before they were migrated. The user doesn't have to do anything different to access the file. When accessed, the migrated file is quickly "demigrated" back to the server's hard disk and opened as usual. The user may notice a delay of a second or two, however, as the file is being demigrated.

Data migration is managed by NetWare's High-Capacity Storage System (HCSS). For an explanation of how to set up and manage HCSS, see Chapter 3.

RESTRICTING USERS' DISK SPACE

You can restrict how much disk space a user can fill up on a particular volume. This can help prevent individual users from using an excessive amount of disk space. To limit the space individual users can use, use the NetWare Administrator and select a Volume object. Choose Details from the Object menu, and then choose the User Space Limits page.

On the User Space Limits page, you can see which users have restricted disk space allowances on this volume. You can see what their restrictions are and how much space they still have available. You can also modify these limits or add other users and restrict their disk space, too.

PURGING AND SALVAGING FILES

In IntranetWare, when files are deleted, they are not actually removed from the server's hard disk. Instead, they are retained in a salvageable state.

Deleted files are usually stored in the same directory from which they were originally deleted. If, however, the directory itself was also deleted, the deleted files are stored in a special directory called DELETED.SAV at the volume's root.

Deleted files are stored in this salvageable state until one of four things happens:

- The file is salvaged, restoring it to its original form.
- The server runs out of free space on the disk and begins to overwrite files that have been deleted for a specified period of time. The oldest deleted files are overwritten first. You can use a SET parameter to set the amount of time the file must have been deleted before it can be overwritten.
- The file is purged by the administrator or user. (When purged, a file is completely removed from the disk and cannot be recovered.) You can purge a file either manually, by using the NetWare Administrator utility, FILER (a DOS-based menu utility), or PURGE (a command-line utility), or you can use the Purge Immediate directory and file attributes to mark a file or directory to be purged immediately upon deletion.
- The Purge Immediately attribute is assigned. Assign the Purge Immediately directory attribute to the volume that contains files you want purged as soon as they are deleted. If you use this attribute, you cannot salvage files you delete from that volume.

Purging and Salvaging Files with NetWare Administrator

To use the NetWare Administrator utility to either purge or salvage a deleted file or directory, complete the steps in the following checklist.

1. From the NetWare Administrator's Browser, select the directory containing the files or directories you want to salvage or purge.
2. From the Tools menu, select Salvage. (This option will let you both salvage and purge files.)

3. In the Include field of the Salvage dialog box that appears, indicate which files you want to see displayed. Specify a file name or use wildcards to indicate several files. A blank line or the wildcard symbols *.* will display all the deleted files in the selected directory.
4. From the Sort Options drop box, specify how you want the displayed files to be sorted: by Deletion Date, Deletor, File Name, File Size, or File Type.
5. From the Source drop box, choose whether you want to see deleted files in your current directory or in a deleted directory.
6. Click the List button to display the files you've specified. Figure 8.1 shows an example of the Salvage dialog box with deleted files listed.
7. From the displayed list, select the files you want to purge or salvage.
8. Click either the Salvage button or the Purge button, depending on what you want to do. If you salvage files from an existing directory, the files are restored to that directory. If you salvage files from a deleted directory, the files are restored at the root directory.
9. When finished, click the Close button.

FIGURE 8.1 *Displaying Salvageable Files in NetWare Administrator*

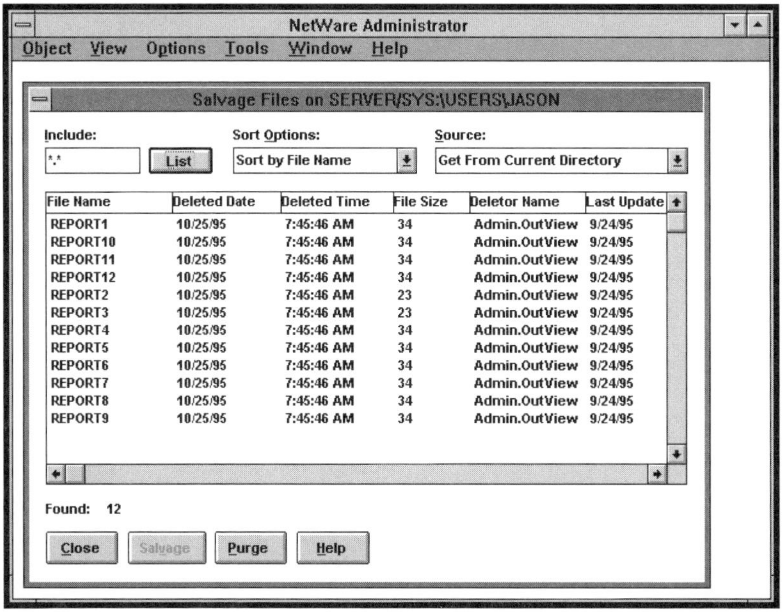

Purging and Salvaging Files with FILER

To use the DOS-based FILER utility to purge or salvage files or directories that have been deleted, complete the steps in the following checklist.

1. At the DOS prompt, enter

   ```
   FILER
   ```

   to start the utility.

2. If you are going to salvage or purge files from a current directory, choose Select Current Directory to make that directory current. To select a different directory, type in the name of the directory you want or press the Insert key to navigate through the file system.

3. (This step is for salvaging only.) To salvage files, choose Salvage Deleted Files.

   a. Choose View/recover deleted files if they are in an existing directory, or choose Salvage from deleted directories if the files are in a deleted directory.

   b. Indicate which files you want to see displayed. Specify a file name or use wildcards (asterisks and question marks) to indicate several files. Use a single asterisk or *.* to display all the deleted files in the selected directory.

   c. Specify how you want the displayed files to be sorted by pressing F3 and choosing an option.

   d. To salvage a single file, highlight the file and press Enter. To salvage multiple files, press the F5 key on each file to mark it, and then press Enter when you've selected all the files you want. If you salvage files from an existing directory, the files are restored to that directory. If you salvage files from a deleted directory, the files are restored at the root directory.

4. (This step is for purging only.) To purge files, choose Purge Deleted Files.

   a. Indicate which files you want to see displayed. Specify a file name or use wildcards (asterisks and question marks) to indicate several files. Use a single asterisk or *.* to display all the deleted files in the selected directory.

   b. Choose whether you want to purge deleted files in only the current directory or in the entire subdirectory structure of the current directory. As soon as you press Enter to select one of the options, the purging begins.

Purging Files with PURGE

To purge deleted files, you can also use the PURGE command-line utility. To purge files using PURGE, use the following command:

```
PURGE path\filename /option
```

Replace *path* with the path to the files you want to purge, and replace *filename* with a file name for the specific files. Wildcards are acceptable. The following *options* can be used with PURGE:

/A	Purges all files in the current directory and in all of its subdirectories
/VER	Displays the version number of PURGE
/?	Displays help screens for PURGE

For example, to purge all the deleted files with the extension .BAT in the current directory only, use the following command:

```
PURGE *.BAT
```

Backing Up and Restoring Files

Files can be lost or damaged in a variety of ways. They can be corrupted by viruses, accidentally deleted by users, overwritten by other applications, or destroyed when a hard disk fails. Despite all the best precautions, you can't always prevent files from being lost.

What you can do, however, is make sure that you always have current backup copies of your network data, so that you can restore files. If you have a carefully planned and executed backup strategy, you can minimize the amount of work that will be lost if you have to restore a file from your archives.

There are many different backup products available on the market. IntranetWare includes a backup solution, called SBACKUP, that you can use, or you can purchase a third-party product that may provide additional features you need. Backup products can back up data onto a variety of storage media, such as tapes and optical disks.

Backing up network files involves more than just making a copy of the files. It's important to use a backup product, such as SBACKUP, that backs up not just the files themselves, but also the NetWare information associated with those files, such as trustee rights, Inherited Rights Filters, and file and directory attributes.

PLANNING A BACKUP STRATEGY

Planning an efficient backup strategy is one of the most beneficial tasks you can do as part of network management. With a good backup strategy, you can limit the time it takes to do backups, ensure that the least amount of working time is lost by your users, and avoid unnecessary headaches from searching for lost files.

Backup strategies can be different for every network. What works for someone else may not work well for you, and vice versa. First, consider the following questions:

- How long do you want to retain old copies of files? Do you want to keep backup files for one month only, and then copy over them? Or do you need to keep backups for twelve months or more?
- How many duplicate copies of the data do you want to keep?
- Where do you plan to store your backups? Noncritical data may be kept on-site (though when storing backups on-site, at least store them in a room separate from the server's room). If some of the data is mission critical, you may need to keep the backups in an off-site location in case of a physical disaster, such as a fire, flood, or earthquake. If the data is critical enough to store off-site but you also want to have immediate access to it, consider making two backups and storing one off-site and the other on-site.

Also take into account the following guidelines, which may help you plan a strategy that makes sense for your network needs:

- In general, don't back up files that change infrequently, such as application files and utilities, as often as files that change frequently.
- Whenever possible, avoid restoring the NDS tree from a backup tape. Instead, use partition replication to restore the NDS tree. See Chapter 5 for more information on partition replication.
- In determining how often to back up critical data that changes frequently, calculate how long you could afford to spend re-creating the information if it was lost. If you can't afford to lose more than a day's worth of work, you should perform daily backups of that information. If losing a week's worth of work is more of a nuisance than a devastating blow, perhaps you don't need to do daily backups.
- Encourage users to store files in network directories instead of on their local hard disks so that you can ensure they get backed up during your backup process. Relying on users to back up their own local files is seldom effective.

- Don't do a full backup of the complete network every night, even though your network data may be critical. Instead, plan a schedule that staggers complete backups with incremental backups, so that you still get full coverage without spending more time and money than necessary. For example, you can do a full backup of the network once a week. Then, once a day, do incremental backups of only those files that have changed. In the event of a total loss of files, you can restore all the files from the weekly backup, and then restore each of the daily tapes to update those files that changed during that week. In this way, you can cover all of your files while minimizing the time each backup session takes during the week.
- Plan a rotation schedule for backup tapes. If you have only one backup tape that you use every week, each time replacing the previous week's backup with the new one, you could unknowingly back up corrupted files onto your single tape, replacing your last good copy. To prevent this type of problem, plan to keep older backup tapes or disks on hand at all times. Many network administrators will use four or more tapes or disks for the same set of files, cycling through them one at a time. Each week, the most outdated tape or disk is used for the new backup. This way, three or more versions of backups are available at any given time. How many tape or disk sets you'll need depends on your rotation schedule. If you want to keep four weeks' worth of daily and weekly backups, you'll need at least 20 sets of tapes or disks — five for each week.
- Keep a backup log. A written record of all backups and your backup strategy can help someone else restore the files if you aren't there. See Appendix D for a worksheet you can use to help document your backups.
- Make sure the backups can be restored! A backup is useful only if the data in it can be successfully restored. Too many people discover a problem with their backups when they're in the middle of an important restoration process. Practice restoring files before you actually need to. By practicing, you may identify problems you didn't realize you had. Don't wait until it is too late.

USING SBACKUP

SBACKUP.NLM is the backup product that ships with IntranetWare. With SBACKUP, you can back up all the different types of files that can be stored on your server: DOS, Macintosh, OS/2, Windows NT, Windows 95, and UNIX.

SBACKUP lets you select the type of backup you want to perform. There are four choices:

- *Full backup.* This option backs up all network files. It removes the Archive Needed file attribute from all files and directories. (This attribute is also called the *modify bit.* It is assigned to a file whenever the file is changed. When the file is backed up, most backup products can remove the attribute so that the next time the file is changed, the attribute is once again assigned.)
- *Differential backup.* This option backs up only files that were modified since the last full backup. It does not remove the Archive Needed attribute from these files.
- *Incremental backup.* This option backs up only files that were modified since the last full or incremental backup. It removes the Archive Needed attribute from these files.
- *Custom backup.* This option lets you specify particular directories to back up or restore. You can specify whether or not to remove the Archive Needed attribute from those files.

Backing Up Files with SBACKUP

To use SBACKUP.NLM to back up files, load SBACKUP.NLM and device drivers for the backup device (tape or disk drive) on a server. This server is called the *host server.* Then load Target Service Agents (TSAs), which also come with the IntranetWare product, on any servers whose files you want to back up. These servers are called *targets.* (TSAs are NetWare Loadable Modules.)

To back up the host server, load both SBACKUP and a TSA on that server. You can back up servers with TSAs on them (targets) from the host server. You do not need to run SBACKUP on the target servers.

Complete the steps in the following checklist to use SBACKUP to back up your network files.

1. Attach the backup device (tape or disk drive) to the host server.
2. Load the necessary backup device drivers on the host server. Then enter the command

   ```
   SCAN FOR NEW DEVICES
   ```

   at the console to register the device with the server. Check the manufacturer's documentation to find out which drivers you need. Place the commands that load the backup device drivers in the server's

STARTUP.NCF file if you want them to load automatically when the server is rebooted.

3. On each target server you want to back up, load the appropriate TSA. Don't forget to load a TSA on the host server that's running SBACKUP if you want to back up the host server itself. Use one of the following TSAs:
   - For NetWare 4.1 and 4.11 target servers, load TSA410.NLM.
   - For NetWare 4.0 target servers, load TSA400.NLM.
   - For NetWare 3.12 target servers, load TSA312.NLM.
   - For NetWare 3.11 target servers, load TSA311.NLM.
   - For NDS, load TSANDS.NLM.
4. Load SBACKUP on the host server.
5. From SBACKUP's main menu, choose Backup.
6. If multiple servers have TSAs loaded, choose the target server that you want to back up.
7. When prompted, enter a user name and password for the target server. You may need to enter the Admin's full context name.
8. If more than one storage device is available, select the backup device you want to use.
9. Specify a location for both the session log and error files. The session log helps SBACKUP locate the backed-up files for later restorations. The error files track any errors that may occur. Either press Enter to accept the default, or press Insert to navigate through the file system and select another location.
10. Select the type of backup you want to do (full, differential, incremental, or custom).
11. (This step is for custom backup only.) If you choose to do a custom backup, several screens appear that enable you to enter information about what you want to back up. You can select specific volumes, directories, and files to be either included or excluded from the backup. Use *exclude* options when you want to back up most of the file system while omitting only a small part. Everything that you don't specifically exclude is backed up. Use *include* options when you want to back up only a small portion of the file system. Everything you don't specifically include is excluded. (When specifying subsets to back up, two options let you exclude or include Major TSA resources.

A Major TSA resource is simply a volume. You can choose to include or exclude volumes, directories, or files.)

12. Enter a description for this backup session.
13. If your backup device can append data to previous sessions on the same media, specify whether you want this session to be appended to the same media as another session or not. If you choose not to append, existing data on the media will be erased and replaced with the new backup session's data.
14. Press F10 and choose whether to start the backup now or later. If you choose to start the backup later, enter the time and date you want it to begin.

Restoring Files with SBACKUP

To use SBACKUP.NLM to restore files, load SBACKUP and device drivers for the backup device on the host server, just as you did when preparing to back up the files. Then load TSAs on any target servers whose files you want to restore.

To restore files with SBACKUP, complete the steps in the following checklist.

1. From SBACKUP's main menu, choose Restore.
2. If multiple servers have TSAs loaded, choose the target server to which you want to restore files.
3. When prompted, enter a user name and password for the target server. You may need to enter the Admin's full context name.
4. If you are restoring files from a session (and you know where its session files are), select Choose a Session to Restore, and then enter the path to the session files and select the session you want.
5. If the session files have been corrupted or deleted, and you want to restore the files directly from a backup media, choose Restore Without Session Files. Then specify a location for the new session log and error files for the restoration session.
6. Select the type of backup device and media from which you want to restore files.
7. Choose whether you want to restore a single file or directory, an entire session, or do a custom restore. Then fill in any information about the files you want to restore.

Working with Volumes

A volume is the highest level in the file system hierarchy, and it contains directories and files. Each NetWare server has at least one volume, SYS, which contains all of the NetWare files and utilities. You can have additional volumes on a server if you want; in fact, a NetWare server can have up to 64 volumes.

When a volume is created on a disk, a *segment* is also created on the disk to hold the volume. If you create two volumes on the disk, the disk will have two segments (also called volume segments). If you later decide to merge the two volumes into one, you will discover that the new single volume contains two segments. If you create a volume that spans multiple hard disks, the portion of the volume on each disk will be contained in a different segment.

Each volume can have up to 32 volume segments, which can all be stored on the same hard disk or scattered across separate disks. Storing volume segments on different disks lets you increase the size of a volume by adding a new hard disk. In addition, by putting segments of the same volume on more than one hard disk, different parts of the volume can be accessed simultaneously, which increases disk input and output. However, the more segments a volume has, the slower performance may be, so use this option carefully.

If you spread volume segments across disks, it is important to mirror the disks so that a single disk's failure won't shut down the entire volume. (For more information about disk mirroring, see Chapter 3.)

One hard disk can hold up to eight volume segments that belong to one or more volumes. However, a single segment cannot span multiple disks.

When you create a physical volume using INSTALL.NLM, a Volume object is automatically created at the same time. The Volume object is placed in the NDS tree, in the same context as the server. By default, the Volume object is named with the server's name as a prefix. For example, if the server's name is Sales, the Volume object for volume SYS is named Sales_SYS.

CREATING AND MOUNTING VOLUMES

You create volumes as part of the installation process when you first install your IntranetWare server. To create additional volumes after the initial installation, use INSTALL.NLM. You can create a new volume out of any free space on the disk. The free space may be space that was never assigned to a volume before, or it may be free space on a new hard disk that's just been added.

After you've created a volume, you must mount it before it can be accessed by network users.

To create a volume, complete the steps in the following checklist.

1. If you're installing a new hard disk, install the hard disk and use INSTALL.NLM to create a new NetWare partition for the disk, which will become the new volume.
2. Load INSTALL.NLM and choose Volume Options.
3. Press the Insert key to see a list of existing volume segments and free disk space.
4. From the list, select any existing free space and press Enter.
5. Enter a name for the new volume (up to 15 characters long). The name can be made up of letters or numbers.
6. If you don't want the new volume to use all the available disk space, select the new volume, press Enter, and type in a new volume size in megabytes.
7. Press F10 to save the new volume information.
8. To mount the volume, choose Mount/Dismount an Existing Volume, and then choose Mount.

You can also mount a volume by using the MOUNT console command. For example, to mount the volume named VOL1, use the following command:

```
MOUNT VOL1
```

To mount all volumes on the server, use the following command:

```
MOUNT ALL
```

DELETING AND DISMOUNTING VOLUMES

Deleting a volume deletes all the files and directories on that volume as well, so be sure you only delete a volume if you don't need the files anymore, or if you have a reliable backup.

To delete a volume, complete the steps in the following checklist.

1. Back up all files on the volume or move them to a different volume, if you want to keep them.
2. If the volume you're going to delete contains HCSS directories, unload the HCSS media first.
3. Dismount the volume you want to delete by typing the following console command (substitute the volume's name for *name*):

   DISMOUNT *name*

4. Load INSTALL.NLM and choose Volume Options.
5. Select the volume you want to delete. (Do not delete volume SYS.)
6. When prompted if you want to delete the volume, answer Yes.

You can also dismount a volume using INSTALL.NLM. To dismount the volume, load INSTALL.NLM and select Volume Options. Then choose Mount/Dismount an Existing Volume, select the volume you want to dismount, and change its status to Dismounted.

INCREASING THE SIZE OF A VOLUME

To increase the size of a volume, you can add a volume segment to an existing volume. To do this, complete the steps in the following checklist.

1. Load INSTALL and select Volume Options.
2. Press Insert to see a list of existing volume segments.
3. From the list, select a segment that has free space and no volume assignment, and press Enter.
4. Choose Make This Segment Part of Another Volume, and press Enter.
5. Choose the volume to which you want to add this segment, and press Enter.
6. Press Esc, and then press F10 to save the new volume information.

ADDING A NAME SPACE TO A VOLUME

By default, IntranetWare servers support DOS, OS/2, Windows NT, and Windows 95. (Previous versions of NetWare supported only the DOS file name format by default.) If you want a volume to store Macintosh, UNIX, or FTAM files, you need to add name space support for those file formats to the volume. Name space support is a feature that extends the volume's storage characteristics, enabling the volume to store the longer file names and additional information that different file formats may contain.

For example, Macintosh name space support enables the volume to store a Macintosh file's resource fork and long file name.

The following name spaces are available for IntranetWare:

- MAC.NAM for Macintosh files
- LONG.NAM for OS/2, Windows NT, and Windows 95 files (this replaces the OS2.NAM and NT.NAM modules available for previous versions of NetWare)

- NFS.NAM (Network File System) for UNIX files
- FTAM.NAM (File Transfer, Access, and Management), which supports the FTAM protocol for remote file access (available separately)

A volume with support for a non-DOS name space requires twice as much memory as a volume with DOS-only files because the name spaces use twice as many directory entries that have to be cached.

To add name space support to a volume, complete the steps in the following checklist.

1. Load the name space loadable module on the server. For example, enter

   ```
   LOAD MAC
   ```

   to load the Macintosh name space, or enter

   ```
   LOAD LONG
   ```

   for the OS/2, Windows NT, or Windows 95 support.

2. Add the name space support to the desired volume by using the ADD NAME SPACE console command. To add the Macintosh name space to the volume VOL1, you would use the following command:

   ```
   ADD NAME SPACE MAC TO VOL1
   ```

Once you've added the name space support to a volume, the only way you can remove the name space support is to run VREPAIR.NLM or delete and re-create the volume.

To see a list of all the volumes on a server and their name spaces, use the VOLUMES console command.

REPAIRING A CORRUPTED VOLUME WITH VREPAIR

Occasionally, a server's hard disk problems may cause minor problems with one or more of the server's volumes. If a volume won't mount, the primary File Allocation Table (FAT) or Directory Entry Table (DET) may be corrupted. VREPAIR.NLM can usually repair these types of volume problems.

NetWare keeps two copies of the FAT and DET. VREPAIR compares the two tables for inconsistencies. If it finds an inconsistency, it uses the most correct table entry to update the incorrect one. Then VREPAIR writes the corrected entry to both the primary and the secondary tables.

VREPAIR can also be used in the following circumstances:

- When a power failure corrupts the volume

- When a hardware problem causes a disk read error
- When bad blocks on the volume cause read or write errors, datamirror mismatch errors, multiple allocation errors, or fatal DIR errors
- When you want to remove a name space from a volume

If a volume doesn't mount when you boot the server, VREPAIR will run automatically and try to repair the volume. If the volume fails while the server is running, you can run VREPAIR manually. (A volume must be dismounted before you can run VREPAIR on it.)

Most volume problems that VREPAIR can fix are hardware related. Therefore, if you repeatedly have to repair the same volume, you should consider replacing the hard disk.

To use VREPAIR.NLM, load it at the server's console. If you are repairing a volume that has a non-DOS name space loaded (or if you're removing a name space from the volume), VREPAIR needs to load another NLM for that name space support. The VREPAIR name space modules are named V_namespace.NLM.

For example, for the MAC name space, VREPAIR looks for a module named V_MAC.NLM. If this module is located in SYS:SYSTEM (which is where it is installed by default), VREPAIR automatically loads it. If this module is in a different location, you'll have to load it manually before running VREPAIR.

You may want to copy VREPAIR and its name space support modules to the server's DOS partition, so that they will be available in case volume SYS has to be repaired.

To run VREPAIR, complete the steps in the following checklist.

1. Make sure the volume you want to repair is dismounted.
2. At the server's console, load VREPAIR. If you want VREPAIR to log any errors it finds in an error log file, add a file name to the end of the LOAD command in the following format:

   LOAD VREPAIR *filename*

3. Choose Repair a Volume to begin trying to fix the volume. (If more than one volume is currently dismounted, you'll have to choose the volume you want to repair.)
4. If you want to change how VREPAIR is displaying errors as it finds them, press F1. Then select option 1 if you don't want VREPAIR to pause after each error. Select option 2 if you want the errors logged in a text file. Select option 3 to stop the repair. Select option 4 to resume the repair.

5. When the repair is finished, choose Yes when asked if you want to write repairs to the disk.
6. If VREPAIR found errors, run it again. Continue running VREPAIR repeatedly until it finds no more errors.
7. After VREPAIR finds no more errors, remount the volume.
8. If the volume still won't mount, delete the volume, re-create it, and then restore all of its files from backups.

VREPAIR may have to delete some files during the repair operation. If it does, it stores those deleted files in new files named VR*nnnnnn*.FIL (where *n* is any number). These files are stored in the directories in which the original files were stored when they were found during VREPAIR's operation.

Files may be deleted if VREPAIR finds problems such as a file with a name that is invalid in DOS, or two files with the same file name.

Protecting Databases with TTS

Transaction Tracking System (TTS) is NetWare's feature for protecting database transactions. With TTS turned on, the transaction is completely backed out so that the database isn't corrupted if a transaction is caught only half-completed when a problem such as a power outage occurs.

When a transaction is backed out, the database is restored to the original state it was in before the transaction began. TTS protects data by making a copy of the original data before it is overwritten by new data. Then, if a failure of some component occurs in the middle of the transaction, TTS restores the data to its original condition and discards the incomplete transaction.

TTS protects the NDS database and the queuing database files from corruption. In addition, you can use it to protect your own database files. If your database application doesn't offer its own form of transaction tracking, NetWare's TTS can provide protection for it. If your database application does offer its own transaction tracking, NetWare's TTS still may benefit you by tracking the transactions in the server. By tracking the file writes in the server, less data is transferred across the network, and NetWare's disk caching system increases performance.

TTS can be used with any application that stores information in records and allocates record locks. It can't be used with applications such as word processors, which don't store data in discrete records.

Because TTS is used to protect the NDS database, TTS is enabled by default.

You should not disable TTS. TTS may become disabled on its own if the SYS volume becomes full because the SYS volume is the volume TTS uses for its backout data. In addition, TTS may become disabled if the server runs out of memory to run TTS. You can see if TTS has been disabled by checking the TTS$LOG.ERR file at the root of the volume.

If TTS has been disabled, you can use the ENABLE TTS console utility to reenable TTS after you correct the problem that caused it to become disabled.

Table 8.2 shows the tasks you can use to manage how TTS works.

TABLE 8.2 *TTS Tasks*

TASK	HOW TO DO IT
Make TTS track a file	Use FLAG, FILER, or NetWare Administrator to assign the file the Transactional file attribute.
Reenable TTS	Use the console command ENABLE TTS.
Make the server automatically back out incomplete transactions without prompting you for input	Load SERVMAN.NLM. Choose Server Parameters, and then choose the Transaction Tracking category. Set the Auto TTS Backout Flag to On. Allow SERVMAN to save the command in the STARTUP.NCF file, and then reboot the server to make the change take effect.
Keep an error log for TTS data	Load SERVMAN.NLM. Choose Server Parameters, and then choose the Transaction Tracking category. Set the TTS Abort Dump Flag to On. Allow SERVMAN to save the command in the AUTOEXEC.NCF file.

Display or change the levels of physical and logical record locks for TTS	Use the SETTTS workstation utility in the following format:
	`SETTTS level`
	For *level*, insert the number of logical or physical locks you want TTS to ignore before tracking the transaction. Use the command:
	`SETTTS /?`
	to see help screens for SETTTS.

Managing Files and Directories

There are several NetWare utilities you can use to work with files and directories. In addition, of course, you can use commands or features of your regular workstation operating system to work with files, such as DOS commands, the Macintosh Filer program, the Windows File Manager, or the Windows 95 Explorer or Network Neighborhood.

Some of the NetWare utilities you can use are explained in the following sections.

FILER UTILITY

FILER is a DOS-based utility that lets you choose tasks from a menu. To execute FILER, enter the command

```
FILER
```

at the workstation's DOS prompt. Then select the tasks from the menus that appear. Press the F1 key for help with each screen. With FILER, you can see and work with the following types of file and directory information:

- List of subdirectories and files within a directory
- Trustees
- File system rights
- File owners
- Creation dates and times
- Available disk space and directory entries for a volume
- File and directory attributes
- Salvageable files

FLAG UTILITY

As explained in Chapter 7, the FLAG utility can be used to view and assign attributes to files and directories. In addition, it can also be used to assign search modes for executable files. To set a search mode for files, use the following command format:

```
FLAG path /M=number
```

For *path*, specify the path to the file or directory whose search mode you want to change. For *number*, insert the number of the search mode you want to be used for the executable files in this path. The search modes are explained in Table 8.3.

TABLE 8.3 *FLAG Search Modes*

SEARCH MODE NUMBER	DESCRIPTION
0	Looks for search instructions in the NET.CFG file (default mode).
1	Searches the path specified in the file. If no path is found, searches the default directory, and then all search drives.
2	Searches the path specified in the file. If no path is found, searches only the default directory.
3	Searches the path specified in the file. If no path is found, searches the default directory. Then, if the open request is read-only, searches the search drives.
4	Not used.
5	Searches the path specified, and then searches all search drives. If no path is found, searches the default directory, and then all search drives.
6	Not used.
7	Searches the path specified. If the open request is read-only, searches the search drives. If no path is found, searches the default directory, and then all search drives.

NCOPY UTILITY

NCOPY is a command-line utility that lets you copy files and directories from one drive or disk to another. To use NCOPY, use the following command format:

```
NCOPY source_path/filename destination_path/file-
name /option
```

The options that can be used with the NCOPY utility are listed in Table 8.4.

TABLE 8.4 *NCOPY Options*

OPTION	DESCRIPTION
/A	(Archive Bit Only) Copies only those files that have the Archive Needed attribute (also called the archive bit). NCOPY does not, however, remove the attribute from the source file, so the file will still have the Archive Needed attribute.
/C	(Copy) Copies files, but does not preserve extended attributes or name space information.
/F	(Force Sparse Files) Forces the operating system to copy sparse files, which aren't normally copied.
/I	(Inform) Notifies the user when extended attributes or name space information can't be copied because the destination volume doesn't support those features.
/M	(Archive Bit Set) Copies files that have the Archive Needed attribute and removes the attribute from the source file. This allows NCOPY to be used as a backup tool.
/R	(Retain Compression) Keeps compressed files compressed, rather than decompressing them during the copy process.
/R/U	(Retain Unsupported Compression) Keeps compressed files compressed even if they are copied to a destination volume that doesn't support compression.
/S	(Subdirectories) Copies all of the subdirectories (except empty subdirectories) as well as the files in the specified path.
/S/E	(Subdirectories, Empty) Copies all the subdirectories, including empty subdirectories, as well as files in the specified path.
/V	(Verify) Verifies that the original and the new files are identical. This option is useful for copies made only on local DOS drives.

For example, to copy all the files from drive G to drive L, use the following command:

```
NCOPY G:*.* L:
```

To copy all of the files, plus the subdirectories (including empty ones) from drive G to drive L, use the following command:

```
NCOPY G:*.* L: /S/E
```

NDIR UTILITY

The NDIR command-line utility lets you list a directory's files, subdirectories, and related information. With it, you can see the following types of information about files and directories:

- List of subdirectories and files within a directory
- Inherited Rights Filters
- Effective file system rights
- File owners
- Creation dates and times
- File sizes
- File and directory attributes
- Archive information
- File version (for Novell files)
- Volume information

With NDIR, you can sort the display of files so that they appear in different orders, such as from largest to smallest, newest to oldest, all those owned by a particular owner, and so on.

To use NDIR, use the following command format:

```
NDIR path /option
```

For example, to list all the files in the directory that is mapped to drive G, use the following command:

```
NDIR G:
```

To display the NDIR help screens, use the following command:

```
NDIR /?
```

The following are some of the most common options:

- To list any files in the directory's subdirectories, add the option /SUB.
- To list only the files in the directory, add the option /FO.
- To list only the subdirectories in the directory, add the option /DO.
- To list files in the order of their size, from smallest to largest, add the option /SORT SI.
- To list files in the order of their size, from largest to smallest, add the option /REV SORT SI.

- To list only the files owned by user Tina, add the option /OW EQ Tina.Sales.Satellite.RedHawk (EQ stands for "equals").
- To list only Macintosh files, add the option /MAC.

THE NETWARE ADMINISTRATOR UTILITY

With NetWare Administrator, which runs in Windows 3.1, OS/2, and Windows 95, you can use the Browser to select files and directories and view information about them, as explained in earlier sections of this chapter. Some of the types of information you can see about files and directories with the NetWare Administrator utility include the following:

- Name spaces
- Size restrictions of directories
- Creation dates and times
- Trustees
- Effective rights
- Inherited Rights Filters
- File and directory attributes
- File owners

RENDIR UTILITY

You can use the RENDIR command-line utility to rename a directory. To use this command, use the following format:

```
RENDIR oldname newname
```

For example, to rename the directory REPORTS to STATUS, use the following command:

```
RENDIR REPORTS STATUS
```

CHAPTER 9

Setting Up NetWare Print Services

Instant Access

Installing

- To install print services using default options (the quick and easy way), use the Print Services Quick Setup feature of the NetWare Administrator utility (which runs in Windows 3.1, OS/2, and Windows 95), and then load PSERVER.NLM on the NetWare server. You can also use the Quick Setup option of PCONSOLE, a menu utility that runs in DOS.
- To install print services using custom settings, use PCONSOLE or the NetWare Administrator utility, and then load PSERVER.NLM on the NetWare server.
- To connect a network printer to a DOS or Windows 3.1 workstation, load NPRINTER.EXE on the workstation.
- To connect a network printer to a Windows 95 workstation, load NPTWIN95.EXE on the workstation.
- To connect a network printer to a NetWare server, load NPRINTER.NLM on the NetWare server.

Defining Print Options

- To tell the printer how to print a job (paper form to use, format, and so on), define print job configurations with the NetWare Administrator utility or the PRINTCON menu utility (which runs in DOS).
- To define print forms (types of paper) for a printer, use the NetWare Administrator utility or the PRINTDEF menu utility (which runs in DOS).
- To define print devices, use the NetWare Administrator utility or the PRINTDEF menu utility.
- To redirect LPT1 to a print queue, put a CAPTURE command in a login script, use NetWare User Tools (which runs in Windows), or configure the application for network printing.

Printing Jobs

- To print files from within an application, simply follow the application's normal printing procedures (make sure the application is configured to print to a network printer).

- To print text files or to print without using an application, use NPRINT.
- To cancel or move a print job that's already in a print queue, use PCONSOLE (select Print Queues, select the queue, and then choose Print Jobs) or the NetWare Administrator utility (select the Print Queue object, choose Details from the Object menu, and then open the Job List page).

NetWare print services enables your network users to share printers that are connected to the network. With NetWare print services loaded, you can increase productivity and save on hardware expenses by allowing users to share a smaller number of printers than you would have to buy if each user had a stand-alone printer. (You may also be able to buy a single, more sophisticated printer instead of multiple lesser-quality printers.) In addition, users don't have to waste time waiting for printers to complete their print jobs before they can resume using an application, as they often do when printing to a directly connected stand-alone printer.

Another benefit is that users can send their print jobs to different printers for different purposes, without having to copy the file they want to print onto a diskette and then physically moving to a different workstation.

NetWare print services also lets you prioritize print jobs, so that important print jobs are sent to the printer ahead of less-important print jobs.

How NetWare Printing Works

In stand-alone printing, a printer is connected directly to the serial or parallel port (usually LPT1) on the workstation. When the user prints a file, the print job goes from the application to the print driver, which formats the job for the specific printer. (The print driver is software that converts the print job into a format that the printer can understand.) Next the print job goes to the LPT port, and then directly to the printer. Often, the application has to wait until the print job is finished before it can resume working.

With NetWare print services, the print job goes to the network instead of directly to the printer, though this process is transparent to users. Then the network takes care of sending the print job to the correct printer.

To accomplish this, NetWare print services employs two features called print queues and print servers. The *print queue* is a special network directory that stores print jobs temporarily before they are printed. Multiple network users can have their jobs stored in the same print queue. The print queue receives all incoming print jobs from various users and stores them in a first-come, first-served order.

The *print server* is a software program, called PSERVER.NLM, which runs on the NetWare server. The print server controls how the print queues and printers work together. The print server takes the jobs from the print queue and forwards them on to the printer when the printer is available.

You can have more than one print queue on a network. Further, you can set up one print queue so that it services several printers (although this can be confusing because you never know which printer will print the job you send). You can also set up a single printer so that it services several print queues. However, it generally simplifies your administration tasks and reduces your users' confusion if you use a one-to-one correspondence between print queues and printers, so that each print queue sends jobs to its own printer.

When you set up NetWare print services, you assign a printer, a print server, and a print queue to each other. Then you redirect the workstation's parallel port to point to a network print queue instead of a directly attached printer.

To redirect the workstation's LPT port, you can use the NetWare utility called CAPTURE (usually placing the CAPTURE command in a login script so that it is executed automatically). You can also use the NetWare User Tools utility (which runs under Windows) to assign LPT1 to a print queue.

Alternatively, most network-aware applications let you set them up so that they redirect print jobs to a print queue themselves. In many cases, you can simply specify a printer in the application, and because the printer, print queue, and print server are all assigned to each other, the job is sent automatically to the correct print queue.

NetWare print services enables printers to be attached directly to the server, attached to various workstations on the network, or attached directly to the network cabling (this last option is currently the most common).

If you attach printers directly to the NetWare server, the server must run an NLM called NPRINTER.NLM. This NLM is a port driver, which is software that routes jobs out of the print queue, through the proper port on the server, to the printer.

If you attach printers to workstations on the network, those workstations must also be running a port driver called NPRINTER.EXE (for DOS and Windows 3.1) and NPTWIN95.EXE (for Windows 95). The workstation's version of NPRINTER or NPTWIN95 works the same way as the server's version, sending print jobs through the port on the workstation to the printer.

Workstations that have printers attached can still be used by workstation users to do regular, day-to-day work. The workstation simply acts as a connection to the network for that printer.

The workstation attached to the printer should still redirect its own LPT1 port to the network so that it uses network printing services like all the other workstations instead of printing directly to the printer. Even if there is a printer attached directly to the workstation, it is usually more efficient to send the print job from the workstation to a network print queue, and then back to the printer. This also allows other workstations to use the printer.

Currently, the most common type of printing connection is to use printers that connect directly to the network cabling, rather than to a server or a workstation. These types of printers, often called *network-direct printers*, may run in either remote printer mode or queue server mode.

Remote printer mode lets the printer function as if it were running its own NPRINTER port driver. It doesn't need to be connected to a workstation; its internal NPRINTER-like software lets it be controlled by the NetWare print server and allows it to take advantage of NDS functionality.

The bindery-based *queue server mode* is used when the printer device has not been designed to work with NDS. This means that you must take care to install the printers, print queues, and the network-direct print devices in the same bindery context. In addition, there may be other restrictions that affect these devices. Be sure to read the manufacturer's documentation for more information about installing these devices.

With NetWare print services, the journey of a print job follows this path:

- The application works with the print driver to format the print job, just as it does in stand-alone mode.
- Instead of going through the LPT port directly to a printer, the print job is redirected to a print queue. If you specify that one print job goes to one printer and another job goes to a second printer, they will both be redirected from the LPT port to the correct print queues.
- When the printer is available, the print server takes the print job from the print queue and sends it to the port driver (such as NPTWIN95.EXE, NPRINTER.EXE, or NPRINTER.NLM) running wherever the printer is connected.
- The port driver then sends the print job to the printer, and the job is printed.

Figure 9.1 illustrates the path a print job takes through the network. In this particular example, the printer is attached to a workstation that is running NPRINTER.EXE.

FIGURE 9.1 *A Print Job's Path through the Network*

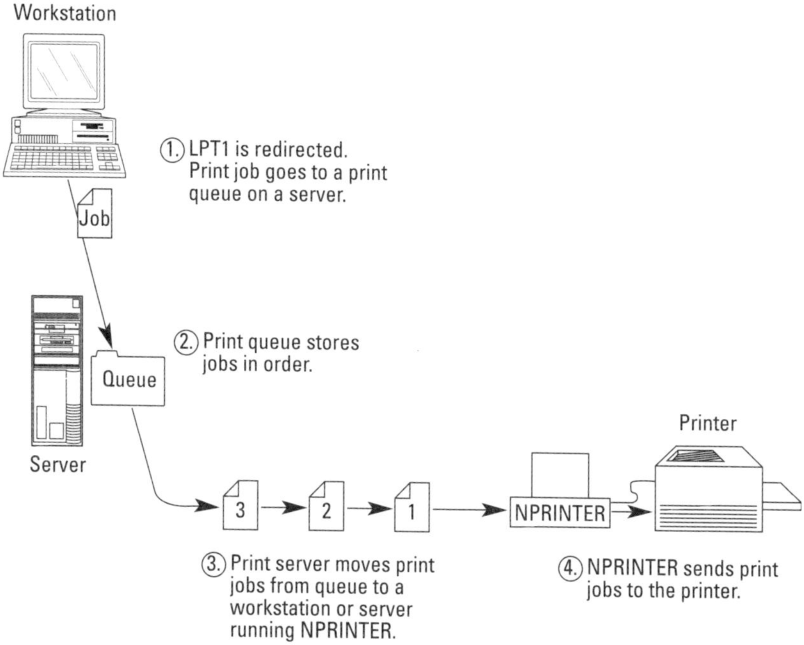
Workstation
1. LPT1 is redirected. Print job goes to a print queue on a server.
Job
2. Print queue stores jobs in order.
Queue
Server
Printer
3
2
1
NPRINTER
3. Print server moves print jobs from queue to a workstation or server running NPRINTER.
4. NPRINTER sends print jobs to the printer.

Planning NetWare Print Services

When you plan how to set up NetWare print services, keep the following guidelines and restrictions in mind:

- In general, PSERVER.NLM uses about 27K of server RAM for each configured printer.
- PSERVER.NLM can service DOS, UNIX, and Macintosh printers.
- A single print server can service up to 255 printers, although performance begins to degrade after about 60 printers or so.
- If you need more than one print server in your network, you can load PSERVER.NLM on additional NetWare servers, and those print servers can service more network printers.

- Printers, print queues, and print servers are all created as NDS objects in the Directory tree.
- To set up and manage print services, you can use the NetWare Administrator utility, which runs on Windows 3.1, OS/2, or Windows 95.
- When you use the CAPTURE utility to redirect an LPT port to a network print queue, you can also use CAPTURE to specify options such as whether or not to print a banner page, whether to use tabs, and so on.
- Instead of using CAPTURE, you may prefer to set up print job configurations. A print job configuration can simplify a user's task of selecting print options by predefining settings such as the designated printer, whether to print a banner page, and the paper form to print on. Print job configurations are stored in databases. Global (or public) print job configuration databases are properties of container objects, and they can be used by multiple users. A private print job configuration database is a property of a user object and can be used only by that user. To create a print job configuration, you can use the NetWare Administrator.
- To define print devices and paper forms to be used in print job configurations, you can use the NetWare Administrator utility. (If the application you are using supports your printer, you do not need to define a print device.)
- To print a job from outside an application (such as printing an ASCII file or a workstation screen), you can use a command-line utility called NPRINT, which runs in DOS.

NOTE

There are three DOS-based utilities, called PCONSOLE, PRINTDEF, and PRINTCON, which can also be used to work with printing services. However, the NetWare Administrator utility contains all the features of these three utilities, and because of its graphical interface, NetWare Administrator is easier to use in many situations. Therefore, most people prefer to use the NetWare Administrator instead. For this reason, PCONSOLE, PRINTDEF, and PRINTCON are not discussed in this chapter.

As you plan your printing setup, decide how many printers you need and where you want to locate them. If you are going to attach printers to workstations, you may want to choose workstations that are not used as heavily as others. In addition, it will be important for the users of those workstations to remember not to turn off the workstation when other users are using the network. Instead, those users should just log out of the network when they are finished using the workstation.

Setting Up NetWare Print Services

There are two different ways to set up NetWare print services for your network:

- Use the Print Services Quick Setup option in the NetWare Administrator utility. This is the quickest, easiest way to set up print services. If you want to set up each printer to service a single print queue, which greatly simplifies printing administration, this is the installation option to use. This option also assigns printers, print servers, and print queues to each other automatically so that there is no chance for you to miss a connection and end up with a broken link somewhere in the print communication chain. After you've set up printing using this quick option, you can modify the setup later.
- Use the NetWare Administrator utility to set up a custom print configuration for a more complex situation.

USING THE QUICK SETUP OPTION

The Print Services Quick Setup option in the NetWare Administrator utility is a fast, efficient way to set up print services.

NOTE

The NetWare Administrator utility runs under Windows 3.1, OS/2, or Windows 95. For instructions on setting up the NetWare Administrator utility on a workstation, see Chapter 5.

To set up print services using the Quick Setup option, complete the steps in the following checklist.

1. Decide where you want to locate your printers and attach them to the server, workstations, or network cabling.
2. From any workstation, log in to the network as user Admin.
3. Launch the NetWare Administrator utility on the workstation.
4. Select the container object that will contain the print server, printers, and print queues. Quick Setup will put them all in the same container,

which will be especially beneficial if users have to access the objects in bindery mode.

5. From the Tools menu, select the Print Services Quick Setup option. The screen that appears shows the default names and information that NetWare Administrator will assign to the print server, printer, and print queue. See Figure 9.2 for an example of the Quick Setup screen.
6. If necessary, change the name of the print server, printer, or print queue.

FIGURE 9.2 *Print Services Quick Setup Screen*

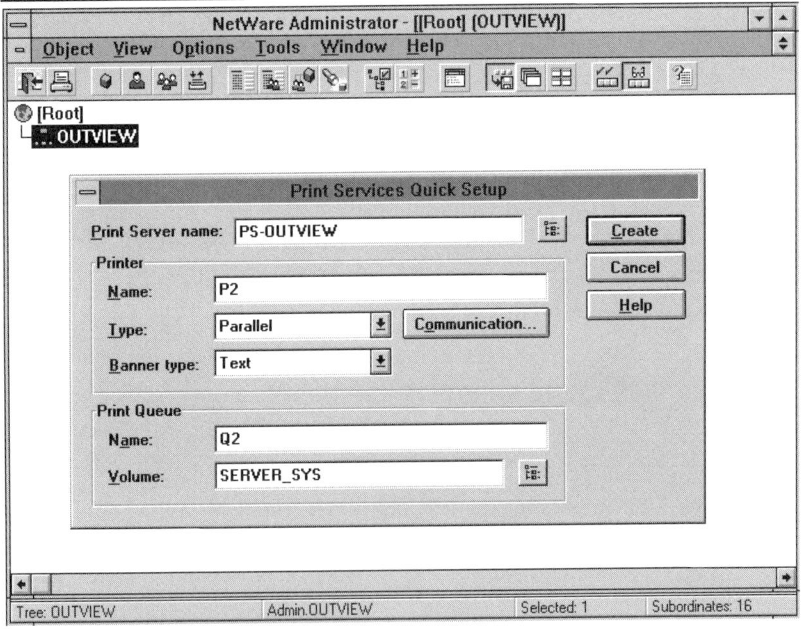

7. Choose the printer type you are using (parallel, serial, UNIX, AppleTalk, or AIO) and fill in any necessary information about that printer type.
8. If necessary, choose a different volume in which to store the print queue.
9. Click Create.

10. Go to the network server that will run the print server (or use Remote Console to access that server's console) and load the print server software using the following command:

    `LOAD PSERVER` *`printserver`*

    where *printserver* is the name of the newly created print server. (Later, you can put the PSERVER command, along with the print server's name, in the NetWare server's AUTOEXEC.NCF file so it automatically loads when the server is rebooted.)

11. If the printer is attached to a network server that is not running PSERVER, load the NPRINTER.NLM on the network server, specifying the print server name and printer number in the NPRINTER command. (This command can also be placed in the NetWare server's AUTOEXEC.NCF file.) If you have more than one printer attached to this server, load NPRINTER multiple times, specifying a different printer number (and print server if necessary) for each printer. For example, to load NPRINTER for printer number 0, which uses print server PS-Tech, use the following command:

    ```
    LOAD NPRINTER PS-Tech 0
    ```

12. If the printer is attached to a workstation, run NPRINTER.EXE (for DOS and Windows 3.1) or NPTWIN95.EXE (for Windows 95) on that workstation.

    a. For DOS and Windows 3.1: Type NPRINTER, followed by the print server name and printer number in the command. (You can include this command in the workstation's AUTOEXEC.BAT file after the login command.) For example, to load NPRINTER for printer number 0, which uses print server PS-Tech, use the following command:

    ```
    NPRINTER PS-Tech 0
    ```

    b. For Windows 95: Start up the NetWare Client32 software on the workstation. From the Network Neighborhood, locate the NPTWIN95.EXE file in SYS:PUBLIC\WIN95. Fill in the Add Network Printer dialog box. (To make sure NPTWIN95 loads every time the workstation reboots, add this file to the Startup folder. Choose Start, then Settings, then Taskbar, and then select the Start Menu Programs tab. Choose Add, and then Browse to find NPTWIN95.EXE. Choose Next, and then Startup. Enter a name for the icon, such as NPRINTER, and choose Finish.)

13. If you have applications that may not redirect workstation ports to a print queue automatically, add a CAPTURE command to the system, profile, or user login script, so that DOS and Windows 3.1 users' LPT ports will be redirected to a network print queue. You may need to specify the queue's full name. For example, to redirect users' LPT1 ports to the queue named Q1, with no banner page, no tabs, no form feed, and a five-second timeout interval, add the following command to the system login script:

    ```
    #CAPTURE L=1 Q=.Q1.Sales.Satellite.RedHawk NB
    NT NFF TI=5
    ```

    (This command should normally be on a single line. It's shown on two lines here because of space constraints.) To capture a port on a Windows 95 workstation, use the Network Neighborhood. Double-click on the printer, and then specify that you want to capture the port. Fill in any necessary information.

14. Configure your applications for printing, specifying queues, and so on. Follow the manufacturer's instructions for setting up the application for network printing.

15. If you want to specify different kinds of paper for different print jobs, set up definitions of paper forms. This is helpful if you use applications that print on different types of paper, such as paychecks, invoices, and so on, and the printer doesn't reset correctly after each type of job.

    To do this, select the container object and choose Details from the Object menu. Then open the Printer Forms page and give the form a name and ID number, and indicate its size (width in characters and length in lines). Now, the print server operator will be notified when a print job requires a different form to be mounted.

    To mount a form, change the paper in the printer, select the Printer object, open Details from the Object menu, open the Printer Status page, and then select Mount Form.

16. If your application isn't designed for network printing, set up print job configurations. Print job configurations tell the printer how the print job should be printed on the paper form you set up in Step 15. Print job configurations can specify items such as whether a banner page will be printed, to which queue the job should be sent, and what paper form to use. To create a print job configuration, select a container object for public configurations or a user object for private configurations. Then, choose Details from the Object menu and open the Print Job Configurations page.

17. If your applications don't recognize your printer (meaning they don't have a printer driver for that type of printer), you may be able to use a printer definition file from Novell, or you may have to create your own printer definition file. See the section "Print Device Definitions" later in this chapter for more information.
18. If you want to modify any information for the printing objects you've created, simply select the object from the NetWare Administrator Browser, choose Details from the Object menu, and edit the fields you want to change.

SETTING UP CUSTOM PRINT SERVICES

If you want to set up a custom printing environment, such as designating multiple queues that will be serviced by a single printer or multiple printers that will service a single queue, use the NetWare Administrator utility.

To set up custom printing services, complete the steps in the following checklist.

1. Decide where you want to locate your printers and attach them to the server, workstations, or network cabling.
2. From any workstation, log in to the network as user Admin.
3. Run the NetWare Administrator utility on the workstation by double-clicking its icon.
4. From NetWare Administrator's Browser, select the container object that you want to contain the printing objects.
5. From the Object menu, choose Create.
6. Select Print Queue. The screen that appears lets you specify information about the print queue you want to create. Choose Directory Service Queue, and then fill in a name for the queue and the volume that will store the queue.
7. Click the Define Additional Properties option. Define any additional information for the queue at this time by opening pages and specifying the appropriate information. For example, you can assign users and queue operators to the queue. By default, the container in which this print queue resides is assigned as a user, so all objects within the container are also users of the queue. The user Admin is the default queue operator (a person assigned to manage the queue). When finished, click OK, and then click the Create button to actually create the queue, and you'll return to the Browser.

8. Again, select the container you're creating the printing objects in, and then choose Create from the Object menu.
9. Select Printer. Enter a name for this printer.
10. Click the Define Additional Properties option. A print queue must be assigned to a printer before the printer can take print jobs from the network. Assign this printer to a print queue by selecting the Assignments page. Click the Add button. Then navigate through the NDS tree using the Directory Context panel and select the print queue you want from the Objects panel.
11. Open additional pages to specify more information for the printer, such as configuration information. When finished, click OK. Then click the Create button to actually create the printer, and you'll return to the Browser.
12. Again, select the container you're creating the printing objects in, and then choose Create from the Object menu.
13. Select Print Server. Enter a name for this print server.
14. Click the Define Additional Properties option. A printer must be assigned to a print server before network printing will work. Assign this print server to a printer by selecting the Assignments page. Click the Add button, navigate through the NDS tree using the Directory Context panel, and then select the printer you want from the Objects panel.
15. Open additional pages to specify more information for the print server as necessary. When finished, click OK. Then click the Create button to actually create the printer, and you'll return to the Browser.
16. Go to the network server that will run the print server (or use Remote Console to access that server's console) and load PSERVER.NLM by typing the following command:

    `LOAD PSERVER` *`printserver`*

    where *printserver* is the name of the newly created print server. (Later, you can put the PSERVER command, along with the print server's name, in the NetWare server's AUTOEXEC.NCF file so it loads automatically when the server is rebooted.)
17. If the printer is attached to a network server that is not running PSERVER, load NPRINTER.NLM on the network server, specifying the print server name and printer number in the NPRINTER command. (This command can also be placed in the NetWare server's AUTOEXEC.NCF file.) If you have more than one printer attached to

this server, load NPRINTER multiple times, specifying a different printer number (and print server if necessary) for each printer.

18. If the printer is attached to a workstation, run NPRINTER.EXE (for DOS and Windows 3.1) or NPTWIN95.EXE (for Windows 95) on that workstation.

    a. For DOS and Windows 3.1: Type NPRINTER, followed by the print server name and printer number in the command. (You can include this command in the workstation's AUTOEXEC.BAT file after the login command.) For example, to load NPRINTER for printer number 0, which uses print server PS-Tech, use the following command:

    ```
    NPRINTER PS-Tech 0
    ```

    b. For Windows 95: Start up the NetWare Client32 software on the workstation. Then, from the Network Neighborhood, locate the NPTWIN95.EXE file in SYS:PUBLIC\WIN95. Fill in the Add Network Printer dialog box. (To make sure NPTWIN95 loads every time the workstation reboots, add this file to the Startup folder. Choose Start, then Settings, then Taskbar, and then select the Start Menu Programs tab. Choose Add, and then Browse to find NPTWIN95.EXE. Choose Next, and then Startup. Enter a name for the icon, such as NPRINTER, and choose Finish.)

19. If you have applications that may not redirect workstation ports to a print queue automatically, add a CAPTURE command to the system, profile, or user login script, so that DOS and Windows 3.1 users' LPT ports will be redirected to a network print queue. You may need to specify the queue's full name. To capture a port on a Windows 95 workstation, use the Network Neighborhood. Find and double-click on the printer, specify that you want to capture the port, and fill in any necessary information.

20. Configure your applications for printing. In many cases, you may be able to simply configure the application to use a particular printer, since IntranetWare will automatically associate the printer with a print queue. Follow the manufacturer's instructions for setting up the application for network printing.

21. If you want to specify different kinds of paper for different print jobs, set up definitions of paper forms. This is helpful if you use applications that print on different types of paper, such as paychecks, invoices, and so on, and the printer doesn't reset correctly after each type of job.

To do this, select the container object and choose Details from the Object menu. Then open the Printer Forms page, give the form a name and ID number, and indicate its size (width in characters and length in lines). Now, the print server operator will be notified when a print job requires a different form to be mounted.

To mount a form, change the paper in the printer, and then select the Printer object. Open Details from the Object menu, open the Printer Status page, and then select Mount Form.

22. If your application isn't designed for network printing, set up print job configurations. Print job configurations tell the printer how the print job should be printed on the paper form you set up in Step 21. Print job configurations can specify items such as whether a banner page will be printed, to which queue the job should be sent, and what paper form to use. To create a print job configuration, select a container object for public configurations or a user object for private configurations. Then, choose Details from the Object menu and open the Print Job Configurations page.
23. If your applications don't recognize your printer (meaning they don't have a printer driver for that type of printer), you may be able to use a printer definition file from Novell, or you may have to create your own printer definition file. See the section "Print Device Definitions" for more information.

PRINT DEVICE DEFINITIONS

Printer drivers are software programs that control printer functions, regulating how printers handle print jobs. Many network-aware applications contain printer drivers for a variety of common printers. If your application doesn't recognize your type of printer, you will either have to use a Novell printer definition file, or you will have to create your own.

To see if IntranetWare came with a printer definition file that you can use, look at the files with the .PDF extension in the SYS:PUBLIC directory. If yours is there, you can import that file into the device database.

To import one of Novell's printer definition files so that you can use it, use the NetWare Administrator utility. Choose the container object, and then choose Details from the Object menu. Open the Print Devices page (shown in Figure 9.3), click Import, and select the correct .PDF file from the SYS:PUBLIC directory.

FIGURE 9.3 *The Print Devices Page*

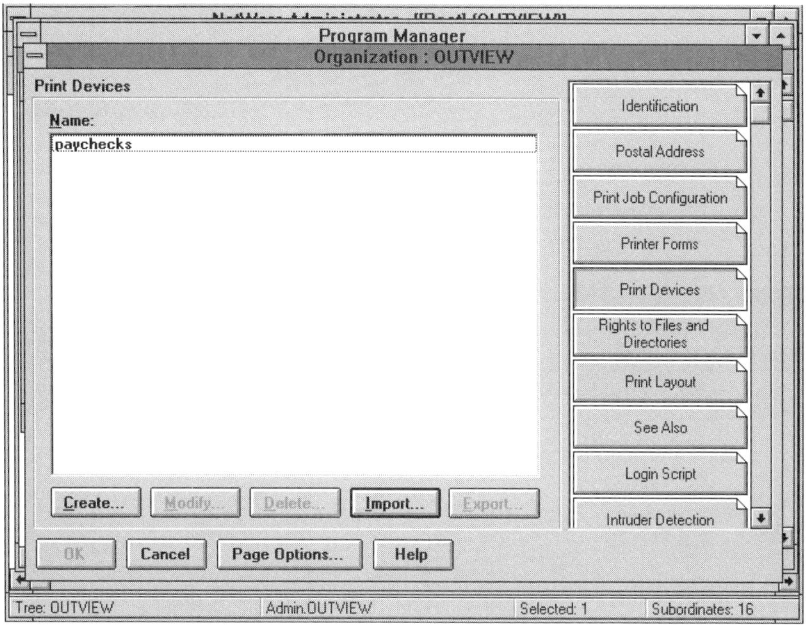

If the driver you need isn't in the SYS:PUBLIC directory, you will have to create your own printer definition file. To do this, select the container object, then choose Details from the Object menu. Open the Print Devices page. Enter a name for the printer definition, and then choose OK. Now click the Modify button. Click on the Create Function or Create Mode buttons to specify the control sequences used by your printer. You will have to refer to the manufacturer's documentation for the control sequences (or printer commands) to use.

After you've created your own printer definition file, you can export it to the SYS:PUBLIC directory (or another location) so that you can then import it to other container objects. To export the definition file, return to the Print Devices page, select the definition you just created, and click Export. Locate the directory where you want to place the file, and then choose OK. The file is named with the first eight characters from the definition's name, plus the .PDF extension. This file can now be imported to other containers' or users' databases.

VERIFYING YOUR PRINTING SETUP

After you've set up your printing services, you can use the NetWare Administrator utility to see a graphical representation of your printing setup. Using this feature, you can see if all your printing objects are assigned to each other correctly.

To see this printing layout diagram, select the container that holds the printing objects, or select the specific print server you're interested in. Choose Details from the Object menu, and then open the Print Layout page. Figure 9.4 shows an example of a print layout diagram.

FIGURE 9.4 *The Print Layout Page*

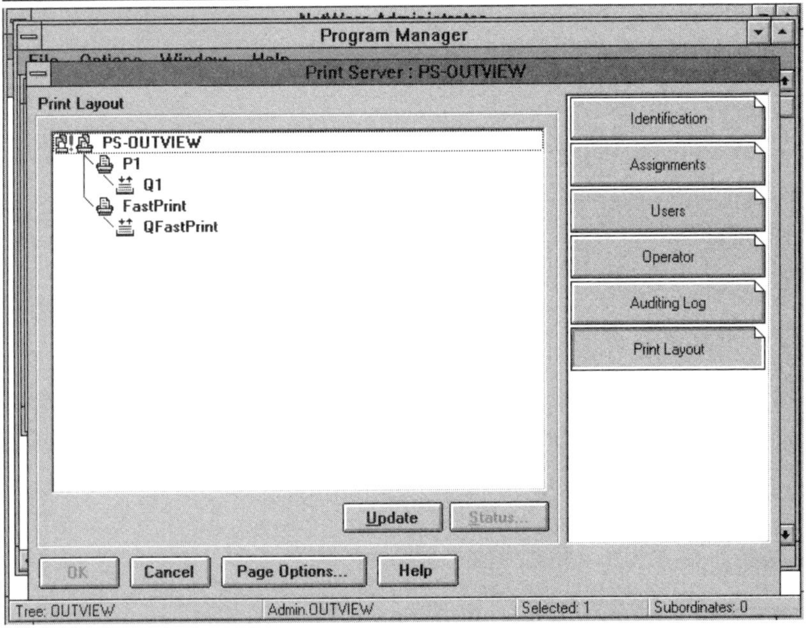

If all you see is a list of print servers, click on a print server to expand the view to show its assigned printers and queues. Lines connecting the printing objects indicate that the objects are assigned to each other correctly. A dashed line connecting them indicates that the connection is good only for this session. When the server is rebooted, the connections will be removed.

If any printing object has an icon with an exclamation mark (!) beside it, there's a problem with that object. (Notice the print server object in Figure 9.4

has an exclamation mark.) Go back through the instructions and see if you missed any steps assigning print queues, print servers, and printers to each other.

You can also right-click on any of the objects to see more information about that particular object.

In addition, you can see the print jobs in a queue by double-clicking the queue object. However, you cannot modify the print jobs from this screen. To modify the print jobs, you have to go back to the NetWare Administrator Browser, select a print queue, and open its Print Jobs page.

Handling Print Jobs

After NetWare print services are set up on the network, users can send their jobs to network print queues as long as they have access to those printers.

A user has access to a queue if he or she is assigned as a print queue user. By default, the container in which a print queue resides is assigned as a user, so all objects within the container are also users of the queue. A print queue user can add jobs to a print queue, see the status of all jobs in the queue, and delete his or her own job from the queue. A queue user cannot delete other users' print jobs from the queue.

A print queue operator is a special type of print queue user who has the ability to manage the print queue. A queue operator can delete other users' print jobs, put them on hold, and so on. The user Admin is the default queue operator.

You can add or remove users and operators from the list of print queue users by using the NetWare Administrator utility. You can also use the same utility to look at the current print jobs in the print queue.

To use the NetWare Administrator utility to change users and operators, select the Print Queue object, choose Details from the Object menu, and then open the Users or Operator page.

To see the current print jobs in the queue, open the Job List page. Here, users can delete their own print jobs or put them on hold. Queue operators can put on hold or delete any users' print jobs. Press the F1 key to read help on each of the available fields in the Job List screen. Figure 9.5 shows the Print Jobs page.

FIGURE 9.5 *Print Jobs in a Print Queue*

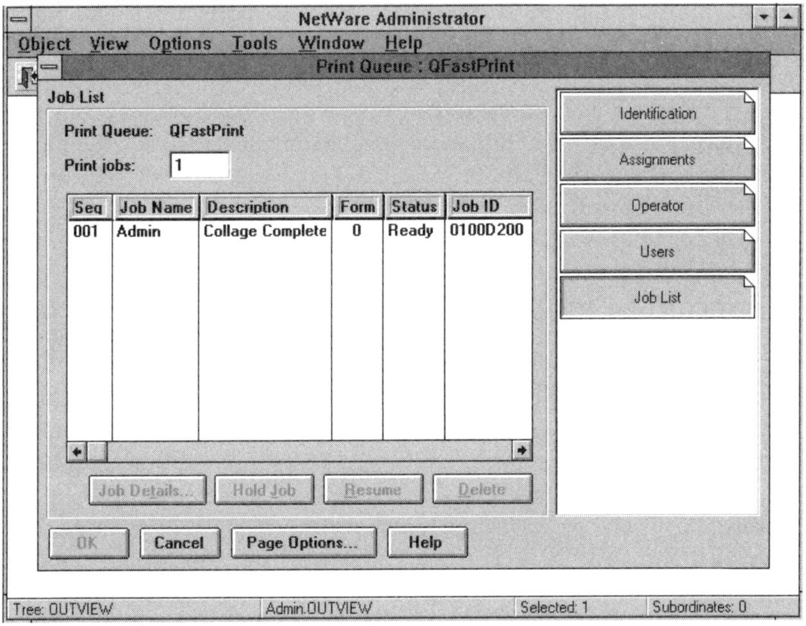

Auditing Print Services

An auditing feature of NetWare print services enables you to track information such as what jobs have been printed, which users sent those jobs, the size of the jobs, the time they were printed, and the printer that was used. This can be useful information if your organization charges users or departments for printing usage.

This information is not tracked by default; you have to enable the printing auditing log in order to track it.

To enable the auditing log, use the NetWare Administrator utility. Select the container object, open its Details page, and then open the Auditing Log page. In this page, you can switch the status to Enabled, and then specify the location where you want the log file stored. (You will have to unload and then reload PSERVER.NLM on the server in order for this change to take effect.)

You can also limit the size of the log file from this page. If the log file reaches its maximum size, or if the volume runs out of room, the log file will stop tracking printing usage. Therefore, it's important to archive or delete the log file regularly so that you don't lose any of the information you need.

To read the auditing log, click the View button in the Auditing Log page.

Unloading PSERVER.NLM

Unloading PSERVER.NLM is very easy. From the NetWare Administrator utility, select the print server object. Then, from the Object menu, choose Details and click Unload.

To reload PSERVER, type the following command at the network server's console:

```
LOAD PSERVER printserver
```

where *printserver* is the name of the newly created print server.

CHAPTER 10

Connecting Mac OS Workstations to a NetWare Network

Instant Access

Installing NetWare Client for Mac OS

- To install NetWare Client for Mac OS server components, use INSTALL.NLM. Select Product Options and select Install NetWare Client for Mac OS.
- To install NetWare Client for Mac OS workstation software, use the Mac OS Clients Installer on the NetWare 4.11 CD-ROM.

Working with NDS Objects

- To see the NDS objects in a Directory tree, mount volumes, configure print jobs, and so on, use the NetWare Directory Browser from a Mac OS workstation.

Printing from a Mac OS Workstation

- To print from a Mac OS Workstation, use the NetWare Directory Browser from the workstation, select the Printer object, and specify any printer configuration information. Then print the file from the application just as you would normally.
- To add helpful information to a PostScript Printer object's properties so that Mac OS users can use the printers without selecting the wrong print driver, loading unnecessary fonts, and so on, use the NetWare Administrator utility.

Logging in to and out of the Network

- To log in to the NDS network, pull down the menu beneath the NetWare Client Tree icon and select Log In.
- To log out, pull down the menu beneath the Tree icon and select Log Out.

Running a Remote Console

- To run a remote console, install the Remote Console software on the Mac OS workstation using the Custom Install option of the Installer. Then, double-click on the Remote Console icon in the NetWare Client Utilities folder.

Managing the Desktop Database

- To manage the desktop database for a network volume, use the MAC-FILE.NLM.

Using HFS CD-ROMs

- To mount HFS CD-ROMs as network volumes, use HFSCD.NLM.
- To configure HFSCD.NLM, use HFSCDCON.NLM.

The NetWare Client for Mac OS is a feature of IntranetWare that allows you to attach workstations running the Mac OS to your NetWare network. Once they are connected to the network, users of these workstations can take advantage of NetWare's security systems, file and print sharing capabilities, NDS objects, and other powerful features.

Earlier versions of NetWare used a product called NetWare for Macintosh to allow Mac OS workstations to attach to a NetWare network. With NetWare for Macintosh, you used the AppleTalk protocol on the network and set up an AppleTalk router in the NetWare server to connect the Mac OS workstations on an AppleTalk network to the rest of the NetWare network. This product is no longer necessary with the new NetWare Client software in IntranetWare.

This new client software allows Mac OS workstations to communicate directly with the network and with NDS using either the IPX/SPX family of protocols (NetWare's default protocols) or the IPX/IP protocol family.

NetWare Client for Mac OS also allows you to run a Remote Console session from this Mac OS workstation, so that you can control the server console without leaving your workstation.

The NetWare Client for Mac OS includes both software that must be installed on each Mac OS workstation, and software that must be installed on the NetWare server.

NOTE

You cannot use a Mac OS computer as a NetWare server; the server must be a PC computer.

With NetWare Client for Mac OS, Mac OS workstations have access to NetWare features without losing the Mac OS "look and feel." Mac OS users still open and work with files, launch applications, send print jobs to printers, and manage their desktops just as they always have. In most cases, the only differences users will notice is that now they can log into the NDS tree so that they can access files on network volumes and other NDS resources, and they can send their print jobs to network printers and queues.

An additional benefit is that PC-based and Mac OS users can share files if they use a common application or an application that can convert files from another format.

The following sections explain how to set up the NetWare Client for Mac OS software on a server and on the workstations.

Installing the Server Components

If you intend to store Mac OS-based applications and files on the NetWare server, you should create a separate volume for Mac OS files when you first install the server. As explained in Chapter 8, in order for a volume to store Mac OS files, it must have the Mac OS name space module loaded. Having a separate volume for Mac OS files can help save server memory, and it may make backups and restores easier to manage.

The following checklist outlines the steps for installing the server components of the NetWare Client for Mac OS.

1. Be sure the NetWare 4.11 CD-ROM is mounted as a volume on the server.
2. From the server console, load INSTALL.NLM, select Product Options, and then select Choose an Item or Product Listed Above.
3. Select Install NetWare Client for Mac OS.
4. Select the source path for the software. This path should be the path to the CD-ROM.
5. Choose either the Easy Install or Custom Install option.
   a. If you choose the Easy Install option, a summary screen shows you what will happen. In general, it shows that the Mac name space will be added to the SYS volume (if it isn't already added), it shows which language will be installed, and it indicates that AUTOEXEC.NCF will be edited to automatically load MACFILE.NLM (which controls the desktop database). If this is the installation you want, press Esc to exit the summary screen, and then select Proceed With The Installation. After the files are all installed, you can exit INSTALL.
   b. If you choose the Custom Install, you will see a list of installation options. These options let you specify which volumes you want to add the Mac name space to, the languages you want to install, whether to load MACFILE.NLM automatically, and so on. Specify the options you want, and then choose Proceed With The Installation when you are ready. After the files are all installed, you can exit INSTALL.

After you've installed the server components, you can set up the NetWare Client software on all the Mac OS computers to turn them into network workstations.

Installing the Workstation Components

If you want users on Mac OS workstations to log in to the network using NDS, each of those users' workstations must have the workstation components of the NetWare Client for Mac OS installed. The client software allows the workstation to communicate with the network, and lets the user log in to the NDS tree. It also allows you to force Macs to use encrypted passwords.

A Mac OS workstation should meet the following system requirements to have NetWare client software installed:

- The Mac OS computer should be an SE or later, with at least 4MB of RAM installed.
- It should be running System 7.1 or better if you want to take advantage of NDS features. (In fact, System 7.5 is preferred because of some of the features in that version of the operating system.)

SELECTING THE NETWORK CONNECTION SOFTWARE

In addition to the requirements listed above, you should have selected the type of network cabling (*network connection type*) that your Mac OS portion of the network will use. Most Mac OS computers currently have EtherTalk support built in. (Older Mac OS computers may have LocalTalk support built in instead.) If your Mac OS computer has EtherTalk built in, you do not need to buy an additional network board for the computer. You can simply use Ethernet cabling to connect the Mac OS workstation, as is, to the network.

Non-EtherTalk network connection types require that you install a network board in the Mac OS workstation, just as you do with PCs. Generally, when you purchase a network board, you also receive from the manufacturer the software (called a *driver*) to run the board. You usually install the network connection driver in the Extensions folder, located in the System folder.

After you choose the network connection type you will use, open the workstation's Network Control Panel. Then select the corresponding AppleTalk network connection to activate the driver. (Even if you are using EtherTalk, check the Network Control Panel to make sure the EtherTalk network connection type is selected.)

There are five different network connection types available. They are listed in Table 10.1.

TABLE 10.1 *Network Connection Types*

NETWORK CONNECTION TYPE	DESCRIPTION
LocalTalk (Built-In)	The LocalTalk connection type used to be built into every Mac OS computer. If you have older Mac OS computers that have LocalTalk, and want to use LocalTalk, you don't need to install a network board in the computer. The computers can connect to each other with just LocalTalk cabling. If you want to access NDS over LocalTalk, you must install the AppleTalk interface for MacIPX, as explained in the section "Using the MacIPX Gateway" later in this chapter. (EtherTalk has replaced LocalTalk in more recent Mac OS computers.)
ARCnet	With ARCnet, you need to install an ARCnet network board in each workstation and a corresponding one in the server. ARCnet does not support IPX or the MacIPX gateway, however, so you can only connect to IntranetWare servers in bindery services mode. Very few, if any, network board manufacturers still make ARCnet boards for Macs, so ARCnet is seldom used.
EtherTalk 1.0 and 2.0	The EtherTalk 2.0 connection type is currently built into every Mac OS computer. (It replaced LocalTalk as the built-in connection type.) EtherTalk is the Mac OS version of Ethernet. If EtherTalk is built into your computer, you do not need to install a separate network board. If your computer has LocalTalk built in, you must install an EtherTalk network board in the workstation. Make sure there is a corresponding Ethernet board in the server. In the Network Control Panel, the icon for EtherTalk 1.0, which is only used in a nonextended AppleTalk network, has single arrows pointing in opposite directions. The icon for EtherTalk 2.0, which supports extended AppleTalk networks, has double arrows pointing in opposite directions.
TokenTalk	With TokenTalk, you need to install a Token Ring network board in each workstation and a corresponding one in the server.

RUNNING THE INSTALLER

The NetWare Client for Mac OS software is located on the NetWare CD-ROM. If your Mac OS workstations have CD-ROM drives, you can insert the CD-ROM directly into the workstations' drives and install the client software from there. If some of your workstations don't have CD-ROM drives, you'll need to make an installation diskette from one of the computers that does have a CD-ROM drive.

To create the installation diskette, insert the NetWare 4.11 CD-ROM into a workstation's drive. Then insert a Mac OS-formatted high-density diskette into the computer's diskette drive, and copy the Mac OS Clients Installer icon from the CD-ROM to the diskette.

To install the client software on the workstation, complete the steps in the following checklist.

1. Insert the NetWare 4.11 CD-ROM or the client installation diskette into the Mac OS workstation's local drive.
2. Double-click on the Mac OS Clients Installer icon. (There should be no other applications, including virus detectors, running on the workstation. The Installer will close any other running applications, including Finder, for you. You may prefer to close them yourself before you begin the installation.)
3. Choose NetWare Client for Mac OS, and then close the title screen that appears.
4. Choose whether you want the Easy Install or the Custom Install option.
   a. If you choose the Easy Install option, all the files you need to connect to the network using IPX/SPX protocols (MacIPX) will be installed. This should be adequate for most installations.
   b. If you want to connect to the network using IP protocols (NetWare/IP), or if you want to install the Remote Console feature on this workstation, choose the Custom Install. In the Custom Install screen, select the items you want to install. To select multiple items, hold down the Command key while you click on your selections. You cannot select both NetWare/IP and MacIPX for the same workstation. Only one protocol family can be used by a single workstation.
5. When the installation is finished, click the Restart button to restart the workstation so that the client software will be activated.

6. (NetWare/IP only) If you installed NetWare/IP support on this workstation, open the NetWare/IP Control Panel (located in the Control Panels folder within the System folder). In this Control Panel, select the network interface you want to use (NetWare/IP), and then click the NetWare/IP icon to specify additional information such as the domain name, the nearest NetWare/IP server, and so on. When finished, close the Control Panel.

Now the Mac OS computer is ready to use as a workstation on the IntranetWare network.

USING THE MACIPX GATEWAY

The MacIPX gateway is a NetWare Client for Mac OS feature that lets Mac OS workstations that are running MacIPX applications on LocalTalk networks (or dialing in using AppleTalk Remote Access) access NDS on a IntranetWare network.

Most users will not have to use a MacIPX gateway.

LocalTalk and AppleTalk Remote Access use only AppleTalk protocols. They do not support IPX. MacIPX software provides support for IPX transport protocols. You don't need to use the MacIPX gateway if you've connected your Mac OS workstations directly to your NetWare network using Ethernet or Token Ring.

When a user logs in to an NDS network, the IPX protocol (NetWare's native network protocol) is used to authenticate the connection. After the authentication is complete, AppleTalk is used for other communications with NetWare.

If a user is logging in to an NDS network from a LocalTalk network or dialing up with AppleTalk Remote Access, where IPX is not supported, the user's workstation has to send IPX packets encapsulated in AppleTalk. The MacIPX gateway receives these encapsulated packets, strips off the AppleTalk data, and forwards the IPX packet to the appropriate node on the IPX network. The gateway also reverses the process, adding AppleTalk encapsulation to IPX packets, to send data from the IPX node to the MacIPX workstation.

To set up the MacIPX gateway, you must use INETCFG.NLM to configure the gateway on the server, and then use the MacIPX Control Panel on each Mac OS workstation to provide MacIPX support.

To configure a MacIPX gateway and set up workstations for MacIPX support, complete the steps in the following checklist.

1. On the server, load INETCFG.NLM.
2. Choose Boards and press Insert.
3. Select MACIPXGW and assign a board name to it. Press Esc to save the settings.
4. Choose Bindings and press Insert.
5. Choose the IPX protocol, and then select the board name you assigned to the MacIPX gateway driver.
6. Specify the network number of the IPX network to which the gateway is attached.
7. When finished, press Esc to save the settings.
8. Use the REINITIALIZE SYSTEM console utility to make the gateway settings take effect.
9. On a Mac OS workstation, open the MacIPX Control Panel. The panel displays icons for each available network interface.
10. Select the appropriate interface and set the appropriate parameters. Choose the AppleTalk interface if the workstation is connected to a LocalTalk cable, or if you want to use AppleTalk Remote Access to dial into the IPX network.
11. Select the zone in which the MacIPX gateway is located, so that the AppleTalk interface will select the correct MacIPX gateway automatically when the workstation is started.
12. Close the Control Panel. The workstation is now prepared for MacIPX gateway support.

Using the NetWare Client for Mac OS

After you've installed the NetWare Client for Mac OS, you can use the workstation to log in to and out of the network, use the NetWare Directory Browser to see NDS objects in the Directory tree, control the server console from a Remote Console session, or send print jobs to a network printer. The following sections explain how to do these tasks.

LOGGING IN TO AND OUT OF THE NETWORK

After you've set up the Mac OS workstation, you can log in to the NDS network using the NetWare Client Tree icon in the menu bar of the workstation.

If you're logged in to the network, the tree icon will have leaves on it. If you are not logged in, the tree will have bare branches. To log in, pull down the Tree menu and select Log In. Then enter your login name and password, and click Log In. (Passwords are not case-sensitive.)

If you click the More Options button, you can specify a different tree or context to use when logging in. The Set Password button lets you change your password.

You can use the Tree menu to log out of the network by selecting the Log Out option.

The Configure option under the Tree menu lets you specify your preferred NDS trees, your context, and login name. The Available button lets you see those trees and contexts that are being held in cache (recently used and still in memory). To use trees that aren't displayed in the cached Available list, use the Find and Add buttons.

The Connections option under the Tree menu lets you disconnect from servers and volumes, without logging out of the NDS tree itself. You can also see information about your connections by clicking the Get Info button. (Another way to disconnect from a volume is to drag its icon to the Trash.)

Once you've logged in to the network, you can work with network files and other services. You can also use the NetWare Directory Browser to mount volumes and work with other NDS objects.

USING THE NETWARE DIRECTORY BROWSER

As part of the NetWare Client for Mac OS software, a NetWare Directory Browser gets installed on the workstation in the NetWare Client Utilities folder. This Browser lets users view the objects in a Directory tree.

To start up the Browser, double-click the NetWare Directory Browser icon in the NetWare Client Utilities folder. If you haven't already logged in to NDS, you'll be asked if you want to now.

The pop-up menu at the top of the Browser screen shows the NDS container you're in currently. You can pop up this menu to select a different container.

The Objects panel displays NDS objects within that container.

The Show Types panel lets you select the types of objects you want to display in the Objects panel. For example, you can choose to list only User and Group objects, or you can select all types.

To open multiple Browsers, so that you can compare objects in different containers, choose New Browser Window from the File menu. To browse through objects in a different tree, select Browse Another Tree from the File menu.

From the Browser, you can work with the NDS objects, such as Volumes and Printers. For example, to mount a volume from within the Browser, you can simply double-click its icon.

If there's a particular printer or print queue you want to select and send a print job to, you can double-click on that Printer or Print Queue object in the Browser and enter the necessary information.

To simplify access to Volume, Printers, and Print Queue objects, you can drag those objects from the Browser to your desktop or a local folder. (Dragging these objects is only supported if you have System 7.5. If you have System 7.1, you must select the object, and then choose Save Selection to Desktop or Save Selection to Folder to accomplish the same thing.)

USING REMOTE CONSOLE FROM A MAC OS WORKSTATION

To use Remote Console from a Mac OS workstation, you must use the Custom Install option of the Mac OS Clients Installer to install the Remote Console software on the workstation. (See the section "Installing the Workstation Components" earlier in this chapter for details.)

Once Remote Console capability is installed, you start a Remote Console session by double-clicking the Remote Console icon on your workstation's desktop.

Like the DOS-based version of Remote Console, you must have the necessary Remote Console NLMs loaded on the server and you must have the Remote Console password before you can start a session. Once you've met those requirements, you can use the Remote Console feature from a Mac OS workstation just as you can from a DOS-based workstation. See Chapter 3 for more information about Remote Console.

TIP

If your Mac OS keyboard does not have function keys (F1, F2, and so on), you can choose Show Function Keys from the Edit menu while you're in a Remote Console session. A palette appears, displaying buttons for the various function keys that Remote Console users can press to navigate through a session. Alternatively, you can use the keystrokes shown in Table 10.2.

TABLE 10.2 *Keystrokes for Navigating through Remote Console*

EXTENDED KEYBOARD	NON-EXTENDED KEYBOARD	DESCRIPTION
Option-F2	Option-Command-2	Closes the session window and displays the server list
Option-F3	Option-Command-3	Moves backwards through active console screens
Option-F4	Option-Command-4	Moves forwards through active console screens
Option-F5	Option-Command-5	Shows the address of the workstation you're using for this session
Ins	Option-Command-i	Inserts information on the screen
Del	Option-Command-d	Deletes information on the screen

You can also select to view an active console screen by choosing one from the Window menu.

PRINTING FROM A MAC OS WORKSTATION

Workstations with NetWare Client for Mac OS installed can send print jobs to compatible NetWare network printers, taking advantage of NetWare's print sharing capabilities.

The NetWare Print Access system extension is installed into the workstation's Extensions folder during the client software installation. This system extension lets supported AppleTalk printer drivers use NetWare printing protocols to handle print jobs.

Printing to a network printer is really no different, as far as the user is concerned, from printing to a directly attached printer.

The first time you want to print a job, you can open the NetWare Directory Browser and double-click the Printer object. This launches the NetWare Print Chooser automatically. You can then select a printer driver if necessary. The NetWare Options button will let you configure the print job, such as specifying if there should be a banner page, notification, and so on. Then, all subsequent print jobs will be sent to that selected printer until you choose a different printer.

Remember, if you want to put the Printer object on your desktop for easier access, you can drag it from the Browser to the desktop (for System 7.5 only) or choose Save Selection to Desktop.

When the user selects a Printer object for printing, the NetWare Client software takes care of sending the print jobs to the network print queue first, so the user doesn't need to worry about print queues at all.

To make the Mac OS workstations use a network printer more efficiently, you should put some information into the Printer object's properties. Information such as the Printer Description Language (PDL) and the printer's supported fonts can be stored in the Printer's object information in NDS so that communication between the printer and the workstation goes smoothly.

The information needed for a PostScript printer can be found by sending a file called PSINFO.PS to that printer. The PSINFO.PS file will print out a list of the printer's key information. You can then use that printout to input information into the Printer object's properties.

To print out the PSINFO.PS file, use the NPRINT utility from a DOS-based workstation. Go to the directory called SYS:SYSTEM\NW-MAC\PSUTILS. Then, use the following NPRINT command, substituting the full NDS name of your printer for *printer*:

```
nprint psinfo.ps p=printer nt nff nb
```

Armed with the information in the PSINFO.PS printout, use the NetWare Administrator utility and open the Printer object's Details page. Fill in the properties that relate to the information in the printout, such as the PDL and the supported fonts.

Rebuilding or Resetting the Desktop Database

One of the server components installed with NetWare Client for Mac OS is MACFILE.NLM. This module controls the desktop for Mac OS files on the server. Occasionally, the desktop may become out of sync or even corrupted. It could get out of sync if, for example, you use a non-Mac OS workstation to restore a large number of files onto the server from a backup. Other possible symptoms that may indicate a problem with the desktop would be missing or damaged icons or icons that fail to launch an application when they're double-clicked.

When this happens, it may help to either rebuild or reset the desktop for that volume. Rebuilding the desktop adds new information to the existing database. Resetting the desktop deletes the existing database and builds a new one from scratch.

To rebuild or reset the desktop, MACFILE.NLM must be loaded. (The installation program loads this NLM automatically, and adds it to the AUTOEXEC.NCF file so it reloads every time the server reboots.)

To rebuild the desktop, type the following command at the server console, substituting the name of the affected volume for *volume*:

```
MACFILE REBUILD DESKTOP ON volume
```

To reset the desktop, use the following command instead:

```
MACFILE RESET DESKTOP ON volume
```

Mounting HPFS-Formatted CD-ROMs

You can mount HPFS-formatted CD-ROMs as a NetWare volume on the network. HPFS (High-Performance File System) CD-ROMs are formatted differently than most PC-based CD-ROMs. To mount an HPFS CD-ROM as a NetWare volume, load HFSCD.NLM. To configure this NLM, use HFSCD-CON.NLM.

Sharing Mac OS and DOS Files

With NetWare Client for Mac OS installed on a NetWare server and on Mac OS workstations, Mac and PC users can see the names of each other's files displayed in file listings or folders, access the same directories, and take advantage of the same NetWare features. (Of course, which files and directories they access depends upon the trustee rights they've been granted. See Chapter 7 for more information about trustee rights.)

However, just because a Mac OS user can see a DOS file doesn't necessarily mean the Mac OS user can open the file. This is because Mac OS and DOS files have completely different formats. NetWare can store both formats (if the Mac OS name space is loaded), but it can't control how applications create files.

With the Mac OS file format, files have two parts:

- The *data fork* portion of the file contains the actual text of the file. This fork corresponds somewhat to a DOS-based file.
- The *resource fork* portion of the file contains information about the file, such as the application used to create the file (which lets you auto-launch a file by double-clicking its icon). In addition, the resource fork

includes information about the type of icon that should be displayed for the file, and so on. DOS and OS/2 files don't have resource forks.

Another difference between DOS and Mac OS files is the rules that govern file names:

- Mac OS names can be up to 31 characters long and can contain spaces and punctuation.
- DOS file names can only consist of 11 characters (an 8-character name, followed by a period, followed by a 3-character extension). In addition, you cannot use spaces or punctuation marks, except for the underscore character (_).

When Mac OS file names are displayed on a PC, those names are shortened to appear in the DOS file name format. The names are shortened for display purposes only and are not actually changed. When you look at the file from a Mac OS, the name still appears in its original format.

These differences, however, do not mean that PC and Mac OS users can never share files. That depends entirely upon the applications that the users are using. Many applications have been created with both a Mac OS and a DOS or Windows version. Most of these applications can take a file from one format and convert it into the other format so that either user can open it.

NOTE

A common mistake new users make is to think that Mac OS users can actually execute PC-based applications or games from a Mac OS workstation. This is not true. Applications can't run on both PCs and Mac OS workstations because of the differences in file format mentioned earlier. However, many applications do have two versions (or more) — one that works on PCs and one that works on Mac OS workstations.

Another option, if the users don't have common applications, is to convert the files into a format that is supported by applications the users do have. For example, if a Mac OS application allows you to save a file in an ASCII format, you can then open the file from a DOS or Windows application that also supports ASCII. However, this process converts only the text in a file; any graphic or formatting elements will be lost.

This means that if your users need to share files, you should make sure that they have applications that can convert files between the two formats. Also, you may want to recommend that Mac OS users use DOS-style file names so the names are comprehensible to PC users.

CHAPTER 11

Managing Protocols

Configuring Protocols

- To configure IPX, TCP/IP, or AppleTalk, use INETCFG.NLM.

Monitoring Protocols

- To monitor IPX, use IPXCON.NLM.
- To monitor AppleTalk, use ATCON.NLM.
- To monitor TCP/IP, use TCPCON.NLM.
- To test the TCP/IP connection between a workstation and a server, use PING.NLM or TPING.NLM on the server.
- To list all the protocols that are currently registered on the server, use the PROTOCOL console utility.

A protocol is a set of defined rules that controls how processes or machines communicate. A protocol regulates how the processes perform activities such as establishing communication, transferring packets of data, and terminating communication.

There are many different types of protocols that have been developed by various organizations to control how information is exchanged across a network. IntranetWare supports many of these protocols.

Discussions about protocols can become very confusing because there are so many different types of protocols, as well as protocols that layer on top of each other. Protocols are associated with several types of properties, such as:

- The network architecture they support, such as a bus- or ring-oriented architecture. Protocols designed for a bus architecture behave differently than protocols designed for a ring architecture.
- Whether they support synchronous or asynchronous transmissions. *Synchronous protocols* use timing to identify transmission of data and are better suited for transmissions that occur at a relatively constant rate. Most mainframe and terminal-handling protocols are synchronous. *Asynchronous protocols* allow data to be transmitted in bursts. These protocols use start and stop bits to mark the individual transmission elements so that the data doesn't have to arrive in its original order. Most network protocols are asynchronous.
- Whether they support connection-oriented or connectionless transmission. A *connection-oriented protocol* establishes a connection between the source and destination. It terminates the connection when the transmission is finished. With such a connection, the data packets only need a destination address. A *connectionless protocol* transmits data across any available path. Packets may take different routes to the destination. Therefore, the packets need both a source and a destination address, and they must be labeled so that they can be reassembled in the correct order when they all arrive at the destination.
- Whether they support character-oriented or bit-oriented transmission. *Character-oriented* (or *byte-oriented*) *protocols* use characters (or bytes) to manage timing and the communication link. These protocols have generally been replaced with more efficient *bit-oriented protocols.*
- The OSI layer at which they function. The OSI Reference Model is described in the next section.

The OSI Reference Model

The International Standards Organization (ISO) has defined a model for allowing any combination of devices to communicate with each other. This model, called the OSI (Open Systems Interconnection) Reference Model, defines seven layers of communication that can occur between devices.

At each layer of the OSI Reference Model, different types of functions must be provided, although the model doesn't dictate *how* those functions must occur. When manufacturers and other organizations implement those functions, they get to determine *how* they are implemented. The protocol is essentially the manufacturer's or organization's definition of how the communication functions required at that level occur.

Figure 11.1 illustrates the seven layers of the OSI Reference Model.

FIGURE 11.1 *The Seven Layers of the OSI Reference Model*

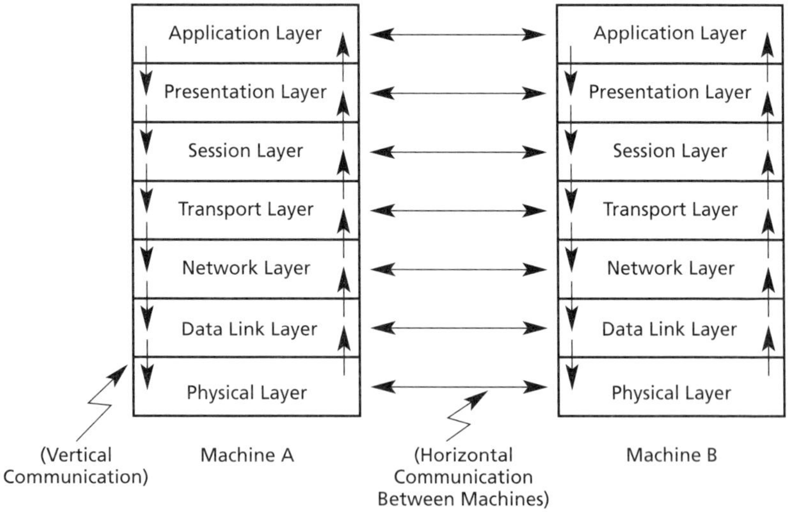

In the OSI Reference Model, a single machine minds its own internal communication by transferring information, such as data packets or service calls, between all seven layers. This is sometimes referred to as vertical communication in the OSI layers.

Two or more machines that want to communicate with each other work horizontally across the OSI layers. They use protocols to let a layer on one machine communicate with the same layer on another machine. The protocol for a particular layer translates the communication between the two machines, whether the machines are using the same program or different programs to send the communications to each other.

The top three layers are sometimes referred to as the *application-* and *service-oriented layers.* These layers control how applications communicate between machines, how connection sessions on the network are managed, and how data packets are encoded for transmission.

The bottom three layers are called the *subnet layers,* or the *communication-* and *network-oriented layers.* These layers control the physical communication between the hardware components, determine hardware and network addresses, find and manage a route between the components, and create packets that fit the network architecture. Relay devices, such as routers or bridges, use only these three layers because they only relay data to other devices.

The middle layer, the *transport layer,* forms the link between the upper three layers and the lower three layers. The transport layer provides the delivery and verification services that allow a session to be maintained.

Some protocols contain functions that actually span more than one layer. The seven layers are described in the following sections.

APPLICATION LAYER

The *application layer* gives applications access to the network. It controls functions such as e-mail services, file transfer, and network management. Application programs are found at this layer.

Some portions of the NetWare Core Protocol (NCP) operate at the application layer. (NCP operates across all the top three layers.) The NetWare server uses NCP to handle workstation requests. In addition, some activities of the NetWare client software operate at this layer to enable the workstation to join the network.

Other examples of application layer protocols include File Transfer Protocol (FTP), X.400 (which specifies protocols for message handling and e-mail services), and Telnet (which provides terminal emulation and remote login support). AppleTalk Filing Protocol (AFP) operates at both the application layer and the next layer down — the presentation layer.

PRESENTATION LAYER

The *presentation layer* works closely with the application layer above, and the session layer below, to present data in a form that applications or users can handle. This layer provides services such as data encryption, data conversion between character sets, and data compression.

AFP operates at this layer and at the application layer. Various TCP/IP protocols, such as File Transfer Protocol (FTP) and Simple Mail Transfer Protocol (SMTP) also have functions that operate at this layer.

SESSION LAYER

The *session layer* maintains a network connection (called a session) during data transmission. Functions at this layer synchronize and sequence the communication and packets being transferred over a network connection, as well as ensure that appropriate security is maintained during the session.

AppleTalk Data Stream Protocol (ADSP), which lets two AppleTalk nodes create a reliable connection for transferring data, is an example of a session layer protocol. NetBIOS and NetBEUI also provide session layer capabilities.

TRANSPORT LAYER

The *transport layer* ensures that packets are transmitted at an acceptable, predefined level of reliability. It assigns numbers to outgoing packets and tracks them at the receiving end to make sure the packets arrived and that they are placed in the correct order for the recipient.

NetWare's Sequenced Packet Exchange (SPX) protocol is a transport layer protocol. SPX provides a connection-oriented link between nodes.

Other examples include TCP and UDP, which are used in most UNIX-based networks, and some of the protocols in the AppleTalk protocol suite: AEP, ATP, NCP, and RTMP.

NETWORK LAYER

Sometimes known as the *packet layer*, the *network layer* determines hardware and network addresses. Once those addresses are determined, protocols at this layer find and establish routes between sources and destinations.

Protocols at the network layer allow applications to communicate over different network links, regardless of differences in frame type, data link protocols, or hardware specifications.

IntranetWare supports the three most commonly used network layer protocols:

- NetWare's Internetwork Packet Exchange (IPX) and the routing protocols it uses: Router Information Protocol (RIP) and Service Advertising Protocol (SAP). IPX is responsible for addressing and routing packets to nodes on the same network or on other networks.
- Internet Protocol (IP), a network layer protocol for the TCP/IP protocol suite. IP uses RIP and OSPF (Open Shortest Path First) for routing.
- Datagram Delivery Protocol (DDP), which provides connectionless service in AppleTalk networks. DDP uses RTMP (Routing Table Maintenance Protocol) and AURP (AppleTalk Update Routing Protocol) for routing.

DATA LINK LAYER

The *data link layer* creates, transmits, and receives data packets in a form that is appropriate for the network architecture. (The form of these packets is often called a *frame* at this layer.) These packets are passed down to the next layer, the physical layer, from which the data is transmitted to the physical layer on the destination machine.

The data link layer is divided into two sublayers. The *logical-link control sublayer* (LLC), which provides an interface for the network layer protocols, is at the top. The *media-access control layer* (MAC), which provides access to a particular physical encoding and transport scheme, is at the bottom.

Network protocols, such as Ethernet, ARCnet, Token Ring, LocalTalk, and FDDI, cover both the data link layer and the physical layer. These are the most common protocols at this layer, and IntranetWare supports them all. AppleTalk protocols used at this layer include EtherTalk Link Access Protocol (ELAP), LocalTalk Link Access Protocol (LLAP), and TokenTalk Link Access Protocol (TLAP).

Serial Line Interface Protocol (SLIP), which can be used to access the Internet over serial lines, and Point-to-Point Protocol (PPP), which provides direct medium-speed communication over serial lines between two machines, are other examples of data link layer protocols.

PHYSICAL LAYER

The *physical layer* defines the mechanical and electrical properties of the network hardware. For example, specifications at this layer define connector pin assignments for cables and connectors, the encoding scheme for electrical 0 and 1 signals in a digital transmission, and the physical connections and signaling methods used by the network hardware.

Protocols Supported by NetWare

By default, IntranetWare supports IPX/SPX when it is installed. However, IntranetWare can also support both IP and AppleTalk. For a workstation to communicate on the network, it must use the same protocol that is being used on the network. Fortunately, servers can be configured to use multiple protocols.

If you want to run your network over IP, you can either add the IP protocol to the server so that the network supports both IPX and IP, or you can specify during the server installation that IP support is installed on the server instead of IPX support. Either way, you can then use NetWare/IP client software to make both PC and Mac OS-based workstations communicate with the server over IP. For PCs, use the NetWare/IP client, which is a version of the NetWare DOS Requester that has been optimized for IP support. For Mac OS workstations, select the NetWare/IP option when installing the Mac Client software.

If you want your network to support AppleTalk, you can add AppleTalk protocol to the server so that the network supports both IPX and AppleTalk. In previous versions of NetWare, if you wanted to attach Mac OS-based workstations to your network, you had to install a product called NetWare for Macintosh on your server. NetWare for Macintosh also required that you install the AppleTalk protocol on the server because the older NetWare client software for Mac OS workstations could communicate only with AppleTalk.

With the newest NetWare Client for Mac OS, which comes in IntranetWare, you no longer need the NetWare for Macintosh product. In most cases, you don't need the AppleTalk protocol either. The NetWare Client for Mac OS supports IPX with a module called MacIPX, which is installed by default during the client's Easy Install option. MacIPX supports Ethernet, Token Ring, and AppleTalk network interfaces. Use AppleTalk only if you have to use a LocalTalk or FDDI cable, or if you are using AppleTalk Remote Access to dial in to the network.

Configuring Protocols on a NetWare Network

When you configure your NetWare network, you will configure primarily two types of protocols:

- Data link protocols (Ethernet, Token Ring, LocalTalk, or FDDI). Configuring these protocols essentially means that you load a LAN driver for a network board and specify a few parameters for the board.
- Network protocols (IPX, IP, or AppleTalk). To add AppleTalk to your NetWare network, load the protocol module called APPLETLK.NLM, specify necessary options, such as an address or whether the server should be a router for that protocol, and then bind the protocol to a LAN driver. To make the network run on the IP protocol family, install the NetWare/IP variation of IntranetWare during the server installation. See the NetWare documentation for more information about installing NetWare/IP.

During server installation, the IPX protocol is automatically configured and bound to the network boards you select (unless you are installing NetWare/IP). After the initial installation, you can either modify the configuration or add protocols to the network.

To configure both data link and network protocols, you can use an NLM called INETCFG. INETCFG is a menu-driven utility that makes it relatively easy to configure the protocols. You can also use the LOAD and BIND console commands (by either typing them at the console or adding them to AUTOEXEC.NCF), but you may find INETCFG easier to work with.

To configure any of the protocols, complete the steps in the following checklist.

1. At the server console, load INETCFG.NLM. You may be asked if you want to transfer your LAN driver, protocol, and remote access commands. What this means is that you move the LOAD and BIND commands from the AUTOEXEC.NCF file to INETCFG's startup files. If you want to manage all your LAN drivers and protocols from INETCFG, choose Yes.
2. From the main menu, select Boards.
3. If you're modifying the configuration for an existing network board, select the board and press Enter. To add a new network board, press Insert and select the appropriate LAN driver for the board.
4. Specify or change any necessary parameters for the network board.
5. Press Esc to save your changes. (You have now configured the data link protocols.)
6. Next, if necessary, select Protocols to configure the network protocol you want this network board and LAN driver to work with.

a. If you are using IPX, you can select IPX to review the configuration settings. IPX is enabled by default, so chances are good you won't need to change any of its parameters.

b. To enable AppleTalk on the network, select AppleTalk. If you have only a single network board in the server and all your network resources can be in a single zone, make sure the AppleTalk Status field says Enabled, and then press Esc and save the changes. If you have multiple network boards or zones, you must configure an AppleTalk router. To do this, change the AppleTalk Status and Packet Forwarding options to Enabled. Then specify whether Packet Forwarding will use Phase 2 addressing (the norm in most AppleTalk networks). Next, change the Internal Network option to Enabled, specify a network number (any single number from 1 to 65,279) in the Network Number option, and specify one or more zones in the Zones option. Finally, when finished configuring the router, press Esc to save the settings.

c. To enable IP on the network, select TCP/IP. Change the TCP/IP Status field to Enabled. Leave the IP Packet Forwarding option set to Disabled if you want this server to act as an end-node, or change it to Enabled if you want this server to act as a router.

7. Now select Bindings to bind the protocol you configured in Step 7 to the LAN driver you configured in Steps 4 and 5.
8. Press Insert, select the protocol you want, and press Enter.
9. From the list, choose the network board to which you want this protocol assigned and press Enter. Depending on the protocol you've chosen, you will be asked for configuration information, such as an IPX network number, a frame type, or an IP address. Enter this information and press Esc when finished to save your changes.
10. Exit INETCFG.
11. To make the new binding take effect, enter the command

    ```
    REINITIALIZE SYSTEM
    ```

    at the console, or restart the server.

Utilities for Monitoring the Protocols

There are several utilities you can use to test and monitor the protocols you've configured on your NetWare network:

- ATCON.NLM lets you monitor information about AppleTalk. ATCON lets you see the status of the AppleTalk Update-based Router protocol, which lets AppleTalk be tunneled through IP. ATCON also lets you view information about network interfaces, manage the error log files, perform a Name Binding protocol (NBP) look-up of network entities, see statistics about AppleTalk packets, display the configuration of the AppleTalk router, and so on. When using ATCON, press the F1 key to read help for each option.
- ATFLT.NLM (AppleTalk filter) lets you restrict how routers see and communicate with other AppleTalk routers.
- AURP.NLM (AppleTalk Update-based Routing Protocol) allows AppleTalk to be tunneled through IP, which lets AppleTalk networks connect to each other through an IP internetwork.
- DHCPCFG.NLM lets you manage the NetWare DHCP service. DHCP (Dynamic Host Configuration Protocol) enables a TCP/IP workstation to get configuration information, such as its IP address and network configuration, automatically from the server.
- FILTCFG.NLM lets you set up and configure filters for IPX, TCP/IP, and AppleTalk protocols. By using filters, you can provide additional network security by limiting what type of information routers broadcast across the network.
- INETCFG.NLM allows you to configure protocols on the server, as explained in the previous section.
- IPCONFIG.NLM lets you configure IP static routes if you are using NetWare/IP.
- IPFLT.NLM (IP filter) lets you restrict how routers see and communicate with other IP routers.
- IPXCON.NLM allows you to monitor information about IPX. With this utility, you can configure SNMP parameters, display IPX statistics and error counts, display information about NLSP, RIP, and SAP on the server, and list information such as known services and destination networks. When using IPXCON, press the F1 key to read help for each option.

- IPXFLT.NLM (IPX filter) lets you restrict how routers see and communicate with other IPX routers.
- IPXPING.NLM lets you send test messages (pings) to another node on the network to see if it is communicating with this server via IPX.
- PING.NLM tests to see if the server can communicate with an IP node on the network. PING sends an ICMP (Internet Control Message Protocol) echo request packet to an IP node.
- PROTOCOL is a console utility you can use to list all the protocols that are currently registered on the server. You can also use this utility to register new protocols and frame types with the server. (You don't need to use this utility to register IPX, IP, or AppleTalk because they are registered automatically during installation or configuration, but you may need to use the PROTOCOL utility if you use a different protocol. See the protocol's manufacturer for more details.)
- REINITIALIZE SYSTEM is a console utility that lets you reenable the multiprotocol router configuration after you've used INETCFG.NLM to make changes to NETINFO.CFG.
- SPXCONFG.NLM lets you configure SPX parameters. You can also configure the same parameters using INETCFG.NLM.
- TCPCON.NLM lets you monitor information about the TCP/IP protocol suite loaded on the server. You can view information about the protocols in the TCP/IP suite, SNMP configuration information, user statistics, and so on.
- TECHWALK.NLM enables you to record INETCFG settings in a file called TECHWALK.OUT in the SYS:ETC directory. It may take this utility anywhere from 5 to 60 minutes to record all your information.
- TPING.NLM sends ICMP packets to an IP node to see if the server can communicate with that node.

CHAPTER 12

Installing and Using Online Documentation

Instant Access

Installing

- To set up online documentation, first set up workstations to access the DynaText viewers, and then install the document collections on the server or the workstations.
- To install a DynaText viewer on a Windows-based workstation, run SETUPDOC.EXE from the workstation and choose the DynaText Viewer option.
- To install a DynaText viewer on a Mac OS workstation, decompress the DYNATEXT.HQX file located on the CD-ROM and copy the resulting DYNATEXT.CFG file to DYNATEXT:DTAPPMAC/*language*. Then rename the DYNATEXT folder to DOCVIEW.
- To install document collections on the server or a workstation, run SETUPDOC.EXE from a Windows-based workstation and choose the Document Collections option. (SETUPDOC.EXE is on the *NetWare 4.11 Online Documentation* CD-ROM.)

Using

- To use the DynaText viewer from a workstation, double-click on the DynaText icon.

In an effort to save trees, bookshelf space, and the administrator's time, most of the documentation for IntranetWare is online, located on a CD-ROM. The only printed documentation included in the IntranetWare package is the documentation you'll need to get your server up and running. The rest of the documentation is located on the CD-ROM.

Having the documentation online enables you to access the documentation from anywhere on the network. Obviously, this is more handy than having to tote two dozen manuals with you to a user's office. In addition, the online documentation's search features can help you locate the information you need quickly.

To enable network users to access the online documentation, you can store the documentation files on the server in a network directory, or you can mount the online documentation CD-ROM as a NetWare volume and access the documentation directly from the CD-ROM. You can also install the documentation files directly onto a workstation. However, other network users won't be able to access the documentation if it's only on your workstation, so most administrators put the documentation into a network directory.

To read the online documentation, you must set up access to the DynaText viewers from each workstation that may be used to access the documentation. The DynaText viewers can be run from a local disk or from the network.

IntranetWare includes DynaText viewers for both Windows (or OS/2) and Mac OS workstations. The following sections describe how to install the online documentation files onto the server and how to install and use the DynaText viewers.

A full set of printed documentation, which you can purchase separately, is also available. To order the printed documentation, you can send in the order form that came in your NetWare box or call 800-336-3892 (in the United States) or 512-834-6905.

Setting Up the Online Documentation

Installing and accessing the online documentation is a two-step process. Using the same utility (SETUPDOC.EXE) from a Windows-based workstation, you can set up DynaText viewers on each Windows-based workstation, and then copy the online documentation files onto each workstation or into a network directory so that network users can access them. (To set up viewers on Mac OS workstations, see the section "Mac OS Workstations" later in this chapter.)

NOTE

The order in which you do these two steps is not important, although if you set up the viewers first, you won't have to configure the viewers to find the right document collections. When you install the document collections, they will be assigned automatically to the viewers that were already set up.

When you install the documentation files, you'll be asked to select the document collections you want. A *document collection* is simply a set of documented information. For example, all of the manuals that were shipped with NetWare 4.1 were contained in a single collection. The manuals in IntranetWare are divided into six different collections: one for manuals about client software, one for reference manuals, and so on.

If you purchase additional NetWare products, those products may have their own collections of documentation. You can add these collections to the same directory so that you can access all of them from the same viewer session. You can also install document collections in more than one language, if you choose.

Setting Up the DynaText Viewer on a Workstation

When you set up the DynaText viewer for a workstation, you can use it to read multiple collections of documentation.

The following sections explain how to set up the DynaText viewer on Windows, OS/2, and Mac OS workstations.

WINDOWS AND OS/2 WORKSTATIONS

The following is a checklist that explains how to set up a DynaText viewer for a Windows or OS/2 (running WIN-OS/2) workstation. You can install the viewer in a network directory or on each individual workstation's hard disk. Once the viewer is set up, you can use this workstation to view the document collections, whether the collections are installed on a network directory, on a CD-ROM mounted as a NetWare volume, or on the workstation itself. (Windows-based workstations should support VGA or SVGA, be running Windows 3.1 or better, and have at least 4MB of memory — although 8MB is preferred.)

1. Make sure the workstation's AUTOEXEC.BAT file contains the command to specify the correct language, such as:

   ```
   SET NWLANGUAGE=ENGLISH
   ```
2. Start Windows or WIN-OS/2.
3. If you are already running SETUPDOC.EXE, click the Install button under the DynaText viewer option. If you are not currently running SETUPDOC.EXE, choose File from the Windows Program Manager, select Run, and then choose SETUPDOC.EXE from the *NetWare 4.11 Online Documentation* CD-ROM's root directory. Then click the Install button for the DynaText viewer.
4. Select the source directory for the DynaText viewer. The utility will display any possible source it finds or thinks you might have, such as the CD-ROM, a server's network directory, your workstation's hard disk, or diskettes. Select the CD-ROM directory.
5. Select the destination directory (where you want to install the DynaText viewer). You can install it on either the local hard disk or in a network directory so that all workstations can access it.
6. Select the language for the viewer to use.
7. Confirm your selections, and the viewer will be installed.
8. When asked if you want to create a viewer icon, select Yes.
9. When you arrive back at the main SETUPDOC menu, click on the Configure Viewer button to make sure the viewer is configured the way you want it.
10. The top list shows the document collections that the viewer is currently configured to access. The bottom list in this screen shows any additional document collections that may be installed but aren't yet assigned to the viewer. To move a collection from the bottom ("Available") list into the top list, double-click on the desired collection. (If you have not yet installed document collections, the list will be blank.)
11. Make sure user access is marked as Shared (instead of Private) if you want all network users to have access to the collections.
12. Keep the language set to Specific (instead of Variable), since you already specified the language you will use in Step 1.
13. When finished, select Save.

14. If you've installed the viewer in a network directory, all you need to do for additional workstations is create viewer icons on their desktops. To create an icon, run SETUPDOC on that workstation, choose Create Icon, select the directory that contains the viewer, and choose OK. Repeat this step for additional workstations.

MAC OS WORKSTATIONS

To set up a Mac OS workstation to use the DynaText viewer, you need a utility that can decompress "BinHexed" StuffIt archives. You can use a StuffIt program from Aladdin Systems, or you can use a freeware utility called StuffIt Expander, which can be obtained from Mac OS bulletin boards and Internet sites. (Whenever you download software from external sources such as bulletin boards, be sure to scan the software for viruses before installing it on your network.)

To set up the viewer, complete the steps in the following checklist.

1. Insert the *NetWare 4.11 Online Documentation* CD-ROM into the Mac OS workstation's CD-ROM drive. (You can also insert it into the server's CD-ROM drive and make sure that it is mounted as either a DOS device or a NetWare volume.)
2. Copy the DYNATEXT.HQX file from the CD-ROM's DOCVIEW:DTAPPMAC:ENGLISH folder (or select another language folder) to the root of your workstation's hard disk.
3. Launch the program that will decompress StuffIt archives.
4. Using the StuffIt program, open and decompress the DYNATEXT.HQX file. This will create a file named DYNATEXT.SIT. Some versions of the StuffIt program may also create a folder called DYNATEXT Folder. If DYNATEXT Folder was not created, select the DYNATEXT.SIT file and decompress it using StuffIt again. That will create the DYNATEXT Folder.
5. Copy the DYNATEXT.CFG file from the DOCVIEW:DTAPPMAC:ENGLISH folder on the CD-ROM to the newly created DYNATEXT:DTAPPMAC:ENGLISH folder on the workstation's hard disk.
6. Delete the DYNATEXT.HQX and the DYNATEXT.SIT files from the workstation.
7. Rename DYNATEXT Folder to DOCVIEW.

8. Set up an alias to the DynaText viewer by browsing to the DynaText program's installation location and clicking on its icon. Then choose Make Alias from the File menu and drag the DynaText alias icon to a convenient location.

Installing the Online Documentation

To install the document collections, complete the following steps.

1. Insert the *NetWare 4.11 Online Documentation* CD-ROM into a workstation's CD-ROM drive.
2. From the Windows Program Manager's File menu, choose Run.
3. Click the Browse button, select SETUPDOC.EXE from the CD-ROM's root directory, and then click OK.
4. From the screen that appears, you can choose to install either the DynaText viewer or the document collections. Click the Install button under Document Collections.
5. Select the source directory for the document collections you want to install. The utility will display any possible source it finds or thinks you might have, such as the CD-ROM, a server's network directory if older document collections already exist, your workstation's hard disk, or diskettes. Select the CD-ROM directory.
6. Select the destination for the document collections. If you want to install the files onto your workstation's hard disk, select your hard disk drive. If you want to install the files onto the network directory on the NetWare server, select that network directory. You can install the NetWare 4.11 document collections into the same directory where older document collections may already exist, so that you can access both sets.
7. Select the document collections you want to install. By default, all the NetWare 4.11 collections are selected.
8. Confirm your selections. The utility will begin copying the document collections to the destination you chose.

Using the DynaText Viewer

After the viewers and the document collections are installed, you can access the online documentation. To do this, double-click on the DynaText icon from your workstation to start up the viewer.

Select one of the NetWare 4.11 collections to list all of the manuals that are included in that collection. To open a manual, simply double-click it. The manual will appear on the workstation screen, with part of the screen showing the book's text and another part of the screen showing the book's Table of Contents.

Once you've opened the book, you can scroll through the text page by page, using the up and down arrow keys or the scroll bar. You can also move quickly to different sections of the book by clicking on a heading in the Table of Contents. If a plus sign appears next to a heading in the Table of Contents, you can click on the plus sign to display the subheadings beneath that topic. In addition, you can search for specific words or phrases in a book by using the Find field.

As you read through the manual's text, you will see references to related information. These references will appear in a different color and will be underlined. If you click on those references, they will take you instantly to the location of the related information, which may be in another section of the manual or in a completely different manual. If the references take you to another manual, DynaText will open that book for you in a new window automatically. To return to the previous book you were reading, close this second book's window.

If you want to return to a previous section you were reading in the same manual, choose Go Back from the Book menu.

CHAPTER 13

Disaster Planning and Recovery

Planning for Disasters

- Write an emergency plan, including emergency contacts and procedures.
- Keep good records of your network, including hardware settings, inventory, and so on.
- When troubleshooting a problem, isolate the problem and try solutions one at a time.

Disasters come in many guises. A disaster that affects your network could be anything from a crashed hard disk on your server, to a security breach, or to a fire that destroys your building. When it comes to computers, a malfunctioning water sprinkler system can cause as much damage as a hurricane.

The best way to recover from a disaster, regardless of what type of disaster it is, is to have planned for one ahead of time. Armed with a disaster plan, good backups, and accurate records of your network, the task of reestablishing your network will not seem nearly as daunting.

Planning Ahead

If you haven't already created a disaster plan, do it today. It doesn't need to be difficult, and it could save you a tremendous amount of wasted time, frustrated users, lost revenue, and sleepless nights. An earthquake or electrical fire isn't going to wait for a convenient time in your schedule to occur, so the sooner you plan for it, the better.

Be sure to document the plan. Write it down, get it approved by your organization's upper management, and then make copies and store them in several locations so that you'll be able to find at least one copy if disaster strikes.

It's important to have a documented plan because having the plan in your head only works if you happen to be around, of course. More important, if you've gotten the CEO to approve your plan to restore the production department's network before the administration department's, you won't have to deal with politics and egos while you're trying to restring cables.

What should be in a disaster plan? Everyone's disaster plan will be different, but there are a few key points to consider when planning yours:

- Decide where you will store your emergency plan. It needs to be in a location where you or others can get to it easily. Ideally, there should be multiple copies of the plan, perhaps assigned to different individuals. Just storing the emergency plan in your office will not be adequate if the building burns down, so you may consider storing a copy off-site, such as in a safety deposit box or even at your home.
- Plan whom to call in case of an emergency and include their names, home phone numbers, pager numbers, and cellular phone numbers in your emergency plan. List key network personnel, such as any network administrators for various branches of the NDS tree, personnel who perform the weekly and daily backups, and so on. You may want to include names of security personnel who should be notified in case of a potential security breach.

- Plan the order in which you will restore service to your company. Who needs to be back online first? Is there a critical department that should be restored before any other? Are there key individuals who need to be reconnected first?
- Once you've identified the key people who need to be reconnected, determine if there is an order to the files or services they'll need. Which servers need to be restored first? What applications must those users have immediately? Which files will they need?
- Document the location of your network records. Where do you keep your hardware inventory, purchase requisitions, backup logs, and so forth?
- Document the location of your network backup tapes or disks. Don't forget to document instructions for restoring files, or indicate the location of the backup system's documentation, in case the backup operator is unavailable. Record your backup rotation schedule so that other people can figure out how to restore files efficiently.
- Include a drawing of the network layout, showing the exact location of cables, servers, workstations, and other computers. Highlight the critical components, so that anyone else reading your plan will know at a glance where to find the priority servers.

In addition to writing a disaster plan, there are other ways you can plan ahead to avert — or at least diminish — a disaster. Some of these preparatory measures include:

- Keeping a faithful schedule of backups, so that files can be restored quickly.
- Implementing disk mirroring (or duplexing), so that a simple hard disk failure in the server won't cause users to lose working time and files because the server is down and they can't do their work.
- Implementing SFT III (mirrored servers) on your mission-critical servers. If you can't afford to have the server go down at all, SFT III can be your best safeguard.
- Using NetWare's TTS (Transaction Tracking System) if you use database applications. TTS ensures that any transactions that are in progress are backed out completely if the server dies or the power goes out, so that the database isn't corrupted.
- Periodically reviewing your network's security, so that you can make sure there are no potential security leaks. Investigate security measures

such as NCP Packet Signature, access rights, and password security to make sure that your network is as secure as you need it to be.

Keeping Good Records of Your Network

Another line in your defense against disaster is to maintain up-to-date records about your network. When something goes wrong with your network, it is much easier to spot the problem if you have accurate documentation.

Good network documentation isn't just helpful in an emergency. Doing paperwork is always a distasteful task, but you'll be thankful you've done it the next time you have to add new hardware to the network, resolve an interrupt conflict, justify your hardware budget to management, get a workstation repaired under warranty, call for technical support, or train a new assistant.

How you track your network information is up to you. You may want to keep a three-ring binder with printed information about the network, or you may prefer to keep the information online in databases or spreadsheets.

However you document your network, be sure you keep the information in more than one location. If a disaster occurs, you don't want to lose your only copy of the information that can help you restore the network quickly. Try to keep copies of your network information in separate buildings, if possible, so that you won't lose everything if you can't access one building.

What kind of network information should you record? Again, networks vary, so your documentation needs will vary, too. The worksheets in Appendix D can help you get started. You can photocopy and use those worksheets, or you can design your own worksheets or databases to keep track of the information you need.

You should maintain the following information:

- An inventory of hardware and software purchases. Record the product's version number, serial number, vendor, purchase date, length of warranty, and so on. This can help you when management asks for current capital assets or budget-planning information. It can also help you with insurance reports and replacements if a loss occurs.
- A record of configuration settings for servers, workstations, printers, and other hardware. This information can save you hours that you would otherwise spend locating and resolving interrupt conflicts.
- A history of hardware repairs. You may want to file all paperwork associated with repairs along with the worksheet that documents your original purchase of the item.

- A drawing of the network layout. If you store this with your disaster plan, you (and others) will be able to locate critical components quickly. On the drawing, show how all the workstations, servers, printers, and other equipment are connected. The drawing doesn't have to be to scale, but it should show each machine in its approximate location. Label each workstation with its make and model, its location, and its user. Show the cables that connect the hardware and show what types of cable they are.
- Batch files and workstation boot files. Use a text editor or other program to print out these files and keep them with the worksheets that document the workstation. You may also want to store copies of the files on diskette. If you need to reinstall the workstation, you can re-create the user's environment quickly if you have archived these files.
- SET parameters. SERVMAN.NLM enables you to save a server's SET parameters to a file. If you've changed the default SET parameters, print out this file, and store the printout and a diskette copy with your network records. This will make it much easier to reinstall the server to the configuration you originally had, if the need arises.
- Backup information. It is very important to record your backup rotation schedule, the location of backup tapes or disks, the names of any backup operators, the labeling system you use on your backup tapes or disks, and any other information someone may need if you're not around to restore the system.

Troubleshooting Tips

Unfortunately, despite the best possible planning, something may still go wrong with your network. The majority of network problems are related to hardware issues — interrupt conflicts, faulty components, incompatible hardware, and so on. However, software creates its own set of problems, such as application incompatibility, Windows bugs and incompatibility, and installation errors.

An endless combination of servers, workstations, cabling, networking hardware, operating systems, and applications makes it impossible to predict and document every possible problem. The best anyone can do is approach the problem with a methodical system for isolating the problem, and then fix it.

The following troubleshooting guidelines can help you isolate the problem and find solutions.

NARROW DOWN THE LIST OF SUSPECTS

First, you need to try to narrow your search to suspicious areas:

- Were there any error messages? If so, look up their explanations in the *NetWare 4.11 System Messages* online manual.
- How many machines did the problem affect?
- Can you identify a particular cabling segment or branch of the Directory tree that has the problem?
- Does the problem occur only when a user accesses a particular application, or does it perhaps occur only when the user executes applications in a particular order?
- If the problem occurred when you installed new workstations or servers on the network, have you checked their network addresses and hardware settings for conflicts with other boards or with machines that already exist on the network? Also double-check the installation documentation to make sure you didn't misspell a command or accidentally skip a step.
- Are the servers and workstations using the same frame type to communicate? If a server is using Ethernet 802.2 and a workstation is using Ethernet 802.3, they won't see each other.
- Are the servers and workstations using compatible NCP Packet Signature levels to communicate?
- If a user is having trouble working with files or applications, have you checked the security features? Does the user have appropriate rights in the necessary directories? Are the files already opened by someone else? Have the files or directories been assigned attributes that restrict the user from some actions?
- Are some of a user's DOS path commands gone? Look in the login scripts for search drive mappings that were mapped without using the INS keyword (which inserts the mapping into the DOS path instead of overwriting existing paths).
- For printing problems, have you checked that the printer, print server, and print queue are all correctly assigned to each other? You can use the NetWare Administrator utility to check your printing setup. Select the print server from the Browser, choose Details from the object menu, and then open the Print Layout page to see whether the print server, printer, and queue are all assigned together correctly.

- Do you have a volume that won't mount? If so, you may need to run VREPAIR.NLM to fix it. VREPAIR is explained in Chapter 8.
- Have you verified that applications are using the correct print drivers for your printers?

CHECK THE HARDWARE

Hardware problems can be relatively common in networks. Network cables are notorious for developing problems, partly because of the abuse they get from being coiled up, walked on, bent around corners, and so on. A network analyzer, such as NetWare LANalyzer, can be a useful tool for diagnosing cable problems. As you diagnose hardware problems, keep the following tips in mind:

- Cables have an annoying tendency to work loose from their connectors, so check all connections between cables and boards first.
- Test suspicious cables by replacing them with cables you know work, and see if the problem persists.
- Make sure cables are terminated correctly, don't exceed length limits, and don't form endless loops in topologies that don't allow that.
- If the problem is with a computer or printer, try disconnecting it from the network and running it in stand-alone mode. If the problem still shows up in stand-alone mode, it's probably not a problem with the network connection. You can then eliminate the network components and concentrate on the configuration of the machine itself.
- Isolate sections of the network segment until the problem disappears. Add each section back to the network until you have identified the problem cable, board, connector, terminator, or other component.
- If the problem occurred when you installed a new workstation or server, or added a board to an existing computer, check hardware settings for conflicts with other boards or with machines that already exist on the network.

REFER TO THE DOCUMENTATION

Forget the jokes about reading the manual only as a last resort. The NetWare online manuals contain explanations of error messages that may occur. In addition, they include troubleshooting tips, configuration instructions, and so on.

Be sure to check the manufacturer's documentation for any network hardware or applications you're using. Some applications have special instructions for installing on a network.

LOOK FOR PATCHES OR WORKAROUNDS

When Novell engineers find a problem with NetWare, they usually either solve the problem with a patch (a piece of software that loads as an NLM on your server and repairs it) or a recommended workaround.

Novell distributes these patches and workarounds on the Novell internet site (www.novell.com) and in the *Novell Support Encyclopedia Professional Volume* (*NSEPro*). See Appendix C for more information about these resources.

TRY EACH SOLUTION BY ITSELF

After you've isolated the problem, try implementing the solutions you've found one at a time. The tendency is to try several possible fixes simultaneously to save time.

Start with the easiest, cheapest solution, and work up from there.

Trying solutions simultaneously may save time in the short run, but it could cost you extra money for unnecessary repairs or replacements. In addition, you won't know for sure what fixed the problem, so you'll have to start from scratch again if the problem reappears on another machine or at another time.

CALL FOR TECHNICAL SUPPORT

There is a wide variety of places you can go to get help, advice, tips, and fixes for your NetWare problems or issues. Appendix C lists several of the resources you should know about. These resources range from Internet user groups, to classes, and to publications that deal with NetWare support issues. If you're looking for more formal technical support, try these ideas:

- You can often find the technical help you need online through the Internet Usenet groups that focus on NetWare or through the Novell forums on the Internet and CompuServe. These forums are moderated by experienced sysops (system operators) and populated by knowledgeable users.
- Try calling your reseller or consultant for help.
- Novell's technical support is available by calling 1-800-858-4000 in the United States, or 1-801-861-4000. However, Novell's technical support is not free. You'll be charged a fee for each incident, so have

your credit card handy. (An incident may involve more than one phone call, if necessary.)

- Before you call technical support, be sure you've tried your other resources first — especially the documentation. It's embarrassing and expensive to have technical support tell you that the answer to your question is on page 25 of the *NetWare 4.11 Installation* manual.

DOCUMENT THE SOLUTION

When you find a solution, write it down and store it with your network documentation. This may prevent you or someone else from going through the same troubleshooting process to fix a similar problem later.

CHAPTER 14

Installing and Using the NetWare Web Server

Reading the Documentation

- To read the Web Server documentation, install a browser (such as Netscape Navigator, which is included with the Web Server) on a workstation and read the HTML formatted documentation from the CD-ROM.

Installing the Web Server

- To specify an IP address for the server and to bind TCP/IP to the network board, use INETCFG.NLM.
- To install the Web Server on the IntranetWare server, use INSTALL.NLM, select Product Options, and choose Install NetWare Web Server.

Configuring the Web Server

- To add a name service to your network, either create a hosts file on your server, or configure your server as a Domain Name Service (DNS) server or as a client of a DNS server.
- To configure the Web Server, use the NetWare Web Manager utility.

The NetWare Web Server 2.5 is an easy-to-install, high performance World Wide Web (WWW) server that comes with IntranetWare. Installation and configuration is so easy that, if you already have TCP/IP configured on your server, you can view the sample NetWare Web Server home page in approximately 15 minutes. If you know how to create your own HyperText Markup Language (HTML) files, you can be viewing your own home page just a few minutes later.

This chapter introduces the NetWare Web Server 2.5 and explains how you can transform your NetWare Web Server into your own custom Internet or intranet Web site.

NOTE

Creating web pages (usually called "authoring") and administering a NetWare Web Server require different skills and are often performed by different people. This chapter focuses on NetWare Web Server administration, but it is undeniable that you can be a much better administrator if you also learn at least some of the basics of web page authoring. Your first indication of this will come when web page authors start linking pages to files all over the server and requesting write permissions. To learn more about web page authoring, consider taking Novell Education Course 654, Web Authoring and Publishing.

What is the NetWare Web Server?

A WWW server, such as the NetWare Web Server, is a file server that serves or *publishes* files in HyperText Markup Language (HTML) format. You read these HTML files from workstations by using client applications called *browsers*. HTML files are text files with special tags (usually enclosed in less-than and greater-than symbols, < >) that tell the browser how to format the file on screen. The main differences between HTML files and standard word processing files are that:

- HTML files do not contain proprietary custom symbols or formatting characters. All formatting is specified with special combinations of ASCII text characters. For example, to indicate that text should be printed in bold, you might use the following command:

  ```
  <B>This will appear as bold text.</B>
  ```

- HTML files can include text or graphic *links*, which users can click on to move to another location in the same file or to another file on any web server in the world.

Many people get confused by the terms HTML and HTTP, and they are overwhelmed when WWW and Internet are also thrown into the same sentence. A WWW web server publishes files in HTML format. A web server communicates with browsers using the HyperText Transfer Protocol (HTTP), which runs over TCP/IP. The Internet is a global network of computers that provide many services, one of which is the WWW.

The NetWare Web Server provides the following features:

- Easy installation and configuration
- A Windows-based administration utility
- NDS Access control for Internet/intranet users and systems
- File security through NDS
- Internet/intranet access logging
- Browser access to NDS trees
- Support for dynamic web pages
- NetBasic for creating Internet scripts
- Netscape Navigator (single-user license in NetWare 4.11, or multi-user license — up to your allowed NetWare user limit — in IntranetWare)

Dynamic web page support allows web page authors to add commands to HTML files that enhance the pages in ways that are not possible with HTML tags. For example, web page authors can add commands that automatically insert variables such as the date or time into a page as it is sent to a browser. Other commands allow web page authors to display animations or perform calculations on data entered by a browser user. The NetWare Web Server supports dynamic web pages with the following features:

- Server Side Include (SSI) commands
- Local Common Gateway Interface (L-CGI)
- Remote Common Gateway Interface (R-CGI)
- BASIC script interpreters
- PERL script interpreters
- Support for Java applets
- Support for JavaScript

Installing the NetWare Web Server

Installing the Web Server consists of configuring the network to support TCP/IP and then running INSTALL.NLM to install the Web Server product.

To set up a NetWare Web Server site, you need the following hardware and software:

- A NetWare 4.11 (or IntranetWare) server with a CD-ROM drive.
- At least 2.5MB of hard disk space for the NetWare Web Server software plus additional disk space for your new HTML files.
- A client workstation running Windows 3.1x, Windows 95, or Windows NT. The workstation must have a 386 processor, 4MB of RAM, and 2.5MB of hard disk space available for the Netscape Navigator browser installation. (You can use a different browser if you prefer.)
- Although you can use Windows word processing tools to create and edit HTML documents, you may want to add HTML authoring software, which would require additional disk space and memory. An HTML authoring tool is not included with the NetWare Web Server.

LOCATING THE WEB SERVER DOCUMENTATION

The Web Server documentation is in HTML format on the *NetWare 4.11 Operating System* CD-ROM. To read or print this documentation, you must use a web browser such as Netscape Navigator (included with the NetWare Web Server) on a workstation.

If you don't have a browser installed yet, complete the steps in the following checklist to install the Netscape Navigator browser on a Windows 3.1x workstation.

1. Insert the *NetWare 4.11 Operating System* CD-ROM into a Windows 3.1x workstation's CD-ROM drive.
2. From the workstation's Program Manager, choose Run from the File menu. Click Browse, and locate the SETUP.EXE file for the Web Server in the following directory: PRODUCTS\WEBSERV\BROWSER\N16E201. Select OK to begin the setup process.

To install the Netscape Navigator on a Windows 95 workstation, complete the steps in the following checklist.

1. Insert the *NetWare 4.11 Operating System* CD-ROM into a Windows 3.1x workstation's CD-ROM drive.
2. From Windows 95, click Start. Then choose Run and locate the SETUP.EXE file for the Web Server in the following directory: PRODUCTS\WEBSERV\BROWSER\N32E201. Select OK to begin the setup process.

After you've installed the viewer, launch it. From the Navigator's File menu, select Open File and select the drive and directory that contains the Web Server documentation (such as the CD-ROM drive or a directory if you've copied the documentation files to the server or the client). Then double-click on the file you want to open.

CONFIGURING TCP/IP

To prepare for NetWare Web Server installation, install IntranetWare on the server and establish IPX and TCP/IP communications between the two. (TCP/IP software is provided with IntranetWare.) Use INETCFG.NLM to specify an IP address for the server and to bind TCP/IP to the network board. Then load the PING NLM on the server and use it to verify TCP/IP communications with the client.

BRINGING UP THE NETWARE WEB SERVER

NetWare Web Server installation is easier than most NetWare installations because the critical configuration is completed when you configure TCP/IP. Simply load INSTALL.NLM on the server, choose Product Options, and then choose Install NetWare Web Server. Follow the instructions that appear on the screen.

When the NetWare Web Server installation is complete, press Alt-Esc at the server console to switch between the following active services:

- Novell HTTP Server 2.5, which is the NetWare Web Server NLM
- Novell Basic language interpreter, for dynamic Web page support
- Novell Perl language interpreter, for dynamic Web page support

You have now created a web site. Any network browser can now view the default home page if the user knows the TCP/IP address of your server.

To view the web site you have just created, start the browser on your client workstation, select Open Location from the file menu, and enter the following Universal Resource Locator (URL):

```
http://server_ip_address
```

After you enter this command with your server IP address, you should see the following web page shown in Figure 14.1.

FIGURE 14.1 *A Sample Web Page*

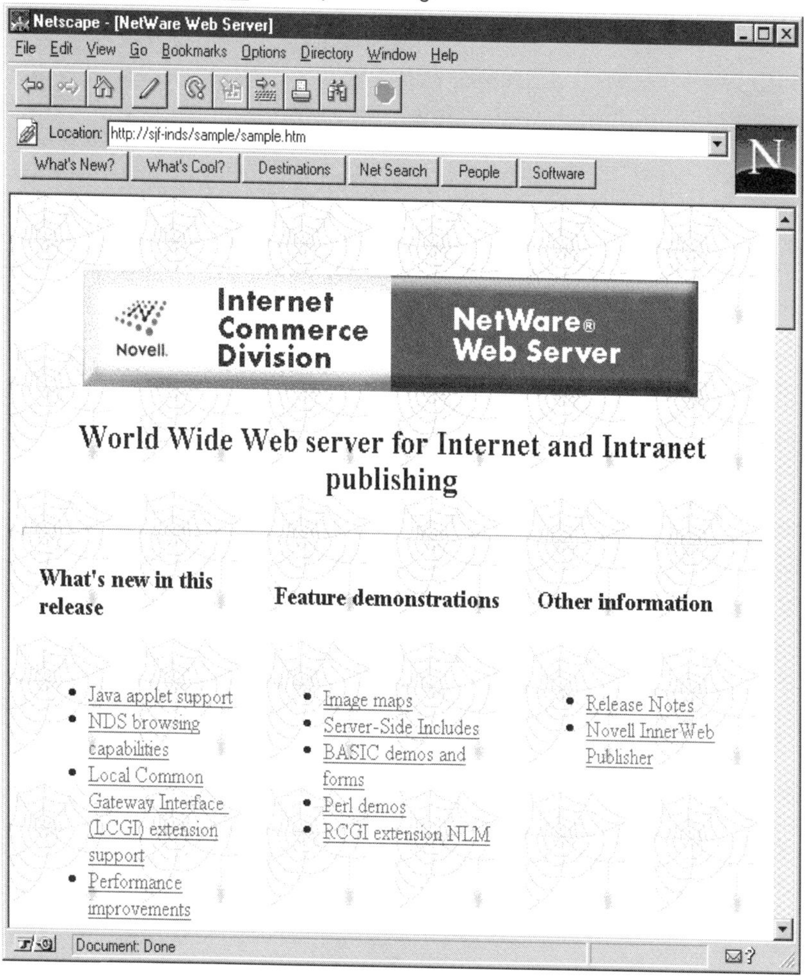

The default web site contains a number of sample pages and links. Browse through these pages to get an idea of what can be published on a NetWare Web Server. To see the HTML commands used to create any page, display the page and then select Document Source from the View menu.

Exploring Your Web Site

You are now a web site manager and, depending on your TCP/IP network connections, your site is available to your organization and possibly the world. Let's take a closer look at what you have.

When you look at the default directory structure of the NetWare Web Server, you'll notice the INDEX.HTM file. This is the default HTML file that web browsers see when they access your site using your IP address. We'll talk about changing the defaults and using names instead of IP addresses later. For now, what you need to know is that this is the entry point for your web site. To create your own home page, start by editing this file or by replacing it with your own INDEX.HTM file.

By default, the INDEX.HTM file is in the SYS:\WEB\DOCS directory, which is the document root directory of your web site. There are at least three root directories on your NetWare Web Server. The one you are most familiar with is the SYS: root directory, which is the NetWare volume root directory.

The NetWare Web Server has two root directories of its own: the server root directory and the document root directory. The server root directory contains all the configuration and control files associated with your web site; these are the files that you don't want your web site visitors to see. The server root directory on any NetWare Web Server is SYS:\WEB and cannot be changed.

The document root directory is the default path to all the files you want to publish. To protect your server configuration files from undesired access, the document root directory should be a subdirectory of the server root directory, or it should be placed on another volume.

NOTE

When browsers access your site, they are restricted to files and directories that are contained in the document root directory — with one exception. You can configure the NetWare Web Server to allow browsers to access user home pages in the users' home directories.

The document root directory can be changed to another directory or another volume, but it should be changed only after careful planning. Many links in the web pages will use relative references that define the path from the document root directory to another file. Carelessly moving the document root can make all your internal web site links invalid, rendering your web site useless.

NOTE

A NetWare Web Server is a live web site; users can connect to it at any time. To avoid user access errors, always edit published web pages offline in your home directory or on another computer. Otherwise your word processor or web authoring tool may lock the file and prevent other users from accessing it. Also, test all links that you create in your Web pages. It's less embarrassing to find the mistakes yourself.

Configuring Name Services

Your web server is up, but your customers (both internal and external) have to remember your server's IP address to access it. Simplify your customers' access by creating a name service.

Name services use a table of IP addresses and names to establish names that can be used in place of IP addresses. Each IP address can be associated with one or more names or aliases.

There are two common ways to add a name service to your network. The easiest is to create a hosts file on your server. The second is to configure your server as a Domain Name Service (DNS) server or as a client of a DNS server. The hosts file approach provides name services only on your network or subnet. DNS provides name services over an entire network or the Internet.

CREATING AND USING A HOST'S FILE

To create a table of IP addresses and host names for your network or subnet, use a text editor to create a file named HOSTS.TXT in the SYS:ETC directory. Create a name table similar to Table 14.1.

TABLE 14.1 *Sample Name Table*

#IP ADDRESS	ALIASES	COMMENTS
ip_address	alias1 alias2	#NetWare Web Server
ip_address	alias3	#jim's pc
ip_address	alias4	#carol's pc

The # character indicates that all text to the right of it is a comment and is to be ignored. Each line starts with the IP address of a host, followed by one or more spaces. The second item on each line is the name you want to assign to the host. You can add several names, but be sure to separate each name with one or more spaces.

USING DOMAIN NAME SERVICES

Domain name service (DNS) is an internet protocol that allows administrators to associate internet addresses with names that people can remember. A DNS server stores the names and their corresponding IP addresses, and responds to clients that need names services. DNS is provided with NetWare/IP and FTP Services for IntranetWare. You can use these products to add DNS to your network, or you can use an existing DNS server.

To configure your NetWare Web Server to use the name services of a DNS server, use a text editor to create a file named RESOLV.CFG in the directory SYS:ETC. Enter the following text in this file:

```
domain domain_name

nameserver IP_address
```

The *domain_name* variable is the name of the domain in which your server is installed. The *IP_address* variable is the IP address of the DNS server. You should be able to get this information from the administrator of the DNS server.

NOTE: To use the services of a DNS server, you must create the RESOLV.TXT file. Installing the DNS server on the same server as your NetWare Web Server does not remove this requirement.

Configuration Tools for Your Web Site

Although the NetWare Web Server does not require configuration, there are a number of configuration changes you may want to make. We describe the following changes in this chapter:

- Controlling access to your web site
- Supporting dynamic web pages
- Supporting long filenames
- Moving the document root directory
- Controlling directory indexing
- Checking site status
- Adjusting the web server processing power

Most of the configuration changes you will want to make can be performed using the NetWare Web Manager utility. Some configuration changes must be entered manually into the configuration files.

USING THE NETWARE WEB MANAGER UTILITY

The NetWare Web Manager utility (WEBMGR.EXE) is installed in the SYS:\PUBLIC directory when the NetWare Web Server is installed. Because this is a Windows-based utility, you may want to create a program icon to launch this for you.

To start the NetWare Web Manager utility and select a NetWare Web Server to manage, complete the steps in the following checklist.

1. From your client computer, map a drive to the SYS volume on your NetWare Web Server.
2. Start the WEBMGR.EXE program in SYS:\PUBLIC using the Windows RUN command or a program icon that you have created.
3. If the Web Server's IP address or domain name appears in the bottom section of the File menu, select the Web Server. If the NetWare Web Server does not appear in the File menu, choose Select Server from the File menu, select the web server root directory, SYS:\WEB, and then click OK.

   After you select the NetWare Web Server, the NetWare Web Server dialog box appears. This is the only dialog box that you can use to change the NetWare Web Server configuration.
4. If the Full Server Name text box does not contain an IP address or a domain name for your server, you must enter it; this information is required. (Domain names are discussed later in this chapter.)
5. Enter the e-mail address of the administrator for this server.
6. After you complete your configuration changes, click OK to save the changes.
7. If you have made changes to the Web Server configuration, the NetWare Web Manager utility will prompt you to restart the server. To activate the changes, click Save & Restart, and then enter the password for the NetWare Web Server.

NOTE

To restart the server using the NetWare Manager utility, you must know the password for the utility and your client must be configured for TCP/IP communications. If these conditions are not met, the utility saves your changes, but does not restart the server.

TIP

To restart the Web Server at the system console prompt, enter the following commands:

```
Unload HTTP
Load HTTP
```

EDITING THE NETWARE WEB SERVER CONFIGURATION FILES MANUALLY

The NetWare Web Server configuration settings are saved in the default configuration files shown in Table 14.2.

TABLE 14.2 *Default Configuration Files*

CONFIGURATION FILE	DESCRIPTION
SYS:\WEB\CONFIG\HTTPD.CFG	This is the principal NetWare Web Server configuration file. This file cannot be moved. It specifies the server name, the Web Server TCP/IP port, the administrator e-mail address, the administrator password, log file options, the location of the other configuration files, and the maximum number of threads to be allocated to the Web Server.
SYS:\WEB\CONFIG\SRM.CFG	This file specifies the resources available to the NetWare Web Server. It defines the locations of the document root directory, any script directories, and any image map directories. The default index filename (Index.htm) is also defined here, as are the indexing options and other resource-related features. The location of this file is specified in HTTPD.CFG by the following directive: ResourceConfig config/srm.cfg

TABLE 14.2 *Default Configuration Files (continued)*

CONFIGURATION FILE	DESCRIPTION
SYS:\WEB\CONFIG\ACCESS.CFG	This is the global web access configuration file, which controls access and indexing options to the directories within your server root. This is also where SSI commands are enabled for a directory. The location of this file is specified in HTTPD.CFG by the following directive: AccessConfig config/access.cfg
path\ACCESS.WWW	This is the local web access configuration file, which controls access to the files within the directory in which it is located. The name of this file is specified in SRM.CFG by the following directive: AccessFileName access.www
SYS:\WEB\CONFIG\MIME.TYP	This is the MIME type configuration file. Each line in this file specifies a Multipurpose Internet Mail Extension (MIME) type and one or more file extensions to be associated with that type. When the browser requests a file, the server refers to the MIME.TYP file to determine if a MIME type has been configured for that extension. If a MIME type is specified, that MIME type is sent to the browser to identify the type of file the server is forwarding. The location of this file is specified in HTTPD.CFG by the following directive: TypesConfig config/mime.typ

Many, but not all, of your configuration changes can be made with the NetWare Web Manager utility, which saves changes to these files. To edit any of these files manually, open a text editor program, make the changes, and save the file. To better understand how the NetWare Web Server uses these files, you may want to view them before and after you make changes with the NetWare Web Manager utility.

Controlling Access to Your Web Site

After you install the NetWare Web Server, everyone that has IP access to your network has the ability to read all the files in your web site. Since you created the web directory structure, you may be the only one who can make changes to web pages. Most web server administrators will need to make some changes to the Web Server access rights. These changes fall into two categories: Web Access Rights and NetWare File System Rights.

CHANGING WEB ACCESS RIGHTS

You can use the NetWare Web Manager utility to limit access to the site or to specific directories (and their subdirectories). You can limit access by restricting the following types of entities:

- Select NDS users
- All valid NDS users
- NDS user groups
- Hostnames
- IP addresses
- IP networks
- Domain names

TIP

You can also limit access to your site using filters provided in IntranetWare or NetWare Multiprotocol Router.

Although the NetWare Web Server offers a variety of access control methods, they are not without their cost. Using any of these methods restricts access to only those users that are explicitly defined to the Web Server, which means you have to define and administer all the users and systems that can access your Web Server.

NOTE

To administer access to NDS user groups, you must edit the ACCESS.CFG file manually. For instructions on this procedure, refer to the NetWare Web Server readme file. The README.TXT file is in the server root directory (SYS:WEB) and on the CD-ROM under the directoryWEBSERV\DISK1.

To restrict access to your Web Server, complete the steps in the following checklist.

1. Start the NetWare Web Server Manager program and select your NetWare Web Server, as described earlier in this chapter.
2. Choose the User Access page (to restrict access by users) or the System Access page (to restrict access based on IP addresses, host names, or domain names) in the dialog box that appears.
3. Select the directory to which you want the restrictions to apply.

NOTE **Remember, you are disabling directory access to everyone who is not specified on this page. If your access list is going to be too large, you might want to reorganize your site so that you can create a smaller access list.**

4. Set the restrictions you want.

   a. If you're restricting access to specific NDS users, mark either the All Valid Users checkbox (to enable access to all valid NDS users) or select a user from the list that appears and click Add to Authorized Users List checkbox (to enable access for a specific user). If you do not enter a context for your users, each user will have to enter a fully distinguished name, starting with a period. To specify the NDS context of the users, enter a context in the NDS Context text box. If you need to support users in multiple contexts, enter the context that is common to all the users. The users will then need to enter their user names relative to this context.

   b. If you're restricting by system access, specify the IP address, full host name, or full domain name to which you want to give directory access. Then select a user from the list that appears and click Add to Authorized Systems List.
5. Click OK to save your changes.
6. If you have made changes to the Web Server configuration, the NetWare Web Manager utility will prompt you to restart the server. To activate the changes, click Save & Restart, and then enter the password for the NetWare Web Server.

NETWARE RIGHTS ISSUES

NetWare rights control who can view the web pages, who can edit and author web pages, and who can change the NetWare Web Server configuration.

Unless you have changed web access rights with the NetWare Web Manager, user Public (in the root container) should have read and file scan access rights to the site root directory and all subdirectories that contain pages, images, or page components that you want the public to view. When planning NetWare access rights for web page authors, remember that the authors will need write, create, and modify access to all directories that contain the files they are publishing.

Table 14.3 lists the default directories to which customers and web authors need rights.

TABLE 14.3 *Directories That Customers and Web Authors Use*

DIRECTORY	GUIDELINES
Document Root Directory	Default location: Sys:\WEB\DOCS
Server Side Include directory	Default location: Sys:\WEB\DOCS\SSI
Images/Graphics	Default location: Sys:WEB\DOCS\IMAGES

Table 14.4 lists the directories that control NetWare Web Server configuration or enable program access to the server volumes. These directories should not be available to the public.

TABLE 14.4 *Directories That the Administrator Uses*

DIRECTORY	GUIDELINES
\Config	Default location: SYS:\WEB\CONFIG Restrict rights to NetWare Web Server administrators. The files in this folder control NetWare Web Server operation and web access rights.
\Maps	Default location: SYS:\WEB\MAPS Restrict rights to the web authors that create image maps. The files in this folder control how user mouse-clicks on a web page graphic are interpreted. Most user mouse-clicks will activate a link to another web page.

TABLE 14.4 *Directories That the Administrator Uses (continued)*

DIRECTORY	GUIDELINES
Scripts directories	Default scripts directories: SYS:\WEB\SCRIPTS, SYS:\WEB\SCRIPTS\PERL Restrict rights to the people responsible for creating and maintaining scripts. Scripts enable the dynamic web pages described later and can write data to your server's hard disk.

Supporting Dynamic Web Pages

When creating dynamic web pages, the first feature you will need to address is the Server Side Include (SSI) command set. Next, you'll need to administer the Common Gateway Interface Scripts.

ADMINISTERING SSI COMMAND USAGE

Server Side Include commands allow web authors to insert variables into their otherwise static web pages. Using a server side include command, the author can dynamically insert text from another file or display the current date and time. The SSI commands supported by the NetWare Web Server are described in the default web pages (INDEX.HTM) provided with the NetWare Web Server. This section describes what you need to know to support the web page authors.

Three rules govern the use of SSI commands in web pages:

- Any file that contains SSI commands must use the .SSI extension.
- An SSI file cannot include text from another SSI file.
- Before any SSI processing occurs, the NetWare Web Server administrator must enable SSI processing for the directory in which the SSI command is stored. (The SYS:WEB\DOCS\SSI directory is enabled when the NetWare Web Server is installed.)

SSI processing is not enabled for all directories because it requires additional processing power from the server and reduces response times for web page viewers. This extra processing time is not excessive, but it is best to enable SSI processing only in those directories where it will be used.

To enable SSI command processing for a directory, complete the steps in the following checklist.

1. Start the NetWare Web Server Manager program and select your NetWare Web Server as described earlier in this chapter.
2. Choose the Directories page in the dialog box that appears.
3. If the directory for which you want to enable SSI commands appears in the Existing Directories box, select it.
4. If the directory you want does not appear in the Existing Directories box, use the Browse button to locate the directory, click Add, and then select your directory in the Existing Directories box.
5. After you have selected the directory, check the Enable Includes checkbox and click Change. (You must click Change. If you click OK instead of Change, it will not change the directory setting.)
6. Click OK to save your changes.
7. If you have made changes to the Web Server configuration, the NetWare Web Manager utility will prompt you to restart the server. To activate the changes, click Save & Restart, and then enter the password for the NetWare Web Server.

SUPPORTING CGI SCRIPTS

The Common Gateway Interface (CGI) is the feature that allows the NetWare Web Server to modify web pages before they are sent to a browser. First, the NetWare Web Server scans an HTML file for SSI commands or commands that reference other programs called scripts. If any SSI commands or scripts are located, the NetWare Web Server processes them, inserts the results in the HTML file, and sends it to the web browser.

Because CGI scripts can write data to your server's hard drives, you should administer their use carefully. Store the script files in directories that the web page users cannot access, and limit create, write, and modify rights to the script programmers. Table 14.5 lists the default directories that store script files.

TABLE 14.5 *Default Directories That Store Script Files*

SCRIPT TYPE	DEFAULT DIRECTORY/NOTES
BASIC RCGI scripts	SYS:WEB\SCRIPTS These are BASIC computer programs. Remote CGI (RCGI) scripts are written to be platform independent so they can be easily adapted to other computer operating systems. This directory is defined in the SRM.CFG file with the following directive: RemoteScriptAlias /scripts/ localhost:8001/scripts
Perl RCGI scripts	SYS:WEB\SCRIPTS\PERL These are Perl computer programs. This directory is defined in the SRM.CFG file with the following directive: RemoteScriptAlias /perl/ localhost: 8002/sys:Web/scripts/perl
LCGI NLM	SYS:WEB\CGI-BIN Local CGI (LCGI) scripts are written to take advantage of a specific computer operating system — in this case, IntranetWare. This directory is defined in the SRM.CFG file with the following directive: RemoteScriptAlias /cgiproc/ localhost: 8003/sys:Web/samples/cgiapp

Moving the Web Server's Document Root Directory

The default location for the document root directory is on the SYS volume under the server root (SYS:\WEB\DOCS). As your web site grows, you may want to move the document root to another volume to avoid filling up the SYS volume.

To move the document root to another volume or directory, complete the steps in the following checklist.

1. Copy the document root directory and all of its subdirectories to the new location.

   Be sure to copy the complete directory structure (using the /s option with NCOPY or XCOPY) so that relative links in the web pages are not invalidated.
2. Start the NetWare Web Server Manager program and select your NetWare Web Server as described earlier in this chapter.
3. Change the Server Root Directory parameter on the Server page to specify the path to the web server document root directory.
4. Click OK to save your changes.
5. If you have made changes to the Web Server configuration, the NetWare Web Manager utility will prompt you to restart the server. To activate the changes, click Save & Restart, then enter the password for the NetWare Web Server.
6. Test your web site links to be sure that the directory move did not invalidate any links.

   All relative links within the document root should work in the new location, as should all explicit references to other web sites.
7. When you are satisfied that the web site is working correctly with the new document root, delete the former document root.

NOTE

You can still view your old document root pages in your browser by entering the domain name and path to the index file in the old root. For example: file:///SYS:/ *path_to_index_file/index_file*. This may be useful while you are troubleshooting links that aren't working.

Controlling Directory Indexing

Directory indexing is a feature that creates an index for a browser when the default directory is missing. If a browser user enters a URL for a file, the browser receives that file. If a browser enters a URL for a directory, one of the following occurs:

- If the default index file (INDEX.HTM) is present, that file is displayed. (The default name is defined in the SRM.CFG file with the DirectoryIndex directive.)

- If the default index file is missing and directory indexing is disabled, no files are found.
- If the default index file is missing and directory indexing is enabled, the server builds an index page that appears at the browser. This page lists all the files in the directory, along with links that can display or download the files.

You can use the NetWare Web Manager utility to manage directory indexing on a directory-by-directory basis. This utility stores your configuration in the ACCESS.CFG file. Table 14.6 lists the index options.

TABLE 14.6 *Index Options*

INDEX OPTION	FUNCTION
Fancy indexing	For each file in a directory, fancy indexing displays the filename listed by conventional indexing and adds an icon, the last modified date, the file size, and a file description.
Icons are links	When fancy indexing is enabled, this option defines the file icons as links so that the browser user can select the file by clicking on the icon.
Scan titles	When fancy indexing is enabled, the Scan titles option causes the server to scan all HTML documents and include the HTML document title in the index as a file description. If this option is disabled, the file description is blank.

To set the directory indexing options for a directory, complete the steps in the following checklist.

1. Start the NetWare Web Server Manager program and select your NetWare Web Server as described earlier in this chapter.
2. Choose the Directories page in the dialog box that appears.
3. If the directory for which you want to set indexing options appears in the Existing Directories box, select it.
4. If the directory you want does not appear in the Existing Directories box, use the Browse button to locate the directory, click Add, and then select your directory in the Existing Directories box.
5. After you have selected the directory, check the Enable Indexing check box.

6. If you want to enable any of the indexing options, check the corresponding check boxes.
7. Click Change, and then click OK to save your changes.
8. If you have made changes to the Web Server configuration, the NetWare Web Manager utility will prompt you to restart the server. To activate the changes, click Save & Restart, and then enter the password for the NetWare Web Server.

Checking Site Status

You can check your site status using the tools listed in Table 14.7.

TABLE 14.7 *Tools for Checking Site Status*

TOOL	PURPOSE
NetWare Web Server console	The Web Server console displays the server and document roots, server statistics, and server status messages, which are recorded in the Web Server error log.
Access log	The access log specifies the IP address or domain name of all users who access your server. It also lists the files that have been accessed. The default configuration of the server records IP addresses in the access log. If you set up the server as a DNS client as described earlier in this chapter, the access log records domain names whenever they are available.
Error log	The error log records the errors and messages that appear on the Web Server console.
Debug log	The debug log records information that you can use to troubleshoot problems with the Web Server.

VIEWING THE NETWARE WEB SERVER CONSOLE

The NetWare Web Server console (see Figure 14.2) is available whenever the Web Server is active, which is whenever the HTTP NLM is loaded. Just press Alt-Esc until the Novell HTTP Server console appears.

FIGURE 14.2 *The NetWare Web Server Console*

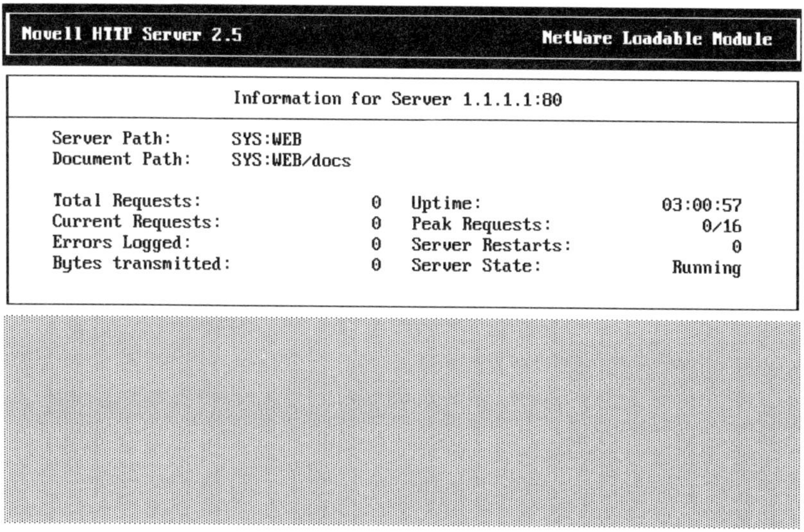

Note the Peak Requests statistic on the Web Server console. This number, 0/16 in this example, lists the maximum number of server threads used (0) and the maximum number of server threads available (16). If the number of server threads used starts to approach the maximum number available, you can configure the NetWare Web Server to use more threads. If you are low on memory and the Web Server is not using many of the allocated threads, you can save memory by reducing the number of allocated threads. These procedures are provided later in this chapter.

VIEWING AND ADMINISTERING LOG FILES

You can use the NetWare Web Manager utility to view and administer log files. To view and administer any log file, complete the steps in the following checklist.

1. Start the NetWare Web Server Manager program and select your NetWare Web Server as described earlier in this chapter.
2. Select the appropriate Open command from the Log menu.
3. Choose the Logs page in the dialog box that appears.
4. Set the log options using the information in Table 14.8.
5. Click OK to save your changes.
6. If you have made changes to the Web Server configuration, the NetWare Web Manager utility will prompt you to restart the server. To activate the changes, click Save & Restart, and then enter the password for the NetWare Web Server.

TABLE 14.8 *Log Options*

LOG OPTION	DESCRIPTION AND USAGE
Log file handling	This option determines whether there are one or more log files. If you select the Do not roll logs option, the NetWare Web Server creates one of each type of log file. When the log file is full, the oldest entries are deleted. If you select the Roll logs as needed option, the Web Server will archive all the log file data when the log gets full, creating an empty log file in which to store new data.
Server debug log options	This option enables or disables the logging of server debug messages.
Maximum log size	This option defines the maximum size of each log file. Notice that the NetWare Web Manager utility calculates the maximum amount of disk space used by the log files and the old logs. This appears on the Logs page.
Maximum number of old logs	This option specifies how many old log files will be created. If you already have filled all the old logs and then you fill the current log, the data in the oldest log file is lost.
Default button	The default button returns all log options to the default options supplied with the NetWare Web Server

Adjusting the Web Server Processing Power

As mentioned earlier, the Web Server console displays the maximum number of threads used by the NetWare Web Server. To provide more performance capacity (at the expense of server memory), you can increase the number of threads available to the Web Server. To reduce the memory required by the Web Server (and decrease the performance capacity of the Web Server), you can decrease the number of threads available.

To adjust the maximum number of threads used by the Web Server, edit the MaxThreads directive in the HTTPD.CFG file. The valid entries are 1 through 255, but entries above 40 may decrease the server performance.

Getting More Information

This chapter has introduced the concepts and administration tasks that will help you establish your web site using the NetWare Web Server. For more information on the NetWare Web Server, refer to one of the following resources:

- The default web pages (INDEX.HTM) provided with the NetWare Web Server
- The *Dynamic Web Page Programmer's Guide*, which describes how to use BASIC and Perl CGI scripts to create dynamic web pages. You can view this guide with your browser by specifying the following URL (replace *x* with the drive letter of the NetWare 4.11 CD-ROM: File:///*x*:/PRODUCTS/WEBSERV/DISK1/WEB/DOCS/ONLINE/WPGUIDE/INDEX.HTM
- The Novell web site, at www.novell.com, for updated information about the NetWare Web Server

CHAPTER 15

Installing the Novell Internet Access Server and FTP Services

Installing and Managing Novell Internet Access Server Components

- To install the Novell Internet Access Server components on the server, use INSTALL.NLM, select Product Options, and choose Install a Product Not Listed. Then specify the path to the *Novell Internet Access Server 4* CD-ROM.
- To configure the IPX/IP gateway on the server, use INETCFG.NLM.
- To install the client support for the IPX/IP gateway on workstations, install NetWare Client32 and choose Additional Options (on Windows 3.1x) or Customize (on Windows 95).
- To work with the IPX/IP gateway object in NDS and to configure access rights, add the IPX/IP gateway snap-in utility to the NetWare Administrator utility by editing the NWADMN3X.INI file.

Installing and Managing FTP Services for IntranetWare

- To install FTP Services for IntranetWare, use INSTALL.NLM, select Product Options, and choose Install a Product Not Listed. Then specify the path to the *FTP Services for IntranetWare* CD-ROM.
- To configure FTP Services for IntranetWare and to create an Anonymous FTP user account, use UNICON.NLM.

Just when we were beginning to get comfortable with the Internet technology, the intranet technology appeared. From a technical standpoint, the intranet is simply a web server that is confined to a private internal network and publishes files to a private audience such as the employees of a corporation. A true WWW server is connected to the Internet and publishes files to the world.

The reason that intranet technology is so popular is that people can use their WWW browsers to view the private information. The intranet server publishes shared information in HTML files that can be created with almost any word processor or text editor and can be viewed with Internet browsers on almost every operating system.

IntranetWare is Novell's comprehensive platform for a modern, full-service intranet. It starts with NetWare 4.11, then adds the following intranet and Internet features:

- *IPX/IP Gateway.* This gateway enables administrators to allow IPX-based workstations to access TCP/IP-based resources, such as FTP and the World Wide Web, without having to install or configure TCP/IP on those workstations. The gateway also lets you implement access control — you can limit users by TCP port number, IP address or the target host, and the time of day.
- *MultiProtocol Router 3.1.* This feature provides WAN (Wide Area Network) connectivity, routing multiple protocols over leased lines, frame relay, or ISDN lines. This capability allows you to connect network users to an Internet Service Provider (ISP).
- *Netscape Navigator.* This is the web browser that lets you locate and read information stored on the Internet or intranet.
- *FTP Services for IntranetWare.* FTP services let you configure FTP access for your intranet.

In your IntranetWare package, you'll find the following CD-ROMs:

- The *NetWare 4.11 Operating System* CD-ROM, which contains the regular NetWare 4.11 product software and the NetWare Web Server. The NetWare Web Server also contains the Netscape Navigator web browser (and a single-user license for the browser).
- The *NetWare 4.11 Online Documentation* CD-ROM, which contains the DynaText documentation for NetWare 4.11.
- The *Novell Internet Access Server 4* CD-ROM, which contains most of the IntranetWare features: the IPX/IP gateway, MultiProtocol Router 3.1

for WAN connectivity, and the Netscape Navigator web browser (multi-user license). This CD-ROM also contains HTML-formatted documentation for the IPX/IP gateway.

- The *FTP Services for IntranetWare* CD-ROM, which contains the FTP services and configuration utilities.

NOTE

To read the HTML-formatted documentation for the Novell Internet Access Server product, use a web browser from a workstation.

For instructions on installing the Netscape Navigator browser that comes with the NetWare Web Server on the *NetWare 4.11 Operating System* CD-ROM, see Chapter 14. For instructions on installing the browser from the *Novell Internet Access Server* CD-ROM, see the *Internet Access Server 4 Quick Reference Guide*, which comes with your IntranetWare kit. The two browsers are identical, and they are placed on both CD-ROMs primarily for convenience.

NOTE

If you have IntranetWare, you are allowed to use as many copies of the web browser as your IntranetWare user license permits. In other words, if you bought a 50-user version of IntranetWare, you can let 50 users use the browser. If you have NetWare 4.11 alone, you have only a single-user license to the browser.

Installing the Novell Internet Access Server Software

Before installing the Novell Internet Access Server software, which will provide the software necessary to run the routing, wan connectivity, and IPX/IP gateway, you must first install a NetWare 4.11 server as usual. Then you can install the Novell Internet Access Server software. During the installation, the Netscape Navigator browser will be copied to the SYS:NETSCAPE so that you can later install it on workstations.

To install Novell Internet Access Server components on the NetWare 4.11 server, complete the following steps.

1. Insert the *Novell Internet Access Server 4* CD-ROM in a drive on the server and mount the CD-ROM as a NetWare volume.
2. At the server console, load INSTALL.NLM.

3. From the Installation Options menu, choose Product Options, then choose Install a Product Not Listed.
4. To specify a path to the installation software, press <F3> and type

   `NIAS4:\NIAS\INSTALL`
5. Choose Install Product. The Install To Servers list displays the local server name. The value in the title reflects the number of servers to be installed. If you want to install Novell Internet Access Server software on a remote server, press Insert to add the server to the list. If an expected server is not displayed, ensure that the latest version of RSPAWN.NLM is loaded on that server. To remove a server from the Install To Servers list, select the server, press Delete, and select Yes at the prompt.
6. From the Install To Servers menu, press Enter and select Yes to begin the installation. Servers are installed in alphabetical order. If you are installing to a remote server, you will be prompted to log in as an administrator. Enter the administrator's full login name and password.
7. When the prompt "Install previously created configuration files?" appears, select No.
8. When prompted for the Novell Internet Access Server license diskette, insert the NetWare 4.11/IntranetWare license diskette in the specified drive and press Enter. Once the login, license, and configuration file information for each server are provided, the installation begins copying files to the destinations.
9. When the installation is completed, you can read the installation log file if you desire. Choose Display Log File. When you're finished reviewing the log, press Esc to return to the Installation Options menu.
10. To verify that the Novell Internet Access Server software installed correctly, choose Product Options from the Installation Options menu, then select Configure/View/Remove Installed Products. The Currently Installed Products list appears, showing entries for the NetWare MultiProtocol Router 3.1 software, WAN Extensions 3.1, and Novell Internet Access Server 4. Press Esc to return to the Installation Options menu.
11. From the Installation Options menu, select NCF Files Options, then choose the Edit STARTUP.NCF file. Modify the STARTUP.NCF file for each installed server to include the following line at the end of the file

if you are using the IntranetWare server to make a WAN connection:

```
SET MINIMUM PACKET RECEIVE BUFFERS=400
SET MAXIMUM PACKET RECEIVE BUFFERS=1000
```

The value of the second parameter can be increased as needed.

12. To exit the installation screen, press Esc and then select Yes to save the changes.
13. Bring down and restart the server to make sure all the correct NLMs are loaded. At the server's console, type:

```
DOWN
RESTART SERVER
```

In addition to updating server NLM files stored in SYS:\SYSTEM, the installation process installs the client files in the SYS:\PUBLIC\CLIENT\WIN95 and SYS:\PUBLIC\CLIENT\WIN31 directories. The Netscape Navigator files are installed in the SYS:\NETSCAPE\32 and SYS:\NETSCAPE\16 directories.

The IPX/IP Gateway

The IPX/IP gateway is an important part of the Novell Internet Access Server components of IntranetWare. With this gateway, IPX-based clients can access the Internet and other IP-based resources without having to install TCP/IP on the workstations themselves. The IPX/IP gateway gets installed on the server as part of the Novell Internet Access Server installation. To take advantage of the gateway, you must install IPX/IP Gateway support on each workstation. Client gateway support is included as an option in the NetWare Client32 installation.

Not having to use TCP/IP on each workstation is a benefit in many cases because there are significant management tasks associated with maintaining TCP/IP workstations. With TCP/IP, you have to manually keep track of and configure many items for each individual workstation, such as the unique IP address, subnet mask, IP addresses of the default router and the domain name servers, and the domain name.

An IPX/IP gateway removes much of the individual management hassles that occur with maintaining TCP/IP workstations by letting you retain IPX on those workstations.

When the IPX/IP gateway is installed on the IntranetWare server, the server runs IPX to communicate with the IPX workstations on the network and TCP/IP so that it can communicate with the Internet. From the viewpoint of a remote host on the Internet, all traffic through the gateway seems to originate from the IP address assigned to the gateway server. Because the IPX/IP gateway uses only a single IP address, regardless of the number of users it supports, the private network is safe from outside interference. Using the Novell IPX/IP Gateway alleviates the difficulties of administering a TCP/IP environment by providing ease of management and centralized control over Internet access.

By using Novell's IPX/IP gateway, you can run only IPX on the network workstations. Compared to IP, IPX is simple to manage. It assigns user connections dynamically, eliminating the need for a registered address to be configured at each desktop. Since IPX addresses are assigned dynamically, workstation IPX address conflicts do not occur. Users can move transparently between IPX networks, and traveling IPX users can roam between multiple networks within an enterprise.

The Novell IPX/IP Gateway allows you to limit access to Internet services by the type of traffic (for example, web browsing or FTP) and by remote host. Either type of restriction can be limited to specific times during the day to reduce "rush hour" traffic on an Internet connection.

CONFIGURING THE IPX/IP GATEWAY

After you've installed Novell Internet Access Server on the server, you can configure the IPX/IP gateway. To do this, complete the following steps.

1. At the server console, load INETCFG.NLM. If you are asked if you want to transfer your LAN driver, protocol, and remote access commands, choose Yes. What this really means is that you will move the LOAD and BIND commands from the AUTOEXEC.NCF file to INETCFG's startup files.
2. From the main menu, select Protocols, then choose TCP/IP, then choose IPX/IP Gateway Configuration.
3. Specify "enabled" in the Enabled for the IPX/IP Gateway field so that the gateway will become operational.
4. If you want to record when clients access a service over the gateway, enable the Client Logging field. The log is stored in a field called GW_AUDIT.LOG in the SYS volume.
5. In the Console Messages field, specify the type of messages you want to display on the gateway logging screen and the gateway status log file (GW_INFO.LOG in the SYS volume). You can choose "Informational, warning, and errors" (the default), "Warnings and errors only," or "Errors only."

6. To enforce access restrictions (which you set using the NetWare Administrator utility), enable the Access Control field.
7. In the Domain Name field, specify the name of the domain in which the gateway is installed. Your Internet Service Provider may provide you with this name.
8. In the Name Server fields, specify the IP addresses of any active domain name servers. Your Internet Service Provider may provide these addresses.
9. Press Esc twice, then log in as user Admin when prompted.
10. If you want to configure the gateway to use leased lines, frame relay, or ISDN lines, complete the following steps (see the documentation that came with Novell Internet Access Server for more specific details about parameters):

    a. Choose Boards from the INETCFG.NLM main menu. Then specify the appropriate WAN driver and configure any necessary parameters.

    b. Choose Network Interfaces from the INETCFG.NLM main menu. Then configure the appropriate WAN interfaces.

    c. Choose WAN Call Directory from INETCFG's main menu and press Ins to configure a new WAN call destination, then configure any necessary parameters.

    d. Choose Bindings from INETCFG's main menu, press Ins, and bind TCP/IP to the appropriate board or driver.

11. Exit INETCFG.NLM and save the changes you made.
12. Reboot the server to make the changes take effect.

After you've enabled and configured the gateway, a gateway server NDS object appears in the NDS tree in the same context as the server on which it is installed. The gateway object's name is the same as the server's name, with -GW added to the end of the name. This gateway object assists gateway clients in locating active IPX/IP gateway servers.

ADDING IPX/IP GATEWAY TOOLS TO THE NETWARE ADMINISTRATOR UTILITY

To work with the IPX/IP gateway object, you'll need to add the gateway's snap-in utility to the NetWare Administrator utility. This will allow NetWare Administrator to recognize the new gateway object and the new access control property that was added to certain objects. (This property is explained later in this chapter.)

The IPX/IP gateway snap-in utility works only with the 16-bit version of NetWare Administrator (which runs on Windows 3.1x).

To add the IPX/IP gateway support to the NetWare Administrator utility on a Windows 3.1 workstation, complete the following steps.

1. If you haven't yet opened the NetWare Administrator utility, open it and close it.
2. From the Windows File Manager on your workstation, double-click on the NWADMN3X.INI file (located in the WINDOWS directory) to open it for editing.
3. Under the heading [Snapin Object DLLs WIN3X], add the following line:

   ```
   IPXGW3X=IPXGW3X.DLL
   ```
4. Save and close the file. Now the NetWare Administrator utility will recognize the IPX/IP gateway object.

CONTROLLING ACCESS TO THE IPX/IP GATEWAY

After the IPX/IP Gateway server is fully installed and configured, you can use the NetWare Administrator utility to give the IPX/IP gateway server access control information for the various objects in the NDS tree. Then you can use NetWare Administrator to set restrictions for users, groups, or containers.

To give the gateway server access control information, use the NetWare Administrator utility to make the following changes to the NDS tree:

- Make the Public object a trustee of the Gateway object, with browse object rights and read and compare property rights (for all properties).
- Make the Public object a trustee of the File Server Object that is running the IPX/IP Gateway, with browse object rights and read and compare property rights for the Network Address property only (under selected properties).
- Make the Gateway object a trustee in the Root object, with browse object rights and read and compare property rights (for all properties).

You control user access through the IPX/IP Gateway by using the NetWare Administrator utility. As the point of connection between a NetWare network and a TCP/IP network, an IPX/IP gateway is in an ideal position to enforce restrictions on traffic between the two networks.

These access restrictions can be stored in two properties that are added to the User, Group, Organization, or Organizational Unit objects when the gateway is enabled:

- The first property, service restrictions, tells the gateway object which applications may be used by the object and which are restricted. These restrictions are based on the port number.
- The second property, host restrictions, tells the gateway which remote hosts are restricted from the object. These restrictions are based on the IP address.

Storing access restrictions in the NDS objects provides a single database of restrictions that all gateway servers share. You do not need to configure access control separately on each gateway. Restrictions are active on all gateways regardless of whether they are applied to an entire organization or created individually for each user.

To place access restrictions on a User, Group, Organization, or Organizational Unit object, use the NetWare Administrator utility and select the object in question. Then choose Details under the Object menu and open the IPX/IP Gateway Service Restrictions page. On this page, you can enter restrictions for this object.

To restrict access to a specific Internet site, place a host restriction on the IP address of that site. To prevent certain types of traffic from being forwarded by the server, create a service restriction for the appropriate port number. For example, you might restrict web browser access to certain hours during the day, but allow FTP or TELNET access during those same hours. You could also place the remote host "www.games.com" off-limits. To prevent news readers from operating across the gateway, you might place a restriction on traffic to port number 119 (News) at any site.

INSTALLING THE IPX/IP GATEWAY CLIENT

The IPX/IP gateway support is installed as an option in the NetWare Client32 workstation software. The following instructions explain how to install this support on Windows 3.1x workstations and Windows 95 workstations.

The Windows 3.1x Client

To configure the IPX/IP gateway support on a Windows 3.1x workstation, you install NetWare Client32 as explained in Chapter 4. During the installation process when the Additional Options screen appears, complete the following steps.

1. Select the NetWare IPX/IP Gateway check box, then select Next to continue.
2. When the Configuration menu for these options appears, enter the appropriate information and select Next to continue.
3. When you've finished, choose OK to restart your computer. When the workstation comes back up, the Novell IPX/IP Gateway Switcher icon appears in the NetWare Tools program group. The gateway switcher program switches the client from gateway operation to native TCP/IP operation (if TCP/IP is available on the client).
4. Double-click the Gateway Switcher icon, then click Enable Gateway to enable the gateway. You can also enter the name of a preferred gateway server if you have more than one gateway installed in the network. If a preferred gateway server is configured, the gateway task will attempt to locate that gateway server through NDS and connect to it. If the preferred gateway server is not available, the gateway client will search for other gateway servers, first in the user's NDS context, then in the bindery of the attached server, then finally it will query for a SAP broadcast of any gateway server.

   Note: There is no linkage between the preferred file server and the preferred gateway server. A user may be attached to file server A while using a gateway server that resides on file server B.

The Windows 95 Client

To configure the IPX/IP gateway support on a Windows 95 workstation, you install NetWare Client32 as explained in Chapter 4. When the installation is finished, complete the following steps.

1. Click on Customize to customize the client.
2. Choose Add.
3. In the Type of Network Component You Want to Install box, double-click on Protocol.
4. In the Manufacturers box, choose Novell, then double-click on Novell NetWare IPX/IP Gateway.

5. Choose OK to exit the Network configuration screen.
6. If you receive a prompt to select a preferred gateway server, click Yes, enter the name of your preferred IPX/IP Gateway server, and select OK. If a preferred gateway server is configured, the gateway task will attempt to locate that gateway server through NDS and connect to it. If the preferred gateway server is not available, the gateway client will search for other gateway servers, first in the user's NDS context, then in the bindery of the attached server, then finally it will query for a SAP broadcast of any gateway server.

   Note: There is no linkage between the preferred file server and the preferred gateway server. A user may be attached to file server A while using a gateway server that resides on file server B.
7. If you asked for additional files, type the location of those files in the Copy Files From box. If you are asked for Client32 files, type in the path to the directory from which you ran SETUP.EXE.
8. Click Yes to restart the computer. The IPX/IP Gateway Switcher program runs automatically during the first restart after installation. This switcher program switches the client from gateway operation to native TCP/IP operation (if TCP/IP is available on the client).
9. To enable the gateway, click the Enable IPX/IP Gateway button, then click OK.

FTP Services for IntranetWare

In addition to the Novell Internet Access Server components, IntranetWare also includes FTP Services. This feature, which is a subset of the NetWare UNIX Print Services 2.11 product, allows NetWare clients to use FTP to work with files on the Internet or intranet.

INSTALLING FTP SERVICES

To install FTP Services for IntranetWare on your server, complete the following steps.

1. Mount the FTP Services CD-ROM as a volume on the NetWare 4.11 server.
2. Load INSTALL.NLM on the server.
3. Choose Product Options, then choose Install a Product Not Listed.

4. Press F3, then type in the following path to the FTP Services files on the CD-ROM:

   `NWUXPS:\NWUXPS`

5. If you are asked to specify a host name, either press Enter to accept the default name displayed or enter the correct host name.
6. Accept the default boot drive (or specify the correct drive from which the server boots).
7. To install the online documentation for FTP Services, choose Yes. This documentation is separate from the regular NetWare online documentation and describes how to install and use FTP Services.
8. If you have already installed the NetWare 4.11 DynaText viewer, choose No when asked if you want to install a new one.

   Note: If you receive the message "hosts.db does not exist," ignore it.

9. When prompted for a user name, enter the ADMIN name and password.
10. Choose the name service option you want to use on this server and answer any prompts necessary for the name service you choose. If you choose to use a local name service, the database that holds the name service information will be stored on this server and will be the master database. You can use the UNICON.NLM utility to work with the master database on a local server. If you choose to use a remote name service, that database will reside on another server. You can use UNICON.NLM only to view the database information but not modify it. You can choose one of the following options:

    - Local DNS and Local NIS. This option stores both master databases on this server.
    - Remote DNS and Remote NIS. This option uses the master databases stored on another server.
    - Remote DNS and Local NIS. This option stores the master NIS database on this server and the DNS database on another server.
    - No DNS and Remote NIS. This option stores the master NIS database on another server and does not provide DNS service at all.

11. Follow any prompts necessary to initialize the name service and the product.
12. To start FTP Services, press Ins and choose FTP Server. FTP Services will start running and will appear in the Running Services menu.
13. To exit the installation program, press Esc as many times as necessary.
14. Restart the server to make the new settings take effect, by typing:

    ```
    DOWN
    RESTART SERVER
    ```

CONFIGURING FTP SERVICES

With FTP Services, users can use FTP to access and transfer files from the intranet or Internet. If you desire, you can create an Anonymous FTP account for users to use. With an Anonymous account, any user can access the FTP service by typing in any password. (Any password will work; the FTP service doesn't actually authenticate the password.)

To configure an Anonymous FTP account, complete the following steps.

1. At the server console, load UNICON.NLM.
2. When prompted, enter the ADMIN user name and password.
3. Choose Manage Services, then choose FTP Server, then choose Set Parameters.
4. Choose Default Name Space and enter NFS. This will install the NFS name space on the server, which will allow the server to store UNIX files.
5. Change the Anonymous User Access field to Yes so that the Anonymous account will be enabled.
6. Choose Anonymous User's Home Directory and change the path from the volume SYS (displayed as /sys) to a directory you prefer to use as the login directory for Anonymous FTP users.
7. When finished, press Esc to exit the installation program and save the changes you've made.
8. Return to the main menu by pressing Esc twice, then choose Perform File Operations, then choose View/Set File Permissions.
9. Enter the path to the Anonymous user's home directory (specified in Step 6) and press F9 to see the permissions (the UNIX equivalent of trustee rights) that have been set for this directory. If the permissions

are not correct, modify them on this screen. The permissions should be:

```
[U = rwx] [G = --] [o = --]
```

10. Press Esc multiple times to exit UNICON and save the changes you've made.
11. Even though you specified the NFS name space in Step 4, you still need to add it to the volume. (You only need to add the name space to the volume once. To see if you've already added NFS name space to a volume, type **VOLUMES** at the server console — the display will show which name spaces are supported on each volume.) If you need to add the name space, type the following command, replacing *volume* with the name of the volume:

    ADD NAME SPACE NFS TO *volume*

CHAPTER 16

IntranetWare Utilities and NLMs

Using Utilities

- IntranetWare workstation utilities are applications or commands you run from a network workstation. There are different utilities for the different tasks you can perform on the network and different utilities for each workstation platform (DOS, Windows 3.1, and so on).
- IntranetWare console utilities are commands you execute from the server's console (or from a Remote Console session running on a workstation). These utilities are generally used to effect the server's operation.
- NLMs (NetWare Loadable Modules) are software modules that you load into the server's operating system to add or change functionality in the server.

You can use many different utilities to monitor, change, or work with an IntranetWare network. This chapter briefly describes these core utilities.

Using IntranetWare Utilities

There are three main types of IntranetWare utilities:

- Workstation utilities, which are applications or commands you run from a network workstation
- Console utilities, which are commands you execute from the server's console (or from a Remote Console session running on a workstation)
- NLMs (NetWare Loadable Modules), which are software modules that you load into the server's operating system to add or change functionality in the server

This chapter lists all of the utilities in alphabetical order, regardless of type. However, each type of utility is executed differently, as explained in the following sections.

NOTE: In many cases, to execute the utility, you simply type the name of the utility. Where there are parameters or options you must enter along with the utility name, the command format to use is indicated.

USING WORKSTATION UTILITIES

How you execute a workstation utility depends on the type of utility it is and the workstation operating system you're using. Workstation utilities are generally used to work with network services, such as the NetWare Directory tree, printing services, and so on.

To execute a NetWare utility that runs in DOS (such as NCOPY), you type the utility's name, plus any additional parameters that may be necessary, at a DOS prompt on the workstation. Some of these utilities may display menus from which you choose the tasks or options you want.

To execute a NetWare utility that runs in Windows, OS/2, or Windows 95 (such as NetWare Administrator), you have to add the utility to your workstation's desktop first. To do this, you use the normal Windows, OS/2, or Windows 95 methods for adding a new application's icon.

The following workstation utilities are described in this chapter.

- ADDICON
- ATOTAL
- AUDITCON
- CAPTURE
- COLORPAL
- CX
- DOSGEN
- DS Migrate
- FILER
- FLAG
- LOGIN
- LOGOUT
- MAP
- MENUCNVT
- MENUMAKE
- MIGPRINT
- MIGRATE
- NCOPY
- NCUPDATE
- NDIR
- NDS Manager
- NETADMIN
- NETUSER
- NetWare Administrator
- NetWare Application Launcher
- NetWare Application Manager
- NetWare File Migration
- NetWare User Tools
- NLIST
- NLS Manager
- NMENU
- NPATH
- NPRINT
- NPRINTER.EXE
- NPTWIN95.EXE
- NVER
- NWXTRACT
- PARTMGR
- PCONCOLE
- PRINTCON
- PRINTDEF
- PSC
- PURGE
- RCONSOLE
- RENDIR
- RIGHTS
- SEND
- SETPASS
- SETTTS
- SETUPDOC
- SYSTIME
- UIMPORT
- WHOAMI
- WSUPDATE

USING CONSOLE UTILITIES

Console utilities, such as MOUNT, are commands that you execute by typing a command at the server's console. You can also execute these utilities from a Remote Console session on a workstation.

In general, you use these commands to change some aspect of the server or to view information about it. Console utilities are built into the operating system, just as internal DOS commands are built into DOS. To read online help for console utilities, use the HELP console utility. Use the following command format, substituting the name of the utility (such as SCAN FOR NEW DEVICES) for *utility*.

```
HELP utility
```

The following console utilities are described in this chapter.

ABORT REMIRROR
ACTIVATE SERVER
ADD NAME SPACE
ALIAS
BIND
BINDERY
BROADCAST
CD
CLEAR STATION
CLS
CONFIG
DISABLE LOGIN
DISABLE TTS
DISMOUNT
DISPLAY NETWORKS
DISPLAY SERVERS
DOWN
ENABLE LOGIN
ENABLE TTS
EXIT
HALT
HCSS
HELP
INITIALIZE SYSTEM
LANGUAGE
LIST DEVICES
LOAD
MAGAZINE
MEDIA
MEMORY
MEMORY MAP
MIRROR STATUS
MODULES
MOUNT
NAME
OFF
PROTOCOL
REGISTER MEMORY
REINITIALIZE SYSTEM
REMIRROR PARTITION
REMOVE DOS
RESET ROUTER
RESTART
RESTART SERVER
SCAN FOR NEW DEVICES
SEARCH
SECURE CONSOLE
SEND
SERVER.EXE
SET
SET TIME
SET TIME ZONE
SPEED
SPOOL
TIME
TRACK OFF
TRACK ON
UNBIND
UNLOAD
UPS STATUS
UPS TIME
VERSION
VOLUMES

USING NLMs

NetWare Loadable Modules (NLMs), such as INSTALL and MONITOR, are software modules that can add functionality to a server, such as allowing the server to support Mac OS files, provide backup services, support different protocols, install new features, and so on.

Many NLMs are installed automatically with the IntranetWare operating system. Others are optional; you can load them if your particular situation requires them.

There are four types of NetWare Loadable Modules that you can use to add different types of functionality to your server: NLMs, name space modules, LAN drivers, and disk drivers. These types of NLMs are described in Chapter 3.

You can load and unload NLMs while the server is running. Many NLMs have their own status screen that displays on the server. To move between NLM screens on the server's console, use Alt-Esc to cycle through the available NLM screens and use Ctrl-Esc to bring up a list of available screens. Then, select the screen you want.

To load NLMs, type the following command, replacing *modules* with the name of the NLM (you do not need to type the .NLM extension in the LOAD command):

```
LOAD module
```

For example, to load MONITOR.NLM, type

```
LOAD MONITOR
```

To unload an NLM, use the UNLOAD command in the same way. For example, to unload MONITOR.NLM, type

```
UNLOAD MONITOR
```

This chapter describes the core NLMs. Many NLMs have related NLMs that automatically load when necessary. These "autoloaded" NLMs are not listed here, as you should never need to load them manually. In addition, there are many NLMs from third-party companies, as well as NLMs from optional Novell products, that can also be used on IntranetWare servers. These NLMs are not listed here, either. See the documentation that comes with these products for more information about their NLMs.

The following NLMs are described in this chapter.

ADSP.NLM
AFP.NLM
AFPCON.NLM
AIOCOMX.NLM
APPLETLK.NLM
ATCON.NLM
ATCONFIG.NLM
ATFLT.NLM
ATPS.NLM
ATPSCON.NLM
ATTOKLLC.NLM
ATXRP.NLM
AURP.NLM
CDROM.NLM
CONLOG.NLM
DHCPCFG.NLM

DS.NLM
DSMERGE.NLM
DSREPAIR.NLM
EDIT.NLM
FILTCFG.NLM
HCSS.NLM
HFSCD.NLM
HFSCDCON.NLM
HFSLFS.NLM
INETCFG.NLM
INSTALL.NLM
IPCONFIG.NLM
IPFLT.NLM
IPXCON.NLM
IPXFLT.NLM
IPXPING.NLM
KEYB.NLM
LONG.NAM
MAC.NAM
MACFILE.NLM
MONITOR.NLM
MPDRIVER.NLM
NETSYNC3.NLM
NETSYNC4.NLM
NFS.NAM
NPAMS.NLM
NPRINTER.NLM
NWIP.NLM
NWIPCFG.NLM
NWPA.NLM
PING.NLM
PSERVER.NLM
PUPGRADE.NLM
REMAPID.NLM
REMOTE.NLM
ROUTE.NLM
RPL.NLM
RS232.NLM
RSPX.NLM
SBACKUP.NLM
SCHDELAY.NLM
SERVMAN.NLM
SPXCONFG.NLM
TCPCON.NLM
TCPIP.NLM
TECHWALK.NLM
TIMESYNC.NLM
TPING.NLM
UNICON.NLM
UPS.NLM
UPS_AIO.NLM
V_LONG.NLM
V_MAC.NLM
V_NFS.NLM
VIEW.NLM
VREPAIR.NLM

The Utilities and NLMs

All of the core IntranetWare utilities and NLMs are explained in the following sections.

ABORT REMIRROR (CONSOLE UTILITY)

Use this utility to stop disk partitions from remirroring. Use the following command format, replacing *number* with the number of the logical disk partition you want to stop from remirroring:

```
ABORT REMIRROR number
```

ACTIVATE SERVER (CONSOLE UTILITY)

Use this utility with SFT III to load the MSENGINE on the servers, which synchronizes the servers' memory and mirrors their disks. See Chapter 3 for more information about SFT III.

ADD NAME SPACE (CONSOLE UTILITY)

Use this utility to add support for a name space (LONG.NAM for OS/2, Windows 95, and Windows NT files, MAC.NAM for Macintosh files, and NFS.NAM for UNIX files). Use the following command format, replacing *name* with the name of the name space module (such as MAC) and *volume* with the volume's name:

```
ADD NAME SPACE name TO volume
```

To display the name spaces currently loaded, type

```
ADD NAME SPACE
```

ADDICON (WORKSTATION UTILITY)

Use this utility on a Windows 3.1 workstation to add icons to the Windows Program Manager. ADDICON can be executed at the DOS prompt or in a login script. It modifies an existing Program Manager group file (named with the extension .GRP) to add the icon to the group's window. Use the following command format, replacing *parameter* with one of the parameters shown in Table 16.1.

```
ADDICON parameter
```

TABLE 16.1 *ADDICON Parameters*

PARAMETER	DESCRIPTION
CMD=*parameters*	Indicates any command parameters necessary for the application.
DESC=*text*	Describes the application (the default is the executable file's name).
EXE=*filename*	Indicates the name of the executable file for the application.
GROUP=*group*	Indicates the name of the Program Manager group.

TABLE 16.1 *ADDICON Parameters (continued)*

PARAMETER	DESCRIPTION
GROUPFILE=*filename*	Specifies the specific .GRP file to modify. Use this parameter instead of the GROUP and WINDOWS parameters.
/H	Displays online help.
ICON=*filename*	Specifies the file that contains the icon if it isn't contained in the executable file for the application.
MIN=*yes/no*	Set to Yes if you want to set the Minimize attribute. (Default is No.)
WINDOWS=*path*	Indicates the path to the Windows directory. If you omit this parameter, ADDICON searches the PATH environment for the WIN.COM file.
WORK=*path*	Indicates the working directory of the application
@*script*	Indicates a script file that contains all the necessary parameters. If you use this parameter, omit all other parameters from the ADDICON command.

ADSP (NLM)

Use this module to load the AppleTalk Data Stream Protocol if you are installing NetWare for Macintosh. This protocol allows applications to communicate over AppleTalk networks. If you are using the NetWare Client for Mac OS, which lets you connect Mac OS workstations directly to the network using IPX, you do not need to use this module. See Chapter 10 for more information.

AFP (NLM)

Use this module to install support for the AppleTalk Filing Protocol 2.0 on the server if you are using the NetWare for Macintosh product to connect Mac OS workstations to your NetWare network via an AppleTalk router. If you are using the NetWare Client for Mac OS, which lets you connect Mac OS workstations directly to the network using IPX, you do not need to use this module. See Chapter 10 for more information.

AFPCON (NLM)

Use this utility to configure the AppleTalk Filing Protocol (AFP.NLM) if you are using the NetWare for Macintosh product to connect Mac OS workstations to your NetWare network via an AppleTalk router. If you are using the NetWare Client for Mac OS, which lets you connect Mac OS workstations directly to the network using IPX, you do not need to use this module. See Chapter 10 for more information.

AIOCOMX (NLM)

Use this module, which is a communications port driver, with utilities such as Remote Console.

ALIAS (CONSOLE UTILITY)

Use this utility to create an alias for a particular console utility or command, so that you can type the alias to execute the utility, rather than the regular utility name. Use the following command format, replacing *alias* with the new command you want to be able to type and *command* with the original utility name or command you want to execute when you type the alias:

```
ALIAS alias command
```

APPLETLK (NLM)

Use this module to load the AppleTalk protocol stack on the server. Use it to create an AppleTalk router on the server to support AppleTalk networks connected to the NetWare network. (Creating an AppleTalk router was the only way to add Mac OS workstations to a NetWare network in previous versions of NetWare. If you are using the NetWare Client for Mac OS, which lets you connect Mac OS workstations directly to the network using IPX, you do not need to use this module. See Chapter 10 for more information.)

ATCON (NLM)

Use this module to monitor and configure the AppleTalk protocol stack and AppleTalk router on the server. ATCON lets you see the status of the AppleTalk Update-based Router protocol, which lets AppleTalk be tunneled through IP. ATCON also lets you see information about network interfaces, manage the error log files, do a Name Binding protocol (NBP) look-up of network entities, see statistics about AppleTalk packets, display the configuration of the AppleTalk router, and so on. When using ATCON, press the F1 key to read help for each option.

ATCONFIG (NLM)

Use this module to configure NetWare for Macintosh after installation. When you use INSTALL.NLM to install NetWare for Macintosh, this NLM is loaded automatically, enabling you to configure the newly installed product. You can also load ATCONFIG.NLM separately later to change the configuration. If you are using the NetWare Client for Mac OS, which lets you connect Mac OS workstations directly to the network using IPX, you do not need to use this module. See Chapter 10 for more information.

ATFLT (NLM)

Use this AppleTalk filter NLM to restrict how routers see and communicate with other AppleTalk routers.

ATOTAL (WORKSTATION UTILITY)

Use this utility to create a report totaling the usage statistics tracked by the accounting feature on a server. To display the totals on a workstation screen, type ATOTAL. To redirect the output of ATOTAL's report to a text file, use the following command format, substituting a file name for *filename:*

```
ATOTAL > filename
```

ATPS (NLM)

Use this module to support AppleTalk Print Services if you are using the NetWare for Macintosh product to connect Mac OS workstations to your NetWare network via an AppleTalk router. If you are using the NetWare Client for Mac OS, which lets you connect Mac OS workstations directly to the network using IPX, you do not need to use this module. See Chapter 10 for more information.

ATPSCON (NLM)

Use this module to configure ATPS.NLM if you are using NetWare for Macintosh. If you are using the NetWare Client for Mac OS, which lets you connect Mac OS workstations directly to the network using IPX, you do not need to use this module. See Chapter 10 for more information.

ATTOKLLC (NLM)

Use this module to support Mac OS workstations on a Token Ring network if you are using the NetWare for Macintosh product to connect Mac OS workstations to your NetWare network via an AppleTalk router. If you are using the NetWare Client for Mac OS, which lets you connect Mac OS workstations directly to the network using IPX, you do not need to use this module. See Chapter 10 for more information.

ATXRP (NLM)

Use this module to allow the NetWare print server to send a print job to an AppleTalk network printer from a NetWare print queue, taking advantage of PSERVER's benefits. ATXRP also allows AppleTalk printers to appear as objects in the NDS tree. If you are using the NetWare Client for Mac OS, which lets you connect Mac OS workstations directly to the network using IPX, you do not need to use this module. See Chapter 10 for more information.

AUDITCON (WORKSTATION UTILITY)

Use this menu utility to configure and view audit trails from a server's volume and container object. This utility lets an auditor see auditing information about NDS and file system or volume events. Auditors cannot, however, open or modify files without appropriate NDS or file system rights.

AURP (NLM)

Use this NLM to allow AppleTalk to be tunneled through IP, which lets AppleTalk networks connect to each other through an IP internetwork. (AURP stands for AppleTalk Update-based Routing Protocol.)

BIND (CONSOLE UTILITY)

Use this utility to assign a protocol such as IPX or AppleTalk to a LAN driver or network board, so that the LAN driver or board knows which protocol to use. Any configuration parameters you specify when you load the LAN driver must also be added to the BIND command so that the protocol is bound to the correct board. Use the following command format, replacing *protocol* with the name of the protocol (such as IPS or APPLETLK), *driver* with the name of the LAN driver or network board, and *parameters* with any necessary driver or protocol parameters:

```
BIND protocol driver parameters
```

The most common protocol parameter for the IPX protocol is:

```
NET=number
```

Replace *number* with the unique network number for the network on which this board is running. (Each network board in a server will have a different network number.)

The most common driver parameters are described in Table 16.2.

TABLE 16.2 *Common Driver Parameters*

DRIVER PARAMETER	DESCRIPTION
DMA=*number*	Indicates the DMA channel the board should use.
FRAME=*type*	Indicates the frame type (Ethernet or Token Ring) this board should use. The available frame types are: Ethernet_802.2 (default) Ethernet_802.3 Ethernet_II Ethernet_SNAP Token-Ring (default) Token-Ring_SNAP
INT=*number*	Indicates the interrupt (in hex) that the board should use.
MEM=*number*	Indicates the memory address the board should use.
NODE=*number*	Indicates the board's node address.
PORT=*number*	Indicates the I/O port the board should use.
SLOT=*number*	Indicates the slot in which the board is installed.

BINDERY (CONSOLE COMMAND)

Use this utility to add or delete a bindery context in the list of bindery contexts this server uses. You can also use the SET BINDERY CONTEXT parameter to set a bindery context, as explained in Chapter 5.

BROADCAST (CONSOLE UTILITY)

Use this utility to send a short message from the server console to users on the network. To send a message to a user, use the following command format, replacing *message* with the message you want displayed (no more than 55 characters long) and *user* with either the name of the user or that workstation's connection number (as seen in MONITOR.NLM):

```
BROADCAST "message" user
```

To send the message to multiple users, separate each user name or connection number with a comma or space. To send the message to all users, don't specify any user name at all. (You can also use the SEND console utility to accomplish the same thing.)

CAPTURE (WORKSTATION UTILITY)

Use this utility to redirect your workstation's LPT port to a network print queue. Many network applications can redirect print jobs to a network print queue automatically, but others don't, so it's often a good idea to put a CAPTURE command in the login script just in case. (See Chapter 9 for more information about printing.)

In general, you can use the following command format, replacing *port* with the number of the LPT port, *queue* with the name of the print queue (you may need to specify the complete Directory name of the queue if it isn't in your own context), and *parameters* with one of the additional parameters listed in Table 16.3.

```
CAPTURE L=port Q=queue parameters
```

TABLE 16.3 *CAPTURE Parameters*

PARAMETER	DESCRIPTION
AU	End capture Automatically. Sends a print job to the printer when you exit the application.
B=*text*	Specifies that a banner page (displaying the *text* you specify) is printed before the print job. The default text is the print job file name.
C=*number*	Specifies how many copies are printed (1 to 999; the default is 1).
CR=*path*	Redirects the print job to a file instead of a printer. Replace *path* with the directory path and name of the file you want to create.
D	Displays details of printing parameters for a capture and shows whether a print job configuration was used.

TABLE 16.3 *CAPTURE Parameters (continued)*

PARAMETER	DESCRIPTION
EC	Ends the Capture. Stops capturing data to the LPT1 port, and if the data was being captured to a file, closes the file. To end a capture to another port, use EC L=*n* and replace *n* with the LPT number. To end a capture and delete the data that was being captured, use ECCA. To end the capture of all LPT ports, use EC ALL.
F=*form*	Specifies the number or name of the form (paper type) that this job should be printed on.
FF	Causes a form feed at the end of a print job, so that the next job prints on the next page. This parameter is necessary only if the application doesn't cause a form feed automatically.
HOLD	Sends a print job to a queue but doesn't print it. To release the Hold, use the NetWare Administrator utility.
J=*name*	Specifies the name of a print job configuration to use. This parameter is necessary only if you don't want to use the default print job configuration.
K	Instructs your workstation to "keep" all captured data in case your workstation loses power while capturing data. The network server will send the captured data to the printer if it detects that your workstation is down.
L=*number*	Specifies which LPT port should be captured (1, 2, or 3).
NA	No Auto Endcap. Prevents the workstation from sending captured data to the printer when you exit an application.
NAM=*name*	Specifies the name that should appear on the banner page (the default is your login name).
NB	Eliminates the banner page.
NFF	Eliminates the form feed.
NNOTI	Prevents a message from appearing on your workstation telling you that the print job is finished. This parameter is necessary only if the print job configuration requests notification and you don't want it.

(continued)

TABLE 16.3 *CAPTURE Parameters (continued)*

PARAMETER	DESCRIPTION
NOTI	Specifies that your workstation receives notification when a print job is finished. This parameter is disabled by default.
NT	No Tabs. This parameter is necessary only if your application has a print formatter, but has problems printing graphics or creates unexpected formats. It allows an application's print formatter to determine how many spaces are in a tab stop.
P=*printer*	Specifies a network printer.
Q=*name*	Specifies a network print queue.
S=*name*	Specifies to which network server a print job should be sent.
SH	Show. Displays a list of your workstation's captured ports and the print queues to which they are redirected.
T=*number*	Specifies how many spaces are in a tab stop. This is necessary only if your application doesn't have a print formatter.
TI=*number*	Specifies the "timeout" — the number of seconds to wait before printing, instead of waiting for the user to exit the application. The default is 0, meaning that timeout is disabled.
/?	Displays help for CAPTURE.

CD (CONSOLE UTILITY)

Use this utility after you've loaded CDROM.NLM to mount a CD-ROM as a volume, dismount a CD-ROM, display a list of all CD-ROMs currently mounted, and so on. The command you use with this utility depends on the task you want to accomplish. The different commands you can use are explained in Table 16.4.

TABLE 16.4 *CD Commands*

CD COMMAND	DESCRIPTION
CD CHANGE *name*	Allows you to remove one CD-ROM and replace it with another. Replace *name* with the name or number of the volume you're changing.

TABLE 16.4 *CD Commands (continued)*

CD COMMAND	DESCRIPTION
CD DEVICE LIST	Displays a list of the CD-ROM drives that are connected to the server and shows the volume names and device numbers of the CD-ROMs in those drives.
CD DIR	Displays a list of the files and directories contained in the CD-ROM's root volume.
CD DISMOUNT *name*	Dismounts a CD-ROM volume. Replace *name* with either the CD-ROM's volume name or number. To eject the CD-ROM, add /EJECT to the end of the command. To remove the index file for the volume, add /PURGE to the end of the command.
CD GROUP *name*	Assigns a NetWare group as a trustee of the CD-ROM volume.
CD HELP	Displays a description of the CD commands you can use.
IMAGE	Lets you mount a CD-ROM image file as a CD, which lets you test the image before making a CD.
CD MOUNT *name*	Mounts a CD-ROM as a NetWare volume, so that network users can access it. Replace *name* with either the CD-ROM's name or number (shown with CD DEVICE LIST).
PURGE	Purges the index and cache files created on the server when a CD-ROM is mounted as a volume. (Dismount all CD-ROM volumes first.)
CD RENAME /D=*number newname*	Renames a CD-ROM volume. To see names of mounted volumes, type **CD RENAME**. To change the volume name, dismount the volume, and then use the CD RENAME command, replacing *number* with the volume's object number (shown with CD DEVICE LIST) and *newname* with the new volume name you want to use.
CD VOLUME LIST	Displays a list of the volumes on each CD-ROM device and shows whether those volumes are mounted.

CDROM (NLM)

Use this module to mount a CD-ROM as a NetWare volume. This NLM supports the High Sierra and ISO 9660 formats, along with HFS (Apple) extensions. (This means you can access Mac files on the CD from a Mac workstation.) After you've loaded this NLM, you can use the CD console utility (explained above) to mount a CD-ROM as a NetWare volume and perform other related tasks.

CLEAR STATION (CONSOLE UTILITY)

Use this command to close a workstation's open files and remove the workstation's connection from the server. This is necessary only if the workstation has crashed and left files open and you can't log out normally. Use the following command format, replacing *number* with the workstation's connection number (as seen in MONITOR.NLM) or the word ALL to clear all connections:

```
CLEAR STATION number
```

CLS (CONSOLE UTILITY)

Use this utility to clear the server's console screen (just as the CLS command works on DOS workstations).

COLORPAL (WORKSTATION UTILITY)

Use this menu utility if your workstation uses a monochrome monitor from a composite color adapter (such as a Compaq or AT&T 6300 computer) and the computer has trouble displaying the NetWare menu utilities in default colors. COLORPAL lets you select the colors in which you want elements of the menus to be displayed. Each color scheme is called a palette.

CONFIG (CONSOLE UTILITY)

Use this utility to see configuration information about the server, such as the server's name, internal network number, loaded LAN drivers, hardware settings, protocols, and the node address of each installed network board.

CONLOG (NLM)

Use this module to capture the console messages that occur during system initialization and send them to a file called CONSOLE.LOG in the SYS:ETC directory. To stop capturing messages in this file, unload CONLOG.

CX (WORKSTATION UTILITY)

Use this utility to move up and down through containers in the Directory tree. This utility is similar to DOS's CD utility, which lets you move around in the file system's subdirectory structure. Use the following command format, replacing *context* with the NDS context you want to move to (such as .MKTG.OUTVIEW) and *parameter* with one of the parameters listed in Table 16.5.

```
CX context /parameter
```

TABLE 16.5 *CX Parameters*

PARAMETER	DESCRIPTION
/A	Includes all objects in the context (use with /T or /CONT).
/C	Causes the display to scroll continuously down the screen.
/CONT	Displays a list of containers in your current context or in the context you specify in the command.
/R	Displays a list of the containers at the root level or changes the context in relation to the root.
/T	Displays a list of the containers below your current context or the context you specify in the command.
/?	Displays help for CX.

DHCPCFG (NLM)

This module lets you manage the NetWare DHCP service. DHCP (Dynamic Host Configuration Protocol) lets a TCP/IP workstation get configuration information such as its IP address and network configuration automatically from the server.

DISABLE LOGIN (CONSOLE UTILITY)

Use this utility to prevent users from logging in to the server (such as when you want to perform maintenance on the server). Users who are already logged in won't be affected, but additional users cannot log in. To allow users to log in again, use ENABLE LOGIN.

DISABLE TTS (CONSOLE UTILITY)

Use this utility to disable TTS (NetWare's Transaction Tracking System). You should not need to disable TTS using this utility unless you are an application developer and have a specific need to do so. If you disable TTS, you can turn it back on using ENABLE TTS.

DISMOUNT (CONSOLE UTILITY)

Use this utility to dismount a volume. Use the following command format, replacing *volume* with the name of the volume you want to dismount:

```
DISMOUNT volume
```

DISPLAY NETWORKS (CONSOLE UTILITY)

Use this utility to display a list of all the networks (shown by their network numbers) that this server recognizes. It also displays how many hops (cable segments between servers or routers) away these networks are and the time (in ticks — approximately $^1/_{18}$ of a second) it takes for a packet to reach these networks.

DISPLAY SERVERS (CONSOLE UTILITY)

Use this command to display a list of all the servers that this server recognizes and records in its router table. It also displays how many hops (cable segments between servers or routers) away those servers are. If you want to see information about a single server or set of servers that start with the same letters, use the following command format, replacing *server* with a server's name (use the wildcard character * to display multiple servers that begin with the same letters):

```
DISPLAY SERVERS server
```

DOSGEN (WORKSTATION UTILITY)

Use this utility to create an image file of a boot disk and store it on the server, so that diskless workstations can access the image and boot from the network instead of from a local disk.

DOWN (CONSOLE UTILITY)

Use this utility to close down the server cleanly, closing any open files, writing any data left in the cache buffers to the disk, and so on. After you've brought down the server, you can use the EXIT command to return the computer to DOS. Then you can safely turn the computer off.

DS (NLM)

This module (along with several related modules, such as DSBACKER.NLM, DSEVENT.NLM, and DSAPI.NLM) loads Novell Directory Services on the server. Networks will generally work more efficiently and have fewer conflicts if all servers in the tree are using the same version of DS.NLM. This NLM is loaded automatically when the server starts up.

DSMERGE (NLM)

Use this module to merge two or more NDS trees into a single tree. (Do not use this utility to merge Directory partitions. This utility should be used only for merging two Directory trees.) You can also use this utility to rename a tree. See Chapter 5 for more information about merging Directory trees.

DS MIGRATE (WORKSTATION UTILITY)

Use this utility to migrate bindery information from a NetWare 2.x or 3.1x server to an existing NetWare Directory tree. This utility is actually an option under the Tools menu of the NetWare Administrator utility. For more information about using DS Migrate, see Chapter 3.

DSREPAIR (NLM)

Use this module to repair possible problems with the NDS database on individual servers. You have to run it on each server that has a problem. DSREPAIR can also perform replica synchronization operations and allow you to see the current status of this server's view of the network or Directory. For more information about using DSREPAIR.NLM, see Chapter 5.

EDIT (NLM)

Use this module to edit text files (such as AUTOEXEC.NCF or STARTUP.NCF) on the server. When you load EDIT, you will be prompted for the path and name of the file to edit.

ENABLE LOGIN (CONSOLE UTILITY)

Use this utility to allow users to log in to the network. This utility is necessary only if you've used DISABLE LOGIN to prevent users from logging in.

ENABLE TTS (CONSOLE UTILITY)

Use this utility to restart TTS (Transaction Tracking System) after the server has disabled TTS. The server will disable TTS if the SYS volume gets too full or if the server doesn't have enough memory to run TTS. (You can also disable TTS manually by using the DISABLE TTS console utility.)

EXIT (CONSOLE UTILITY)

Use this command after using the DOWN command. EXIT will return the server to DOS. (If you removed DOS from the server using the REMOVE DOS command, EXIT will reboot the server instead of going to DOS.)

FILER (WORKSTATION UTILITY)

Use this menu utility to work with files, directories, and volumes on the network. You can display information about these files, directories, and volumes, and modify file system security.

FILTCFG (NLM)

Use this module to set up and configure filters for IPX, TCP/IP, and AppleTalk protocols. Filters provide additional network security by limiting what type of information is broadcast across the network by routers.

FLAG (WORKSTATION UTILITY)

Use this utility to view and assign attributes to files and directories and to assign search modes for executable files. To use FLAG to set file and directory attributes, use the following command format:

```
FLAG path attributes /options
```

For *path*, indicate the path to the directory or file whose attributes you're changing. For *attributes*, insert the list of attributes you want to assign. See Chapter 7 for a description of these parameters.

To use FLAG to assign search modes for executable files, use the following command format:

```
FLAG path /M=number
```

For *path*, specify the path to the file or directory whose search mode you want to change. For *number*, insert the number of the search mode you want to be used for the executable files in this path. For instructions on setting search modes, see Chapter 8.

HALT (CONSOLE UTILITY)

Use this utility with SFT III to stop the IOEngine in one server and force the other server to take over.

HCSS (NLM)

Use this module to load support for HCSS (High-Capacity Storage System) on the server, which allows you to use an optical jukebox as file storage for the network. For more information about HCSS, see Chapter 8.

HCSS (CONSOLE UTILITY)

Use this utility to control HCSS support once you've loaded HCSS.NLM. See Chapter 8 for more information about HCSS.

HELP (CONSOLE UTILITY)

Use this utility to display help for console utilities. To see a list of available console utilities, type HELP at the server console. To display help for a specific console utility, use the following format, replacing *utility* with the name of the console utility whose help file you want to read:

```
HELP utility
```

HFSCD (NLM)

Use this module to allow NetWare to mount an HPFS-formatted (High Performance File System) CD-ROM as a NetWare volume.

HFSCDCON (NLM)

Use this module to configure HFSCD.NLM, which allows you to use HPFS-formatted CD-ROMs as NetWare volumes.

HFSLFS (NLM)

Use this module with the CDROM.NLM module to allow CDROM.NLM to support HPFS-formatted CD-ROMs.

INETCFG (NLM)

Use this module to configure both data link and network protocols. INETCFG is a menu-driven module that makes it relatively easy to configure the protocols. You can also use the LOAD and BIND console commands (either typing them at the console or adding them to AUTOEXEC.NCF), but you may find INETCFG easier to work with.

INITIALIZE SYSTEM (CONSOLE UTILITY)

Use this utility to execute commands in NETINFO.CFG and to enable the multiprotocol router configuration.

INSTALL (NLM)

Use this utility to install IntranetWare on a server. You can also use it to upgrade a NetWare 3.1x or 4.x server to IntranetWare, as well as to modify an existing IntranetWare server, create or modify volumes, install additional products such as the NetWare Web Server, replace hard disks, or modify disk partitions.

IPCONFIG (NLM)

Use this module to configure IP static routes if you are using NetWare/IP.

IPFLT (NLM)

Use this IP filter NLM to restrict how routers see and communicate with other IP routers.

IPXCON (NLM)

Use this module to monitor information about IPX. With this utility, you can configure SNMP parameters, display IPX statistics and error counts, display information about NLSP, RIP, and SAP on the server, and list information such as known services and destination networks. When using IPXCON, press the F1 key to read help for each option.

IPXFLT (NLM)

Use this IPX filter NLM to restrict how routers see and communicate with other IPX routers.

IPXPING (NLM)

Use this module to send test messages (pings) to another node on the network to see if it is communicating with this server via IPX. You will need to specify the target node's IPX internal network number and its node number.

KEYB (NLM)

Use this module to indicate the type of keyboard that is attached to your server. The default type of keyboard supported by IntranetWare is the type used in the United States with English. Different countries and languages may require different types of keyboards. If you aren't using a United States keyboard with English, use the following command format to specify a different keyboard type, replacing *country* with the name of the country you want to choose:

```
LOAD KEYB country
```

To see a list of the countries from which you can choose, load KEYB without specifying any country.

LANGUAGE (CONSOLE UTILITY)

Use this utility to change the language that displays when NLMs are loaded at the server console. This utility will not change the language of the operating system or of NLMs that are already loaded; it affects only those NLMs that are loaded after this utility is executed.

To display the current language being used by NLMs, type **LANGUAGE**.

To display a list of all available languages, type **LANGUAGE LIST**.

To change the language to be used by subsequently loaded NLMs, use the following command format, replacing *name* with either the name or number of the language:

```
LANGUAGE name
```

LIST DEVICES (CONSOLE UTILITY)

Use this utility to display a list of all the storage devices you have installed on the server, such as CD-ROM drives, disk drives, and tape drives.

LOAD (CONSOLE UTILITY)

Use this utility to load NLMs (NetWare Loadable Modules) on the server. Use the following command format, replacing *module* with the name of the NLM you're loading (you don't need to include the .NLM extension in the module name):

```
LOAD module
```

To unload a module, use the UNLOAD console utility.

LOGIN (WORKSTATION UTILITY)

Use this utility to log in to the network. LOGIN authenticates you to the network and it can also execute login scripts to set up your work environment. There are two versions of this utility. The DOS-based version is a command you execute at the DOS prompt of your workstation. For DOS, use the following command format, replacing *tree* with either a Directory tree name or a server name (this is not necessary if you want to log in to the default tree or server) and *username* with your login name:

```
LOGIN tree/username
```

The NetWare GUI Login utility is a graphical utility that you can use from Windows 3.1 or Windows 95. To log in to the network from Windows 3.1, double-click on the NetWare GUI Login program icon and specify a login name and a password. (The Login Program for Windows 3.1 is installed as part of the Client32 software for DOS and Windows.) From Windows 95, right-click the desired server or tree, click Authenticate, and then enter a login name and password.

For more information about logging in to the network and login scripts, see Chapter 6.

LOGOUT (WORKSTATION UTILITY)

Use this utility to log out of the network. To log out of the network completely, type LOGOUT. To log out of a specific server, use the following command format, replacing *server* with the server name (you will remain logged in to any other servers you've been logged in to already):

```
LOGOUT server
```

LONG.NAM (NLM)

Use this module to load support for OS/2, Windows NT, and Windows 95 long file names on the server. After you've loaded this module, use the ADD NAME SPACE console command to assign the name space to a particular volume.

MAC.NAM (NLM)

Use this module to load support for Mac OS long file names and file formats on the server. After you've loaded this module, use the ADD NAME SPACE console command to assign the name space to a particular volume.

MACFILE (NLM)

Use this module to control the desktop for Mac OS files on the server. For more information about using this module, see Chapter 10.

MAGAZINE (CONSOLE UTILITY)

If the server prompts you to insert a new media magazine during some task, use this utility to indicate to the server that you've inserted or removed a media magazine. Use the following command format, replacing *parameter* with one of the parameters listed in Table 16.6.

```
MAGAZINE parameter
```

TABLE 16.6 *MAGAZINE Parameters*

PARAMETER	DESCRIPTION
Inserted	Tells the server you've inserted the media magazine.
Not Inserted	Tells the server that you have not inserted the media magazine.
Removed	Tells the server that you have removed the media magazine.
Not Removed	Tells the server that you have not removed the media magazine.

MAP (WORKSTATION UTILITY)

Use this utility to map drive letters on the workstation to network directories. You can execute MAP commands at the workstation's console, or you can put MAP commands in a login script, so that the same drives are mapped every time the user logs in. The MAP utility and drive mappings are explained fully in Chapter 6.

MEDIA (CONSOLE UTILITY)

If the server prompts you to insert a specified storage medium during some task, use this utility to indicate to the server that you've inserted or removed the medium. Use the following command format, replacing *parameter* with one of the parameters listed in Table 16.7.

```
MEDIA parameter
```

TABLE 16.7 *MEDIA Parameters*

PARAMETER	DESCRIPTION
Inserted	Tells the server you've inserted the medium.
Not Inserted	Tells the server that you have not inserted the medium.
Removed	Tells the server that you have removed the medium.
Not Removed	Tells the server that you have not removed the medium.

MEMORY (CONSOLE UTILITY)

Use this utility to see the total amount of memory in the server.

MEMORY MAP (CONSOLE UTILITY)

Use this utility to see how much of the server's memory is allocated to DOS and to the server.

MENUCNVT (WORKSTATION UTILITY)

If you have menu programs that you created in NetWare 3.11 using the older MENU utility (whose files have the extension .MNU), use this utility to convert them into the newer-style menu programs supported by IntranetWare's NMENU utility. (A different menu system was used in NetWare 3.11 and earlier versions than the Saber derivative used in IntranetWare.) For more information about upgrading menu programs, see Chapter 6.

MENUMAKE (WORKSTATION UTILITY)

Use this utility to create a menu program for users to use when they work on the network. Create a text utility with the necessary commands first, and then run this utility to compile the text file into a menu program. Use the following command format, replacing *file* with the name of the text file (leave off the file's extension when you type its name):

```
MENUMAKE file
```

For more information about creating menu programs, see Chapter 6.

MIGPRINT (WORKSTATION UTILITY)

Use this utility to migrate NetWare 2.x or NetWare 3.x printers, print queues, print job configurations, and print servers to an IntranetWare Directory tree. During a server upgrade, the printing objects are not upgraded from previous versions of NetWare to the Directory tree by default. You must use this utility to migrate those objects.

Use the following command format, replacing *source* with the name of the server from which you're migrating printing information, *destination* with the name of the IntranetWare server, *volume* with the name of the volume that will hold the print queues (only if you don't want to use the default SYS volume), and *file* with the name of an output file to store messages about the migration (only if you don't want to use the default file, called MP*nnn*.RPT):

```
MIGPRINT /S=source /D=destination /VOL=volume
/O=file
```

MIGRATE (WORKSTATION UTILITY)

Use this utility to migrate NetWare 2.x bindery information to an IntranetWare Directory tree. For more information about using MIGRATE, see Chapter 3.

MIRROR STATUS (CONSOLE UTILITY)

Use this utility to list all the disk partitions on the server and to display their mirror status. Five states are possible:

- *Being remirrored.* This means the disk partition is being synchronized with another and will soon be mirrored.
- *Fully synchronized.* This means the disk partitions are mirrored and working correctly, so that both partitions contain identical data.
- *Not mirrored.* This means the disk partition isn't mirrored with any other partition.
- *Orphaned state.* This means the disk partition used to be mirrored with another, but isn't now. The integrity of this partition's data may not be ensured anymore.
- *Out of synchronization.* This means the two disk partitions that are mirrored do not have identical data and therefore need to be remirrored.

MODULES (CONSOLE UTILITY)

Use this utility to display a list of all the NLMs currently loaded on the server. If you want to see information about a single NLM or set of NLMs that start with the same letters, use the following command format, replacing *module* with an NLM's name (use the wildcard character * to display multiple NLMs that begin with the same letters):

```
MODULES module
```

MONITOR (NLM)

Use this module to monitor the server's performance. This is one of the most frequently used management utilities for NetWare servers. In addition to letting you track and modify your server's performance characteristics, it lets you run a screen saver on the console and lock the console so that a password is required to use it. To load MONITOR.NLM, use the following command format, replacing *parameter*, if necessary, with one of the optional parameters listed in Table 16.8.

```
LOAD MONITOR parameter
```

TABLE 16.8 *MONITOR Parameters*

PARAMETER	DESCRIPTION
L	Locks the server console when MONITOR is loaded. Use the Admin user's password to unlock the console.
M	Activates the screen saver only if MONITOR's screen is currently displayed on the console. Without this option, the screen saver will activate regardless of what screen is currently displayed.
N	Disables the screen saver.
T*nnn*	Sets the number of seconds of keyboard inactivity MONITOR waits before activating the screen saver. Replace *nnn* with the number of seconds. The default is 600 seconds if the console is unlocked, 60 seconds if the console is locked.

MOUNT (CONSOLE UTILITY)

Use this utility to mount a volume on a server so that network users can access it. Use the following command format, replacing *volume* with the volume's name (or with ALL to mount all volumes):

```
MOUNT volume
```

MPDRIVER (NLM)

Use this module to enable processors in a multiprocessor server. You can use this module only if you have installed the NetWare SMP (Symmetric MultiProcessing) version of IntranetWare on your server. Use the following command format, replacing *number* with the number of the processor you want to enable, or with the word ALL to enable all licensed processors:

```
LOAD MPDRIVER number
```

MSERVER (.EXE)

This executable file loads an SFT III server. For more information about SFT III NetWare, see Chapter 3.

NAME (CONSOLE UTILITY)

Use this utility to display the server's name.

NCOPY (WORKSTATION UTILITY)

Use this utility to copy files and directories from one drive or disk to another. To use NCOPY, use the following command format:

```
NCOPY source/filename destination/filename /para-
meters
```

For more information and a description of the parameters that can be used with the NCOPY utility, see Chapter 8.

NCUPDATE (WORKSTATION UTILITY)

Use this utility to automatically update a workstation's NET.CFG file with a new name context if you have moved or renamed the user's container. You can execute this utility from a login script if desired.

NDIR (WORKSTATION UTILITY)

Use this utility to list a directory's files, subdirectories, and related information. More importantly, use it to see information such as Inherited Rights Filters, effective file system rights, file owners, file and directory attributes, archive information, and Volume information. To use NDIR, use the following command format:

```
NDIR path /parameter
```

To display the NDIR help screens, use the following command:

```
NDIR /?
```

For more information about NDIR and a description of its most common parameters, see Chapter 8.

NDS MANAGER (WORKSTATION UTILITY)

Use this utility to analyze and repair (if necessary) Directory partitions and replicas. This utility can be executed by itself or as a feature of the NetWare Administrator utility under the Tools option.

NDS Manager automatically executes DSREPAIR.NLM for repair options, so you may prefer to use NDS Manager from a workstation instead of using DSREPAIR from the console.

By default, NDS Manager is not part of NetWare Administrator, but you can easily add it. If you don't want to add it to NetWare Administrator, you must add NDS Manager to your workstation desktop as its own icon before you can use it. For more information about NDS Manager, see Chapter 5.

NETADMIN (WORKSTATION UTILITY)

This is the DOS-based version of the NetWare Administrator utility. It is much more limited than the NetWare Administrator, but you can still use it to work with NDS objects, login scripts, and so on.

NETSYNC3 (NLM)

Use this module on a NetWare 3.1x server to synchronize its bindery objects with an IntranetWare server, so that you can manage the NetWare 3.1x users from NetWare Administrator. For more information about NetSync, see Chapter 5.

NETSYNC4 (NLM)

Use this module to turn an IntranetWare server into a host for a NetSync network of NetWare 3.1x servers. For more information about NetSync, see Chapter 5.

NETUSER (WORKSTATION UTILITY)

Use this utility from a DOS-based workstation to perform common network tasks such as selecting print queues, sending messages to other users, changing passwords, mapping drive letters to directories, and logging in and out of the network. There is also a Windows-based version of this utility, called NetWare User Tools. (Most Windows 95 users will use the Windows Explorer and Network Neighborhood instead of NETUSER or the NetWare User Tools to complete network tasks.)

For more information about NETUSER, see Chapter 6.

NETWARE ADMINISTRATOR (WORKSTATION UTILITY)

Use this utility to manage your network. With NetWare Administrator, which runs in Windows 3.1, OS/2, or Windows 95, you can do tasks such as:

- Creating, deleting, or modifying NDS objects
- Setting up printing services
- Assigning NDS rights
- Modifying login scripts

Before you can use NetWare Administrator, you need to install it on your workstation. The Windows version of NetWare Administrator (which can also run on OS/2) is called NWADMN3X.EXE, and it's located in SYS:PUBLIC. The Windows 95 version is called NWADMN95.EXE, and it can be found in SYS:PUBLIC\WIN95. For information on setting up NetWare Administrator on your workstation, see Chapter 5.

NETWARE APPLICATION LAUNCHER (WORKSTATION UTILITY)

Use the NetWare Application Launcher to allow users to easily find and launch network applications.

Once you have the NetWare Application Launcher set up on each user's workstation, you can use NetWare Administrator to make an application become an object in the NDS tree. Then, the icon for the Application object will appear automatically on the desktop of each user you assign to that application.

The users don't need to know where the application is; they don't need to map drives or enter launch parameters; and you don't need to update login scripts. When you update the application, the icons in all the desktops will continue to point to the new application.

For more information and instructions on setting up the NetWare Application Launcher, see Chapter 6.

NETWARE APPLICATION MANAGER (WORKSTATION UTILITY)

Use this utility to set up Application objects so that users can execute them from the NetWare Application Launcher installed on their workstations. This utility is actually executed as a feature of the NetWare Administrator utility when you create an Application object. You don't execute this utility separately. For more information about creating Application objects and setting up the NetWare Application Launcher, see Chapter 6.

NETWARE FILE MIGRATION (WORKSTATION UTILITY)

Use this utility to migrate data files from a NetWare 3.1x server to an existing IntranetWare server. You will use this utility after you have migrated all of the NetWare 3.1x server's bindery information to the IntranetWare server. For more information, see Chapter 3.

NETWARE USER TOOLS (WORKSTATION UTILITY)

Use this utility from a Windows 3.1-based workstation to perform common network tasks such as selecting print queues, sending messages to other users, changing passwords, mapping drive letters to directories, and logging in and out of the network. There is also a DOS-based version of this utility, called NETUSER. (Most Windows 95 users will use the Windows Explorer and Network Neighborhood instead of NETUSER or the NetWare User Tools to complete network tasks.)

For more information about NetWare User Tools, see Chapter 6.

NFS.NAM (NLM)

Use this module to load support for UNIX long file names on the server. After you've loaded this module, use the ADD NAME SPACE console command to assign the name space to a particular volume.

NLIST (WORKSTATION UTILITY)

Use this utility to display a variety of information about network objects such as users, groups, servers, and volumes. Use the following command format, replacing *class* with the type of object you want to display (such as SERVER, USER, or GROUP):

```
NLIST class
```

You can also specify a specific object name (or use wildcards to list those that begin with the same letters) by using the following command format:

```
NLIST class=name
```

You can use additional parameters and variations of this command to display many kinds of information. To read help screens and see examples of NLIST commands, type:

```
NLIST /? ALL
```

NLS MANAGER (WORKSTATION UTILITY)

Use this utility to manage NetWare Licensing Services (NLS). You can use NLS Manager to install license certificates, create metering certificates, display licensing information, and so on. Because no third-party applications have taken advantage of this feature as of this book's printing, this feature is not described in this book. See the documentation that came with your IntranetWare package for more information.

NMENU (WORKSTATION UTILITY)

Use this utility to execute a menu program that you've created using the menu creation feature in IntranetWare (described in Chapter 6). Use the following command format, replacing *filename* with the path and name of the menu file:

```
NMENU filename
```

To have workstations automatically execute the menu program when users log in, add the following line to the end of the login script:

```
EXIT "NMENU filename"
```

NPAMS (NLM)

Use this module on the MSEngine of an SFT III server to allow a CD-ROM to be mounted as a NetWare volume.

NPATH (WORKSTATION UTILITY)

Use this utility to see the search path that a particular utility is using. This lets you determine why your workstation can't find a particular file, why it's finding the wrong version of the file, or why it's executing in a foreign language. Use the following command format, replacing *utility* with the name of the utility whose search sequence you want to see, *filename* with the name of the file your workstation says it can't find, and *parameter* with any of the parameters listed in Table 16.9.

```
NPATH utility filename /parameter
```

TABLE 16.9 *NPATH Parameters*

PARAMETER	DESCRIPTION
A	All. Lists the path to all occurrences of the file.
D	Details. Displays the language, version number, date, and time of the file.
Uni	Displays all paths to Unicode files.
/Uni /D	Unicode Details. Displays the country code and code page for your workstation, the utility's needed Unicode files, and the path to the first occurrence of each file.

NPRINT (WORKSTATION UTILITY)

Use this utility to print a job from outside of an application (such as printing an ASCII file or a workstation screen). Use the following command format, replacing *parameters* with parameters from Table 16.10.

```
NPRINT parameters
```

TABLE 16.10 *NPRINT Parameters*

PARAMETER	DESCRIPTION
B=*text*	Specifies that a banner page (displaying the *text* you specify) is printed before the print job. The default text is the print job file name.
C=*number*	Specifies how many copies are printed (1 to 65,000; the default is 1).
D	Displays the printing parameters for the print job and shows whether a print job configuration was used.
DEL	Specifies that the file is deleted after it's printed.

TABLE 16.10 *NPRINT Parameters (continued)*

PARAMETER	DESCRIPTION
F=*form*	Specifies the number or name of the form (paper type) that this job should be printed on.
FF	Causes a form feed at the end of a print job so that the next job prints on the next page. This parameter is necessary only if the application doesn't already cause a form feed.
HOLD	Sends a print job to a queue but doesn't print it. To release the Hold, use the NetWare Administrator utility.
J=*name*	Specifies the name of a print job configuration to use. This parameter is necessary only if you don't want to use the default print job configuration.
NAM=*name*	Specifies the name that should appear on the banner page (the default is your login name).
NB	Eliminates the banner page.
NFF	Eliminates the form feed.
NNOTI	Prevents a message from appearing on your workstation telling you that the print job is finished. This parameter is only necessary if the print job configuration requests notification and you don't want it.
NOTI	Specifies that your workstation receives notification when a print job is finished. Disabled by default.
NT	No Tabs. Allows an application's print formatter to determine how many spaces are in a tab stop. This parameter is necessary only if your application has a print formatter but has problems printing graphics or creates unexpected formats.
P=*name*	Specifies a printer.
Q=*name*	Specifies a network print queue.
S=*name*	Specifies which network server to send a print job to.
T=*number*	Specifies how many spaces are in a tab stop. This parameter is necessary only if your application doesn't have a print formatter.
/?	Displays help for NPRINT.

NPRINTER.EXE (DOS/WINDOWS 3.1 WORKSTATION UTILITY)

Use this utility to load a port driver, which is software that routes jobs out of the print queue, through the proper port on a DOS or Windows 3.1 workstation, to the printer. See Chapter 9 for more information about printing.

NPRINTER (NLM)

Use this module to load a port driver, which is software that routes jobs out of the print queue, through the proper port on a server, to the printer. See Chapter 9 for more information about printing.

NPTWIN95.EXE (WINDOWS 95 WORKSTATION UTILITY)

Use this utility to load a port driver, which is software that routes jobs out of the print queue, through the proper port on a Windows 95 workstation, to the printer. See Chapter 9 for more information about printing.

NVER (WORKSTATION UTILITY)

Use this utility to display the version number of the following types of programs running on the workstation or server: NetBIOS, IPX and SPX, LAN drivers, NetWare Client software, the workstation's operating system, and the version of NetWare on the server.

NWIP (NLM)

Use this module to support NetWare/IP on the server. For more information about NetWare/IP, refer to the documentation that came with your IntranetWare package.

NWIPCFG (NLM)

Use this module to configure the NetWare/IP server software, start the NetWare/IP service, or configure the server as a NetWare Domain Name System (DNS) client.

For more information about NetWare/IP, refer to the documentation that came with your IntranetWare package.

NWPA (NLM)

Use this module to allow the server to support the NetWare Peripheral Architecture, which allows disk drivers and CD-ROM drivers to work with NetWare.

NWXTRACT (WORKSTATION UTILITY)

Use this utility to extract an individual file from the NetWare 4.11 CD-ROM and copy it to a network directory or your hard disk. The files on the CD-ROM are compressed, so you cannot simply copy the file directly from the CD-ROM. This utility will locate the file on the CD-ROM, decompress it, and then copy it to the location you specify.

The NWXTRACT utility is located on the CD-ROM in the following directory: PRODUCTS\NW411\INSTALL\IBM\ostype\XXX\ENGLISH. (Replace ostype with either DOS or OS2, depending on which operating system your workstation is using. You can also replace ENGLISH with the language directory you prefer.) To use NWXTRACT, first go to this directory on the CD-ROM. Then, use the following command format, replacing *source* with the path to the CD-ROM, *filename* with the name of the file you want, and *destination* with the path you want the file copied to (or omit the destination if you want it copied to the default location on the server):

```
NWXTRACT source filename destination /parameters
```

Replace *parameters* with one of the following, if necessary:

- S=*server* — Replace *server* with the name of the server to which you want the file copied.
- T=*type* — Copies files of the specified *type*: DOS, MAC, OS2, SER (server), UNX, or WIN.

To read the online help, type

```
NWXTRACT /?
```

OFF (CONSOLE UTILITY)

Use this utility to clear the server's console screen. You can also use the CLS utility to accomplish the same thing.

PARTMGR (WORKSTATION UTILITY)

Use this utility to manage Directory partitions and replicas. You may prefer to use the NDS Manager utility to work with Directory partitions and replicas because NDS Manager is more graphical and easy to use, and it also automatically launches DSREPAIR.NLM when necessary. See Chapter 5 for more information about using NDS Manager.

PCONCOLE (WORKSTATION UTILITY)

Use this menu utility to set up and modify printing services. However, you may prefer to use the NetWare Administrator utility to work with printing services because its graphical interface is often easier to use. See Chapter 9 for more information about using NetWare Administrator's printing features.

PING (NLM)

Use this module to test if the server can communicate with an IP node on the network. PING sends an ICMP (Internet Control Message Protocol) echo request packet to an IP node.

PRINTCON (WORKSTATION UTILITY)

Use this utility to create and use print job configurations. However, you may prefer to use the NetWare Administrator utility to set up print job configurations because its graphical interface is often easier to use. See Chapter 9 for more information about using NetWare Administrator's printing features.

PRINTDEF (WORKSTATION UTILITY)

Use this utility to define the printer you're using, if necessary, and to define paper forms (types of paper such as paychecks, invoices, legal size paper, and so on). However, you may prefer to use the NetWare Administrator utility to work with printer definitions and paper forms because its graphical interface is often easier to use. See Chapter 9 for more information about using NetWare Administrator's printing features.

PROTOCOL (CONSOLE UTILITY)

Use this utility to list all the protocols that are currently registered on the server by simply typing PROTOCOL.

You can also use this utility to register new protocols and frame types with the server. You don't need to use this utility to register IPX, IP, or AppleTalk because they are registered automatically during installation or configuration, but you may need to use this utility if you use a different protocol. See the protocol's manufacturer for more details. To use this utility, use the following command format, replacing *protocol* with the name of the protocol, *frame* with the frame type, and *id* with the Protocol ID (PID, also called Ethernet Type, E-Type, or SAP) number assigned to the protocol:

```
PROTOCOL REGISTER protocol frame id
```

PSC (WORKSTATION UTILITY)

Use this utility to control print servers and network printers. This utility allows you to execute many of the same functions as PCONSOLE and the NetWare Administrator utility, but in a command-line format so that the commands can be used in a batch file. Use one of the following command formats:

```
PSC PS=printserver parameters
```

or

```
PSC P=number parameters
```

Replace *printserver* with the name of the print server you want to control, or replace *number* with the number of the printer you want to control. Replace *parameters* with any of the parameters from Table 16.11.

TABLE 16.11 *PSC Parameters*

PARAMETER	DESCRIPTION
AB	Abort. Aborts the current print job and deletes it from the print queue.
CD	Cancel Down. If you chose the option in PCONSOLE or NetWare Administrator to have the printer go down after current print jobs are finished, this command will prevent the printer from going down.
FF	Form Feed. Causes a form feed to occur if the printer has stopped or paused.
L	Displays a tree layout of how printing is currently set up.
M *character*	Mark. Prints a line of the character you specify so that you can see on which line the printer will begin printing. The default character is *.
MO F=*form*	Mount Form. Indicates to the printer that you have mounted a new form on the printer. Replace *form* with the number of the form you mounted.

(continued)

TABLE 16.11 *PSC Parameters (continued)*

PARAMETER	DESCRIPTION
PAU	Pause. Pauses the printer.
PRI	Private. Changes the printer to a local printer, removing it from the print server's list of network printers so that only the workstation to which the printer is attached can use it.
SHA	Shared. Removes the PRI (Private) attribute so that the printer can once again be used by other network users.
STAR	Start. Restarts a paused or stopped printer.
STAT	Status. Displays the status of the print server's printers.
S=*server*	Specifies which NetWare server contains the print server you want to manage.
STO	Stop. Stops a printer and deletes the current print job from the print queue.

PSERVER (NLM)

Use this module to load a print server on the server so that the print server can regulate network print queues and printers. Use the following command format, replacing *name* with the name of the print server you created by using the NetWare Administrator utility:

```
LOAD PSERVER name
```

See Chapter 9 for more information about using PSERVER.

PUPGRADE (NLM)

Use this module to upgrade NetWare 3.1x print servers and printers to IntranetWare Directory objects and to upgrade NetWare 3.1x PRINTCON and PRINTDEF databases to the format used by IntranetWare. You must run PUPGRADE after you've upgraded the rest of your NetWare 3.1x server and bindery information to IntranetWare if you want to upgrade your printing objects.

PURGE (WORKSTATION UTILITY)

Use this utility to permanently erase files from the server. Usually, when files are deleted, they are retained in a salvageable state until the server needs the disk space and automatically purges them. To completely remove these files without waiting for the server to run out of disk space, you can use the PURGE utility. Use the following command format, replacing *path* with the path to the files you want to purge and *filename* with a file name for the specific file or files (wildcards are acceptable):

```
PURGE path\filename /option
```

If desired, you can replace *option* with one of the following:

- /A — Purges all files in the current directory and all of its subdirectories
- /? — Displays help screens for PURGE

For more information about purging and salvaging files, see Chapter 8.

RCONSOLE (WORKSTATION UTILITY)

Use this utility to set up a Remote Console session from a workstation. For more information about Remote Console and using RCONSOLE, see Chapter 3.

REGISTER MEMORY (CONSOLE UTILITY)

Use this utility on ISA (AT bus) servers to register memory above 16MB so that NetWare can address it. This command is unnecessary for EISA or MCA computers because NetWare automatically registers memory above 16MB on EISA machines. On a PCI computer, NetWare recognizes up to 64MB.

Use the following command format, replacing *start* with the hexadecimal address of where the memory above the limit begins (16MB starts at 1000000, 64MB starts at 4000000) and *length* with the hexadecimal length of the memory above 16MB or 64MB (see Table 16.12 for some *length* numbers for different amounts of memory):

```
REGISTER MEMORY start length
```

NOTE

Hexadecimal numbers can use the numerals 0 through 9 and the letters A through F.

TABLE 16.12 *Length Values for Memory*

MEMORY ABOVE THE MINIMUM (16MB OR 64MB)	LENGTH
4	400000
8	800000
12	C00000
16	1000000
20	1400000
24	1800000
48	3000000
96	6000000
112	7000000
240	F000000
384	18000000
984	3D800000
2936	B7800000
2984	BA800000

REINITIALIZE SYSTEM (CONSOLE UTILITY)

Use this utility to reenable the multiprotocol router configuration after you've used INETCFG.NLM to make changes to NETINFO.CFG.

REMAPID (NLM)

Use this module on NetWare 3.1x servers that are being managed by NetSync. This module is used to control how passwords are synchronized. You shouldn't unload it because you will have to change every user's password on the server. (Make sure REMAPID.NLM is loaded by the AUTOEXEC.NCF file to ensure that it doesn't get removed if you remove NetSync. The command to load REMAPID should have been added to the file during NetSync installation.) For more information about NetSync, see Chapter 5.

REMIRROR PARTITION (CONSOLE UTILITY)

Use this utility to restart the remirroring process if something halted the server's remirroring of its disk partitions. Use the following command format, replacing *number* with the number of the disk partition you want to remirror:

```
REMIRROR PARTITION number
```

REMOTE (NLM)

Use this module to allow an IntranetWare server to support Remote Console sessions from a workstation. See Chapter 3 for more information about using Remote Console.

REMOVE DOS (CONSOLE UTILITY)

Use this utility to remove DOS from the server's memory. This prevents anyone from using commands or files on the server's DOS partition. It also frees up the memory that DOS was using.

RENDIR (WORKSTATION UTILITY)

Use this utility to rename a directory. Use the following command format, replacing *oldname* with the original directory name (or a period if you want to rename your current directory) and *newname* with the name to which you want the directory renamed:

```
RENDIR oldname newname
```

RESET ROUTER (CONSOLE UTILITY)

Use this utility to clear the router table and force a new table to be built on the server, updating any changes to servers or routers that have gone down or come back up. Because the table is automatically rebuilt every two minutes, you need to use this utility only if you don't want to wait for the next automatic rebuild.

RESTART (CONSOLE UTILITY)

Use this utility with SFT III to reload a stopped IOEngine while the IOEngine in the other server continues to run. You can also use this utility to force an SFT III server to switch from being primary to secondary.

RESTART SERVER (CONSOLE UTILITY)

Use this utility to restart the server after you have brought it down.

RIGHTS (WORKSTATION UTILITY)

Use this utility to see your effective rights in a directory. Use the following command format, replacing *path* with the path to the directory or path you want (you can omit the path if you want to see your rights in your current directory) and *parameters* with any of the parameters shown in Table 16.13.

```
RIGHTS path /parameters
```

TABLE 16.13 *RIGHTS Parameters*

PARAMETER	DESCRIPTION
C	Causes the display to scroll continuously down the screen.
F	Displays the Inherited Rights Filter (IRF).
I	Shows from where the inherited rights came.
NAME=*username*	Replaces *username* with the name of a user or group whose rights you want to see or change.
S	Lets you see or change subdirectories below the current directory.
T	Displays trustee assignments for a directory.

ROUTE (NLM)

Use this module to allow IntranetWare to support an IBM bridge on a Token Ring network using Source Routing. Load this module once for every Token Ring network board you have installed in your server. Use the following command format, replacing *parameters* with one or more of the parameters shown in Table 16.14.

```
LOAD ROUTE parameters
```

TABLE 16.14 *ROUTE.NLM Parameters*

ROUTE.NLM PARAMETER	DESCRIPTION
BOARD=*number*	Indicates the network board's number, if the Token Ring LAN driver wasn't the first LAN driver loaded.
CLEAR	Clears all information from the Source Routing table so that it can be rebuilt with updated information.
DEF	Causes frames (packets) with unknown destination addresses to be forwarded as All Routes Broadcast packets, which means they won't be sent across Single Route IBM bridges.
GBR	Causes General Broadcast frames to be sent as All Routes Broadcast frames, instead of being sent as Single Route Broadcast frames.
MBR	Causes Multicast Broadcast frames to be sent as All Routes Broadcast frames, instead of being sent as Single Route Broadcast frames.
NAME=*board*	Specifies the name of the network board.
REMOVE=*number*	If a bridge has gone down, use this parameter to remove a node address from the server's Source Routing table, forcing the server to find a new route.
RSP=*response*	Indicates how the server must respond to a broadcast request. Replace *response* with: NR (Not Required). Default: Respond to all requests directly. AR (All Routes). Respond with an All Routes Broadcast frame. SR (Single Route). Respond with a Single Route Broadcast frame.
TIME=*seconds*	Determines how often to update the server's Source Routing table. Default: 03. Range: 03 to 255.

(continued)

TABLE 16.14 *ROUTE.NLM Parameters (continued)*

ROUTE.NLM PARAMETER	DESCRIPTION
UNLOAD	Removes Source Routing support from a network board. (Specify the board you want first by using the BOARD=parameter, and then use this UNLOAD parameter.)
XTX=*number*	Sets how many times to transmit on a timed-out route using the old route. Default: 02. Range: 00 to 255.

RPL (NLM)

Use this module to allow diskless workstations to boot from the server instead of from a local boot disk.

RS232 (NLM)

Use this module to allow the server to support Remote Console sessions over an asynchronous connection (via a modem). See Chapter 3 for more information about running Remote Console. Use the following command format, replacing *port* and *baud* with the appropriate communications port number (1 or 2) and baud rate being used by your modem:

```
LOAD RS232 port baud
```

RSPX (NLM)

Use this module to allow the server to support Remote Console sessions over a direct network connection (in other words, if the workstation is connected directly to the network and doesn't require a modem to access the server). See Chapter 3 for more information about running Remote Console.

SBACKUP (NLM)

Use this module to back up and restore data from the network. To use SBACKUP, you must also have a TSA (Target Service Agent) loaded on the server you intend to back up or restore. See Chapter 8 for more information about using SBACKUP.

SCAN FOR NEW DEVICES (CONSOLE UTILITY)

Use this utility to cause the server to look for and recognize any new storage devices (disk drives, CD-ROM drives, and so on) that may have been added since the server was booted.

SCHDELAY (NLM)

Use this utility to list all server processes and see which ones have consistently high Load values. If you want to change some of the values on the scheduling information screen, you may find it easier to use the Scheduling Information option of MONITOR.NLM. See Chapter 3 for more information about using MONITOR.

SEARCH (CONSOLE UTILITY)

Use this utility to set the paths that a server should search through when looking for an .NCF (configuration) file or an NLM. The default search path is SYS:SYSTEM. If volume SYS isn't mounted, the default search path becomes the DOS boot directory on the server. To display the server's current search paths, simply type SEARCH. To add a search path, use the following command format, replacing *path* with the directory path you want the server to search:

```
SEARCH ADD path
```

To delete a search path, use the following command format, replacing *number* with the number of the search drive you want to remove (drive numbers are displayed when you type SEARCH):

```
SEARCH DEL number
```

SECURE CONSOLE (CONSOLE UTILITY)

Use this utility to prevent anyone from loading NLMs from anywhere but SYS:SYSTEM. (This prevents unauthorized users from loading NLMs from an area where they may have more rights than in SYS:SYSTEM, such as from a diskette in the server's diskette drive.) This utility also prevents anyone from accessing the operating system's debugger from the server's keyboard and allows only the administrator to change the server's date and time. To disable this feature, reboot the server.

SEND (WORKSTATION UTILITY)

Use this utility to send a short message from your workstation to other users on the network. To send a message to a user or group, use the following command format, replacing *message* with the message you want displayed (no more than 44 characters long) and *user* with the name of the user or group:

```
SEND "message" user
```

To send the message to multiple users or groups, separate each name with a comma.

SEND (CONSOLE UTILITY)

Use this utility to send a short message from the server console to users on the network. To send a message to a user, use the following command format, replacing *message* with the message you want displayed (no more than 55 characters long) and *user* with either the name of the user or that workstation's connection number (as seen in MONITOR.NLM):

```
SEND "message" user
```

To send the message to multiple users, separate each user name or connection number with a comma or space. To send the message to all users, don't specify any user name at all. (You can also use the BROADCAST console utility to accomplish the same thing.)

SERVER (.EXE)

This is the command that loads the NetWare server from DOS. You can add the command SERVER to the server's AUTOEXEC.BAT file so that the server loads automatically when the computer is booted.

SERVMAN (NLM)

Use this utility to set server parameters, also called SET parameters, to optimize your server's performance. SET parameters control things such as how buffers are allocated and used, how memory is used, and so on. You can change these parameters by loading SERVMAN.NLM and selecting the SET parameters you want from menus. SERVMAN will automatically save the command in the correct server startup file. For more information about SET parameters, see Appendix B.

SET (CONSOLE UTILITY)

Use this utility to change performance parameters on the server. You may prefer to use the SERVMAN.NLM to change SET parameters because SERVMAN allows you to select the parameters from menus rather than having to type long commands. SET commands can also be added to the AUTOEXEC.NCF and STARTUP.NCF files so that they are executed every time the server is rebooted. For more information about SET parameters, see Appendix B.

SET TIME (CONSOLE UTILITY)

Use this utility to change the server's date and time. Use the following command format:

SET TIME *month/day/year hour:minute:second*

SET TIME ZONE (CONSOLE UTILITY)

Use this utility to change the server's time zone information. Use the following command format, replacing *zone* with the three-letter abbreviation for your time zone (such as EST, CST, MST, or PST), *hours* with the number of hours you are east or west of Greenwich Mean Time (use a - sign before the number if you're east), and *daylight* with the three-letter abbreviation for your area's daylight saving time (only if you are currently on daylight saving time):

SET TIMEZONE *zone hours daylight*

For example, to set the time zone to Eastern Daylight Saving Time, type

```
SET TIMEZONE EST5EDT
```

SETPASS (WORKSTATION UTILITY)

Use this utility to change your network password. When you execute this utility, follow the prompts to type in your old and new passwords.

SETTTS (WORKSTATION UTILITY)

Use this utility to set the number of logical and physical record locks that TTS (NetWare's Transaction Tracking Service) ignores before beginning to track a transaction. This utility lets TTS work with an application that requires you to set new transaction beginning points. (Most applications do not require this utility.)

Use the following command format, replacing *logical* with the number of logical record locks you want TTS to ignore and *physical* with the number of physical record locks you want TTS to ignore:

```
SETTTS logical physical
```

SETUPDOC (WORKSTATION UTILITY)

Use this utility to install the IntranetWare online documentation and the documentation viewers. See Chapter 12 for more information on using SETUPDOC.

SPEED (CONSOLE UTILITY)

Use this utility to display the server's processor speed.

SPOOL (CONSOLE UTILITY)

Use this utility to display or create spooler mappings so applications that print to printer numbers will direct their print jobs to print queues instead. Most current network applications do not require this utility to be executed. If used, this utility also specifies the default print queue for NPRINT and CAPTURE. Use the following command format, replacing *number* with the printer number (which will also be the spooler number) and *queue* with the name of the print queue:

```
SPOOL number TO QUEUE queue
```

SPXCONFG (NLM)

Use this module to configure SPX parameters. You can also configure the same parameters using INETCFG.NLM. To display help screens for using SPXCONFG, use the following command:

```
LOAD SPXCONFG H
```

SYSTIME (WORKSTATION UTILITY)

Use this utility to synchronize a workstation's time with the server's time. Use the following command format, replacing *server* with the name of the server to which you want your workstation synchronized:

```
SYSTIME server
```

TCPCON (NLM)

Use this module to monitor information about the TCP/IP protocol suite loaded on the server. You can view information about the protocols in the TCP/IP suite, SNMP configuration information, user statistics, and so on.

TCPIP (NLM)

Use this module to load TCP/IP support on the network server. For more information about using TCP/IP and NetWare/IP, refer to the documentation that came with your IntranetWare package.

TECHWALK (NLM)

Use this module to record INETCFG settings in a file called TECHWALK.OUT in the SYS:ETC directory. It may take this utility anywhere from 5 to 60 minutes to record all your information. If you want to record configuration information for a specific NLM, use the following command format, replacing *module* with the name of the NLM:

```
LOAD TECHWALK module
```

TIME (CONSOLE UTILITY)

Use this utility to display the server's date, time, daylight saving time status, and time synchronization information. (To change the date or time, use the SET TIME console utility. To change the server's time zone information, use the SET TIMEZONE console utility.)

TIMESYNC (NLM)

This module is automatically loaded when the server boots, and it is used to control the server's time services. You should not need to load or unload this module.

TPING (NLM)

Use this module to send ICMP packets to an IP node to see if the server can communicate with that node. Use the following command format, replacing *host* with the symbolic host name or IP address of a TCP/IP system, *size* with the size (in bytes) of the ICMP packets, and *retries* with the number of times the packet should be sent to the host if it doesn't reply to the first (default is 5):

```
LOAD TPING host size retries
```

TRACK OFF (CONSOLE UTILITY)

Use this utility to turn off the display of routing information (which is displayed if you used the TRACK ON console utility).

TRACK ON (CONSOLE UTILITY)

Use this utility to display the routing information that your server is broadcasting and receiving.

UIMPORT (WORKSTATION UTILITY)

Use this utility to create User objects in the Directory database by importing user information from another database. Use the following command format, replacing *controlfile* with the name of the file that contains information on how to load user data into the directory and *datafile* with the name of the text file that contains the actual user data (property values):

```
UIMPORT controlfile datafile
```

UNBIND (CONSOLE UTILITY)

Use this utility to unbind a protocol, such as IPX or APPLETLK, from a network board. Use the following command format, replacing *protocol* with the name of the protocol, *driver* with the name of the LAN driver or network board from which you want the protocol unbound, and *parameters* with the same parameters you originally specified when you loaded the driver (so that the UNBIND command knows exactly which LAN driver or network board you intend):

```
UNBIND protocol FROM driver parameters
```

See the explanation of the BIND console utility for more information about driver parameters.

UNICON (NLM)

Use this module to manage the NetWare Domain Name System and the NetWare/IP Domain SAP/RIP Service if you have installed NetWare/IP on your server. For more information about NetWare/IP, refer to the documentation that came with your IntranetWare package.

UNLOAD (CONSOLE UTILITY)

Use this utility to unload an NLM that's been previously loaded. Use the following command format, replacing *module* with the name of the NLM you want to unload (you can omit the .NLM extension of the NLM's file name):

```
UNLOAD module
```

UPS (NLM)

Use this module to allow the server to be supported by a UPS (Uninterruptible Power Supply). Some UPS manufacturers supply their own software to be used instead of UPS.NLM. If so, you do not need to use UPS.NLM. See Chapter 3 for more information about using a UPS with your server.

UPS_AIO (NLM)

Use this module instead of UPS.NLM if your UPS is attached to your server's serial port. See Chapter 3 for more information about using a UPS with your server.

UPS STATUS (CONSOLE UTILITY)

Use this utility to display the status of a UPS that is attached to your server. When you use this utility, you can see the type of power the server is currently using (regular power or the UPS's battery), the discharge time remaining (how much time the server can safely run on the UPS's battery power), the battery's status (recharged, low, or being recharged), the recharge time remaining, and the current network power status.

UPS TIME (CONSOLE UTILITY)

Use this utility to change the amount of time required to discharge and recharge a UPS battery. The discharge time is the amount of time that the server can run on the battery's power if commercial power stops. The recharge time is the amount of time required to fully recharge a battery after it's been used. See the UPS manufacturer's documentation for the recommended times for your UPS.

When you execute this utility, you will be asked to specify the amount of recharge and discharge time necessary.

V_LONG (NLM)

This module is used by VREPAIR.NLM to repair volumes that use the LONG.NAM name space module. LONG.NAM allows the server to support Windows NT, Windows 95, and OS/2 long file names and formats, and it is loaded by default when you install IntranetWare. You may want to copy this support module, along with VREPAIR, to the server's DOS boot partition so you can use them even if volume SYS is down. (VREPAIR and its support modules are located in SYS:SYSTEM by default.)

V_MAC (NLM)

This module is used by VREPAIR.NLM to repair volumes that use the MAC.NAM name space module. MAC.NAM allows the server to support Mac OS long file names and formats. If you store Mac OS files on your server, you may want to copy this support module, along with VREPAIR, to the server's DOS boot partition so you can use them even if volume SYS is down. (VREPAIR and its support modules are located in SYS:SYSTEM by default.)

V_NFS (NLM)

This module is used by VREPAIR.NLM to repair volumes that use the NFS.NAM name space module. NFS.NAM allows the server to support UNIX long file names and formats. If you store NFS files on your server, you may want to copy this support module, along with VREPAIR, to the server's DOS boot partition so you can use them even if volume SYS is down. (VREPAIR and its support modules are located in SYS:SYSTEM by default.)

VERSION (CONSOLE UTILITY)

Use this utility to see the version of NetWare that is running on the server.

VIEW (NLM)

Use this module to display a file on the server console. You cannot edit or create a file with VIEW.NLM, however. You must use EDIT.NLM to edit or create a file. Use the following command format, replacing *filename* with the name of the file you want to see:

```
LOAD VIEW filename
```

VOLUMES (CONSOLE UTILITY)

Use this utility to display a list of all the volumes currently mounted on the server. The display also indicates which name spaces are supported by each volume.

VREPAIR (NLM)

Use this module to repair minor problems with a volume or to remove a name space from a volume. If the server detects a volume problem when it boots, it will run VREPAIR automatically. You can also run VREPAIR manually if you need to, but you can only run it on dismounted volumes. VREPAIR also requires the name space support modules (V_MAC.NLM, V_LONG.NLM, or V_NFS.NLM) if the volume supports any of those name spaces.

You may want to copy VREPAIR.NLM and these support modules to the server's DOS boot partition so you can use them even if volume SYS is down. (VREPAIR and its support modules are located in SYS:SYSTEM by default.)

Use the following command format, replacing *name* with the name of the volume you want to repair:

```
LOAD VREPAIR name
```

WHOAMI (WORKSTATION UTILITY)

Use this utility to display information such as the servers you're logged into, your login name on each of those servers, and the times you logged in. To see a list of all the servers you're logged into, simply type WHOAMI. To see more detailed information, use the following command format:

```
WHOAMI /ALL
```

WSUPDATE (WORKSTATION UTILITY)

Use this utility to update files on users' workstations. WSUPDATE compares the dates of the files on the workstation with the source files on the server and copies the newer version to the workstation if necessary. Use the following command format, replacing *source* with the path and name of the source file you want to use to update the workstation, *destination* with the workstation drive on which you want the utility to look for the older file, and *parameters* with any of the parameters listed in Table 16.15.

```
WSUPDATE source destination /parameters
```

TABLE 16.15 *WSUPDATE Parameters*

PARAMETER	DESCRIPTION
C	Copies the newer file over the old and doesn't keep a backup copy of the old file.
F=*path\filename*	Sends WSUPDATE to a file that contains commands for updating the workstation's files.
/I	Makes WSUPDATE interactive so that it asks the user whether to update an old file (Default).
L=*path\filename*	Creates a log file containing the messages generated during updates.
N	Creates a new path and file if an older version doesn't already exist.
R	Renames the old file with the extension .OLD and then copies the new file to the workstation.
S	Searches for the old files in all subdirectories of the workstation's drive.
V=*drive*	Updates the workstation's CONFIG.SYS file.

APPENDIX A

NET.CFG Parameters

The NET.CFG file on a workstation configures the NetWare DOS Requester (VLMs) and LAN driver for the workstation's needs. Because NET.CFG is used to configure a variety of aspects of your workstation, it can be quite simple or fairly involved.

NET.CFG is created by the NetWare DOS Requester installation. It is located in the NWCLIENT directory and can be edited with a text editor.

NET.CFG must be formatted with headings for various categories of configuration parameters. Each heading must be flush with the left margin; commands beneath that heading are indented once. (The only exception to these formatting conventions is NETBIOS commands. They are all flush with the left margin.) It doesn't matter if you use uppercase or lowercase in the commands in NET.CFG. (The examples in this chapter use mixed case for readability.)

The following is a sample NET.CFG file that was created to configure an NE2000 network board to use port 300, interrupt 3, and the 802.2 Ethernet frame type. Notice that the file is divided by headings. The Link Driver NE2000 heading contains indented lines that specify the information for that driver. The NetWare DOS Requester heading contains indented lines that specify general items for the Requester. Each heading is preceded by a blank line, which makes it easier to read the file. The NET.CFG file that will be created when you first install the NetWare DOS Requester will vary from this sample, depending on your configuration.

```
LINK DRIVER NE2000
     Port 300
     Int 3
     Frame Ethernet_802.2

NETWARE DOS REQUESTER
     NetWare Protocol=NDS, BIND
     First Network Drive=F
```

There are fifteen categories of NET.CFG parameters:

- Desktop SNMP
- Link Driver
- Link Support
- Named Pipes
- NetBIOS
- NetWare DOS Requester

- NetWare DOS TSA
- Protocol IPX
- Protocol ODINSUP
- Protocol RFCNBIOS
- Protocol RPL
- Protocol SPX
- Protocol TCPIP
- TBMI2
- Transport Provider IPX (or UDP)

The following sections explain the available parameters for each of these categories.

Desktop SNMP Parameters

Desktop SNMP parameters configure the desktop SNMP option. To use these parameters, add the Desktop SNMP heading to the NET.CFG file, and then place each parameter command beneath the heading, indented as shown.

```
DESKTOP SNMP
     parameter
```

The following parameters can be used with this heading:

- **Asynchronous timeout *number*** Sets the timeout (in ticks) for asynchronous connections. When an SNMP manager requests data from a managed object, the desktop SNMP waits the specified amount of time before trying to cancel a request. Default: 20 (about 1.2 seconds).
- **Control community "*name*"** Specifies the control community, which is the read-write community that is allowed to do SET operations. Enclose the *name* in quotation marks. Default: Public. Values: Public, Private, or other name.
- **Enable control community *status*** Specifies which control communities can be used to gain access. Default: Specified. Values: Specified, Any, Off, or Omitted.
  - **Specified** Only the community in the Control Community command is allowed.

- **Any** Any community is allowed.
- **Off** Access for this community type is disabled.
- **Omitted** If "Omitted" is used, Desktop SNMP defaults to "Specified" and looks for a specified community. If none is found, the default community becomes the Public community.

- **Enable monitor community *status*** Specifies which monitor communities can be used to gain access. Default: Specified. Values: Specified, Any, Off, or Omitted.
  - **Specified** Only the community in the Monitor Community command is allowed.
  - **Any** Any community is allowed.
  - **Off** Access for this community type is disabled.
  - **Omitted** If "Omitted" is used, Desktop SNMP defaults to "Specified" and looks for a specified community. If none is found, the default community becomes the Public community.
- **Enable trap community *status*** Specifies which trap communities can be used to gain access. Default: Specified. Values: Specified, Off, or Omitted. ("Any" is not a possible value for this parameter.)
  - **Specified** Only the community in the Trap Community command is allowed.
  - **Off** Access for this community type is disabled.
  - **Omitted** If "Omitted" is used, Desktop SNMP defaults to "Specified" and looks for a specified community. If none is found, the default community becomes the Public community.
- **Monitor community "*name*"** Specifies the monitor community, which is the read-only community that is allowed to do GET and GET NEXT operations. Enclose the *name* in quotation marks. Default: Public. Values: Public, Private, or other name.
- **Snmpenableauthentrap *on/off*** When set to On, tells the Desktop SNMP to send a trap message if an unauthorized user tries to use SNMP to get or change data that SNMP manages. Default: Off.
- **Syscontact "*name*"** Specifies the name of the person who should be notified if the workstation needs maintenance. Enclose the *name* in quotation marks. You can enter a name and phone number or other information, such as "Ray Snow ext. 3354."

- **Syslocation "*location*"** Specifies the physical location of the workstation. Enclose the *location* in quotation marks. Enter any location, such as "West wing 2nd floor."
- **Sysname "*name*"** Specifies the user's login name or TCP/IP host name, if available, such as "lksmith." Enclose the *name* in quotation marks.
- **Trap community "*name*"** Specifies the trap community. Enclose the *name* in quotation marks. Default: Public. Values: Public, Private, or other name.

Link Driver Parameters

Link Driver parameters configure hardware and software options for the workstation's LAN driver. They also allow you to specify frame types and protocols for the LAN driver.

To use these parameters, add the Link Driver heading to the NET.CFG file, and then place each parameter command beneath the heading, indented as shown here. Substitute the name of your LAN driver, such as NE2000 or 3C523, for *driver* in the heading.

```
LINK DRIVER driver

    parameter
```

The following parameters can be used with this heading:

- **Accm *address*** Sets whether the PPP protocol should use ACCM (asynchronous control character map). Replace *address* with the correct address for the remote host. Default: FFFFFFFF.
- **Accomp *yes/no*** When set to Yes, tells the PPP protocol whether to compress the address and control field of the PPP header. Default: No.
- **Alternate** Specifies an alternate network board.
- **Authen pap *username password*** Tells the PPP protocol to use authentication (based on the Password Authentication Protocol — PAP). PPP uses the username and password to identify the local system to the peer host.
- **Baud *rate*** Specifies the baud rate for the SLIP_PPP driver. Default: 2400. Values: 300, 1200, 2400, 4800, 9600, 14400, 19200, or 38400.

- **Bus ID *name number*** Specifies the bus into which the network board is inserted. Used with LAN drivers that support multiple bus types. Replace *name* with the name of the LAN driver, such as NE2000. The default value for *number* (-1 0FFh) makes the LAN driver search each bus for a supported network board and then initialize the first board found. Default: -1 0FFh. Example values are as follows:

ISA	0
MCA	1
EISA	2
PCMCIA	3
PCI	4
VL (VESA Local)	5

- **Counter *protocol timeout config# term# nak#*** Specifies a *protocol,* which can be LCP (Link Control Protocol), IPCP (Internet Protocol Control Protocol), or PAP (Password Authentication Protocol). Sets the protocol's timeout value (in seconds) for retransmitting request packets (*timeout*), the maximum number of retries for sending a configuration request (*config#*), the maximum number of retries for sending a terminate request (*term#*), and the maximum number of retries for sending a configuration NAK (*nak#*).
- **Dial *number*** Specifies the phone number for the SLIP_PPP driver to call when it is loaded. Used only when the Direct parameter is set to No. Values: Any dial modifiers supported by your modem, up to 30 characters.
- **Direct *yes/no*** Specifies whether the SLIP or PPP link is direct. Set to No only if you use the Dial or Listen parameters. Default: Yes.
- **Dma [#1 or #2] *number*** Configures the network board's DMA channels. Select #1 or #2 to specify which of the configurable DMA channels you're configuring, and then specify the DMA channel you want it to use. For example, to set the first configurable channel to use DMA channel 3, type **dma #1 3**.
- **Frame *frametype* [*mode*]** Sets the frame type the LAN driver will use. Can also set the address mode to either LSB (canonical addressing mode) or MSB (noncanonical addressing mode) for LAN drivers that support this. Default frame types:
  - For Ethernet drivers: Ethernet_802.2
  - For Token Ring drivers: Token-Ring
  - For TCP/IP SLIP_PPP drivers: SLIP

- **Ipaddr *address*** Specifies the IP addresses for PPP in dotted decimal notation, such as 129.46.01.5. If the remote host did not specify an address in its configuration request, the specified address in this parameter is used. Default: none.
- **Irq [#1 or #2] *number*** Sets the interrupt (IRQ) that the network board will use. Use #1 or #2 to specify the network board you're configuring, and then replace *number* with the interrupt number you want to assign. Recommended values: 3, 5, or 7 for most network boards, to avoid conflicting with other hardware. See the manufacturer's documentation for more information.
- **Link stations *number*** Specifies the number of link stations needed for the LANSUP driver. Used with the IBM LAN Support Program. Default: 1.
- **Listen** Indicates the passive end of a modem connection for the SLIP or PPP protocol.
- **Magic *number*** Specifies a number used by the SLIP_PPP driver as a seed number to generate a unique number for process recognition. This parameter enables you to detect looped-back links and other problems. Default: Disabled.
- **Max frame size *number*** Specifies the maximum frame size, in bytes, that the NTR2000 and LANSUP LAN drivers can send out onto the network.
  - Default for NTR2000: 4222 bytes, or 2174 if the network board has 8K or shared RAM available.
  - Default for LANSUP: 1150 bytes, or 1496 if you're using the IBM LAN Support Program with an Ethernet LAN driver.
  - Values: Between 638 and 17,954 for a line speed of 16 Mbps. Between 638 and 4464 for a line speed of 4 Mbps. Value includes number of bytes in a data packet, plus bytes in the largest possible header (currently 126 bytes — 52 bytes for LAN driver header plus 74 bytes for protocol header).
- **Mem [#1 or #2] *address length*** Sets the memory range that the network board can use. Specify the board by typing either #1 or #2. Replace *address* with the hex starting address of the memory used by the network board. If necessary, replace *length* with the number of hex paragraphs (16 bytes each) of the memory address range.
- **Mru *number* m** Specifies the maximum receive and transmit units (MRU) for the SLIP or PPP protocol. Add the optional "m" to the com-

mand if the SLIP_PPP driver should assume a worst-case scenario for character mapping, in which data bytes in a packet are mapped into 2 bytes each. Default for PPP: 1500. Default for SLIP: 1006. Values: 76 to 1500.

- **Node address *address* [*mode*]** Sets the hex address number for the network board, which overrides the hard-coded address. Can also set the address mode to either LSB (canonical addressing mode) or MSB (noncanonical addressing mode) for LAN drivers that support this.
- **Open** Allows the LANSUP file to increase the frame size for a Token Ring driver for networks using the IBM LAN Support Program.
- **Open *mode*** Specifies the active or passive open mode for LCP (Link Control Protocol) and IPCP (Internet Protocol Control Protocol) for networks using the PPP protocol. Default: Active. Values: Active or Passive.
- **Pcomp *yes/no*** When set to Yes, tells the PPP protocol to compress the protocol field of the PPP header. Default: No.
- **Port [#1 or #2] *address* [*number*]** Sets the hex address for the starting I/O port and, if necessary, the number of ports in the range. Use #1 or #2 to specify the appropriate network board.
- **Protocol *name ID type*** Adds additional protocols to the LAN driver. *Name* is the new protocol's name. *ID* is the protocol's hex ID number. *Type* is the protocol's frame type. See Table A.1 for a list of protocols with their frame types and ID numbers.
- **Saps *number*** Sets the number of Service Access Points needed by the LANSUP driver. Used with the IBM LAN Support Program. Default: 1.
- **Slot *number*** Specifies the board's slot number so the driver doesn't have to scan the slots to find the board.
- **Tcpipcomp [vj *or* no] *slots number*** Uses VJ (Van Jacobson) header compression for the SLIP or PPP protocols. If you do not want VJ compression, set this parameter to No. If you want VJ compression, enter VJ, and specify the conversation slot you want and whether to compress the slot ID (when *number* is 0, do not compress slot ID; when *number* is 1, compress slot ID). Default: No compression. If you set compression to VJ, defaults: slots = 16, number = 0. If you set compression to VJ, values: slots = 1 to 16, number = 0 or 1.

TABLE A.1 *Protocols with Their Frame Types and ID Numbers*

FRAME ID	FRAME TYPE	PROTOCOL	PROTOCOL ID NUMBER	DESCRIPTION
0	VIRTUAL_LAN	IPX/SPX	0	Use where no Frame ID/MAC envelope is necessary.
1	LOCALTALK	AppleTalk	0	Apple LocalTalk frame
2	ETHERNET_II	IPX/SPX	8137h	Ethernet using a DEC Ethernet II envelope
2	ETHERNET_II	XNS	600h	Ethernet using a DEC Ethernet II envelope
2	ETHERNET_II	AARP	80F3h	Ethernet using a DEC Ethernet II envelope
2	ETHERNET_II	AppleTalk	809Bh	Ethernet using a DEC Ethernet II envelope
2	ETHERNET_II	ARP	806h	Ethernet using a DEC Ethernet II envelope
2	ETHERNET_II	RARP	8035h	Ethernet using a DEC Ethernet II envelope
2	ETHERNET_II	IP	800h	Ethernet using a DEC Ethernet II envelope
3	ETHERNET_802.2	IPX/SPX	E0h	Ethernet (802.3) using an 802.2 envelope
3	ETHERNET_802.2	RPL	FCh	Ethernet (802.3) using an 802.2 envelope
3	ETHERNET_802.2	SNA	04h	Ethernet (802.3) using an 802.2 envelope
3	ETHERNET_802.2	NetBIOS	F0h	Ethernet (802.3) using an 802.2 envelope
4	Token-Ring	IPX/SPX	E0h	Token Ring (802.5) using an 802.2 envelope
4	Token-Ring	RPL	FCh	Token Ring (802.5) using an 802.2 envelope

(continued)

TABLE A.1 *Protocols with Their Frame Types and ID Numbers (continued)*

FRAME ID	FRAME TYPE	PROTOCOL	PROTOCOL ID NUMBER	DESCRIPTION
4	Token-Ring	SNA	04h	Token Ring (802.5) using an 802.2 envelope
4	Token-Ring	NetBIOS	F0h	Token Ring (802.5) using an 802.2 envelope
5	ETHERNET_802.3	IPX/SPX	00h	IPX 802.3 raw encapsulation
6	802.4	IPX/SPX	N/A	Token-passing bus envelope
7	RESERVED			Reserved for future use
8	GNET	IPX/SPX	E0h	GatewayG/Net frame envelope
9	PRONET-10	IPX/SPX	N/A	Proteon ProNET I/O frame envelope
10	ETHERNET_SNAP	IPX/SPX	8137h	Ethernet (802.3) using an 802.2 envelope with SNAP
10	ETHERNET_SNAP	XNS	600h	Ethernet (802.3) using an 802.2 envelope with SNAP
10	ETHERNET_SNAP	AARP	80F3h	Ethernet (802.3) using an 802.2 envelope with SNAP
10	ETHERNET_SNAP	AppleTalk 8000	7809Bh	Ethernet (802.3) using an 802.2 envelope with SNAP
10	ETHERNET_SNAP	ARP	806h	Ethernet (802.3) using an 802.2 envelope with SNAP
10	ETHERNET_SNAP	RARP	8035h	Ethernet (802.3) using an 802.2 envelope with SNAP

TABLE A.1 *Protocols with Their Frame Types and ID Numbers (continued)*

FRAME ID	FRAME TYPE	PROTOCOL	PROTOCOL ID NUMBER	DESCRIPTION
10	ETHERNET_SNAP	IP	800h	Ethernet (802.3) using an 802.2 envelope with SNAP
11	Token-Ring_SNAP	IPX/SPX	8137h	Token Ring (802.5) using an 802.2 envelope with SNAP
12	LANPAC_II	IPX/SPX	N/A	Racore frame envelope
13	ISDN	IPX/SPX	N/A	Integrated Services Digital Network (not available)
14	NOVELL_RX-NET	IPX/SPX	FAh	Novell RX-Net envelope
17	OMNINET/4	IPX/SPX	N/A	Corvus frame envelope
18	3270_COAXA	IPX/SPX	N/A	Harris Adacom frame envelope
19	IP	IPX/SPX	N/A	IP Tunnel frame envelope
20	FDDI_802.2	IPX/SPX	E0h	FDDI using an 802.2 envelope
20	FDDI_802.2	RPL	FCh	FDDI using an 802.2 envelope
20	FDDI_802.2	SNA	04h	FDDI using an 802.2 envelope
21	IVDLAN_802.9	IPX/SPX	N/A	Commtex, Inc. frame envelope
22	DATACO_OSI	IPX/SPX	N/A	Dataco frame envelope
23	FDDI_SNAP	IPX/SPX	8137h	FDDI using 802.2 with a SNAP envelope
23	FDDI_SNAP	XNS	600h	FDDI using 802.2 with a SNAP envelope

(continued)

TABLE A.1 *Protocols with Their Frame Types and ID Numbers (continued)*

FRAME ID	FRAME TYPE	PROTOCOL	PROTOCOL ID NUMBER	DESCRIPTION
23	FDDI_SNAP	AARP	80F3h	FDDI using 802.2 with a SNAP envelope
23	FDDI_SNAP	AppleTalk	809Bh	FDDI using 802.2 80007 with a SNAP envelope
23	FDDI_SNAP	ARP	806h	FDDI using 802.2 with a SNAP envelope
23	FDDI_SNAP	RARP	8035h	FDDI using 802.2 with a SNAP envelope
23	FDDI_SNAP	IP	800h	FDDI using 802.2 with a SNAP envelope
24	IBM_SDLC	Unknown		Novell frame type
25	PCO_FDDITP	Unknown		PC Office frame type
26	WAIDNET	Unknown		Hyper communications frame type
27	SLIP	Unknown		Novell frame type
28	PPP	Unknown		Novell frame type
29	RANGELAN	Unknown		Proxim frame type
30	X.25	Unknown		Novell frame type
31	Frame_Relay	Unknown		Novell frame type
32	IWI_BUS-NET_SNAP	Unknown		Integrated Workstations frame type
33	SNA_LINKS	Unknown		Novell frame type
34	WAN_Client_LAN	Unknown		Novell frame type

(Table reprinted from *NetWare Client for DOS and MS Windows Technical Reference* manual, 1994, Novell, Inc. All rights reserved. Used with permission.)

Link Support Parameters

Link Support parameters configure options for the Link Support Layer (LSL.COM), such as the size of packet receive buffers, the size of memory pool buffers, and so on.

To use these parameters, add the Link Support heading to the NET.CFG file, and then place each parameter command beneath the heading, indented as shown here.

```
LINK SUPPORT
    parameter
```

The following parameters can be used with this heading:

- **Buffers *number* [*size*]** Sets the number of communication buffers (if applicable) and the size (in bytes) of receive buffers that LSL.COM can handle. The buffer size should be the same size as the largest packet size that your workstation receives over the network.
  - For IPX Default *number*: 0 (IPX uses its own buffers and does not need the LSL to provide buffers for it.) Default *size*: 1500.
  - For TCP/IP Default *number*: 8. Default *size*: 1500.
  - For LSL Default *number*: none. Default *size*: 1514.
- **Max boards *number*** Sets the maximum number of logical boards LSL.COM can maintain. Default: 4. Values: 1 to 16.
- **Max stacks *number*** Sets the maximum number of logical protocol stack IDs that LSL.COM can support. Default: 4. Values: 1 to 16.
- **Mempool *number* [K]** Configures the size of the memory pool buffers (in bytes) for some protocols (not used with IPXODI). Include the K option to indicate the value is in kilobytes.

Named Pipes Parameters

Named Pipes parameters regulate how a workstation interacts with a Named Pipes server.

To use these parameters, add the Named Pipes heading to the NET.CFG file, and then place each parameter command beneath the heading, indented as shown here.

```
NAMED PIPES
    parameter
```

The following parameters can be used with this heading:

- **Np max comm buffers *number*** Indicates the maximum number of communication buffers that the extender can use when communicating with the Named Pipes server. Default: 6. Values: 4 to 40.
- **Np max machine names *number*** Sets the DOSNP software for peer mode and specifies how many Named Pipes servers the extender can communicate with. Sets the maximum number of Named Pipes servers that the DOSNP software can maintain in a local name table. Default: 10. Values: 4 to 50.
- **Np max open named pipes *number*** Sets the maximum number of Named Pipes that the workstation can have open simultaneously. Default: 4. Values: 4 to 128.
- **Np max sessions *number*** Sets the maximum number of Named Pipes servers that the extender can communicate with in default mode. Not used in peer mode. Default: 10. Values: 4 to 50.

NetBIOS Parameters

NetBIOS parameters let you configure NetBIOS sessions, buffers, and broadcasts.

To use these parameters, you don't need to add a NetBIOS heading to the NET.CFG file. Each NetBIOS command can be entered flush with the left margin.

```
NETBIOS parameter
NETBIOS parameter
```

The following NetBIOS parameters can be used:

- **Netbios abort timeout *number*** Sets the time, in ticks, NetBIOS waits for a response before ending a session. Default: 540 (approximately 30 seconds).
- **Netbios broadcast count *number*** Sets how many queries or claims NetBIOS broadcasts for the name being used by the application. When multiplied by NetBIOS Broadcast Delay number, sets the time required to broadcast a name resolution packet across the network. With

NetBIOS Internet On, default: 4. With NetBIOS Internet Off, default: 2. Values: 2 to 65,535.

- **Netbios broadcast delay *number*** Sets how many ticks NetBIOS waits between query or claim broadcasts. When multiplied by NetBIOS Broadcast Count number, sets the time required to broadcast a name resolution packet across the network. With NetBIOS Internet On, default: 36. With NetBIOS Internet Off, default: 18. Values: 18 to 65,535.
- **Netbios commands *number*** Specifies the number of NetBIOS commands that can be buffered in the NetBIOS driver at a time. Default: 12. Values: 4 to 250.
- **Netbios internet *on/off*** Speeds up packets when set to Off if you are using NetBIOS applications on a single network. If using multiple networks through bridges, leave On. Default: On.
- **Netbios listen timeout *number*** Sets the time, in ticks, NetBIOS waits before requesting another packet to make sure the connection is still valid. Default: 108 (approximately 6 seconds). Values: 1 to 65,535.
- **Netbios receive buffers *number*** Sets the number of IPX receive buffers that NetBIOS uses. Default: 6. Values: 4 to 20.
- **Netbios retry count *number*** Specifies how many times NetBIOS resends a packet to establish a NetBIOS session with a remote partner. With NetBIOS Internet On, default: 20. With NetBIOS Internet Off, default: 10. Values: 4 to 20.
- **Netbios retry delay *number*** Specifies how long, in ticks, NetBIOS waits between sending packets to establish a session. Default: 10 (approximately 0.5 seconds). Values: 10 to 65,535.
- **Netbios send buffers *number*** Sets the number of IPX send buffers that NetBIOS uses. Default: 6. Values: 4 to 250.
- **Netbios session *number*** Specifies the maximum number of simultaneous NetBIOS sessions. Default: 32. Values: 4 to 250.
- **Netbios verify timeout *number*** Sets the interval, in ticks, between packets sent to keep a connection open. Default: 54 (approximately 3 seconds). Values: 4 to 65,535.
- **Npatch *offset, value*** Patches any location in the NETBIOS.EXE data segment with the specified value. *Offset* is the number of the data segment you want patched. *Value* is the number of the data segment with which you want to patch it.

NetWare DOS Requester Parameters

NetWare DOS Requester parameters configure the NetWare DOS Requester and VLM files.

To use these parameters, add the NetWare DOS Requester heading to the NET.CFG file, and then place each parameter command beneath the heading, indented as shown here.

```
NETWARE DOS REQUESTER
    parameter
```

The following parameters can be used with this heading:

- **Auto large table=*on/off*** When set to On, creates a connection table of 178 bytes per connection for bindery reconnects. When set to Off, creates a small table of 34 bytes. Default: Off.
- **Auto reconnect=*on/off*** When set to On, AUTO.VLM reconnects the workstation after a connection has been broken. Default: On. (You must also load AUTO.VLM and RSA.VLM. Bind Reconnect = On must also be set for bindery reconnections.)
- **Auto retry=*number*** Sets the time AUTO.VLM waits before retrying. Default: 0. Values: 0 (no retries) to 3640.
- **Average name length=*number*** Sets the average length (number of characters) of server names, which is used to create a table to store those names. Default: 48. Values: 2 to 48.
- **Bind reconnect=*on/off*** Rebuilds bindery connections after a connection has been broken. (You must also load AUTO.VLM, and Auto Reconnect = On must be set to make autoreconnection work.)
- **Broadcast retries=*number*** Specifies how many times the NetWare DOS Requester broadcasts a request. Default: 3. Values: 1 to 255.
- **Broadcast send delay=*number*** Specifies how long, in ticks, the NetWare DOS Requester waits before performing the next function. Default: 0. Values: 0 to 255.
- **Broadcast timeout=*number*** Specifies how long, in ticks, the NetWare DOS Requester waits between broadcast retries. Default: 2. Values: 1 to 255.
- **Cache buffers=*number*** Specifies the number of cache buffers used for local caching. Default: 5. Values: 0 to 64.

- **Cache buffers size=*number*** Sets the size of cache buffers used by FIO.VLM. Default: Media maximum minus 64 bytes. Values: 64 to 4096 bytes. See the manufacturer's documentation for your media type's cache buffer size.
- **Cache writes=*on/off*** Specifies whether writes are cached. Default: On.
- **Checksum=*number*** Sets level at which NCP packets are validated. Default: 1. Values: 0 = disabled; 1 = enabled but not preferred; 2 = enabled and preferred; 3 = required.
- **Confirm critical error action=*on/off*** Specifies how network-critical error messages, intended for the NetWare DOS Requester, are handled by Windows. Default: On. Values: On = message displays the server that has lost the connection, and you are prompted to cancel or retry before Windows responds; Off = Windows may intercept critical errors and automatically respond to error messages intended for the NetWare DOS Requester.
- **Connections=*number*** Sets the maximum number of connections. Default: 8. Values: 2 to 50.
- **Dos name="*name*"** Specifies the name of DOS on the workstation. Enclose the *name* in quotation marks. Default: MSDOS.
- **Eoj=*on/off*** Determines whether files, locks, semaphores, and so on are automatically closed at the end of a job. Default: On.
- **Exclude vlm=*path\vlm*** Specifies a VLM file that should not load. Replace *path\vlm* with the path to and the name of the VLM you don't want to load.
- **First network drive=*letter*** Specifies which drive letter will be the first network drive. Default: First available. Values: A to Z.
- **Force first network drive=*on/off*** If set to On, ensures that, after the user logs out, the SYS:LOGIN directory is mapped to the same drive letter specified in the First Network Drive command. If set to Off, this command maps SYS:LOGIN to the drive letter from which the user logged out. Default: Off.
- **Handle net errors=*on/off*** Sets how network errors are handled. Default: On. Values: On = interrupt 24 handles errors; Off = NET_RECV_ERROR is returned.
- **Large internet packets=*on/off*** Allows maximum packet size to be used. Default: On.

- **Lip start size *number*** Sets the packet size in bytes. Used when starting LIP negotiations. Default: 0 (0 = Off). Values: 576 to 655535.
- **Load conn table low=*on/off*** Specifies whether the connection table is loaded in high or conventional memory. Set to On *only* if you are using the initial release of NetWare 4.0 utilities. Default: Off.
- **Load low conn=*on/off*** If set to Off, makes CONN.VLM load in upper memory, which saves memory but decreases performance. Default: On.
- **Load low ipxncp=*on/off*** If set to Off, makes IPXNCP.VLM load in upper memory, which saves memory but decreases performance. Default: On.
- **Load low redir=*on/off*** If set to Off, makes REDIR.VLM load in conventional memory, which increases performance but sacrifices memory. Default: Off.
- **Local printers=*number*** Tells the workstation how many local printers are attached. Default: 3. Values: 0 to 9. Set to 0 to prevent Shift-Print Screen from hanging the workstation if CAPTURE isn't in effect.
- **Lock delay=*number*** Specifies how long, in ticks, the NetWare DOS Requester waits before trying to get a lock. Default: 1. Value: 0 to 255.
- **Lock retries=*number*** Specifies how many times the NetWare DOS Requester tries to get a lock on the network. Default: 1. Values: 0 to 255.
- **Long machine type="*name*"** Specifies the type of computer being used. Enclose the *name* in quotation marks. Used by the %MACHINE variable in login script drive mappings. Default: IBM_PC.
- **Max tasks=*number*** Sets the maximum number of simultaneously active tasks. Default: 31. Values: 5 to 254.
- **Message level=*number*** Sets which messages are displayed during load. Default: 1. Values: 0 = copyright and critical errors; 1 = warning messages; 2 = load information for VLMs; 3 = configuration information; 4 = diagnostic information. (Each message level also displays the previous level's messages.)
- **Message timeout=*number*** Sets how long, in ticks, broadcast messages remain on the screen before being cleared. Default: 0. Values: 0 (wait for user intervention) to 10,000 (approximately 9 minutes).
- **Minimum time to net=*milliseconds*** Overrides the time-to-net value defined by the local router during connections. Used on bridged WAN

or satellite links with time-to-net values set too low for workstations to make a connection. Default: 0. Values: 1 to 65,535.

- **Name context="*context*"** Sets the user's current location, or context, in the NDS tree. Enclose the *context* in quotation marks. Default: The root of the NDS tree.
- **Netware protocol=*list*** Sets the order in which NetWare protocols (NDS, BIND, and PNW) are used. Lets you prioritize protocols for login or load order. Separate protocols by a comma or space. Default order: NDS BIND PNW.
- **Network printers=*number*** Specifies how many LPT ports can be captured. Default: 3. Values: 0 to 9. (If set to 0, PRINT.VLM will not load.)
- **Pb buffers=*number*** Turns Packet Burst on and off. Default: 3. Values: 0 (0 = Off) to 10.
- **Pburst read windows size=*number*** Specifies the read buffer size, in bytes, for Windows. Default: 16. Values: 3 to 128.
- **Pburst write windows size=*number*** Specifies the write buffer size, in bytes, for Windows. Default: 10. Values: 3 to 128.
- **Preferred server="*server*"** Specifies which server to attach to first. Enclose the *server* in quotation marks. Default: none.
- **Preferred tree="*tree*"** Specifies which Directory tree to attach to first. Enclose the *tree* in quotation marks. Default: none.
- **Preferred workgroup="*workgroup*"** Specifies which Personal NetWare workgroup to attach to first. Used only with Personal NetWare. Enclose the *workgroup* in quotation marks. Default: none.
- **Print buffer size=*number*** Sets the size, in bytes, for the print buffer. Default: 64. Values: 0 to 256.
- **Print header=*number*** Specifies the size, in bytes, of the buffer to hold initialization information for each print job. Default: 64. Values: 0 to 1024.
- **Print tail=*number*** Specifies the size, in bytes, of the buffer to hold reset information after a print job. Default: 16. Values: 0 to 1024.
- **Read only compatibility=*on/off*** If set to On, allows a read-only file to be opened with a read-write access call. Default: Off.
- **Responder=*on/off*** If set to Off, makes the workstation ignore broadcasts and diagnostic communication, which reduce the NetWare DOS Requester's use of conventional memory. Default: On.

- **Search mode=*number*** Sets the search mode for finding files in directories. Default: 1. Values: 0 to 7.
- **Set station time=*on/off*** If set to On, the workstation's time is synchronized to the time of the server to which it first attaches. Default: On.
- **Short machine type="*name*"** Sets the computer name to determine which overlay files to use. Enclose the *name* in quotation marks. Default: IBM.
- **Show dots=*on/off*** If set to On, displays dots (. and ..) for parent directories in Windows 3.x. Default: Off.
- **Signature level=*number*** Sets the level of NCP Packet Signature security. Default: 1. Values: 0 = no signing; 1 = signs if server requests; 2 = signs if server can sign; 3 = required.
- **True commit=*on/off*** Specifies whether the commit NCP is sent on DOS commit requests. Default: Off.
- **Use defaults=*on/off*** When set to Off, lets you override default loading of VLMs and specify exact files to load. Default: On.
- **Vlm=*path\vlm*** Loads a VLM file. Replace *path\vlm* with the path to and the name of the VLM you want to load.
- **Workgroup net=*address*** Specifies an address for a workgroup that resides on a network segment outside your local network. Used only with Personal NetWare. Change this parameter only with Personal NetWare utilities.

NetWare DOS TSA Parameters

NetWare DOS TSA parameters let you configure the DOS TSA (Target Service Agent) software. The DOS TSA lets you back up a DOS-based workstation using SBACKUP.NLM.

To use these parameters, add the NetWare DOS TSA heading to the NET.CFG file, and then place each parameter command beneath the heading, indented as shown here.

```
NETWARE DOS TSA
     parameter
```

The following parameters can be used with this heading:

- **Disk buffers *number*** Specifies the size, in bytes, of disk buffers. Default: 1. Values: 1 to 30.

- **Drives *letter*** Specifies which hard disk drives are being managed by the TSA. Separate multiple drive letters with a space. Default: C.
- **Password *name*** Sets a unique password for the workstation. Default: none.
- **Stack size *number*** Sets the stack size, in bytes, for the TSA. Use only if the available RAM on the workstation is extremely limited. Default: 2048. Values: 512 to 4096.
- **Tsa server name *server*** Specifies the network server to which this workstation should attach.
- **Workstation name *name*** Identifies this workstation's unique name.

Protocol IPX Parameters

Protocol IPX parameters configure the IPX protocol.

To use these parameters, add the Protocol IPX heading to the NET.CFG file, and then place each parameter command beneath the heading, indented as shown here.

```
PROTOCOL IPX
    parameter
```

The following parameters can be used with this heading:

- **Bind *driver*** Binds the protocol to a LAN driver. *Driver* is the LAN driver name or logical board number.
- **Int64 *on/off*** If set to Off, allows an application to use interrupt 64h. Default: On.
- **Int7a *on/off*** If set to Off, allows an application to use interrupt 7Ah. Default: On.
- **Ipatch *offset*, *value*** Allows an address in IPXODI.COM to be patched with the specified byte offset value.
- **Ipx packet size limit *number*** Sets the maximum size, in bytes, of packets to reduce wasted memory. Default: 4160 or the size specified by the LAN driver, if smaller. Values: 576 to 6500.
- **Ipx retry count *number*** Specifies the number of times a workstation resends a packet that failed. Default: 20.

- **Ipx sockets *number*** Sets the maximum number of sockets that IPX can have open. Default: 20.

Protocol ODINSUP Parameter

The Protocol ODINSUP parameter allows the NDIS protocol stack (used with Extended Services and LAN Services) to communicate using ODI Token Ring or Ethernet drivers.

To use this parameter, add the Protocol ODINSUP heading to the NET.CFG file, and then place the parameter command beneath the heading, indented as shown here.

```
PROTOCOL ODINSUP
    parameter
```

The following parameter can be used with this heading:

- **Bind *driver*** Binds the ODINSUP protocol to an ODI LAN driver. *Driver* is the Token Ring or Ethernet LAN driver name or logical board number.

Protocol RFCNBIOS Parameter

The Protocol RFCNBIOS parameter lets you configure RFCNBIOS, which implements the NetVIOS B-node protocols as defined in RFC 1001 and 1002.

To use this parameter, add the Protocol RFCNBIOS heading to the NET.CFG file, and then place the parameter command beneath the heading, indented as shown here.

```
PROTOCOL RFCNBIOS
    parameter
```

The following parameter can be used with this heading:

- **Remotename *number ip_address*** Specifies an IP address on a different broadcast network. This address is preloaded in the NetBIOS name cache. Replace *number* with the number of addresses that should be reloaded in the NetBIOS name cache. Replace *ip_address* with the IP (Internet Protocol) address assigned to this workstation.

Protocol RPL Parameters

Protocol RPL parameters configure the RPL protocol stack.

To use these parameters, add the Protocol RPL heading to the NET.CFG file, and then place each parameter command beneath the heading, indented as shown here.

```
PROTOCOL RPL
    parameter
```

The following parameters can be used with this heading:

- **Bind *driver*** Binds the protocol to an ODI LAN driver that uses the IEEE 802.2 frame type. Use only when running RPL on enhanced Remote Boot PROMs. *Driver* is the LAN driver name or logical board number. Default: RPL binds to the first Ethernet or Token Ring LAN driver it finds.
- **Buffers *number*** Sets the number of receive buffers to configure. Default: 5. Values: 4 to 40.
- **Cache size *number*** Specifies the maximum amount of memory to use for loading the BOOTCONF.SYS file. Default: none.

Protocol SPX Parameters

Protocol SPX parameters configure the SPX protocol.

To use these parameters, add the Protocol SPX heading to the NET.CFG file, and then place each parameter command beneath the heading, indented as shown here.

```
PROTOCOL SPX
    parameter
```

The following parameters can be used with this heading:

- **Minimum spx retries *number*** Sets the minimum number of unacknowledged transmit requests that occur before assuming the connection has failed. Default: 20. Values: 0 to 255.
- **Spx abort timeout *number*** Sets the time, in ticks, that SPX waits for a response before terminating a connection. Default: 540 (approximately 30 seconds).

- **Spx connections *number*** Sets the maximum number of simultaneous SPX connections a workstation can have. Default: 15.
- **Spx listen timeout *number*** Sets the time, in ticks, that SPX waits for a packet before requesting another packet to make sure the connection is still valid. Default: 108 (approximately 6 seconds).
- **Spx verify timeout *number*** Sets the interval, in ticks, between packets that SPX sends to verify a connection is working. Default: 54 (approximately 3 seconds).

Protocol TCPIP Parameters

Protocol TCPIP parameters configure the TCP/IP protocol.

To use these parameters, add the Protocol TCPIP heading to the NET.CFG file, and then place each parameter command beneath the heading, indented as shown here.

```
PROTOCOL TCPIP
    parameter
```

The following parameters can be used with this heading:

- **Bind *driver* [*number frametype network*]** Binds the TCP/IP protocol to a LAN driver. *Driver* is the LAN driver name. *Number* is the board number when you have two boards with the same name. *Frametype* is the frame type for your network connection. *Network* is a descriptive name for this network connection.
- **Ip_address *address* [*name*]** Specifies this workstation's IP address. *Name* is a descriptive name for this network connection.
- **Ip_netmask *address* [*name*]** Specifies this workstation's default subnetwork mask if subnetworks are being used. *Name* is a descriptive name for this network connection.
- **Ip_router *address* [*name*]** Specifies the default router address for all packets being sent to remote networks. *Name* is a descriptive name for this network connection.
- **Nb_adapter [0 or 1]** Sets the network board to use when binding NetBIOS to the TCP/IP protocol stack. Default: 0. Values: 0 = first network board; 1 = second network board.

- **Nb_brdcast [0 or 1]** Sets the format of IP broadcasts sent by the RFCNBIOS.EXE program. Default: 1. Values: 0 = broadcast address uses zeros for the host portions of the IP address; 1 = broadcast address uses 255 for the host portions of the IP address.
- **Nb_commands *number*** Sets the maximum number of asynchronous NetBIOS commands. Default: 8. Values: 0 to 80.
- **Nb_domain *name*** Sets the name of the logical domain for a NetBIOS workstation.
- **Nb_sessions *number*** Specifies the maximum number of simultaneous NetBIOS sessions. Default: 4. Values: 0 to 64.
- **No_bootp** Forces the workstation to bypass any network BOOTP server (which provides TCP/IP configuration data) and use RARP (Reverse Address Resolution Protocol) to identify the workstation's IP address.
- **Path tcp_cfg *path*** Indicates the directories that contain the database configuration files HOSTS, NETWORKS, SERVICES, and RESOLV.CFG. This command works with the same syntax as the DOS PATH command. Default path: C:\NET\TCP.
- **Raw_sockets *number*** Sets the maximum number of raw IP sockets (connections). Default: 1.
- **Tcp_sockets *number*** Sets the maximum number of concurrent TCP (Transmission Control Protocol) sockets (connections). Default: 8. Values: 0 to 64.
- **Udp_sockets *number*** Sets the maximum number of UDP (User Datagram Protocol) sockets (connections). Default: 8. Values: 0 to 32.

TBMI2 Parameters

TBMI2 parameters configure the workstation's task-switching environment. To use these parameters, add the TBMI2 heading to the NET.CFG file, and then place each parameter command beneath the heading, indented as shown here.

```
TBMI2
    parameter
```

The following parameters can be used with this heading:

- **Data ecb count *number*** Sets the number of data ECBs (event control blocks) allocated by DOS programs needing virtualization. Default: 60. Values: 10 to 89.
- **Ecb count *number*** Sets the number of nondata ECBs allocated by DOS programs needing virtualization. Default: 20. Values: 10 to 255.
- **Int64 *on/off*** If set to Off, allows an application to use interrupt 64h. Default: On.
- **Int7a *on/off*** If set to Off, allows an application to use interrupt 7Ah. Default: On.
- **Use max packets** Lets TBMI2 use the maximum IPX packet size.
- **Using windows 3.0** Lets TBMI2 use TASKID, which identifies tasks in each DOS BOX as separate tasks.

Transport Provider IPX (or UDP) Parameter

The Transport Provider parameter lets you specify the trap target address for SNMP desktops. The two Desktop SNMP transport providers, STPUDP.COM and STPIPX.COM, read the configuration file to find trap targets on the network.

To use this parameter, add either the Transport Provider IPX or Transport Provider UDP heading to the NET.CFG file, and then place the parameter command beneath the heading, indented as shown here. (The example shows the Transport Provider IPX heading.)

```
TRANSPORT PROVIDER IPX
     parameter
```

The following parameter can be used with this heading:

- **Trap target *address*** Specifies the management workstation address so that the workstation can receive traps sent by Desktop SNMP. Replace *address* with either the IPX address (for the IPX transport) or the IP address (for the UDP/IP transport) of the management workstation.

APPENDIX B

SET Parameters

When you first install IntranetWare, the operating system is tuned by default so that its performance is optimized for most systems. Occasionally, you may find that your system could benefit by modifying some aspect of the server's operation.

For this reason, you can use numerous parameters to change the way the server handles things such as memory or file locks. These parameters, called SET parameters, can be set in three different ways:

- At the server console, using the SET console command. Parameters set this way are in effect only until the server is rebooted.
- In the server startup files, using STARTUP.NCF and AUTOEXEC.NCF. Parameters set in these files remain in effect when the server is rebooted.
- In SERVMAN.NLM, which enables you to select the parameters you want from menus instead of typing in complete SET commands at the console. SERVMAN.NLM can also automatically update the STARTUP.NCF and AUTOEXEC.NCF files.

In most cases, you probably will not need to change any SET parameters. However, if you need to change them, each SET parameter is explained in this appendix.

The thirteen categories of SET parameters are as follows:

- Communication
- Directory Caching
- Directory Services
- Disk
- Error Handling
- File Caching
- File System
- Locks
- Memory
- Miscellaneous
- NCP
- Time
- Transaction Tracking

The following sections explain the available SET parameters for each of these categories.

Communication Parameters

Communication parameters configure the way the operating system handles communication buffers. The following communication parameters are available:

- **IPX netbios replication option=*number*** Sets how replicated NetBIOS broadcasts are handled by the IPX router. Default: 2. Values: 0 = no replication of broadcasts; 1 = replicate broadcasts (causes duplicate broadcasts when there are redundant routes); 2 = replicate broadcasts, but suppress duplicate broadcasts; 3 = same as 2, but do not replicate to WAN links.

  Can be set in AUTOEXEC.NCF or at the console.

- **Load Balance Local LAN=*on/off*** Turns load balancing on or off. Default: Off.

  Can be set in STARTUP.NCF or at the console.

- **Maximum packet receive buffers=*number*** Sets the maximum number of packet receive buffers the server can allocate. Default: 100. Values: 50 to 4294967295.

  Can be set in STARTUP.NCF, AUTOEXEC.NCF, or at the console.

- **Minimum packet receive buffers=*number*** Sets the minimum number of packet receive buffers that the server can allocate. This number is allocated automatically when the server is booted. Default: 50. Values: 10 to 4294967295.

  Can be set in STARTUP.NCF only.

- **Maximum physical receive packet size=*number*** Sets the largest size of packets that can be transmitted. Default size is acceptable for Ethernet and Token Ring boards. If some boards on the network can transmit more than 512 bytes of data per packet, use the largest packet size. Default: 4202 bytes. Values: 618 to 24682 bytes.

  Can be set in STARTUP.NCF only.

- **Maximum interrupt events=*number*** Sets the maximum number of interrupt time events (such as IPX routing) that occur before a thread switch is guaranteed to have occurred. Default: 10. Values: 1 to 1000000.

  Can be set in AUTOEXEC.NCF or at the console.

- **Reply to get nearest server=*on/off*** When set to On, this server will respond to workstations that request a connection to their nearest server. Default: On.

  Can be set in STARTUP.NCF, AUTOEXEC.NCF, or at the console.

- **Number of watchdog packets=*number*** Sets the number of watchdog packets the server sends to an unresponsive workstation before clearing the workstation's connection. Default: 10. Values: 5 to 100.

  Can be set in AUTOEXEC.NCF or at the console.

- **Delay between watchdog packets=*time*** Sets the time the server waits before sending each watchdog packet. Default: 59.3 sec. Values: 9.9 sec to 10 min 26.2 sec.

  Can be set in AUTOEXEC.NCF or at the console.

- **Delay before first watchdog packet=*time*** Sets the time the server waits before sending the first watchdog packet to an unresponsive workstation. Default: 4 min 56.6 sec. Values: 15.7 sec to 14 days.

  Can be set in AUTOEXEC.NCF or at the console.

- **New packet receive buffer wait time=*seconds*** Sets the time the operating system waits after allocating the minimum number of buffers before granting the next packet receive buffer. Default: 0.1 sec. Values: 0.1 to 20 sec.

  Can be set in AUTOEXEC.NCF or at the console.

- **Use old watchdog packet type=*on/off*** Sets server to use type 0 instead of type 4 watchdog packets. Use this option if you use older router hardware that filters out type 4 IPX packets. Default: Off.

  Can be set in AUTOEXEC.NCF or at the console.

- **Console display watchdog logouts=*on/off*** When set to On, a console message is displayed when a workstation's connection is cleared by the watchdog. Default: Off.

  Can be set in AUTOEXEC.NCF or at the console.

Directory Caching Parameters

Directory Caching parameters enable you to configure how directory cache buffers are used to optimize access to frequently used directories. A *directory cache buffer* is a portion of server memory that holds a directory entry that is accessed frequently. A directory entry held in memory is accessed faster than a directory entry stored on the hard disk. The following Directory Caching parameters are available:

- **Dirty directory cache delay time=*seconds*** Specifies how long a directory table write request is kept in memory before it is written to disk. Default: 0.5 sec. Values: 0 to 10 sec.

  Can be set in AUTOEXEC.NCF or at the console.
- **Maximum concurrent directory cache writes=*number*** Sets the maximum number of write requests that can be stored before the disk head begins a sweep across the disk. Default: 10. Values: 5 to 500.

  Can be set in AUTOEXEC.NCF or at the console.
- **Directory cache allocation wait time=*time*** Specifies how long the server waits after allocating one directory cache buffer before allocating another one. Default: 2.2 sec. Values: 0.5 sec to 2 min.

  Can be set in AUTOEXEC.NCF or at the console.
- **Directory cache buffer nonreferenced delay=*time*** Sets how long a directory entry is held in cache before it is overwritten. Default: 5.5 sec. Values: 1 sec to 5 min.

  Can be set in AUTOEXEC.NCF or at the console.
- **Maximum directory cache buffers=*number*** Sets the maximum number of directory cache buffers that the server can allocate. Prevents the server from allocating so many directory cache buffers that other server processes run out. Default: 500. Values: 20 to 20000.

  Can be set in AUTOEXEC.NCF or at the console.
- **Minimum directory cache buffers=*number*** Sets the minimum number of directory cache buffers to be allocated by the server before the server uses the Directory Cache Allocation Wait Time to determine if another directory cache buffer should be allocated. Allocating buffers too quickly will cause the server to eat up memory resources during peak loads. Waiting too long may cause a delay in file searches. This wait time creates a leveling factor between peak and low access times. Default: 20. Values: 10 to 8000.

  Can be set in AUTOEXEC.NCF or at the console.
- **Maximum number of internal directory handles=*number*** Sets the maximum number of directory handles that are available to internal NLMs that use connection 0. A directory handle is allocated each time

an NLM accesses a file or directory. Allocating directory handles decreases the time required to gain access rights. Default: 100. Values: 40 to 1000.

Can be set in STARTUP.NCF or at the console.

- **Maximum number of directory handles=*number*** Sets the maximum number of directory handles that each connection can obtain. Default: 20. Values: 20 to 1000.

  Can be set in STARTUP.NCF or at the console.

Directory Services Parameters

Directory Services parameters enable you to configure NDS maintenance characteristics. The following NDS parameters are available:

- **NDS trace to screen=*on/off*** When set to On, the NDS trace screen, which displays information about NDS events, is turned on. Default: Off.

  Can be set in AUTOEXEC.NCF or at the console.

- **NDS trace to file=*on/off*** When set to On, the NDS trace information is sent to a file in the SYS:SYSTEM directory, named DSTRACE.DBG by default. Default: Off.

  Can be set in AUTOEXEC.NCF or at the console.

- **NDS trace filename=*path\filename*** Specifies a different path or file name for the NDS trace file. Default: SYSTEM/DSTRACE.DBG.

  Can be set in AUTOEXEC.NCF or at the console.

- **NDS client NCP retries=*number*** Sets the number of NCP retries that are sent before the NDS client is disconnected from a connection. Default: 3. Values: 1 to 20.

  Can be set in AUTOEXEC.NCF or at the console.

- **NDS external reference life span=*hours*** Sets the number of hours that unused external references (local IDs assigned to users when they access other servers) can exist before they are removed. Default: 192. Values: 1 to 384.

  Can be set in AUTOEXEC.NCF or at the console.

- **NDS inactivity synchronization interval=*minutes*** Sets how many minutes can elapse between exhaustive synchronization checks. Set high (up to 240 minutes) if replicas have to synchronize across WAN connections to reduce network traffic. Default: 30. Values: 2 to 1440.

Can be set in AUTOEXEC.NCF or at the console.

- **NDS synchronization restrictions=*on/off, versions*** When set to Off, the server synchronizes with all versions of NDS that are available on the network. When this parameter is set to On, the server synchronizes with only the versions of NDS specified (such as "On, 489, 492"). Default: Off.

  Can be set in AUTOEXEC.NCF or at the console.

- **NDS servers status=*up/down*** Sets the status of all Server objects in the local NDS database as either up or down, so that you can force the network to recognize that a particular server is up when the network thinks it is down. Default: none.

  Can be set in AUTOEXEC.NCF or at the console.

- **NDS janitor interval=*minutes*** Specifies how often, in minutes, the janitor process runs. The janitor process cleans up unused records, reclaims disk space, and purges deleted objects. Default: 60. Values: 1 to 10080.

  Can be set in AUTOEXEC.NCF or at the console.

- **NDS backlink interval=*minutes*** Specifies how often, in minutes, backlink consistency is checked. Backlinks indicate that an object in a replica has an ID on a server where the replica does not exist. Default: 780. Values: 2 to 10080.

  Can be set in AUTOEXEC.NCF or at the console.

- **NDS trace file length to zero=*on/off*** When set to On, the server deletes the contents of the NDS trace file but does not delete the trace file itself. To delete the file contents, also set the NDS Trace to File parameter to On, so that the file will be open for the deletion process. Default: Off.

  Can be set in AUTOEXEC.NCF or at the console.

- **NDS does not synchronize with=*on/off, versions*** When set to On, prevents synchronization with any of the versions of NDS specified. This prevents older, unsupported versions of NDS from corrupting later versions through feature changes and other incompatibilities. Default: On, 290, 291, 296, 332, 463, 477.

  Can be set in AUTOEXEC.NCF or at the console.

- **Check equivalent to me=*on/off*** When set to On, checks a user's Equivalent To Me attribute during authentication. Default: Off.

  Can be set in AUTOEXEC.NCF or at the console.

- **Bindery context=*context;context;...*** Specifies which containers and their objects will be used as the server's "bindery" when the server provides bindery services. You can include up to 16 containers as part of this server's bindery context. Separate each context with a semicolon. Default: The bindery context set for this server during installation, if one was set.

  Can be set in STARTUP.NCF or at the console.

Disk Parameters

Disk parameters enable you to control Hot Fix redirection, which helps protect data on the server from hard disk failures. The following disk parameters are available:

- **Enable disk read after write verify=*on/off*** Specifies whether data written to disk is compared with the data in memory to verify its accuracy. If set to On, this parameter tells the driver to perform the highest level of read-after-write verification that it can. If set to Off, this parameter turns off any form of read-after-write verification that the driver may do. The disk controller may have a built-in function that performs read-after-write verification. If so, leave this parameter set to Off. Default: Off.

  Can be set in STARTUP.NCF, AUTOEXEC.NCF, or at the console.

- **Remirror block size=*number*** Specifies the remirror block size in multiples of 4K. Default: 1 (4K). Values: 1 to 8 (1 = 4K, 2 = 8K, 3 = 12K, and so on).

  Can be set in AUTOEXEC.NCF or at the console.

- **Concurrent remirror requests=*number*** Specifies how many simultaneous remirror requests can occur per logical disk partition. Default: 4. Values: 2 to 32.

  Can be set in STARTUP.NCF only.

- **Mirrored devices are out of sync message frequency=*minutes*** Specifies how often devices are checked for out-of-sync status. Default: 30. Values: 5 to 9999.

Can be set in STARTUP.NCF, AUTOEXEC.NCF, or at the console.

- **Sequential elevator depth=*number*** Sets the maximum number of sequential requests that the Media Manager will send to the same device. If another device in the mirror group is idle when the first device contains this number of requests, Media Manager will begin sending requests to the idle device. Default: 8. Values: 0 to 4294967295.

  Can be set in STARTUP.NCF, AUTOEXEC.NCF, or at the console.

- **Ignore disk geometry=*on/off*** When set to On, allows the creation of nonstandard and unsupported partitions on the server's hard disk. Default: Off.

  Can be set in STARTUP.NCF, AUTOEXEC.NCF, or at the console.

- **Enable IO handicap attribute=*on/off*** When set to On, allows drivers and applications to set and use an attribute to inhibit (or handicap) read requests from one or more devices. When turned off, NetWare is able to treat the device like any other device. Do not turn this parameter on unless instructed to by the manufacturer. Default: Off.

  Can be set in STARTUP.NCF, AUTOEXEC.NCF, or at the console.

Error Handling Parameters

Error Handling parameters let you manage the server, volume, and TTS error log files. The server log file is named SYS$LOG.ERR. The volume log file is named VOL$LOG.ERR. The TTS log file is named TTS$LOG.ERR. The following parameters are available:

- **Server log file state=*number*** Specifies what action to take when the log file reaches its maximum size. Default: 1. Values: 0 = take no action; 1 = delete the log file; 2 = rename the log file.

  Can be set in STARTUP.NCF, AUTOEXEC.NCF, or at the console.

- **Volume log file state=*number*** Specifies what action to take when the log file reaches its maximum size. Default: 1. Values: 0 = take no action; 1 = delete the log file; 2 = rename the log file.

  Can be set in STARTUP.NCF, AUTOEXEC.NCF, or at the console.

- **Volume TTS log file state=*number*** Specifies what action to take when the log file reaches its maximum size. Default: 1. Values: 0 = take no action; 1 = delete the log file; 2 = rename the log file.

Can be set in STARTUP.NCF, AUTOEXEC.NCF, or at the console.

- **Server log file overflow size=*number*** Specifies the maximum size (in bytes) of the log file. Default: 4194304. Values: 65536 to 4294967295.

  Can be set in STARTUP.NCF, AUTOEXEC.NCF, or at the console.

- **Volume log file overflow size=*number*** Specifies the maximum size (in bytes) of the log file. Default: 4194304. Values: 65536 to 4294967295.

  Can be set in STARTUP.NCF, AUTOEXEC.NCF, or at the console.

- **Volume TTS log file overflow size=*number*** Specifies the maximum size (in bytes) of the log file. Default: 4194304. Values: 65536 to 4294967295.

  Can be set in STARTUP.NCF, AUTOEXEC.NCF, or at the console.

- **Enable deadlock detection=*on/off*** When set to On, detects deadlocks in the SMP spin lock code. Only use when debugging an NLM because results may be in error depending on the hardware and the behavior of the spin locks. Default: Off.

  Can be set in STARTUP.NCF, AUTOEXEC.NCF, or at the console.

- **Auto restart after abend delay time=*number*** Sets the time, in minutes, that the server will wait before automatically shutting down and restarting after an abend occurs. Default: 2. Values: 2 to 60.

  Can be set in STARTUP.NCF, AUTOEXEC.NCF, or at the console.

- **Auto restart after abend=*number*** Determines whether the server automatically shuts down and restarts itself if an abend occurs. Default: 1. Values: 0 = the server does not restart itself; 1 = the server determines the abend's cause and then either keeps the computer running or shuts it down and restarts; 2 = the server always shuts down and restarts.

  Can be set in STARTUP.NCF, AUTOEXEC.NCF, or at the console.

File Caching Parameters

File Caching parameters enable you to configure how file cache buffers are used to optimize access to frequently used files. A file cache buffer is a portion of server memory that holds a file or portion of a file that is accessed frequently. A file in memory is accessed faster than a file on the hard disk. The following File Caching parameters are available:

- **Read ahead enabled=*on/off*** When set to On, background reads can be done during sequential file access so that blocks are placed into the cache before they are requested. Default: On.

  Can be set in AUTOEXEC.NCF or at the console.

- **Read ahead LRU sitting time threshold=*time*** Sets the time the server will wait before doing a read ahead. (LRU means Least Recently Used.) Default: 10 sec. Values: 0 sec to 1 hour.

  Can be set in AUTOEXEC.NCF or at the console.

- **Minimum file cache buffers=*number*** Sets the minimum number of cache buffers that must be reserved for file caching. Default: 20. Values: 20 to 2000.

  Can be set in AUTOEXEC.NCF or at the console.

- **Maximum concurrent disk cache writes=*number*** Sets the maximum number of write requests that can be stored before the disk head begins a sweep across the disk. Default: 50. Values: 10 to 4000.

  Can be set in AUTOEXEC.NCF or at the console.

- **Dirty disk cache delay time=*seconds*** Sets how long the server will keep a write request in memory before writing it to the disk. Default: 3.3 sec. Values: 0.1 sec to 10 sec.

  Can be set in AUTOEXEC.NCF or at the console.

- **Minimum file cache report threshold=*number*** Sets how close to the minimum number of allowed buffers the system can drop before a warning message is sent. Default: 20. Values: 0 to 2000.

  Can be set in AUTOEXEC.NCF or at the console.

File System Parameters

File System parameters enable you to configure components of the file system, such as volume disk space warnings, file purging, and file compression. The following parameters are available:

- **Minimum file delete wait time=*time*** Specifies how long a deleted file must be stored before it can be purged. Default: 1 min 5.9 sec. Values: 0 sec to 7 days.

  Can be set in AUTOEXEC.NCF or at the console.

- **File delete wait time=*time*** Sets the maximum amount of time a deleted file must be stored in a salvageable state. After this time has elapsed, the file can be purged if the space is needed. Default: 5 min 29.6 sec. Values: 0 sec to 7 days.

  Can be set in AUTOEXEC.NCF or at the console.
- **Allow deletion of active directories=*on/off*** When set to On, a directory can be deleted even if a user has a drive mapped to it. Default: On.

  Can be set in AUTOEXEC.NCF or at the console.
- **Maximum percent of volume space allowed for extended attributes=*number*** Limits the percentage of disk space that can be used to store extended attributes. Default: 10. Values: 5 to 50.

  Can be set in STARTUP.NCF, AUTOEXEC.NCF, or at the console.
- **Maximum extended attributes per file or path=*number*** Specifies the maximum number of extended attributes that can be assigned to a file or a subdirectory (path) on any of the server's volumes. Default: 16. Values: 4 to 512.

  Can be set in AUTOEXEC.NCF or at the console.
- **Fast volume mounts=*on/off*** When set to On, allows the server to mount volumes more quickly by not checking certain, less important fields. Turn this parameter on only if the volume was dismounted normally the last time. Default: On.

  Can be set in STARTUP.NCF, AUTOEXEC.NCF, or at the console.
- **Maximum percent of volume used by directory=*number*** Limits the percentage of disk space that can be used as directory space. Default: 13. Values: 5 to 85.

  Can be set in AUTOEXEC.NCF or at the console.
- **Immediate purge of deleted files=*on/off*** Specifies whether files are purged immediately when they are deleted or stored in a salvageable state. If set to On, this parameter purges deleted files immediately, and they cannot be salvaged. Default: Off.

  Can be set in AUTOEXEC.NCF or at the console.
- **Maximum subdirectory tree depth=*number*** Sets the maximum level of subdirectories the server can support. Default: 25. Values: 10 to 100.

  Can be set in STARTUP.NCF only.

- **Volume low warn all users=*on/off*** When set to On, all users are notified when the free space on a volume reaches a minimum level. Default: On.

  Can be set in AUTOEXEC.NCF or at the console.

- **Volume low warning reset threshold=*number*** Specifies the number of disk blocks above the Volume Low Warning Threshold value that must be freed up to reset the low volume warning. This parameter controls how often you receive the low volume warning if your free space is fluctuating around the threshold. Default: 256. Values: 0 to 100000.

  Can be set in AUTOEXEC.NCF or at the console.

- **Volume low warning threshold=*number*** Sets the minimum amount of free space (in blocks) that a volume can have before it issues a warning that it is low on space. Default: 256. Values: 0 to 1000000.

  Can be set in AUTOEXEC.NCF or at the console.

- **Turbo FAT re-use wait time=*time*** Sets how long a turbo FAT (File Allocation Table) buffer stays in memory after an indexed file is closed. Default: 5 min 29.6 sec. Values: 0.3 sec to 1 hour 5 min 54.6 sec.

  Can be set in AUTOEXEC.NCF or at the console.

- **Compression daily check stop hour=*hour*** Specifies the hour when the file compressor stops searching volumes for files that need to be compressed. If this value is the same as the Compression Daily Check Starting Hour value, the search starts at the specified starting hour and continues until all compressible files have been found. Default: 6 (6:00 a.m.). Values: 0 (midnight) to 23 (11:00 p.m.).

  Can be set in STARTUP.NCF, AUTOEXEC.NCF, or at the console.

- **Compression daily check starting hour=*hour*** Specifies the hour when the file compressor begins searching volumes for files that need to be compressed. Default: 0 (midnight). Values: 0 to 23 (11:00 p.m.).

  Can be set in STARTUP.NCF, AUTOEXEC.NCF, or at the console.

- **Minimum compression percentage gain=*number*** Specifies the minimum percentage that a file must be able to be compressed in order to remain compressed. Default: 20. Values: 0 to 50.

  Can be set in STARTUP.NCF, AUTOEXEC.NCF, or at the console.

- **Enable file compression=*on/off*** When set to On, file compression is allowed to occur on volumes that were previously enabled for compression during installation. (Just because a volume is enabled for compression doesn't mean compression will actually occur. This parameter must be turned on for compression to occur. For more information about file compression, see Chapter 8.) Default: On.

  Can be set in STARTUP.NCF, AUTOEXEC.NCF, or at the console.

- **Maximum concurrent compressions=*number*** Specifies how many volumes can compress files at the same time. Increasing this value may slow down server performance during compression times. Default: 2. Values: 1 to 8.

  Can be set in STARTUP.NCF, AUTOEXEC.NCF, or at the console.

- **Convert compressed to uncompressed option=*number*** Specifies how a compressed file is stored after it has been accessed. Default: 1. Values: 0 = always leave the file compressed; 1 = leave the file compressed after the first access within the time frame defined by the Days Untouched Before Compression parameter; then leave the file uncompressed after the second access. 2 = change the file to uncompressed after the first access.

  Can be set in STARTUP.NCF, AUTOEXEC.NCF, or at the console.

- **Decompress percent disk space free to allow commit=*number*** Specifies the percentage of free disk space that is required on a volume before committing an uncompressed file to disk. This helps you avoid running out of disk space by uncompressing files. Default: 10. Values: 0 to 75.

  Can be set in STARTUP.NCF, AUTOEXEC.NCF, or at the console.

- **Decompress free space warning interval=*time*** Specifies the interval between warnings when the volume doesn't have enough disk space for uncompressed files. Default: 31 min 18.5 sec. Values: 0 sec (which turns off warnings) to 29 days 15 hours, 50 min 3.8 sec.

  Can be set in STARTUP.NCF, AUTOEXEC.NCF, or at the console.

- **Deleted files compression option=*number*** Specifies how the server handles deleted files. Default: 1. Values: 0 = don't compress deleted files; 1 = compress deleted files during the next day's search; 2 = compress deleted files immediately.

  Can be set in STARTUP.NCF, AUTOEXEC.NCF, or at the console.

- **Days untouched before compression=*days*** Specifies how many days a file or directory must remain untouched before being compressed. Default: 14. Values: 0 to 100000.

  Can be set in STARTUP.NCF, AUTOEXEC.NCF, or at the console.
- **Allow unowned files to be extended=*on/off*** When set to On, files can be changed even if their owner has been deleted. Default: On.

  Can be set in STARTUP.NCF, AUTOEXEC.NCF, or at the console.

Locks Parameters

Locks parameters enable you to configure how workstations and the server work with file and record locks. The following parameters are available:

- **Maximum record locks per connection=*number*** Sets the number of record locks a workstation can use simultaneously. Default: 500. Values: 10 to 100000.

  Can be set in AUTOEXEC.NCF or at the console.
- **Maximum file locks per connection=*number*** Sets the number of opened and locked files a workstation can use simultaneously. Default: 250. Values: 10 to 1000.

  Can be set in AUTOEXEC.NCF or at the console.
- **Maximum record locks=*number*** Sets the number of record locks the server can support simultaneously. Default: 20000. Values: 100 to 400000.

  Can be set in AUTOEXEC.NCF or at the console.
- **Maximum file locks=*number*** Sets how many opened and locked files the server can support simultaneously. Default: 10000. Values: 100 to 100000.

  Can be set in AUTOEXEC.NCF or at the console.

Memory Parameters

Memory parameters let you configure how the server's memory is managed. The following parameters are available:

- **Allow invalid pointers=*on/off*** When set to On, invalid pointers are allowed to map in a nonexistent page with only one notification.

Default: Off.

Can be set in STARTUP.NCF, AUTOEXEC.NCF, or at the console.

- **Read fault notification=*on/off*** When set to On, the console and error log file are notified of emulated read page faults. Default: On.

  Can be set in STARTUP.NCF, AUTOEXEC.NCF, or at the console.
- **Read fault emulation=*on/off*** When set to On, specifies that a read that occurs from a nonpresent page is emulated. Default: Off.

  Can be set in STARTUP.NCF, AUTOEXEC.NCF, or at the console.
- **Write fault notification=*on/off*** When set to On, the console and error log file are notified of emulated write page faults. Default: On.

  Can be set in STARTUP.NCF, AUTOEXEC.NCF, or at the console.
- **Write fault emulation=*on/off*** When set to On, specifies that a write that occurs from a nonpresent page is emulated. Default: Off.

  Can be set in STARTUP.NCF, AUTOEXEC.NCF, or at the console.
- **Garbage collection interval=*time*** Sets the maximum time between garbage collections. Default: 15 min. Values: 1 min to 1 hour.

  Can be set in STARTUP.NCF, AUTOEXEC.NCF, or at the console.
- **Number of frees for garbage collection=*number*** Sets the minimum number of times memory must be freed up before a garbage collection can occur. Default: 5000. Values: 100 to 100000.

  Can be set in STARTUP.NCF, AUTOEXEC.NCF, or at the console.
- **Minimum free memory for garbage collection=*bytes*** Sets the fewest number of free allocation bytes required for garbage collection. Default: 8000. Values: 1000 to 1000000.

  Can be set in STARTUP.NCF, AUTOEXEC.NCF, or at the console.
- **Alloc memory check flag=*on/off*** When set to On, the server is set to do corruption checking in the alloc memory nodes. Default: Off.

  Can be set in STARTUP.NCF, AUTOEXEC.NCF, or at the console.
- **Auto register memory above 16 megabytes=*on/off*** When set to On, the server automatically adds memory above 16MB that can be detected on EISA-bus computers. This parameter should be set to Off if you are using a network board or disk controller board that uses an online DMS or AT bus. Default: On.

  Can be set in STARTUP.NCF only.

- **Reserved buffers below 16 meg=*number*** Sets a number of cache buffers in lower memory for device drivers that cannot access memory above 16MB. Default: 200. Values: 8 to 300.

  Can be set in STARTUP.NCF only.

Miscellaneous Parameters

The Miscellaneous parameters set a variety of server options. The following parameters are available:

- **Command line prompt default choice=*on/off*** Sets the default input for the "?" (conditional execution) console command. Default: On. Values: On (for Y) and Off (for N).

  Can be set in STARTUP.NCF, AUTOEXEC.NCF, or at the console.

- **Command line prompt time out=*seconds*** Sets the number of seconds the command line ? command prompt will wait before using the default answer. If set to zero, the prompt will not time out. Default: 10. Values: 0 to 4294967295.

  Can be set in STARTUP.NCF, AUTOEXEC.NCF, or at the console.

- **Sound bell for alerts=*on/off*** When set to On, a sound emits whenever an alert message appears on the server's console screen. Default: On.

  Can be set in AUTOEXEC.NCF or at the console.

- **Replace console prompt with server name=*on/off*** When set to On, the server's name is displayed as the console prompt on the server's screen. Default: On.

  Can be set in STARTUP.NCF, AUTOEXEC.NCF, or at the console.

- **Alert message nodes=*number*** Determines how many alert message nodes are preallocated. Default: 20. Values: 10 to 256.

  Can be set in STARTUP.NCF, AUTOEXEC.NCF, or at the console.

- **Worker thread execute in a row count=*number*** Determines how many times in a row the scheduler dispatches new work before allowing other threads to execute. Default: 10. Values: 1 to 20.

  Can be set in AUTOEXEC.NCF or at the console.

- **Halt system on invalid parameters=*on/off*** When set to On, the system stops whenever invalid parameters or conditions are detected.

When this parameter is set to Off, the system displays an alert message but continues running if an invalid parameter is detected. Default: Off.

Can be set in STARTUP.NCF, AUTOEXEC.NCF, or at the console.

- **Upgrade low priority threads=*on/off*** When set to On, low-priority threads are scheduled at regular priority. Some modules can freeze low-priority threads, which may cause problems such as shutting down file compression. Default: Off.

  Can be set in AUTOEXEC.NCF or at the console.

- **Display relinquish control alerts=*on/off*** When set to On, messages are displayed when an NLM uses the server's processor for more than 0.4 seconds without giving up control to other processes. This command is useful if you are writing your own NLMs and want to see if your NLM is using the CPU correctly. Default: Off.

  Can be set in STARTUP.NCF, AUTOEXEC.NCF, or at the console.

- **Display incomplete IPX packet alerts=*on/off*** When set to On, alert messages are displayed when IPX receives incomplete packets. Default: On.

  Can be set in STARTUP.NCF, AUTOEXEC.NCF, or at the console.

- **Display old API names=*on/off*** When set to On, messages are displayed when API calls from older versions of NetWare are used by an NLM. If you receive these messages, you may want to contact the NLM's manufacturer for an upgrade that uses the faster, newer APIs. Default: Off.

  Can be set in STARTUP.NCF, AUTOEXEC.NCF, or at the console.

- **CPU hog timeout amount=*time*** Sets the amount of time the system waits before terminating a process that has not relinquished control of the CPU. If set to zero, this option is disabled. Default: 1 min. Values: 0 sec to 1 hour.

  Can be set in STARTUP.NCF, AUTOEXEC.NCF, or at the console.

- **Developer option=*on/off*** When set to On, options that are associated with a developer environment are enabled. Default: Off.

  Can be set in STARTUP.NCF, AUTOEXEC.NCF, or at the console.

- **Display spurious interrupt alerts=*on/off*** When set to On, error messages are displayed when the server hardware creates an interrupt that has been reserved for another device's interface board. If you receive this error, remove all add-on boards and run SERVER.EXE (the

NetWare operating system). If the message doesn't appear after you remove everything, add the boards one at a time until you locate the board that is generating the message. Then contact the board's vendor or manufacturer for assistance. Default: On.

Can be set in STARTUP.NCF, AUTOEXEC.NCF, or at the console.

- **Display lost interrupt alerts=*on/off*** When set to On, error messages are displayed when a driver or board makes an interrupt call but drops the request before it's filled. To identify the problem driver, unload all drivers, and then reload them one at a time. When you locate the driver that is generating the message, contact the driver's manufacturer. Default: Off.

  Can be set in STARTUP.NCF, AUTOEXEC.NCF, or at the console.

- **Pseudo preemption count=*number*** Sets how many times threads can make file read or write system calls before they are forced to relinquish control. Default: 10. Values: 1 to 4294967295.

  Can be set in AUTOEXEC.NCF or at the console.

- **Global pseudo preemption=*on/off*** When set to On, all threads are forced to use pseudo preemption. Default: Off.

  Can be set in AUTOEXEC.NCF or at the console.

- **Minimum service processes=*number*** Sets the minimum number of service processes the server can allocate without waiting for the amount of time specified in the New Service Process Wait Time parameter. Default: 10. Values: 10 to 500.

  Can be set in AUTOEXEC.NCF or at the console.

- **Maximum service processes=*number*** Sets the maximum number of service processes the server can create. Increase this parameter if the number of service processes (as shown in MONITOR.NLM) is at the maximum. Default: 50. Values: 5 to 1000.

  Can be set in AUTOEXEC.NCF or at the console.

- **New service process wait time=*seconds*** Determines how long the server waits to allocate another service process after receiving an NCP request. If a service process is freed up during this time, a new one will not be allocated. Default: 2.2 sec. Values: 0.3 to 20 sec.

  Can be set in AUTOEXEC.NCF or at the console.

- **Automatically repair bad volumes=*on/off*** When set to On, VREPAIR will run automatically on a volume that fails to mount. Default: On.

Can be set in STARTUP.NCF, AUTOEXEC.NCF, or at the console.

- **Enable SECURE.NCF=*on/off*** When set to On, causes the SECURE.NCF file to be executed when the server boots. This file is used to set configuration parameters necessary for a C2-security compliant system. See the NetWare security documentation for more information. Default: Off.

  Can be set in STARTUP.NCF, AUTOEXEC.NCF, or at the console.

- **Allow audit passwords=*on/off*** When set to On, allows audit password requests to be used. Default: Off.

  Can be set in AUTOEXEC.NCF or at the console.

- **Allow unencrypted passwords=*on/off*** When set to On, the server will accept unencrypted passwords. Turn on this parameter only if your network includes servers running NetWare 2.11 or earlier. If you have servers running NetWare 2.12 or 2.2, copy the NetWare 3.1*x* utilities to those servers and leave this parameter off, so that passwords will be encrypted. Default: Off.

  Can be set in AUTOEXEC.NCF or at the console.

NCP Parameters

NCP (NetWare Core Protocol) parameters enable you to configure NCP packets, control boundary checking, and change NCP Packet Signature security levels on the server. The following parameters are available:

- **NCP file commit=*on/off*** When set to On, an application is allowed to issue a File Commit NCP and flush the file immediately from cache to disk. Default: On.

  Can be set in AUTOEXEC.NCF or at the console.

- **Display NCP bad component warnings=*on/off*** When set to On, NCP bad component alert messages are displayed. Default: Off.

  Can be set in STARTUP.NCF, AUTOEXEC.NCF, or at the console.

- **Reject NCP packets with bad component=*on/off*** When set to On, the server rejects NCP packets that fail component checking. Default: Off.

  Can be set in STARTUP.NCF, AUTOEXEC.NCF, or at the console.

- **Display NCP bad length warnings=*on/off*** When set to On, NCP bad-length alert messages are displayed. Default: Off.

Can be set in STARTUP.NCF, AUTOEXEC.NCF, or at the console.

- **Reject NCP packets with bad lengths=*on/off*** When set to On, the server rejects NCP packets that fail boundary checking. Default: Off.

  Can be set in STARTUP.NCF, AUTOEXEC.NCF, or at the console.

- **Maximum outstanding NCP searches=*number*** Determines the maximum number of NCP directory searches that can be performed at the same time. Default: 51. Values: 10 to 1000.

  Can be set in AUTOEXEC.NCF or at the console.

- **NCP packet signature option=*number*** Sets the server's NCP Packet Signature security level. See Chapter 7 for more information about NCP Packet Signature levels. Default: 1. Values: 0 to 3.

  Can be set in STARTUP.NCF, AUTOEXEC.NCF, or at the console.

- **Enable IPX checksums=*number*** Sets the IPX checksum level. Default: 1. Values: 0 = no checksums; 1 = checksums performed if enabled on the client; 2 = checksums required.

  Can be set in STARTUP.NCF, AUTOEXEC.NCF, or at the console.

- **Allow change to client rights=*on/off*** When set to On, a job server is allowed to assume a client's rights for NCP Packet Signature. If you are concerned that a job or print server may forge packets, turn off this parameter. Default: On.

  Can be set in STARTUP.NCF, AUTOEXEC.NCF, or at the console.

- **Allow LIP=*on/off*** When set to On, support for Large Internet Packets is enabled. Default: On.

  Can be set in STARTUP.NCF, AUTOEXEC.NCF, or at the console.

Time Parameters

Initially, you set up time services on the server during installation. Time services are controlled by TIMESYNC.NLM, which is loaded automatically when the server is started up. To modify time synchronization after installation, you can use the Time and Time Synchronization SET parameters.

Depending on which time-related SET parameters you are modifying, you may need to add them to either AUTOEXEC.NCF or to the time synchronization file, TIMESYNC.CFG, if you want them to be in effect when the server is rebooted.

All SET parameters that start with the word "TIMESYNC" must be added to the TIMESYNC.CFG file. The others can be added to AUTOEXEC.NCF. With most of the parameters, you can modify the appropriate file using SERVMAN.NLM, but a few of the parameters must be added directly to TIMESYNC.CFG using EDIT.NLM instead of SERVMAN. This information is indicated in the list shown here.

The following parameters are available:

- **Timesync add time source=*server*** Specifies which server should be used as a time source.

  Can be set in TIMESYNC.CFG only, using either SERVMAN or EDIT.

- **Timesync configuration file=*path\filename*** Specifies the directory and file name of the time synchronization configuration file if it is not SYS:SYSTEM\TIMESYNC.CFG.

  Can be set in TIMESYNC.CFG only, using either SERVMAN or EDIT.

- **Timesync configured sources=*on/off*** When set to On, the server ignores SAP (Service Advertising Protocol) time sources and instead accepts time sources configured with the TIMESYNC Time Source parameter. When this parameter is set to Off, it causes the server to listen to any advertising time source. Default: Off.

  Can be set in TIMESYNC.CFG only, using either SERVMAN or EDIT.

- **Timesync directory tree mode=*on/off*** When set to On, time synchronization ignores SAP (Service Advertising Protocol) packets that don't originate from within the server's Directory tree. When this parameter is set to Off, the server accepts SAP packets from any time source on the network, regardless of the tree from which it originates. If SAP is turned on, this parameter should also be set to On. Default: On.

  Can be set in TIMESYNC.CFG only, using either SERVMAN or EDIT.

- **Timesync hardware clock=*on/off*** When set to On, Primary and Secondary time servers set the hardware clock, and Single Reference and Reference servers set their time from the hardware clock at the start of each polling interval. Only set this parameter to Off if this server uses an external time source such as a radio clock. Default: On.

  Can be set in TIMESYNC.CFG only, using either SERVMAN or EDIT.

- **Timesync polling count=*number*** Determines the number of time packets to exchange while polling. Increasing this number may increase unnecessary traffic on the network. Default: 3. Values: 1 to 1000.

  Can be set in TIMESYNC.CFG only, using either SERVMAN or EDIT.

- **Timesync polling interval=*seconds*** Determines the polling interval in seconds. All servers in the tree must use the same polling interval. Default: 600. Values: 10 to 2678400 (31 days).

  Can be set in TIMESYNC.CFG only, using either SERVMAN or EDIT.

- **Timesync remove time source=*server*** Removes a server from the time source list, thus preventing it from being a time source.

  Can be set in TIMESYNC.CFG only, using EDIT.NLM only.

- **Timesync reset=*on/off*** When set to On, all servers are removed from the time source list, and time synchronization is reset. The parameter automatically resets itself to Off. Default: Off.

  Can be set in TIMESYNC.CFG only, using EDIT.NLM only.

- **Timesync restart flag=*on/off*** When set to On, you can reload TIMESYNC.NLM without rebooting the server. Default: Off.

  Can be set in TIMESYNC.CFG only, using either SERVMAN or EDIT.

- **Timesync service advertising=*on/off*** When set to On, SAP (Service Advertising Protocol) is turned on, meaning Single Reference, Reference, and Primary time sources advertise using SAP. Only set this parameter to Off if you are configuring a custom list of time sources. Default: On.

  Can be set in TIMESYNC.CFG only, using either SERVMAN or EDIT.

- **Timesync synchronization radius=*milliseconds*** Determines the maximum time (in milliseconds) that a server is allowed to vary from the synchronized time while still being considered synchronized. Do not set this parameter for under 2 seconds (2000 milliseconds) unless you have an application that uses synchronized timestamps that will not tolerate a 2-second deviation between time sources. Default: 2000. Values: 0 to 2147483647.

  Can be set in TIMESYNC.CFG only, using either SERVMAN or EDIT.

- **Timesync time adjustment=*+or- hour:minute:second [at month/day/year hour:minute:second]*** Determines when a time adjustment will take place. This parameter does not apply to Secondary time servers. Use sparingly to correct networkwide time errors. Overuse can corrupt time synchronization. The default date and time is six polling intervals or one hour (whichever is longer) from the current time. Default: None scheduled.

  Can be set in TIMESYNC.CFG only, using either SERVMAN or EDIT.

- **Timesync time source=*server*** Specifies a server as a time source. If used at the console, and no server name is entered, the parameter displays the list of configured servers.

  Can be set in TIMESYNC.CFG only, using either SERVMAN or EDIT.

- **Timesync type=*type*** Specifies the type (Reference, Primary, and so on) of the default time source. Default: Single (for Single Reference). Values: Single, Reference, Primary, or Secondary.

  Can be set in TIMESYNC.CFG only, using either SERVMAN or EDIT.

- **Timesync write parameters=*on/off*** When set to On, parameters specified by the TIMESYNC Write Value parameter are written to the TIMESYNC.CFG file. Default: Off.

  Can be set in TIMESYNC.CFG only, using either SERVMAN or EDIT.

- **Timesync write value=*number*** Specifies which parameters are written by the TIMESYNC Write Parameters parameter to the TIMESYNC.CFG file. Default: 3. Values: 1 = write internal parameters only; 2 = write configured time sources only; 3 = write both parameters and configured time sources.

  Can be set in TIMESYNC.CFG only, using either SERVMAN or EDIT.

- **Time zone=*zone*** Specifies the abbreviation for this server's time zone, its offset from UTC (Universal Coordinated Time, which used to be called Greenwich Mean Time), and the abbreviation for this server's time zone that is used when daylight saving time is in effect. Example: *zone* is MST7MDT for Mountain Standard Time in the U.S.A. Mountain Standard Time is offset 7 hours from UTC, and the abbreviation used when daylight saving time is in effect is MDT.

  Can be set in STARTUP.NCF, AUTOEXEC.NCF, or at the console.

- **Default time server type=*type*** Specifies the type of time server for this server. Values: Single (for Single Reference), Reference, Primary, or Secondary.

  Can be set in STARTUP.NCF, AUTOEXEC.NCF, or at the console.

- **Start of daylight savings time=*date time*** Indicates the day that daylight saving time begins locally. (You must also set the ending date with the End of Daylight Savings Time parameter.) To specify the beginning of daylight saving time so that it recurs every year, enclose the date and time in parentheses, and use the following format: (April Sunday First 2:00:00 a.m.).If you do not enclose the date in parentheses, the change will occur only in the current year. "April Sunday First" indicates that the change occurs on the first Sunday in April. Default: (April Sunday First 2:00:00 a.m.).

Can be set in AUTOEXEC.NCF or at the console.

- **End of daylight savings time=*date time*** Indicates the day that daylight saving time ends locally. (You must also set the starting date with the Start of Daylight Savings Time parameter.) To specify the end of daylight saving time so that it recurs every year, enclose the date and time in parentheses, and use the following format: (October Sunday Last 2:00:00 a.m.).If you do not enclose the date in parentheses, the change will occur only in the current year. "October Sunday Last" indicates that the change occurs on the last Sunday in October. Default: (October Sunday Last 2:00:00 a.m.).

  Can be set in AUTOEXEC.NCF or at the console.

- **Daylight savings time offset=*+or- hour:minute:second*** Specifies the offset applied to time calculations when daylight saving time is in effect, causing UTC time to be recalculated from local time. Default: +1:00:00.

  Can be set in STARTUP.NCF, AUTOEXEC.NCF, or at the console.

- **Daylight savings time status=*on/off*** When set to On, this parameter indicates that daylight saving time is currently in effect. If this parameter is set to On, also set the Daylight Savings Time Offset parameter. Changing this parameter does not change the local time on the server.

  Can be set in STARTUP.NCF, AUTOEXEC.NCF, or at the console.

- **New time with daylight savings time status=*on/off*** When set to On, the local time on the server is adjusted by adding or subtracting the time indicated in the Daylight Savings Time Offset parameter. Default: Off.

  Can be set in AUTOEXEC.NCF or at the console.

Transaction Tracking Parameters

Transaction Tracking parameters enable you to configure NetWare's Transaction Tracking System. The following parameters are available:

- **Auto TTS backout flag=*on/off*** When set to On, incomplete transactions can be backed out automatically when a downed server is rebooted. Default: On.

  Can be set in STARTUP.NCF only.

- **TTS abort dump flag=*on/off*** When set to On, the TTS$LOG.ERR file is created to record backout data in the event of a failure. Default: Off.

  Can be set in AUTOEXEC.NCF or at the console.

- **Maximum transactions=*number*** Specifies how many transactions can occur simultaneously across all connections. Default: 10000. Values: 100 to 10000.

  Can be set in AUTOEXEC.NCF or at the console.

- **TTS unwritten cache wait time=*time*** Sets the time that a block of transactional data can be held in memory. Default: 1 min 5.9 sec. Values: 11 sec to 10 min 59.1 sec.

  Can be set in AUTOEXEC.NCF or at the console.

- **TTS backout file truncation wait time=*time*** Sets the minimum amount of time that allocated blocks remain available for the TTS backout file. Default 59 min 19.2 sec. Values: 1 min 5.9 sec to 1 day 2 hours 21 min 51.3 sec.

APPENDIX C

Sources of More Information and Help

Whenever a product becomes as popular and as widely used as NetWare, an entire support industry crops up around it. If you are looking for more information about NetWare, you're in luck. You can go to a variety of places for help.

NetWare information is as local as your bookstore or local user group, and as international as the Internet forums that focus on NetWare. It can be as informal as an article in a magazine, or as structured as a college course. This appendix describes the ways you can get more information or technical support for NetWare:

- General Novell product information
- Novell on the Internet
- Novell technical support
- The *Novell Support Encyclopedia*
- DeveloperNet, Novell's developer support
- *Novell Application Notes*
- Novell Education classes and CNE certification
- NetWare Users International (NUI)
- Network Professional Association (NPA)

General Novell Product Information

The main Novell information number, 1-800-NETWARE, is your inroad to all types of information about Novell or its products.

By calling this number, you can obtain information about Novell products, the locations of your nearest resellers, pricing information, technical support (see the section "Novell Technical Support" later in this chapter), and so on.

To order the printed manuals for IntranetWare, you can use the order form that came in your IntranetWare box, or you can call 800-336-3892 (in the United States) or 512-834-6905.

Novell on the Internet

There is a tremendous amount of information about Novell and NetWare products, both official and unofficial, on the Internet. Officially, you can obtain the latest information about Novell from Novell's web site on the Internet.

Unofficially, there are several active user forums that deal specifically with NetWare or generally with computers. There are also Novell forums on CompuServe.

The Novell Internet and CompuServe forums offer users access to a wide variety of information and files dealing with NetWare and other Novell products, such as GroupWise. You can receive information such as technical advice from sysops (system operators) and other users, updated files and drivers, and the latest patches and workarounds for known problems in Novell products.

The Novell site also provides a database of technical information from the Novell Technical Support division, as well as information about programs such as Novell Education classes and NetWare Users International (NUI). There is also marketing and sales information about the various products that Novell produces.

The Novell site is managed by Novell employees and by sysops who have extensive knowledge about NetWare. Public forums can be quite active, with many experienced users offering advice to those with problems.

To get technical help, post a message and address it to the sysops. (Don't send the sysops a personal e-mail message asking for help — the public forums are the approved avenue for help.)

To access Novell information on CompuServe, you need a CompuServe account. There is no additional monthly fee for using the Novell forums, although you are charged the connection fee (at an hourly rate) for accessing the service (GO NETWIRE).

If you have a connection to the Internet, you can access The Novell site through one of the following communication options:

- World Wide Web: http://www.novell.com/
- Gopher: gopher.novell.com
- File Transfer Protocol (FTP): anonymous FTP to ftp.novell.com

(Users in Europe should replace .com with .de.)

Novell Technical Support

If you encounter a problem with your network that you can't solve on your own, there are several places you can go for help:

- Try calling your reseller or consultant.
- Go online and see if anyone in the online forums or Usenet forums knows about the problem or can offer a solution. The knowledge of

people in those forums is broad and deep. Don't hesitate to take advantage of it and don't forget to return the favor if you know some tidbit that might help others.

- Call Novell technical support. You may want to reserve this as a last resort simply because Novell technical support charges a fee for each incident (an incident may involve more than one phone call, if necessary). The fee depends on the product for which you're requesting support.

When you call technical support, make sure you have all the necessary information ready, such as the versions of NetWare and any utility or application you're using, the type of hardware you're using, network or node addresses and hardware settings for any workstations or other machines being affected, and so on. You'll also need a major credit card.

To get in touch with Novell's technical support, call 1-800-858-4000 in the United States or 1-800-861-4000.

The Novell Support Encyclopedia

A subscription to the *Novell Support Encyclopedia Professional Volume* (*NSEPro*) can update you every month with the latest technical information about Novell products. The NSEPro is a CD-ROM containing technical information such as:

- Novell Technical Information Documents
- Novell Labs hardware and software test bulletins
- Online product manuals
- *Novell Application Notes*
- All available NetWare patches, fixes, and drivers
- The Novell Buyer's Guide
- Novell corporate information such as event calendars and press releases

The *NSEPro* includes Folio information-retrieval software that enables you to access and search easily through the NSEPro information from your workstation using DOS, Mac OS, or Microsoft Windows.

To subscribe to the *NSEPro*, contact your Novell Authorized Reseller or Novell directly at 1-800-377-4136 (in the United States and Canada) or 303-297-2725.

DeveloperNet: Novell's Developer Support

Developers who create applications designed to run on NetWare may qualify to join Novell's program for professional developers, called DeveloperNet. Subscription fees for joining DeveloperNet vary, depending on the subscription level and options you choose. If you are a developer, some of the benefits you can receive by joining DeveloperNet are:

- The Novell SDK (Software Development Kit) CD-ROM, which contains development tools you can use to create and test your application
- The DeveloperNet Handbook
- Special technical support geared specifically toward developers
- *Novell Developer Notes*, a bimonthly publication from the Novell Research department that covers software development topics for NetWare products
- Discounts on various events, products, and Novell Press books

For more information, to apply for membership, or to order an SDK, call 800-REDWORD or 801-861-5281, or contact the program administrator via e-mail at devprog@novell.com. More information is available online on CompuServe (GO THE NOVELL SITE) or on the World Wide Web at http://developer.novell.com.

Novell Application Notes

Novell's Research Department produces a monthly publication called *Novell Application Notes*. Each issue of *Novell Application Notes* contains research reports and articles on a wide range of topics. The articles delve into topics such as network design, implementation, administration, and integration.

A year's subscription costs $95 ($135 outside the United States).

To order a subscription, call 800-377-4136 or 303-297-2725.

Novell Education Classes and CNE Certification

Are you looking for a way to learn about NetWare in a classroom setting, with hands-on labs and knowledgeable instructors? Novell offers a variety of classes on various aspects of running NetWare networks.

NetWare classes are taught at over 1,000 Novell Authorized Education Centers (NAECs) throughout the world. They are also taught at more than 100 NAEPs (Novell Authorized Education Partners), which are universities and colleges that teach these courses.

These classes often offer the best way to get some direct, hands-on training in just a few days. Some of the classes are also available in Computer-Based Training (CBT) form, in case you'd rather work through the material at your own pace, on your own workstation, than attend a class.

These classes also help prepare you if you want to become certified as a CNE, signifying that you are a Novell NetWare professional.

The Novell CNE program provides a way to ensure that networking professionals meet the necessary criteria to adequately install and manage NetWare networks. To achieve CNE status, you take a series of exams on different aspects of NetWare. In many cases, you may want to take the classes Novell offers through its NAECs to prepare for the exams, but the classes aren't required.

The classes and exams you take depend somewhat on the level of certification you want to achieve. Although there are certain core exams that are required for all levels, you may also take additional "electives" to achieve the certification and specialization you want.

The following levels of certification are available:

- CNA (Certified Novell Administrator). This certification is the most basic level. It prepares you to manage your own NetWare network. It does not delve into the more complex and technical aspects of NetWare. If you are relatively new to NetWare, the class offered for this certification is highly recommended.
- CNE. This certification level ensures that you can adequately install and manage NetWare networks. While pursuing your CNE certification, you "declare a major," meaning that you choose to specialize in a particular Novell product family. For example, you may become a NetWare 4 CNE or a GroupWise CNE.

- Master CNE. This certification level allows you to go beyond CNE certification. To get a Master CNE, you declare a "graduate major." These areas of specialization delve deeper into the integration- and solution-oriented aspects of running a network than the CNE level.
- CNI (Certified Novell Instructor). CNIs are authorized to teach NetWare classes through NAECs. The tests and classes specific to this level ensure that the individual taking them will be able to adequately teach others how to install and manage NetWare.

The ECNE (Enterprise CNE) level has been phased out. The ECNE level's series of tests emphasized aspects of networking encountered in larger, enterprisewide networks, such as routing, gateways, Novell Directory Services, and so on.

The Master CNE program replaces the ECNE level and adds more flexibility to the type of specialization the candidate can pursue. If you've already achieved ECNE status, you retain the title, and Novell still recognizes it. However, Novell stopped certifying new ECNEs on September 30, 1995.

CNEs and Master CNEs qualify for membership in the Network Professional Association (NPA), which is explained later in this Appendix.

For more information about Novell Education classes or to find the nearest NAEC near you, call 1-800-233-3382.

To purchase a CBT version of a class, contact your nearest NAEC.

There are also numerous organizations that provide classes and seminars on NetWare products. Some of these unauthorized classes are quite good. Others are probably of lower quality, because Novell does not have any control over their course content or instructor qualifications. If you choose an unauthorized provider for your NetWare classes, try to talk to others who have taken a class from the provider before, so you'll have a better idea of how good the class is.

NetWare Users International (NUI)

NetWare Users International (NUI) is a nonprofit association for networking professionals. With more than 250 affiliated groups worldwide, NUI provides a forum for networking professionals to meet face to face, to learn from each other, to trade recommendations, or just to share war stories.

By joining the NetWare user group in your area, you can take advantage of the following benefits:

- Local user groups that hold regularly scheduled meetings

- A discount on Novell Press books through *NetWare Connection* magazine and also at NUI shows
- *NetWare Connection,* a bimonthly magazine that provides feature articles on new technologies, network management tips, product reviews, NUI news, and other helpful information
- NUInet, NUI's home page on the World Wide Web at http://www.nuinet.com (also accessible from Novell's regular web site, www.novell.com), which provides NetWare 3 and NetWare 4 technical information, a calendar of NUI events, and links to local user group home pages
- Regional NUI conferences, held in different major cities throughout the year (with a 15 percent discount for members)

The best news is, there's usually no fee or only a very low fee for joining an NUI user group.

For more information or to join an NUI user group, call 800-228-4NUI or send a fax to 801-228-4577.

For a free subscription to *NetWare Connection,* fax your name, address, and request for a subscription to 801-228-4576. You can also mail NUI a request at:

NetWare Connection
P.O. Box 1928
Orem, UT 84059-1928
USA

Network Professional Association (NPA)

If you've achieved, or are working toward, your CNE certification, you may want to join the Network Professional Association (NPA), formerly called CNEPA. The NPA is an organization for network computing professionals. Its goal is to keep its members current with the latest technology and information in the industry.

If you're a certified CNE, you can join the NPA as a full member. If you've started the certification process, but aren't finished yet, or if you are a CNA, you can join as an associate member (which gives you all the benefits of a full member except for the right to vote in the NPA's elections).

When you join the NPA, you can enjoy the following benefits:

- Local NPA chapters (more than 100 worldwide) that hold regularly scheduled meetings that include presentations and hands-on demonstrations of the latest technology

- *Network News,* a monthly publication that offers technical tips for working with NetWare networks, NPA news, classified ads for positions, and articles aimed at helping CNEs make the most of their careers
- Discounts on NPA Satellite Labs (satellite broadcasts of presentations)
- Product discounts from vendors
- Hands-On Technology Labs (educational forums at major trade shows and other locations sponsored by local NPA chapters)
- Discounts or free admission to major trade shows and conferences

Membership in NPA costs $150 per year. For more information or to join NPA, call 801-379-0330.

APPENDIX D

Worksheets

Keeping accurate and up-to-date documentation about the various aspects of your network can save you a tremendous amount of time and energy if something goes wrong. You can photocopy and use the worksheets in this section to begin documenting your network. If you prefer, you can design your own forms or databases for tracking important information such as hardware and software inventory, NDS information, and your backup schedules.

Worksheet A: Server Installation and Configuration

Server name: ______________________________

Make and model: ______________________________

Current location: ______________________________

Serial number: ______________________________

Memory: ______________________________

Server's internal IPX network number: ______________________________

Directory tree name: ______________________________

Type of time sync server: ______________________________

Server's time zone: ______________________________

Server's name context in the Directory tree: ______________________________

Protocols

IPX/SPX: Yes __ No __

TCP/IP: Yes __ No __

AppleTalk: Yes __ No __

Network Board

Type: ______________ Node address: ______________

LAN driver: ______________ Frame type: ______________

Settings: ______________________________

IP address (for TCP/IP only): ______________________________

Subnet mask (for TCP/IP only): ______________________________

Network Board

Type: ______________ Node address: ______________

LAN driver: ______________ Frame type: ______________

Settings: ______________________________

IP address (for TCP/IP only): ______________________________

Subnet mask (for TCP/IP only): ______________________________

Network Board

Type: ______________ Node address: ______________

LAN driver: ______________ Frame type: ______________

Settings: ______________________________

IP address (for TCP/IP only): ______________________________

Subnet mask (for TCP/IP only): ______________________________

Network Board

Type: ______________________ Node address: ____________

LAN driver: ________________ Frame type: ______________

Settings: ____

IP address (for TCP/IP only): ____________________________

Subnet mask (for TCP/IP only): __________________________

Hard disk size: ____

DOS partition size: ______________________________________

Disk mirrored? Yes __ No __

Disk duplexed? Yes __ No __

SFT III installed? Yes __ No __

CD-ROM drive? Yes __ No __

Disk Controller Board

Name: ____

Disk drive name: ______________________________

Settings: ____

Other Boards

Name: ____

Settings: ____

Name: ____

Settings: ____

Name: ____

Settings: ____

Name: ____

Settings: ____

Comments: ____

____

____

____

Worksheet B: Volumes

Server name: ______________________________

SYS Volume

Size: ______________________________

Name spaces: ______________________________

File compression on? Yes __ No __

Data migration on? Yes __ No __

Block suballocation on? Yes __ No __

Other volume (name): ______________________________

Size: ______________________________

Name spaces: ______________________________

File compression on? Yes __ No __

Data migration on? Yes __ No __

Block suballocation on? Yes __ No __

Other volume (name): ______________________________

Size: ______________________________

Name spaces: ______________________________

File compression on? Yes __ No __

Data migration on? Yes __ No __

Block suballocation on? Yes __ No __

Other volume (name): ______________________________

Size: ______________________________

Name spaces: ______________________________

File compression on? Yes __ No __

Data migration on? Yes __ No __

Block suballocation on? Yes __ No __

Comments: ______________________________

____

____

____

____

____

Worksheet C: Hardware and Software Purchases

Product: ______________________________

Serial number: ______________________________

Version number: ______________________________

Vendor name: ______________________________

Address: ______________________________

____

Phone: ______________________________

Fax: ______________________________

Manufacturer name: ______________________________

Address: ______________________________

____

Phone: ______________________________

Fax: ______________________________

Purchase date: ______________________________

Purchase order number: ______________________________

Purchase price: ______________________________

Warranty card sent in? Yes __ No __ Not applicable __

Length of warranty: ______________________________

Current location of product: ______________________________

Comments: ______________________________

____

____

____

____

____

Worksheet D: Hardware Maintenance

Product: ____

Serial number:____

Repair date: ____

Purchase order number: __________________________________

Repair vendor name: _____________________________________

Address: ____

____

Phone: ____

Fax: ____

Repair cost: ____

Repaired under warranty? Yes __ No __

New warranty granted? Yes __ No __

Warranty expiration date: ______________________________

Comments: ____

____

____

____

____

____

Worksheet E: Time Synchronization Servers

NDS Directory tree: ____________________

Single reference server: ____________________

Reference server: ____________________

Primary servers: ____________________

____

____

____

____

____

____

____

____

Comments: ____________________

____

____

____

____

____

Worksheet F: Hot Fix Bad Block Tracking

Server: ______________________________

Disk: ______________________________

Total redirection area: ____________________

Date: __________ Redirection blocks used: __________

Date: __________ Redirection blocks used: __________

Date: __________ Redirection blocks used: __________

Date: __________ Redirection blocks used: __________

Date: __________ Redirection blocks used: __________

Date: __________ Redirection blocks used: __________

Date: __________ Redirection blocks used: __________

Date: __________ Redirection blocks used: __________

Date: __________ Redirection blocks used: __________

Date: __________ Redirection blocks used: __________

Date: __________ Redirection blocks used: __________

Date: __________ Redirection blocks used: __________

Date: __________ Redirection blocks used: __________

Date: __________ Redirection blocks used: __________

Date: __________ Redirection blocks used: __________

Date: __________ Redirection blocks used: __________

Date: __________ Redirection blocks used: __________

Date: __________ Redirection blocks used: __________

Date: __________ Redirection blocks used: __________

Date: __________ Redirection blocks used: __________

Date: __________ Redirection blocks used: __________

Date: __________ Redirection blocks used: __________

Date: __________ Redirection blocks used: __________

Date: __________ Redirection blocks used: __________

Date: __________ Redirection blocks used: __________

Date: __________ Redirection blocks used: __________

Date: __________ Redirection blocks used: __________

Date: __________ Redirection blocks used: __________

Date: __________ Redirection blocks used: __________

Comments: ______________________________

____

____

____

____

____

Worksheet G: Workstation Installation and Configuration

Workstation's user and/or location:____________________

Make and model: ____________________

Serial number:____________________

Memory: ____________________

Size of floppy disk drives: A:__________ B:__________

Size of hard disk: C:__________ D:__________

CD-ROM drive? Yes __ No __

PC

- DOS version: __________
- Windows version: __________
- OS/2 version: __________
- Windows NT version: __________
- Windows 95 version: __________

Mac OS

- System version: __________
- Filer version: __________

NetWare client software version:____

Network Board

- Type: __________ Node address: __________
- LAN driver:__________ Frame type: __________
- Settings: ____________________

Network Board

- Type: __________ Node address: __________
- LAN driver: __________ Frame type: __________
- Settings: ____________________

Other Boards

- Name:____________________
- Settings: ____________________
- Name:____________________
- Settings: ____________________
- Name:____________________
- Settings: ____________________
- Name:____________________
- Settings: ____________________

Comments: ____________________

____

____

Worksheet H: Backup Schedule

Server name (of server backed up): ______________________

Server location: ______________________

Backup system used (hardware and software): ______________________

____

____

Location of backup media: ______________________

____

____

Backup schedule: ______________________

Full backup: ______________________

Incremental backup: ______________________

Differential backup: ______________________

Custom backup: ______________________

If custom backups are done, describe: ______________________

____

____

____

Media rotation schedule: ______________________

____

____

Media labeling instructions: ______________________

____

____

Primary backup administrator name: ______________________

Phone numbers: ______________________

____

____

Secondary backup administrator name: ______________________

Phone numbers: ______________________

____

Comments: ______________________

____

____

____

Worksheet I: Printer Installation and Configuration

Printer object's full name: ______________________________

Make and model: ______________________________

Current location: ______________________________

Serial number: ______________________________

Directory tree name: ______________________________

Printer number: ______________________________

Print queues assigned: ______________________________

____

____

____

Print server assigned: ______________________________

How is the printer attached: To server __ To workstation __ Direct __

Print queue operators: ______________________________

Print server operators: ______________________________

Printer type (parallel, serial, AppleTalk, etc.): ______________________________

Interrupt mode (polled or specific IRQ): ______________________________

Parallel printer configuration

Port (LPT1, LPT2, or LPT3): ______________________________

Poll: ______________________________

Interrupt (LPT1=7, LPT2=8): ______________________________

Serial Printer Configuration

Port (COM1 or COM2): ______________________________

Baud rate: ______________________________

Word size: ______________________________

Stop bits: ______________________________

Parity: ______________________________

XON/XOFF: ______________________________

Poll: ______________________________

Interrupt (COM1=4, COM2=3): ______________________________

Comments: ______________________________

____

____

____

____

IDG BOOKS WORLDWIDE LICENSE AGREEMENT

Important — read carefully before opening the software packet(s). This is a legal agreement between you (either an individual or an entity) and IDG Books Worldwide, Inc. (IDG). By opening the accompanying sealed packet containing the software disk(s), you acknowledge that you have read and accept the following IDG License Agreement. If you do not agree and do not want to be bound by the terms of this Agreement, promptly return the book and the unopened software packet(s) to the place you obtained them for a full refund.

1. **License.** This License Agreement (Agreement) permits you to use one copy of the enclosed Software program(s) on a single computer. The Software is in "use" on a computer when it is loaded into temporary memory (i.e., RAM) or installed into permanent memory (e.g., hard disk, CD-ROM, or other storage device) of that computer.

2. **Copyright.** The entire contents of the disk(s) and the compilation of the Software are copyrighted and protected by both United States copyright laws and international treaty provisions. You may only (a) make one copy of the Software for backup or archival purposes, or (b) transfer the Software to a single hard disk, provided that you keep the original for backup or archival purposes. The individual programs on the disk(s) are copyrighted by the authors of each program respectively. Each program has its own use permissions and limitations. To use each program, you must follow the individual requirements and restrictions detailed for each in the Appendix of this Book. Do not use a program if you do not want to follow its Licensing Agreement. None of the material on the disk(s) or listed in this Book may ever be distributed, in original or modified form, for commercial purposes.

3. **Other Restrictions.** You may not rent or lease the Software. You may transfer the Software and user documentation on a permanent basis provided you retain no copies and the recipient agrees to the terms of this Agreement. You may not reverse engineer, decompile, or disassemble the Software except to the extent that the foregoing restriction is expressly prohibited by applicable law. If the Software is an update or has been updated, any transfer must include the most recent update and all prior versions.

4. **Limited Warranty.** IDG warrants that the Software and disk(s) are free from defects in materials and workmanship for a period of sixty (60) days from the date of purchase of this Book. If IDG receives notification within the warranty period of defects in material or workmanship, IDG will replace the defective disk(s). IDG's entire liability and your exclusive remedy shall be lim-

ited to replacement of the Software, which is returned to IDG with a copy of your receipt. This Limited Warranty is void if failure of the Software has resulted from accident, abuse, or misapplication. Any replacement Software will be warranted for the remainder of the original warranty period or thirty (30) days, whichever is longer.

5. **No Other Warranties.** To the maximum extent permitted by applicable law, IDG and the author disclaim all other warranties, express or implied, including but not limited to implied warranties of merchantability and fitness for a particular purpose, with respect to the Software, the programs, the source code contained therein and/or the techniques described in this Book. This limited warranty gives you specific legal rights. You may have others which vary from state/jurisdiction to state/jurisdiction.

6. **No Liability For Consequential Damages.** To the extent permitted by applicable law, in no event shall IDG or the author be liable for any damages whatsoever (including without limitation, damages for loss of business profits, business interruption, loss of business information, or any other pecuniary loss) arising out of the use of or inability to use the Book or the Software, even if IDG has been advised of the possibility of such damages. Because some states/jurisdictions do not allow the exclusion or limitation of liability for consequential or incidental damages, the above limitation may not apply to you.

7. **U.S. Government Restricted Rights.** Use, duplication, or disclosure of the Software by the U.S. Government is subject to restrictions stated in paragraph (c) (1) (ii) of the Rights in Technical Data and Computer Software clause of DFARS 252.227-7013, and in subparagraphs (a) through (d) of the Commercial Computer — Restricted Rights clause at FAR 52.227-19, and in similar clauses in the NASA FAR supplement, when applicable.

Index

NUMBERS AND SYMBOLS

A

B

D

E

F

G

H

(continued)

(continued)

(continued)

Q

R

S

T

U

(continued)

(continued)